T0383330

FORENSIC ODONTOLOGY

FORENSIC ODONTOLOGY

PRINCIPLES AND PRACTICE

Edited by

THOMAS J. DAVID

Forensic Odontology Consultant, Georgia Bureau of Investigation, Division of Forensic Sciences, Decatur, GA, United States;
Clinical Assistant Professor, Department of General Dentistry, Forensic Dentistry Fellowship, The University of Tennessee
Graduate School of Medicine, Knoxville, TN, United States

JAMES M. LEWIS

Forensic Odontology Consultant, Alabama Department of Forensic Sciences, Madison, AL, United States;
Assistant Professor, Department of General Dentistry, Forensic Dentistry Fellowship,
The University of Tennessee Graduate School of Medicine, Knoxville, TN, United States;
Adjunct Faculty, Center for Education and Research in Forensics,
The University of Texas Health Science Center at San Antonio, San Antonio, TX, United States

ACADEMIC PRESS

An imprint of Elsevier

Academic Press is an imprint of Elsevier
125 London Wall, London EC2Y 5AS, United Kingdom
525 B Street, Suite 1800, San Diego, CA 92101-4495, United States
50 Hampshire Street, 5th Floor, Cambridge, MA 02139, United States
The Boulevard, Langford Lane, Kidlington, Oxford OX5 1GB, United Kingdom

Library of Congress Cataloging-in-Publication Data
A catalog record for this book is available from the Library of Congress

British Library Cataloguing-in-Publication Data
A catalogue record for this book is available from the British Library

ISBN: 978-0-12-805198-6

For information on all Academic Press publications visit our website at
https://www.elsevier.com/books-and-journals

Working together
to grow libraries in
developing countries

www.elsevier.com • www.bookaid.org

Publisher: Mica Haley
Acquisition Editor: Elizabeth Brown
Editorial Project Manager: Joslyn Chaiprasert-Paguio & Pat Gonzalez
Production Project Manager: Priya Kumaraguruparan
Cover Designer: Mark Rogers

Typeset by TNQ Books and Journals

Dedication

I would like to thank three individuals who have played an important role in my professional success in Forensic Odontology. First and foremost, I would like to thank Dr. Ed Herschaft for his encouragement in motivating me to become a diplomate of the American Board of Forensic Odontology (ABFO) and become actively involved in organized forensic odontology. Secondly, I would like to thank Dr. David Senn for his continuous leadership by example. He always endeavors to make those around him, myself included, strive for excellence in forensic odontology and all that they do. I would also like to thank Dr. Paula Brumit not only for her diligence and work ethic in education as well as her selfless devotion to the ABFO, but, more importantly, for passing along what she has learned to others as a means of maintaining the never-ending quest for excellence in forensic odontology.

Finally, I would like to thank my wife Donna, whose constant support has been invaluable to my success. She has persistently sacrificed countless hours of personal and family time over the years without complaint. In addition, she has always been willing to provide valuable feedback for my many forensic endeavors. She has been by my side through both success and heartache. Regardless, she has always been there for me, a guiding light and shining beacon of faithfulness and love. Many people have said "behind every successful man is a woman." In my case, I would say "beside this successful man is his wife," because she has been alongside me the entire time. Donna, I can never thank you enough for what you have done for me!

Thomas J. David

Professionally, I wish to thank three individuals who have greatly influenced me over the years. First, to Dr. Roy Cowan, who mentored and encouraged me to strive for perfection and accept only excellence as a dental practitioner. To Dr. David Senn, who provided educational opportunity, mentorship, and continues to inspire me to grow professionally in the endeavor to improve the field of forensic odontology. And to Dr. Richard Weems, who has been a wonderful forensic colleague opening doors for me to practice forensics.

But primarily, I dedicate this book to my late loving wife, Teri, who encouraged me to pursue my passions in life and sacrificed for me to do so:

> When you really love someone…you will fight for them to the end
> And you have to make it work; no matter how far you have to bend
>
> You are going to have to hold on tight and never, never let them go
> And if you are not willing to do just that; then the love will not grow
>
> If you start to play games with the other persons heart and emotions
> You will end up losing their love for you…when all is set into motion
>
> When it comes to true love; listen to the sages and take their advice
> Never take someone's love for granted…for true love takes sacrifice
>
> — William John Palmer

James M. Lewis

Contents

4. Forensic Dental Photography

MARK L. BERNSTEIN, FRANKLIN D. WRIGHT

5. Disaster Victim Identification

PETER W. LOOMIS

6. Missing and Unidentified Persons
JAMES P. FANCHER, PETER HAMPL

7. Domestic Violence
JOHN D. MELVILLE, JOHN D. MCDOWELL

8. Assessment of Dental Age
JAMES M. LEWIS, KATHLEEN A. KASPER

14. Forensic Odontology Related Specialties

CRAIG O'CONNOR, MELISSA MOURGES, MURRAY K. MARKS, DARINKA MILEUSNIC-POLCHAN, HEATHER WALSH-HANEY

Educational Outcomes   297

EDWARD E. HERSCHAFT

Index   313

List of Contributors

Robert E. Barsley Professor, Department of Diagnostic Sciences, LSUHSC School of Dentistry, New Orleans, LA, United States; Chief Forensic Odontologist, Jefferson Parish Coroner, New Orleans, LA, United States; New Orleans Forensic Center, Orleans Parish Coroner, New Orleans, LA, United States

Mark L. Bernstein Professor of Pathology and Oral Pathology, Dept. of Surgical and Hospital Dentistry, University of Louisville Dental School, Louisville, KY, United States; Forensic Dental Consultant, Medical Examiner's Office, Louisville, KY, United States

Thomas J. David Forensic Odontology Consultant, Georgia Bureau of Investigation, Division of Forensic Sciences, Decatur, GA, United States; Clinical Assistant Professor, Department of General Dentistry, Forensic Dentistry Fellowship, The University of Tennessee Graduate School of Medicine, Knoxville, TN, United States

J.C. Upshaw Downs Medicolegal consultant, forensX, LLC Savannah, Georgia

James P. Fancher Forensic Odontology Consultant: Bexar County Medical Examiner's Office, San Antonio, TX, United States; Central Texas Autopsy, Lockhart, TX, United States; Forensic Anthropology Center at Texas State University, San Marcos, TX, United States; Faculty – Forensic Dentistry Fellowship, Center for Education and Research in Forensics, The University of Texas Health Science Center at San Antonio, San Antonio, TX, United States

Scott Hahn Federal Bureau of Investigation, Special Agent (Ret.); United States Navy, Dental Corps, Captain (Ret.)

Peter Hampl Forensic Odontology Consultant: Pierce County Medical Examiner's Office, Tacoma, WA, United States; Spokane County Medical Examiner's Office, Spokane, WA, United States; Disaster Mortuary Operational Response Team (Region X), United States; Blake Emergency Services, Combs, High Peak, England; FBI's National Dental Image Repository (Review Panel), United States

Edward E. Herschaft Department of Biomedical Sciences, UNLV School of Dental Medicine, Las Vegas, NV, United States; Forensic Odontology Consultant, Clark County Office of the Coroner/Medical Examiner, Las Vegas, NV, United States

Kathleen A. Kasper Forensic Odontology Consultant, Tarrant County Medical Examiner's District, Fort Worth, TX, United States

James M. Lewis Forensic Odontology Consultant, Alabama Department of Forensic Sciences, Madison, AL, United States; Assistant Professor, Department of General Dentistry, Forensic Dentistry Fellowship, The University of Tennessee Graduate School of Medicine, Knoxville, TN, United States; Adjunct Faculty, Center for Education and Research in Forensics, The University of Texas Health Science Center at San Antonio, San Antonio, TX, United States

Peter W. Loomis Forensic Odontology Consultant, New Mexico Office of the Medical Investigator, Albuquerque, NM, United States; Faculty - University of New Mexico School of Medicine, Albuquerque, NM, United States

Murray K. Marks Associate Professor, Department of General Dentistry, University of Tennessee Medical Center, Knoxville, TN, United States; Forensic Anthropologist, Regional Forensic Center, Knoxville, TN, United States

John D. McDowell Distinguished Fellow of the American Academy of Forensic Sciences, Professor and Director Oral Medicine and Forensic Sciences, University of Colorado School of Dental Medicine, Aurora, CO, United States; Professor, School of Medicine, Department of Family Medicine, University of Colorado Health Sciences Center, Aurora, CO, United States

John D. Melville Chief, Division of Child Abuse Pediatrics, Medical University of South Carolina, Charleston, SC, United States

Roger D. Metcalf Chief of the Human Identification Laboratory, Tarrant County Medical Examiner's District, Fort Worth, TX, United States; Assistant Professor, Center for Education and Research in Forensics, The University of Texas Health Science Center at San Antonio, San Antonio, TX, United States

Darinka Mileusnic-Polchan Chief Medical Examiner for Knox & Anderson Counties, Regional Forensic Center, Knoxville, TN, United States

James A. Misselwitz Vice President ECBM, LLP, West Conshohocken, PA, United States; President, PLM & JAM Associates Inc., Millsboro, DE, United States; Board member of CLEW (Consultants, Lawyers, and Expert Witnesses), Malvern, PA, United States

Melissa Mourges Chief, Forensic Sciences/Cold Case Unit, Manhattan DA's Office, New York, NY, United States

Craig O'Connor Criminalist IV, Assistant Technical Leader of DNA Operations, Department of Forensic Biology, New York City Office of Chief Medical Examiner, New York, NY, United States

Haskell M. Pitluck Retired Circuit Court Judge, State of Illinois, 19th Judicial Circuit, Crystal Lake, IL, United States

Jacqueline S. Reid Forensic Odontology Consultant: Middlesex Regional Medical Examiner's Office, North Brunswick, NJ, United States; Northern Regional Medical Examiner's Office, Newark, NJ, United States; Program Director, Chief, Hospital Dentistry, Robert Wood Johnson University Hospital, General Practice Residency in Dentistry, New Brunswick, NJ, United States

Bruce A. Schrader Forensic Odontology Consultant, Lubbock County Medical Examiner's Office, Lubbock, TX, United States; Center for Education and Research in Forensics, The University of Texas Health Science Center at San Antonio, San Antonio, TX, United States

Alexander Simpson Associate Director, California Innocence Project, San Diego, CA, United States; Adjunct Faculty, California Western School of Law, San Diego, CA, United States

Michael P. Tabor Chief Forensic Odontologist, Davidson County, State of Tennessee, Nashville, TN, United States

Heather Walsh-Haney Forensic Anthropologist, Program Leader & Associate Professor, Florida Gulf Coast University, Department of Justice Studies, Fort Myers, FL, United States

Richard A. Weems University of Alabama School of Dentistry, Forensic Odontology Consultant, Jefferson County Chief Medical Examiner, Birmingham, AL, United States; Faculty – Forensic Dentistry Fellowship, The University of Tennessee Graduate School of Medicine, Knoxville, TN, United States

Franklin D. Wright Forensic Odontology Consultant, Hamilton County Coroner's Office, Cincinnati, OH, United States

Biographies

Thomas J. David, DDS, earned his dental degree from Emory University School of Dentistry in 1977. He has maintained a dental practice since that time in the Atlanta metropolitan area. He is a member of the American Society of Forensic Odontology (ASFO), a fellow of the American Academy of Forensic Sciences (AAFS), and a diplomate of the American Board of Forensic Odontology (ABFO). He has served as chair of the Odontology Section of AAFS and president of the ABFO and has also served on the editorial board of the Journal of Forensic Sciences (JFS). He has authored articles in various periodicals, including the JFS. He has also authored chapters in a number of textbooks, including multiple editions of the Manual of Forensic Odontology as well as the second edition of Forensic Dentistry.

Dr. David is a consultant in Forensic Odontology to the Georgia Bureau of Investigation (GBI), Division of Forensic Sciences, and the State of Georgia Medical Examiner's Office. He also holds a faculty appointment as a clinical assistant professor in the Department of General Dentistry of the Graduate School of Medicine of the University of Tennessee Health Science Center at Knoxville. He provides instruction for the Forensic Odontology Fellowship program and the University of Tennessee biennial Symposium "All That Remains."

James M. Lewis, DMD, attended the University of Alabama and earned his dental degree from the School of Dentistry, University of Alabama, Birmingham, in 1985. He has maintained a general dentistry practice since that time, exclusively in Madison, AL, since 1986.

Dr. Lewis completed a fellowship in Forensic Odontology from the Center for Education and Research in Forensics, the University of Texas Health Science Center at San Antonio in 2001. As a forensic odontologist, he assisted in victim identification in New York following the World Trade Center attack; and since 2003, he has served as a consultant to the Alabama Department of Forensic Sciences (ADFS). And is a volunteer to the Alabama Office of Emergency Preparedness in relation to its mass disaster response group.

Dr. Lewis is a fellow of the Odontology Section of the American Academy of Forensic Sciences (AAFS), became board certified by the American Board of Forensic Odontology (ABFO) in 2008, has served on the Board of Governors of the American Society of Forensic Odontology (ASFO) and president of the organization in 2012. For ABFO, he served as member and chair of the Dental Age Assessment Committee, 2008–15; as a member of the Certification and Examination Committee, 2011–15; Bitemark Evidence and Patterned Injury Committee, 2008–15 and 2017; and currently holds the office of ABFO Secretary. He is currently appointed to the Odontology Subcommittee, Organization of Scientific Area Committees for Forensic Science (OSAC), National Institute of Standards and Technology (NIST).

Dr. Lewis is on faculty as an assistant professor in the Department of General Dentistry, fellowship in Forensic Odontology at the University of Tennessee, Graduate School of Medicine, and adjunct faculty for the Center for Education and Research in Forensics (CERF), fellowship in Forensic Odontology; and the Southwest Symposium on Forensic Dentistry. He has authored textbook chapters and articles in peer-reviewed journals on forensic odontology.

Foreword

I have been privileged to be a professor emeritus at The University of Texas School of Dentistry at Houston and have been in the forensic field for almost 50 years. I taught forensic odontology for most of those years, both at the dental school and the Armed Forces Course and other venues. There have been many changes and it pleases me when a new book on the subject is being published. One of the joys of a teacher is when an idea is planted in a student who eventually comes forward with a new technique, or from his/her research proves or disproves a problem area. The American Board of Forensic Odontology, which assures the legal and other professions in the science the individuals doing the examinations and techniques have had adequate training to satisfy the requirements of the case at hand, chose me as one of the founding members. The authors of each chapter were carefully chosen to reflect that same knowledge, training, and have done research in their particular area of their chapter to bring you, the reader, up to date on the latest in the particular field. Most areas are noncontroversial and they will be presented and researched as accepted techniques. In some areas where a difference of opinions exists, they will attempt to evaluate all aspects of the problem and the research and things written about the area and perhaps even give you their interpretation and the reasons behind their opinion. Like any forensic discipline, there are some areas in forensic odontology that need further research and either acceptance, change, or perhaps are no longer useful due to forensic advances in the field. If you are an interested dentist or student in this field, I welcome you and know that this text will be of great use and a learning situation for you. For others, such as detectives, attorneys, or other interested parties, I hope you find a great deal of help in the areas you are researching and that this text aids in the situation you are presently investigating. The research and articles are current and can help you in your examinations.

My desire for you is that you will find the forensic field and particularly forensic odontology as exciting and rewarding as I have over these many years. It is very gratifying to be able to make a positive identification of an individual and provide the medical examiner or corner an opinion to bring closure to a family and loved ones. Serving as an expert witness is another challenge and helps to bring information to the judge or jury that is tasked with deciding a legal challenge.

Paul G. Stimson, D.D.S., M.S

Forensic Sciences and Forensic Identification

Scott Hahn[1,2], Melissa Mourges[3], Alexander Simpson[4,5]

[1]Federal Bureau of Investigation, Special Agent (Ret.); [2]United States Navy, Dental Corps, Captain (Ret.); [3]Chief, Forensic Sciences/Cold Case Unit, Manhattan DA's Office, New York, NY, United States; [4]Associate Director, California Innocence Project, San Diego, CA, United States; [5]Adjunct Faculty, California Western School of Law, San Diego, CA, United States

OUTLINE

A LAW ENFORCEMENT PERSPECTIVE

Forensic Science entails the practical applications of specific, repeatable methodologies and analyses for use in investigative and legal processes. Specifically, forensic science constitutes many scientific analytical specialties by which physical evidence (or a physical derivative of testimonial evidence) is examined and exploited to ascertain and assimilate facts for ultimate prosecution or defense in legal cases and provide actionable intelligence in ongoing investigations. The analytical products of forensic science can be inculpatory, exculpatory, or neutral regarding ongoing investigations, yet equal investigative effort and scientific application of principles are required of involved practitioners to minimize potential bias.

Forensic analysis can be performed on body chemistry, weapons, projectiles, tire prints, vehicle paint, tool marks, broken glass, adhesive tape, ropes and lines, and chemicals (not an exhaustive list). While the products of these

Forensic Odontology
http://dx.doi.org/10.1016/B978-0-12-805198-6.00001-3

analyses can provide information that, along with cumulative use of other physical evidence, may assist with identification of subjects, victims, and/or decedents, these disciplines do not directly identify the corpus of specific human beings.

Forensic identification comprises this backbone of scientific methodology to assist the legal system (and society as a whole) with determining the name or individuality of human decedents, victims, perpetrators, and/or suspects. Scientific disciplines/analytical methodologies that can facilitate forensic identification include (but are not limited to): DNA analysis, forensic odontology, forensic pathology, forensic anthropology, forensic document examination of handwriting, and fingerprint examination. In this broader definition of forensic identification, the methodology does not rely on a direct examination of the human(s) in question, but can be accomplished via an intermediary event or substance, such as with handwriting comparison and analysis.

Forensic document examination/handwriting comparison and analysis, in this example, conducts an examination on the known, uncontested handwriting of an individual, as compared to that of a questioned document. If the two correspond in individualizing characteristics to such a degree that it could not occur by coincidence; while (at the same time) exhibiting no inexplicable variations or disparities, these findings would identify that individual as the source of the handwriting. This discipline could not, however, identify the deceased remains of that individual as the handwriting source.

Forensic identification based upon comparison of human anatomy and/or human chemistry is limited to the disciplines of DNA analysis, forensic odontology, forensic pathology, forensic anthropology, and fingerprint examination. Serialized implants recovered as a result of autopsy can also provide identification via comparison with device registrations completed by practitioners upon insertion/placement.

Anthropological and odontological examination and analysis of postmortem skeletal and dental tissue (wherein a positive identification is not possible) can provide information as to a human's approximate age, stature, sex, occupation, and/or ethnic group. Odontological and anthropological evaluation of living humans can provide information as to age estimation. This is particularly important regarding immigration status of minors versus "legal-aged" adults. Additional anthropological analysis of living humans can provide clues as to potential ethnic backgrounds or origins, environmental effects, and group or cadre likenesses to assist in such endeavors as refugee status and vetting.

Forensic identification of victims and/or subjects by bitemarks on the human corpus is another area of analysis conducted by forensic odontologists. These types of injuries can be inflicted by either the attacker, or the victim on the attacker (as a means of self-defense). There are also instances wherein bitemarks are self-inflicted. While it is not possible to obtain a positive identification from a bitemark in an open population of potential "biters," information preserved from the injury/injuries in these situations can assist investigations and the legal system in the following ways:

1. The injury location can be used for targeted DNA collection and analysis.

2. The injury can be used by investigators as a discussion point during interview/interrogation.

3. The injury can give an indication as to the violence involved at the time of its infliction by nature of the amount of tissue damage.

4. Patterned injury analysis and bitemark comparison may lead to inclusion or exclusion of suspects.

From the law enforcement/practical perspective, the use of forensic science to analyze physical evidence collected from crime scenes is well established and an indispensable aspect of any criminal investigation. The products of the forensic analysis are utilized both actively during the investigative process and later during the courtroom proceedings to help ascertain guilt or innocence. The investigators and technicians, who recognize and collect evidence, cannot always analyze it for its intrinsic value in the field. The specialties and specialists performing the follow-up forensic analysis provide the scientific methodology, which allows evidence to be admitted in court, and the interpretive expertise to explain how the analysis of the evidence is relative to the case at hand.

Tactical forensic identification of nonhuman components of crime scenes/terrorist attacks is possible via the rapid forensic exploitation of a particular explosive or device in the field (or the nearest rear echelon evaluation area). This analysis can provide actionable intelligence that could give enough advanced warning (bomb maker's signature, appearance of IED containers, purchase of unique raw materials) to allow authorities in potential future attack zones to target/narrow their search and preventative activities to a more "known quantity," thus possibly intercepting the device and rendering it safe.

From an operational perspective, the rapid employment of human forensic identification can not only enhance investigations but also help to prevent future adverse events by providing actionable intelligence to tactical elements pursuing perpetrators of a terrorist attack or other violent acts. The rapid identification of deceased terrorists on the battlefield (now capable through enhanced DNA techniques as well as battlefield forensic odontology) provides war fighters with unique battle damage assessments and intelligence personnel with adversarial connectivity information.

Forensic identification has limitations, which are known to practitioners and should be made known to all end users. For forensic identification to be useful in criminal investigations, and to stand up to challenges of the legal system, it must be applied dispassionately to ensure derived data/information are free from bias. Applicable statistical analysis and repeatability, in the end, is the measure of accuracy of any scientific method employed…and forensic identification must maintain the highest standards in this regard.

A "positive identification" through forensic analysis carries much weight, and should be able to stand up to scientific and legal scrutiny. Forensic identification often speaks for those who cannot speak for themselves: deceased victims of homicides, transportation mishaps, and terrorist attacks. A positive identification can bring closure to families, assist with the settling of estates, and provide additional information for substantive investigations.

A PROSECUTION PERSPECTIVE

Forensic odontology has two main components, identification of human remains and bitemark analysis and comparison, typically for use in criminal cases. While identification of human remains, both in individual and mass disaster situations, generates little controversy, bitemark analysis and comparison is at the center of a heated debate over whether it is sufficiently reliable for use in court.

Bitemark analyses and comparisons have been accepted in state courts since at least 1954, see *Doyle v. State*, 159 Tex. Crim 310, 263 S.W. 2d 799. In that case, a defendant bit into a piece of cheese at the request of police, and those bitemarks were compared to bitemarks left in cheese at the scene of a grocery store burglary. A local dentist testified, based on plaster casts and photos of the two sets of bitemarks, that they were made by the same set of teeth. An appellate court upheld that conviction. A California court upheld a conviction in a murder case when a lodger in a rooming house strangled his landlady and knifed her in the vagina. She had deep bitemarks on her nose. Impressions from the wounds on her nose were taken after exhumation, and a dentist took impressions of the suspect's teeth. A team of three dentists working together concluded the defendant's teeth were a match to the bitemark. Finding that the trial court properly admitted the testimony under the *Frye* test for expert testimony, the Court took a very practical approach:

> What is significantly different about the evidence in this case is this: the trier of fact, here the court, was shown models, photographs, X-rays and dozens of slides of the victim's wounds and defendant's teeth. It could see what we have seen in reviewing the exhibits to determine the admissibility of evidence. First, for example, the extent to which the appearance of wounds changed between the time that the autopsy was performed and the time that the body was exhumed in Dallas. Second, the extent to which the purported bitemarks appear to conform generally to obvious irregularities in defendant's teeth. Thus, the basic data on which the experts based their conclusions were verified by the court. Further, in making their painstaking comparisons and reaching their conclusions, the experts did not rely on untested methods, unproven hypothesis, intuition or revelation. Rather, they applied scientifically and professionally established techniques—X-rays, models, microscopy, photography—to the solution of a particular problem, which, though novel, was well within the capabilities of those techniques. In short, in

admitting the evidence, the court did not have to sacrifice its independence and common sense in evaluating it. *People v. Marx, 54 Cal. App. 3d, 100, 126 Cal. Rptr.350 (December 29, 1975).*

Bitemark analysis and comparison testimony is admissible in all 50 states and the federal court system. This common sense approach is typical of trial court judges, who must evaluate whether to admit expert testimony in scientific, medical, or technical fields. A basic question is this: what constitutes evidence? The basic answer is that evidence consists of information that is material and relevant to a particular issue and that would be helpful to the trier of fact, typically the jury or judge.

There are a wide variety of disciplines in which testimony from experts, those with appropriate training and experience, would be helpful to a jury. Confronted with a situation where victims or suspects have bitemarks, a judge is fully justified in admitting expert testimony, both for the prosecution and the defense, as an aid to the jury to help them determine, if possible, when, under what circumstances, and by whom the bitemarks were inflicted.

There has been a movement, spearheaded by postconviction advocacy groups, to preclude such testimony altogether.[1] These groups cite the 2009 National Academy of Science (NAS) advisory report, *"Strengthening Forensic Science in the United States: A Path Forward"* to support their claim that forensic odontology is scientifically unsound. Nothing in the NAS report supports that conclusion, and no jurisdiction in the United States has outlawed bitemark testimony in response to the NAS report.[2]

---

[1] Most criminal statutes offer postconviction relief upon proof of "newly discovered evidence" that could reasonably be expected to have changed the outcome of the case. Postconviction groups urge that if forensic odontology is declared "junk science" in even one jurisdiction, that will constitute the "newly discovered evidence" necessary for postconviction relief in many courtrooms. In the majority of these very old cases, prosecutors cannot retry defendants who have had their convictions set aside in this manner, due to the passage of time, fading memories, and the incapacity or deaths of witnesses.

[2] The Texas Forensic Science Commission has called for a "moratorium" on such testimony, as discussed below. http://www.fsc.texas.gov.

First, it is important to look at what the NAS report does *not* do. The report does not claim to be an authoritative treatise on any forensic science. The 286-page report expends less than 4 pages on a discussion of forensic odontology (NAS report at 173–177). The brief treatment of forensic odontology is not surprising, given that the "NAS committee decided early in its work that it would not be feasible to develop a detailed evaluation of each forensic discipline in terms of scientific underpinning, levels of development and ability to provide evidence to address the major types of questions raised in criminal and civil litigation." (NAS report at 7). Nor was the report authored by experts in each forensic field; while the committee had numerous academicians and statisticians, no forensic odontologists made the cut. Nor does the NAS report state that forensic odontology as a field should be discredited. Nowhere does the NAS report urge, as detractors of forensic odontology suggest, that forensic odontology is based on technologies not accepted by the relevant scientific community. To the contrary, the NAS report states that there are well-established guidelines for the collection of evidence, for example, various forms of photography, computer enhancement, electron microscopy, and swabbing for serology and DNA that are firmly grounded and noncontroversial. While the report notes that bitemarks on the skin will change over time and can be distorted by the elasticity of skin, the unevenness of the surface bite and swelling and healing, these are features that are well understood by forensic odontologists and their analyses and comparisons take those and many other factors into account.

The NAS report notes the significance of bitemark analysis and comparison, citing the fact that bitemarks are seen most often in cases of homicide, sexual assault, and child abuse. Nowhere does the report state or even imply that forensic odontology should be deemed inadmissible under either *Frye* or *Daubert*. That point was discussed by Justice Harry Edwards, the Chief Justice for the D.C. Circuit and cochairman of the NAS committee. In his address to Congress regarding the report, he said, "The question of whether forensic evidence in a particular case is admissible under applicable law is not coterminus with the question of whether there are studies confirming the scientific validity and reliability of a forensic science discipline."[3]

Both federal and state courts have interpreted the NAS report as acknowledging the need for further research and regulation in forensic science, *not* as an affirmative directive demanding judges "to take the drastic step of excluding long-accepted forms of expert evidence," *United States v. Stone*, 2012 U.S. Dist. LEXIS 8973 (2012). In *Pettus v. United States*, 37 A. 3d 213, (D.C. 2012), the D.C. Court of Appeals rejected the argument that the NAS report amounts to a critique and repudiation of the supposed science underlying all forensic analysis based on pattern matching, except for DNA. The Court found, "The report is much more nuanced than that… the goal is not to hold other disciplines to DNA's high standards," since, "… it is unlikely that most other current forensic methods will ever produce evidence as discriminating as DNA." (id at 226). The Court further noted, "Yet in virtually no instance…does the report imply that evidence of forensic expert identifications should be excluded from judicial proceedings until the particular methodology has been validated." (id at 226). Widener Law School did a survey of 65 court decisions mentioning the NAS report; in none of these did the court preclude pattern matching evidence.[4]

---

[3] http://www.nationalacademies.org/includes/OSEdwards.pdf.

[4] Jules Epstein, 2014. Preferring the 'Wise Man' to Science: The Failure of Courts and Non-Litigation Mechanisms to Demand Validity in Forensic Matching Testimony, vol. 20. Widener Law Review.

Critics claim there is a lack of empirical and statistical data to demonstrate error rate, the uniqueness of human dentition or the ability of human skin to transfer and maintain a pattern. However, forensic odontology is not a hard science like chemistry or DNA analysis, where researchers can sit at a lab bench and perform the same experiments over and over to establish ground truths. Each bitemark is a unique event. Even consecutive bitemarks inflicted rapidly between the same biter and victim will be different, as the victim reacts to pain by moving away as quickly as possible, and each movement changes the relative position of biter and victim. It is not possible to inflict severe, violent bites on human subjects for research purposes. The difficulties in constructing useful models for bitemark scenarios have been starkly illustrated by problems encountered by researchers.

Forensic odontology is an observational science, where the skill and experience of the forensic dentist informs his good judgment in a particular case. In this way, forensic odontology is much like forensic pathology. Pathologists cannot investigate the effects of gunshot wounds by lining people up and shooting them; nor can they determine the lethal dose of fentanyl by increasing the dosage on volunteers until someone dies. Instead, practitioners wait for victims of gunshots, overdoses, and violent bites to come into the hospital or morgue to make their observations.

Critics also cite a series of studies as proof that skin cannot reliably retain bitemarks, and that dentitions are not unique. Both studies have been discredited as being poorly designed and inapplicable to real life conditions, and testimony regarding those studies has been discounted in court.[5]

Those studies involved the use of "defrosted" refrigerated human cadavers that were subjected to being pinched by a device constructed of stone tooth models set in Home Depot vise grips. The lack of vital reaction in the cadavers, as well as differences between the vise-grip device and the mechanics of actual human jaws and teeth, deprived the studies of real life application. In another set of studies, flatbed scans of tooth models subjected to a Procrustes statistical shape analysis failed to demonstrate lack of uniqueness.[6]

Recognizing that errors in testimony by a few forensic dentists have been implicated in some exonerations of individuals convicted of crimes by evidence that included bitemark testimony, the American Board of Forensic Odontology (ABFO), the Department of Justice, and the National Institute of Standards and Technology are working to better articulate standards and conclusions to ensure that forensic dentists follow best practices to ensure accurate and conservative results.

Prompted by a letter of complaint from a postconviction advocacy group in February 2016, the Texas Forensic Science Commission issued a

---

[5] *State v. Prade* No. CR1998-02-0463 (Ohio Com. Pl. January 29, 2013, at 11–13); *People v. Clarence Dean*, Ind. No. 4555/2007, J. Wiley, New York County Supreme Court, September 5, 2013.

[6] Bush, M.A., Miller, R.G., Bush, P.J., Dorion R.B.J., 2009. Biomechanical factors in human dermal bitemarks in a cadaver model. Journal of Forensic Sciences 54 (1),167–176; Miller, R.G., Bush, P.J., Dorion, R.B.J., Bush, M.A., 2009. Uniqueness of the dentition as impressed in human skin: a cadaver model. Journal of Forensic Sciences 54 (4), 909–914; Bush, M.A., Thorsrud, K., Miller, R.G., Dorion, R.B.J, Bush, P.J., 2010. The response of skin to applied stress: investigation of bitemark distortion in a cadaver model. Journal of Forensic Sciences 55 (1), 71–76; Bush, M.A., Bush, P.J., Sheets, H.D., 2011. Statistical evidence for the similarity of the human dentition. Journal of Forensic Sciences 56 (1), 118–123; Bush, M.A., Bush, P.J., Sheets, H.D., 2011. Similarity and match rates of the human dentition in 3 dimensions: relevance to bitemark analysis. International Journal of Legal Medicine 125 (6), 779–784.

"moratorium" on the use of bitemark testimony in court. This presents a significant problem on many fronts because bitemark analysis, when properly performed with appropriate collection, analysis, use of terminology, and conservative conclusions, is vital to the legal system. Bitemarks can demonstrate pain, violence, the age and timing of an injury, whether there was a single incident or pattern of abuse; or whether a bite was inflicted by an animal, child, or adult. Importantly, where the bitemark is distinctive, showing both class and individual characteristics, it can be used to develop a biter profile and exclude or include a particular suspect, and allow the forensic dentist to demonstrate in detail the features that led to this conclusion.

A "moratorium" on bitemark analysis and comparison evidence leaves many questions unanswered. Will evidence be collected or ignored? When a person with a suspected bitemark comes into the ER or the morgue, who decides if it will be swabbed for DNA? What happens when DNA does not provide a clear answer to the identity of the assailant, such as the many child abuse cases in which a caregiver can plausibly claim their DNA would be expected to be present on a child's body? What happens when too much time has passed for DNA collection or when, as a victim's body decomposes, his/her own DNA obliterates that of the biter? What about the many "mandated reporters" who see victims of suspected bites? What suspicions are they permitted to report? What will support those reports? Who will document the bitemark evidence? Taking photos of bitemarks is a highly technical skill, requiring specific camera angles, use of ABFO scales, and, in many cases, the use of UV or other alternate light sources. Harvesting bitemarks on the skin of deceased victims is also highly technical. Who will be called to perform these tasks if all the forensic odontologists are sent packing?

Who will collect timely models from suspects? It does no good to collect a suspect's models after a lengthy delay, during which teeth may have been broken, pulled, restored, or replaced. And, in cases where no suspect is developed for a significant length of time, what can one tell a defendant who justifiably insists his rights were violated and his ability to defend himself hampered by a failure to document and preserve evidence?

And even if evidence *is* collected, basic due process concerns require that evidence be processed and analyzed. Who will produce the hollow volume overlays and other computer images that aid in the comparison between bitemark and suspected biter? Whether in the context of a criminal trial that could result in the loss of freedom, or a child welfare proceeding to determine safe custody of a child, it is impossible to walk into a courtroom and plausibly explain that although evidence was collected, no qualified expert ever examined it.

While it is extremely unlikely that police could identify by bitemarks alone the killer of a New Year's Eve reveler in New York's Times Square (where there is an "open population" of an almost infinite number of potential suspects), that is simply not true in every case. In the typical child abuse scenario, where the victim comes to the ER or the morgue with bitemarks, the small circle of caregivers, generally, make up the "closed population" of potential suspects. In the usual case, all the caregivers are suspects, and evidence that some suspects are excluded and one suspect is included, and the detailed reasons why, is important evidence that must be made available to everyone. All the suspects, the investigators, the prosecutors, the defense attorneys, and the triers of fact rely on this evidence to help establish the truth.

A DEFENSE PERSPECTIVE

Thirty years ago, forensic investigation was spoken of almost religiously, a multibranched philosophy that could—with enough practice, enough patience, and enough attention to detail—positively identify who committed a crime beyond a reasonable doubt. The abilities of forensic experts to solve crimes were so strongly believed that they became the subject of countless television shows, both real and fictional. "CSI" alone has four spin-off series, each more spectacular than the last, all of them depicting dedicated and (more importantly) altogether unerring crime scene analysts who always found their man by the end of the hour. Forensic investigation was seen, in the eyes of the public at least, as nothing short of a miracle for police work. It could be used to solve cold cases that had previously stymied law enforcement; it could completely destroy a defendant's alibi; it could definitively prove guilt by analyzing a piece of evidence invisible to the naked eye.

As Associate Director of the California Innocence Project, and having worked in criminal defense for more than 15 years, I have more than a passing familiarity with the forensic sciences and forensic investigation but, at the beginning, I fell into the same beliefs that the general public had about it. I believed, as most people did, two things. First and foremost, I believed that forensic science was largely infallible and that all forensic science disciplines were largely the same—that ballistics were as rigorously tested and researched as fingerprint evidence; that bitemark evidence was as verifiable as DNA testing and able to withstand the same scrutiny and review. Second, and perhaps more importantly, I believed that forensic science was, like all other sciences, impartial. I believed that in any forensic case, the goal and ultimate purpose was to seek out and determine the truth, in whatever form, through rigorous testing, constant

questioning, and meticulous refinement and reassessment. Science, after all, has no agenda, no purpose other than to discover the truth, whatever that may be. I believed forensic science was the same: that the purpose was to discover the perpetrator through the available evidence—and if the available evidence (and the analysis of that evidence) showed the perpetrator was the suspect, or indeed, someone other than the suspect, so be it.

As to this last point, I also believed the converse: if the forensic analysis could not determine who the perpetrator was, then the analyst would simply say that no conclusion could be made. In other disciplines, scientists do this all the time. A scientist may hope that a particular medicine will lower blood pressure but after testing he/she may realize it does not work the way he/she hoped it would. He/she may try to refine, or retest, or control for other variables, but, in the end, it may simply be that the drug is a dead end, or the science is not there yet, and he/she moves on to another drug, satisfied at the very least that another avenue has been pursued and eliminated on the quest to find the truth.[7] I believed that forensic science worked essentially the same.

As I worked in the criminal justice system, however, and as I researched more and more into forensic science, I realized that my two beliefs were not reflective of the reality of how forensics is used in crime scene investigations. I will discuss these beliefs below, but I should note that one of the biggest differences between forensic science and other sciences is that it can be incredibly fallible and partial, if not in how it is designed then certainly in how it is used.

---

[7] This idealistic view of science—and the concept that science works to eliminate incorrect hypotheses as much as discover correct ones—has deep roots. Thomas Edison has reportedly said, in reference to the many times he had not been able to produce a working, long-lasting light bulb, "I have not failed 10,000 times. I have successfully found 10,000 ways that will not work." (The World Bank. 1994, World Development Report, 1994: Infrastructure for Development. New York, N.Y.: Oxford University Press.) However, there are numerous other publications that question whether Edison ever actually said this. It is likely apocryphal, but it does reflect how the general public views science and the scientific method.

This is because forensic science serves the criminal justice system, and the criminal justice system is all about proving someone is or is not the perpetrator. It is (at least in this country) explicitly adversarial, and both sides try very hard to "win" a case through the available tools they have at their disposal. Forensic science is one of those tools that the prosecution or defense use to win the case, not to solve the mystery, and this ultimate goal of forensic science sets it apart from other scientific disciplines. In astronomy, for example, scientists may attempt to determine the distance between one star and another, or how large a particular galaxy is at its widest distance. But nobody goes to prison if Alpha Centauri is 4.37 light-years away, and nobody is acquitted if the Andromeda galaxy is 220,000 light-years across. In forensic science, as opposed to other sciences, determining who the perpetrator may be is actually a secondary goal; its primary goal is to develop reliable evidence to obtain a conviction or an acquittal.

In 2001, I began working on the case of William "Bill" Richards,[8] an individual who had been convicted of the murder of his wife, Pamela. The murder occurred at their home in the High Desert area of San Bernardino, California, and was particularly brutal; Pamela had been strangled and her skull had been crushed by two cinder blocks found next to her body. Bill had come home from a long day of work to discover his wife's body on the ground outside their trailer; she had died earlier that evening at some point. No eyewitnesses saw the crime, no confession, and no direct evidence to identify the killer.

Despite this lack of direct evidence, law enforcement focused their attention on Bill almost immediately, bringing Bill in for questioning and—because it was dark out—abandoning the crime scene and the body until the next day. When they returned, much of what could have been gained through forensic analysis was lost. Investigators did not take a core temperature of the body at any point, making time of death estimation less accurate. Dogs had partially buried Pamela's body, destroying valuable trace and other evidence that could have been collected and processed. Believing they had their man, and believing they could extract a confession from Bill, law enforcement investigators ignored even the possibility of forensic testing and investigation in many respects.[9]

Bill did not confess and, based on the available evidence, the prosecution was unable to secure a conviction after three trials.[10] For the fourth trial, law enforcement needed to rely on forensic science to "solve" the case. An analysis of the body at autopsy had revealed an injury mark on Pamela's right hand, a half-crescent shaped pattern, which looked like it might be a bitemark. Investigators sent a photo of the mark to a forensic odontologist, who observed that the mark had distinct characteristics, and matched a unique feature of Bill's lower teeth: the lower right canine tooth was out of alignment with the other teeth and had never emerged fully from the gum.[11] The odontologist testified at Bill's fourth trial that based on this, "it might be one or two or less" out of a hundred people who would have this dental irregularity, and that the mark on Pamela's hand was a

---

[8] More information can be found at: https://californiainnocenceproject.org/read-their-stories/william- richards/.

[9] It is this type of consideration for forensic science that I referenced earlier, when discussing how the goal of obtaining a conviction is its primary goal first and foremost. Unless it can help to secure the conviction, it is largely meaningless to law enforcement, and it is ignored.

[10] In re Richards, 2012. 55 Cal.4th 948, 955.

[11] See footnote 10.

human bitemark "consistent with" this irregularity.[12] Bill was convicted.

Years later, the California Innocence Project spoke to the expert to see whether his testimony would be the same as when he testified at Bill's fourth trial. One of the issues was that the photograph the expert had seen was off-angle from the injury, distorting the injury mark seen in the photo. The expert acknowledged the angular distortion in the photograph of the mark on the victim's hand, and he examined other photographs depicting other, similar injuries on Pamela's body.[13] Based on these new considerations, he explained he was no longer sure "…that photograph depicts a bitemark."[14] Further, the expert acknowledged he should never have used the "one or two or less" language in his testimony, as it was "not scientifically accurate."[15] Ultimately, he concluded that "[his] opinion today is that [Bill's] teeth…are not consistent with the lesion on the hand."[16] Our office challenged the conviction on these and other grounds, arguing the fact that the expert had recanted his prior testimony, which meant the prior testimony was false and should never have been introduced in the first place, thus prejudicing his original trial. The court agreed, finding him innocent and ordering him released from prison. Bill's conviction was reversed.

Unfortunately for Bill, however, his story did not end there. The prosecution appealed the reversal, and won the appeal; the case went all the way up to the California Supreme Court for hearing. In a 4-3 decision, the Court found the expert's testimony—either his original testimony at the original trial, or his new testimony in which he recanted—to be neither true nor false because he was an expert, and expert testimony is really only their own opinion after all:

> Expert opinion is qualitatively different from eyewitness testimony and from physical evidence. Expert witnesses are by definition witnesses with "special knowledge, skill, experience, training, or education" in a particular field, and they testify "in the form of an opinion." The word "opinion" implies a subjective component to expert testimony.

> Given, on the one hand, the subjective component of expert opinion testimony and, on the other hand, the possibility that advances in science and technology might prove an earlier-held opinion to be objectively untrue, it is critical to define what precisely is meant by "false" when the false evidence standard is applied to expert opinion testimony.

> When an expert witness gives an opinion at trial and later simply has second thoughts about the matter, without any significant advance having occurred in the witness's field of expertise or in the available technology, it would not be accurate to say that the witness's opinion at trial was *false*. Rather, in that situation there would be no reason to value the later opinion over the earlier. Therefore, one does not establish false evidence merely by presenting evidence that an expert witness has recanted the opinion testimony given at trial.[17]

This came as quite a surprise to all of us because it meant two things. First, the Court seemed to be saying that when an expert in forensic science stated that Person X was the perpetrator because his DNA was a match to the biological material found at the crime scene,

[12] See footnote 10.

[13] See footnote 10 at 957.

[14] See footnote 13.

[15] See footnote 13 at 956.

[16] See footnote 13 at 957.

[17] See footnote 13 at 962–963, citations removed, emphasis in original.

this determination was definitively less valuable as testimony—less persuasive, less reliable, and less credible—than the testimony of an eyewitness. The Court seemed to believe expert testimony was "subjective" and the testimony of an eyewitness was "objective," which meant the Court believed there was at least a component of scientific analysis that involved the expert just guessing about what the evidence showed.

Second, the Court's reasoning meant that even if an expert were wrong—if, for example, he/she honestly misread the results, or if he/she discovered some error in the calculations—he/she could never go back and correct the mistake; or at the very least, it would not do any good. Once an expert testified that the results showed the person was the perpetrator; that was that: an individual could not get his or her conviction reversed merely by showing the expert was wrong, even if the expert themselves came forward to say so.

The Court's reasoning was particularly interesting, because it seemed to be saying both that forensic science was essentially guesswork and that it was essentially inviolate. The California Legislature recognized the severe problems with the Court's ruling, and 2 years later it passed a bill reversing the decision.[18] Bill went back into court and, earlier this year, the Court reversed itself, finding the changes in the law meant his conviction should be reversed.[19] Bill was allowed to go home, 23 years after his arrest, a free man at last.

The *Richards* case highlighted one of the main problems with forensic science: at the end of the day, its purpose is to be used in court, but courts have obviously had trouble with how to use it properly. Part of this problem has to do with

the two beliefs I referenced earlier in this chapter. Unfortunately, experts in forensic science are fallible, just as any other witnesses are fallible, and they can be wrong in their testimony, just as any other witnesses can be wrong. The difference, however, is that experts present themselves as having "special knowledge, skill, experience, training, or education"[20] in a particular field, and thus they are perceived as far less likely to be wrong about their testimony. This perception is obviously inaccurate as experts are human, after all, and their opinion can vary considerably, even within a particular field, which I will discuss below. Part of this perception is exacerbated by the second belief: that forensic science has no agenda or bias, and thus when an expert testifies about their analysis, they are only testifying because the science dictates the testimony. This second belief, discussed below, is not necessarily inaccurate, but small changes in how forensic science is treated and processed can dramatically reduce or even eliminate potential bias in the system.

Forensic Science Is Infallible

As previously noted, forensic science has previously been held up as being able to do almost impossible things, to identify the perpetrator when no other evidence is available, to solve a case when all other avenues have failed. To be sure, depending on the case, forensic evidence can do all of the things. But in recent years, forensic disciplines have come under increasing scrutiny and suspicion. Forensics has gone from being seen as largely infallible to being seen as deeply troubling in many respects. The use and misuse of forensic evidence has,

[18] Senate Bill 1058 (Leno), passed in 2013 and effective 2014, was sponsored by the California Innocence Project. A copy of the text can be found here: http://leginfo.legislature.ca.gov/faces/billNavClient.xhtml?bill_id=201320140 SB1058.

[19] In re Richards, 2016. 63 Cal.fourth 291, 311.

[20] In re Richards, supra, 55 Cal.fourth at 962.

unfortunately, contributed to a number of wrongful convictions. Some of these wrongful convictions would be unbelievable in fiction.[21] Some people have spent decades in prison for crimes they did not do. Some, unfortunately, have been executed.[22] These convictions and their reversals have upset confidence in the criminal justice system generally, and in forensic investigation specifically.

It was not always like this, of course. Forensic science, or the use of scientific theories to solve crimes, has been in existence since ancient times—indeed, since before the scientific method was given a name. But it has not been until the twentieth century that forensic evidence has been used in earnest, with the advent of rigorous evidence collection and investigation techniques being applied to areas as diverse as fingerprint comparison (first articulated in the eighteenth century, but later developed in earnest in 1904),[23] modern tool-mark analysis (seemingly always a part of crime scene investigation, but fully articulated by 1930),[24] bitemark analysis (used since at least 1937),[25] hair comparison (promulgated by the FBI since 1973),[26] and arson science (in 1977).[27] Armed with these new techniques, law enforcement investigators were able to rely confidently on the science behind crimes and the clues left at a crime scene, and prosecutors were able to build a case—and secure a conviction—against defendants who were entirely unaware of the mountain of evidence they had against them.

With the advent of these new techniques, criminal investigations—and the criminal justice system as a whole—took on an entirely new dimension, at least for the most serious cases. Crimes previously thought to be unsolvable, either because there were no witnesses or because there was no confession, now became entirely solvable and almost commonplace. Fingerprint evidence alone was often enough to prove a suspect was guilty beyond a reasonable doubt. In cases where forensic evidence was not enough to prove guilt, it could often be used to persuade the defendant to admit guilt, or to take a plea to avoid what could be an embarrassing and unwinnable trial.

For most of the twentieth century, forensic science could comfortably be called nothing more than an unmitigated success. It led to accuracy, consistency, and reliability, and, most importantly, it produced results. Juries could rely upon forensic experts to give scientific explanations of crimes and the state of the evidence in an impartial and unbiased way, and this made them more reliably consistent and predictable. Prosecutors, defense attorneys, and judges needed no longer to leave cases up to chance, dependent on the credibility of witnesses, or the vagaries of their memory to prove their case in court. Witnesses, after all, are unreliable.

[21] In the Matter of an Investigation of the West Virginia State Police Crime Laboratory, Serology Division, 190 W.Va. 321, 438 S E.2 d 501 (1993).

[22] Possley, March 19, 2015. Prosecutor Accused of Misconduct in Death Penalty Case, Washington Post, p. A3.

[23] Gale, 2005. Friction Ridge Skin and Personal Identification: A History of Latent Fingerprint Analysis, World of Forensic Science.

[24] Hamby, Summer 1999. The History of Firearm and Tool-mark Identification. Association of Firearm and Tool Mark Examiners, 30th Anniversary Issue, 31 (3).

[25] Wasim, Seminar: Forensic Odontology. Forensic India.

[26] Fraser, December 13, 2015. A History of Problems in Cases with Microscopic Hair Comparison. Montana Standard.

[27] Lentini, 2012. The Evolution of Fire Investigation and Its Impact on Arson Cases, ABA Magazine, Criminal Justice. vol. 27, no. 1, Spring.

They can forget key details, or contradict earlier statements; they can be biased, or have ulterior motives; they may have criminal records, and may make deals with authorities in exchange for their testimony. Experts rely on analysis, not memory; their reports are the products of that analysis, not of bias or motive; they do not testify because doing so means they avoid criminal charges in an unrelated case.

The benefits of forensic science and expert testimony were thus readily apparent, and it was, of course, not all one-sided. Defendants and defense attorneys were also able to use these same techniques to establish doubt in a case, and in many high profile cases, forensic evidence was the linchpin to a successful defense even when the prosecution's evidence seemed insurmountable. This, again, showed how integral forensic evidence had become: it had the power not just to convict the guilty but to prove the accused was actually innocent of the crime.

In the 1980s the world of forensic science took an enormous step forward. DNA evidence, and DNA testing, revolutionized the criminal justice system, in more ways than one. It is unquestionably the closest thing to definitive proof of guilt or innocence we currently have. If a person's DNA were found at the crime scene, then the question was no longer whether the analyst accurately compared the fingerprint exemplars to the partial; or whether the tire tread found at the scene was similar enough to the tires from the suspect's car. The question was not whether the DNA test was wrong or the person was the perpetrator; as DNA testing became more sophisticated, the likelihood that DNA results were incorrect became statistically insignificant. DNA was, and still is, the king of forensic science and investigation.

The advent of DNA testing had some unexpected consequences, however, for the rest of forensic science. Other areas of forensic testing

were devised primarily by law enforcement, by police officers and investigators who were trying to solve crimes, applying their intellect and their reason to make sense of the clues left at the scene. DNA testing originated from the mind of a mammalian geneticist who had nothing to do with the law or with crime scene investigation until his discovery that variations in the genetic code between individuals could help to identify and distinguish them from one another.[28]

The difference in the origin of these disciplines is important, in a number of key respects. Other areas of forensic testing were designed to decipher "clues" at a crime scene and to assist law enforcement's investigation of a case; indeed, often, forensic science is used to create additional evidence to support an investigator's theory that a suspect committed a crime. An odontologist, for example, is often asked to look at an injury on a victim and give an opinion as to whether it is a bitemark and whether a particular suspect's teeth could have made the mark; the expert relies on his or her experience as a dentist to give an opinion about the likelihood that the suspect could have done so. Depending on the experience of the expert, and what information he or she chooses to take into account or disregard, an expert may say the suspect's dentition is "consistent with" or "inconsistent with" the injury. Experts looking at the same injury may disagree considerably, and may even disagree about whether the injury is even a bitemark at all. But even the best odontologist in the world cannot look at a bitemark and tell investigators *who the suspect is* without being able to compare it to a known individual. An expert cannot look at an injury and say, for example, that this bite was caused by Mr. John Johnson of Bismarck, North Dakota, who lives on Elm Avenue.

DNA testing, on the other hand, can. DNA testing, and the DNA database, have given the criminal justice system the ability to solve

[28] Marshall, September 9, 2009. DNA Pioneer's 'Eureka' Moment. BBC News.

cases even when there is no suspect. If investigators discover a profile at the crime scene, that profile can be uploaded into the Combined DNA Index System (CODIS) and that profile can be compared to see if it is a match to someone in the database. This difference alone sets DNA testing apart from almost all other forensic disciplines. There is no arson database, for example, where law enforcement investigators can input an arson "profile" into the system and have that system spit out a previously unknown suspect.[29] Forensic odontologists can compare remains to dental records to determine victims in a plane crash, but they cannot input a dentition "profile" into an index of known suspects to determine the true culprit.

DNA testing differs from other forensic sciences in another way. It relies on statistical probability, meaning that an analyst can confidently state that the likelihood someone other than the suspect having the same genetic profile is one in billions, or on in trillions, or one in quadrillions, more than the population of the planet. Of course there are limits to DNA testing, and DNA testing is not the panacea to the criminal justice system any more than any other forensic science is. But the advent of DNA testing meant that the differences between it and other forensic disciplines were thrown in stark relief. If fiber analysis, for example, could not provide investigators with the type of certainty that DNA testing could, what amount of certainty could it provide? Upon what is that certainty based? If the evidence relied

upon by other forensic experts is qualitatively different in some way from evidence relied upon by DNA experts, how is it different? If it is not certain to the same extent or degree, could the testimony given by forensic experts in countless trials across the country be reliable or credible?

For much of the last 2 decades, these questions were answered slowly, on a case-by-case basis. Researchers looking at the forensic sciences published many papers and articles addressing deficiencies in one area or another, but they did not produce system-wide reform. Research into arson science, for example, could be used to overturn the conviction of George Souliotes,[30] but that research did not mean arson investigators across the country decided altogether to revise their manuals, or look back into other cases where similar testimony was given, or to call for a moratorium on particular techniques or testimony. For those involved in criminal justice reform, this was distressing but not surprising. Change—especially in the law—is slow to come, and the questions raised by DNA concerning the other forensic sciences were not easily answerable.

In this century, however, comprehensive research has been conducted into almost all aspects of forensic science. The results were the 2009 publication from the NAS entitled "*Strengthening Forensic Science in the United States: A Path Forward*,"[31] and was intended to serve as an assessment of forensic science and to provide recommendations on how to improve those sciences to better serve the

---

[29] There are arson databases, of course, such as the Arson and Explosives Incidents Database (AEXIS) Files kept by the Bureau of Alcohol, Tobacco, and Firearms. However, unlike CODIS, which collects and stores DNA profiles from offenders and crimes, it is simply a repository of "information on incidents of suspected arson and explosions in the United States" and US territories.

[30] Ahumada, July 3, 2013. Former Modesto Landlord Is Free After 16 Years in Prison. The Modesto Bee.

[31] Strengthening Forensic Science in the United States: A Path Forward, Committee on Identifying the Needs of the Forensic Sciences Community, 2009. National Research Council. This publication can be found at https://www.ncjrs.gov/pdffiles1/nij/grants/228091.pdf.

criminal justice system. The publication covered sciences such as fingerprint analysis, shoeprint and tire track identification, tool mark and firearms identification, hair and fiber evidence analysis, forensic odontology, and bloodstain pattern analysis. The report is far too long to recount here, but importantly, the authors noted many of the disciplines relied on subjective interpretation to arrive at conclusions; that statistics or percentages do not exist for some sciences; that significant differences can exist between experts regarding the same piece of evidence; that conclusions were often overstated at trial; and that standardized training or material is often nonexistent.[32]

More recently, a report from the President's Council of Advisors on Science and Technology (PCAST) looked specifically into the science behind forensic odontology, fingerprint analysis, hair analysis, DNA, firearms analysis, and shoeprint identification.[33] The report drew similar conclusions as the NAS report, finding that, with the exception of DNA testing, there were concerns in other sciences, with the subjectivity of analysts; a lack of research; a lack of standards; and generally advancing the proposition that more needed to be done to make these disciplines scientifically sound and reliable.

If anything, the research into the forensic sciences is just beginning, and these studies show how the face of forensic science may change yet again in the coming years. But in the short term, these reports demonstrate the need to reconsider how we think about forensic science, and more importantly, how juries and triers of fact assess the statements and testimony of forensic experts in court cases.

Forensic Science Is Impartial

As noted above, forensic science is believed by many (myself included, previously) to be impartial and unbiased. This is partially due to the general public perception of what forensic science is, and aforementioned television shows aside, this is by no means a new phenomenon; Sir Arthur Conan Doyle was regaling his readers with the tales of his star forensic detective Sherlock Holmes since the late nineteenth century. The concept of an unbiased and impartial forensic scientist applying his skills to the evidence—without care for the result or whether those results would force investigators to rethink the entire case—has been around for a very long time.

In reality, however, the concept of forensic investigation has never been truly impartial. Since its inception, it has been used to develop evidence of guilt in a criminal investigation, generally an investigation of a particular suspect. This is by design: it is the responsibility of the state (the prosecutor and the investigating

---

[32] The NAS followed up its publication with another report a few years later addressing issues with eyewitness identification and eyewitness identification procedures used by law enforcement. See "Identifying the Culprit: Assessing Eyewitness Identification," Committee on Scientific Approaches to Understanding and Maximizing the Validity and Reliability of Eyewitness Identification in Law Enforcement and the Courts; Committee on Science, Technology, and Law; Policy and Global Affairs; Committee on Law and Justice; Division of Behavioral and Social Sciences and Education; National Research Council, 2014. This publication can be found at http://www.innocenceproject.org/ wp-content/uploads/2016/02/NAS-Report-ID.pdf. As the focus of this book is on forensic sciences, however, this follow-up report is beyond the scope of this chapter.

[33] Report to the President: Forensic Science in Criminal Courts: Ensuring Scientific Validity of Feature-Comparison Methods, 2016. Executive Office of the President, President's Council of Advisors on Science and Technology. This publication can be found at https://www. whitehouse.gov/sites/default/files/microsites/ostp/PCAST/pcast_forensic_science_report_final.pdf.

agency) to develop evidence against a suspect and prove the case against the suspect beyond a reasonable doubt. The defense has no responsibility to develop evidence of innocence, and many a defendant has been acquitted solely because the prosecution could not prove its case, without the defense calling a single witness. Because of this, many forensic science laboratories are often housed in police stations, or in prosecutor's offices. There are independent laboratories, to be sure, but there are no state laboratories housed in public defender offices. Thus the concept of forensic science is to assist the state in the development of its case, and this means it is not designed to be impartial.

For the vast majority of forensic investigations, the purpose of and methods used in forensic science are also partial. As noted *ante*, most forensic sciences cannot determine who the perpetrator is unless law enforcement already has a suspect in mind. A shoeprint found at the scene does not tell an investigator that Sam Smith of Elkhorn, Indiana committed the crime. But if investigators believe Sam Smith may have committed the crime, then an analyst can tell investigators whether Sam Smith's shoes match the print found at the scene. Thus, forensic science generally confirms or corroborates other evidence, even if that other "evidence" is the suspicion of the investigators that someone committed the crime. It does not solve crime without something more. At best, it acts in tandem with other evidence to cement the case against someone. But if there is nothing else for investigators to go on, no amount of microscopic fiber analysis will point investigators in the right direction. Traditionally, then, the purpose of and methods used in forensic science are also biased, since they are used much more often to build the case against a suspect.

Two caveats should be mentioned here. First, and to reiterate, DNA testing (and, to a lesser extent, fingerprint comparison) is fundamentally different than most other sciences in this regard, since the testing can, in fact, tell investigators

who the suspect is without any other corroborating evidence. This is not to say that DNA investigations are completely impartial, and DNA results are often only as good as the person interpreting them. But they do differ from other forensic sciences based on the database alone. Second, and more importantly, forensic science has often been used to exonerate someone, or to convince investigators the suspect is innocent even before charges are filed. But it could hardly be argued that the amount of times forensic science is used to exonerate the innocent is on par with the amount of times it is used to convict the guilty. Forensic investigation is used far more in criminal investigations by law enforcement and prosecutors than it is used by defense attorneys and defendants. This means that the science is inherently skewed one way, toward prosecutions more often than it is toward exoneration.

This bias creeps into almost everything in forensic investigation, even down to how laboratories interact with the two sides. There have been countless times in my career when I have asked an "independent" crime lab to tell me about evidence in a case, only to be told I need to go through the prosecutor first. I have had analysts tell me that, if they had their way, they would tell me the results or give me the reports—but that the Sheriff has a policy that the information will not be disclosed without prior approval. Often, I do not even get a call back. But the district attorney has no problem getting all of this information without so much as a formal request, and sometimes by simply walking down the hall to the next door.

As forensic science evolves, it is my ardent hope that this status quo is disrupted considerably, and that all forensic laboratories become truly independent and impartial, as committed to discovering the truth—to exonerating the innocent and to convicting the guilty—as television says they are. This would ensure all sides have faith in the integrity of the science and, as a result, faith in the justice system as a whole.

CONCLUSION

Although this chapter points out concerns for forensic science, it is by no means an attempt to criticize or dismiss forensic investigation altogether. Rather, I hope that with the advent of additional research, applied technologies, and scientific advancements, we will look back on the early 21st century as the dawn of a new era in criminal investigation, where forensic science can be used to definitively identify perpetrators, exonerate the innocent, and improve the justice system for all who come in contact with it.

CHAPTER

2

History and Scope of Forensic Odontology

Bruce A. Schrader[1,2]

[1]Forensic Odontology Consultant, Lubbock County Medical Examiner's Office, Lubbock, TX, United States; [2]Center for Education and Research in Forensics, The University of Texas Health Science Center at San Antonio, San Antonio, TX, United States

INTRODUCTION

Not unexpectedly, the scope of forensic odontology has expanded as the science and delivery of dentistry has progressed. The first cases regarded as being dental identifications were crude and nonscientific by today's standards. They were based upon visual identification or the examiner's memory of the decedent's antemortem condition. The historical cases of dental forensics are well documented and reported in a multitude of previous writings. These instances include early dental identifications, identifications undertaken as part of mass fatality incidents (MFIs), bitemarks, expert witness testimony, age assessment, and human abuse. The purist would contend that these early cases employed nonscientific techniques; but the

accepted practice was based on the materials and methods available at that time. In retrospect, some would argue that these identifications are invalid. It is also likely that many of these historical cases would not have been allowed in court due to the inability of defense experts to present evidence. Despite the methods employed at that time, they laid the foundation for the beginning of what we know as forensic odontology.

HISTORY

It has been stated previously that the first bitemark case of historical relevance involved the "original sin" in the Garden of Eden when Eve was beguiled by the serpent (King James Bible; Brumit and Stimson, 2010). The support of the evidence lies in written records that have been passed down through the ages. The validity of that record will not be argued in this chapter.

One of the first cases involving a dental identification involves the observation of a dental anomaly in an individual. The education and training of the "odontologist" can certainly be questioned, but the result was a positive identification. Well, at least there was enough evidence to convince the examiner that the person of interest matched the dentition of the purported person. This case involves the Roman Empress Agrippina (AD 49) who used a known peculiarity in a dentition to confirm that the dismembered head brought for her review was indeed that of Lollia Paulina (Brumit and Stimson, 2010; Lipton et al., 2013). Obviously, the dental examiner, Agrippina was not a trained odontologist; but during this period of history, it would not be wise to argue the findings of the case with the examiner, as the temperament of the examiner might have deleterious effects on the inquisitor's life (Lipton et al., 2013).

Other historic positive identifications of deceased persons using their dentition have been made following battles. In several cases the identification was made by individuals who were familiar with the deceased. This was found to be the situation in the identification of the Earl of Shrewsbury in 1453 following the Battle of Castillon. In 1477, Charles the Bold, the Duke of Burgundy, was killed in the Battle of Nancy and was identified by his page that recognized spaces from teeth lost due to trauma. In 1758, Peter Halket was killed in battle and was buried. Several years following his burial, his body was exhumed and his own son provided the positive identification of the skeletonized remains. It appears the first dental identification performed by an individual recognized as a "dentist" was performed by Paul Revere. In 1776, Dr. Joseph Warren was killed in the Battle of Breed's Hill from a gunshot wound to his face leaving him unrecognizable. Dr. Warren was identified from a dental prosthesis Paul Revere had fabricated and placed (Brumit and Stimson, 2010; Lipton et al., 2013). The notable item in each of the cases to this point is all were performed by individuals without a formal dental education and in each case without confirmation by another person with the same or similar training.

The first documented use of a forensic dental expert witness was in 1814 in Scotland. This case involved multiple defendants alleged to have robbed the grave of Mrs. McAlister to use the body for medical dissection. In this case, the husband provided the wife's denture to Dr. James Alexander for comparison to the "unknown" individual. In his testimony, Dr. Alexander, the treating dentist and maker of the appliance, testified it fit the cadaver to the exclusion of any others. One opposing expert, Dr. James Scott, was called upon to examine the evidence for the defense and testified to the contrary. He testified the mouth had remaining teeth that were loose and decayed. A second witness called by the defense, Dr. Robert Nasmyth, stated that the appliance could and did fit several other cadavers (Brumit and Stimson, 2010; Lipton et al., 2013). It is interesting to consider what might have occurred in the chain of custody of the evidence in this case or what the personal thought or calibration of the "standard of care" might have been for those involved in the case.

In 1831 in London there was an accusation of the murder of a woman named Caroline Walsh at the hands of Elizabeth Ross. Following the alleged abduction and murder of Walsh, a woman appeared on the streets of London claiming to be Caroline Walsh. The defendant, Elizabeth Ross, claimed her innocence in the matter as the presumed homicide victim was in fact alive. Witnesses in the trial testified the missing woman had a healthy anterior dentition and this newly found Caroline Walsh was missing several anterior teeth with healed ridges. The court convicted Elizabeth Ross and she was executed for the crime despite no evidence of a body (Brumit and Stimson, 2010; Lipton et al., 2013).

In 1849, two Harvard professors, Dr. George Parkman and Dr. John Webster, were involved in some business dealings in which Webster was known to owe a large sum of money to Parkman. Dr. Parkman, known to be very timely, missed a dinner appointment and it was assumed shortly thereafter that Dr. Webster was responsible for his disappearance. Initial inspection of Dr. Webster's property did not reveal incriminating evidence. Subsequent searches of his property revealed a portion of a mandible and a dental prosthesis. Dr. Nathan Cooley Keep stated he had created the prosthesis and testified about the process and circumstances surrounding the appliance for Dr. Parkman. Dr. Keep was able to produce a dental model to demonstrate how the denture fit the model and display the adjustments he had made to the appliance. Dr. John Webster was sentenced to hanging for the homicide of Dr. Parkman. Webster confessed to the murder hoping to commute his sentence. He stated he had struck Parkman but had not intended to kill him. The court considered Webster's request and it was denied. This case is considered to be the first time a dental expert offered testimony in a case in the United States (Brumit and Stimson, 2010; Lipton et al., 2013).

SCOPE

Forensic odontology has many disciplines in which a practitioner becomes involved. Primarily, a dentist is called upon to perform dental identification of an unknown or confirmation of a deceased person's identity. This same methodology is also used in MFIs. Additional areas where the odontologist can be helpful are child/elder abuse recognition, bitemark analysis, age assessment, and reviewing casework for standard of care cases. There is always a possibility the odontologist will be called upon to relay their findings to the appropriate court under sworn testimony either as a deposition or in a court of law.

The majority of the general public is only aware of forensic odontology cases involving identification of a decedent by dental records. This is the most common type of case encountered by the forensic dentist, even a board-certified odontologist having experience and training in all disciplines of the profession. The forensic odontologist offers expertise in comparing dental records of a known individual to the dentition of an unidentified person. This comparative analysis is the basis for dental identifications and is the same practice used in the identification of an individual or multiple people in an MFI. The evaluation includes all available antemortem records for the known person. This would include any records available through dental visits for the individual including: patient registration forms, health histories, treatment plans, progress notes from office visits, insurance claims, billing records, photographs, dental models, and of course, all radiographs taken of the individual during the course of their care.

People often ask what the interest is in "dead people." It is unfortunate many forensic cases involve the death of an individual; however, there are instances in all disciplines of the practice of forensic odontology where there is an opportunity to assist and work with living individuals. You will certainly consider an MFI an exception to that statement, so allow me to address it first. Consider there is an MFI involving a total of 50 fatalities. In the process of collecting antemortem records and information from friends and families after the incident, there are dental records for 51 persons collected for comparison to the deceased. During this process, the dental team was able to positively identify all 50 persons recovered leaving one of the 51 records as being excluded from the remains collected. Although this does not confirm the person belonging to the one remaining record is still living, it only confirms he/she is not among the deceased group. In each of the other forensic odontology disciplines, it is possible to perform analysis on either a living or a deceased individual.

Age assessment casework most generally involves efforts to establish the approximate age of an individual, which may assist in identification of the missing and unidentified. Additionally, legal authorities may want to ascertain if an individual has attained the age of majority within a jurisdiction. This estimation can be critical in cases where the subject needs to be appropriately placed or detained in a juvenile or adult facility. Additionally, this work may assist the trier of fact in determining if an individual is to be tried for a crime as an adult or a juvenile. Age assessment can be important in determining the status of an individual for potential deportation. For example, in the United States, undocumented persons having reached the legal age of majority are generally detained and deported. Dental age assessment is a useful adjunct in determining the potential identity of an individual by offering an age range as an adjunct to identification. There are many known dental techniques, destructive and nondestructive, to estimate age. The different techniques are discussed extensively in Chapter 8.

During routine dental visits it is possible that dentists will encounter children or adults who are victims of domestic abuse. Abuse can present itself in various forms including unusual bruising or patterned injuries not consistent with normal activities or accidents. There is also the potential of encountering patients considered victims of neglect. This might be a "gray" area for some as one might consider neglect to be another version of abuse. Failure to treat a known pathologic dental condition (neglect) is a form of abuse as compared to physical maltreatment of an individual. Human abuse will be discussed more extensively in Chapter 9.

In some instances of assault, the victim or the assailant will use his/her dentition as a weapon. Human skin is an elastic material that deforms under the pressure of external forces placed by a tool or a dentition. Despite human skin being a poor medium as a dental impression material, useful information can be obtained in evaluation of the injuries. Through evaluation of the patterned injury and reviewing information surrounding the occurrence of the injury, it is possible to determine what potentially made the patterned injury. For example, the dentition of a dog or a cat bite will have a significantly different appearance than one of a human bitemark. The human dentition may leave characteristic patterned injuries on the skin. Persons who are potential suspects as the maker of a bitemark can be excluded as perpetrators due to inconsistencies between the dentition and the bitemark. For example, a suspect might be missing a tooth or multiple teeth, a tooth or teeth may be rotated, or fractured. If the bitemark was determined to have been caused by an "orthodontically correct" dentition and the suspected dentitions are not "normally aligned," these persons would be excluded from having inflicted the patterned injury. The practice of bitemark analysis has become a topic of great interest in the forensic community over the last several years. This is partially due to several previous bitemark cases being overturned by other evidence or administrative findings. The methods and techniques used in bitemark evaluation continue to be reviewed and revised by the forensic odontology community in general and the American Board of Forensic Odontology (ABFO) in particular. The desire is to standardize the evaluation and analytic process of patterned injuries for those who might be called upon to examine injuries created by a dentition. This topic will be discussed more extensively in Chapter 9.

When involved with any of the type of forensic casework, there is always the possibility the forensic odontologist will be called upon to provide a sworn testimony related to their actions, findings, or reports. This process might involve a simple review of your findings in a dental identification case or something as complex as demonstrating and explaining one's findings in a bitemark evaluation of a patterned injury in a homicide case. The forensic odontologist may be called upon by an attorney to review dental records, treatments, and results of treatment by another dentist. Normally, this involves potential or filed litigation against a provider. In a standard of care case there has likely been some type of unexpected outcome from dental treatment where a patient is seeking action or retribution against the dentist. Occasionally, the odontologist is requested to review a case by the medical examiner to assist in determining a cause or manner of death.

In closing, all disciplines of forensic odontology should be conducted after training and education to become familiar with the methodologies, standards, guidelines, and responsibilities of a prudent forensic odontology practitioner. Wherever possible, a dentist with interest in forensic odontology should attempt to find a mentor to assist in his/her education as well as to learn and discover his/her own limitations. In the following chapters, you will find additional information on all aspects of forensic odontology. Take note of what you read in these sections. These chapters will help you understand potential issues you may encounter and learn how to handle these situations appropriately.

References

Brumit, P.C., Stimson, P.G., 2010. History of forensic dentistry. In: Senn, D.R., Stimson, P.G. (Eds.), Forensic Dentistry, second ed. Taylor and Frances Group, Boca Raton, FL, pp. 11−24.

King James Bible. Genesis (Chapter 3).

Lipton, B.E., Murmann, D.C., Pavlik, E.J., 2013. Hisory of forensic odontology. In: Senn, D.R., Weems, R.A. (Eds.), Manual of Forensic Odontology, fifth ed. Taylor and Frances Group, Boca Raton, FL, pp. 1−39.

Dental Identification & Radiographic Pitfalls

Peter W. Loomis[1,2], *Jacqueline S. Reid*[3,4,5], *Michael P. Tabor*[6], *Richard A. Weems*[7,8]

[1]Forensic Odontology Consultant, New Mexico Office of the Medical Investigator, Albuquerque, NM, United States; [2]Faculty - University of New Mexico School of Medicine, Albuquerque, NM, United States; [3]Forensic Odontology Consultant: Middlesex Regional Medical Examiner's Office, North Brunswick, NJ, United States; [4]Northern Regional Medical Examiner's Office, Newark, NJ, United States; [5]Program Director, Chief, Hospital Dentistry, Robert Wood Johnson University Hospital, General Practice Residency in Dentistry, New Brunswick, NJ, United States; [6]Chief Forensic Odontologist, Davidson County, State of Tennessee, Nashville, TN, United States; [7]University of Alabama School of Dentistry, Forensic Odontology Consultant, Jefferson County Chief Medical Examiner, Birmingham, AL, United States; [8]Faculty — Forensic Dentistry Fellowship, The University of Tennessee Graduate School of Medicine, Knoxville, TN, United States

OUTLINE

INTRODUCTION

Along with determining the cause and manner of death, the Medical Examiner or Coroner (ME/C), has the legal authority and statutory responsibility to identify the deceased and issue a death certificate. The identification of a living amnesiac is the responsibility of local, state, or federal law enforcement agencies. Although it is ultimately these agencies that certify the identification to determine whether the scientific information available justifies the declaration of a positive identification and issuance of a death certificate, it is the forensic odontologist that provides their opinion of the identity, as it relates to forensic odontology. Those opinions are based upon guidelines established by the forensic odontology community and are based on scientific best practices.

The determination of a positive identification of unknown human remains or a living amnesiac by comparative dental analysis requires careful documentation of the unidentified remains or amnesiac, as well as obtaining dental/medical records from the dentists or physicians who treated the patient. The procedures and techniques used to reconcile this information (e.g., radiographs, photographic images, charts, and treatment progress notes) have been established by numerous forensic organizations including the American

Board of Forensic Odontology (ABFO), American Society of Forensic Odontology (ASFO), British Association of Forensic Odontology (BAFO), Disaster Mortuary Operational Response Team (DMORT), INTERPOL's Disaster victim identification (DVI) Forensic Odontology Subcommittee, as well as many other groups.

The positive identification of an individual is important for multiple reasons that include the following.

For Deceased Persons

- To assist family members go through the grieving process, providing some measure of relief, knowing that their loved one has been found.
- A death certificate annotated with a positive identification is necessary to settle business and personal affairs.
- Estate transfer, settlement of probate, and execution of wills, disbursement of life insurance benefits, remarriage of spouse, and child custody issues can be delayed for years by legal proceedings if a positive identification cannot be rendered.
- Criminal investigation and potential prosecution in a homicide case may not proceed without a positive identification of the victim.

For the Living Amnesiac

- A positive identification is vital to reunite a living amnesiac with their family members.

SCIENTIFIC METHODS OF IDENTIFICATION

The rationale for human identification is based on the hypothesis that every person has a unique phenotype, and thus a decedent's biometric data and physical changes that occur during their lifetime can be compared with antemortem biometric/medical/dental records of the presumed decedent or living amnesiac to establish a positive identification.

All methods of identification involve comparing the postmortem evidence of the decedent with known antemortem data. If a presumed identification has been established by context and circumstance, then antemortem biometric data obtained on the individual may be compared to the postmortem evidence to establish a positive identification.

There are five generally accepted methods used to identify deceased persons and most require a presumptive identification to allow for the direct comparison of antemortem and postmortem evidence. Depending on the condition of the remains and availability of antemortem data, each method has advantages or shortcomings and all are dependent on the existence of antemortem data. If there is no presumptive identity of the individual, careful examination of the remains may provide clues to the examiner, which might limit the pool of potential persons, eventually leading to identification.

TECHNIQUES OF HUMAN IDENTIFICATION

Visual

Visual identification is a method that is not scientific but may be used by the ME/C when the remains are intact, nondecomposed, and viewable, and/or the death was witnessed. However, changes in appearance from illness, the circumstances of death (fire, trauma, disruption, etc.), and postmortem taphonomic effects (decomposition, mummification, saponification, skeletonization, animal predation/scavenging, insect activity) render visual identification unreliable in many instances. Tattoos, scars, piercings, subdermal body modification, and soft-tissue abnormalities included in this method may be useful for identification if the tissue is intact. Personal effects found with the remains or at the scene (ID cards, jewelry, cell phones etc.) should never be used to make an identification, but are important clues for a presumptive identification that may direct the investigator to obtain antemortem data to allow for a scientifically based identification.

Ridgeology (Fingerprints)

A biometric method of human identification is commonly used when the soft tissue of the fingers is intact, an adequate impression or image of the friction ridges can be obtained, and antemortem fingerprint records are available. Burned, severely decomposed, skeletal, and fragmented remains may not readily exhibit fingerprints. Fingerprint (ridgeology) identification has the advantage of a large known national and international database and it does not require a presumptive identification to obtain antemortem information.

The largest fingerprint database in the world is the Federal Bureau of Investigation (FBI) Integrated Automated Fingerprint Identification System (IAFIS), with more than 34 million civil and 70 million criminal fingerprint files. The Department of Homeland Security (US-VISIT) maintains a fingerprint database with over 67 million files, and INTERPOL maintains an AFIS system for its 188 member countries of 233,000 files. Fingerprint identification is often the most expedient method for human identification if the fingers can be printed and if antemortem fingerprint records are available.

Anthropology/Radiology

Anthropology/Radiology is another biometric method of identification that relies on the unique characteristics of the skeleton, comparing postmortem radiographic imaging with antemortem imaging and written records. Radiographs of bony anomalies, healed fractures, pathological lesions, medical/surgical hardware, or unusual qualities of the skeleton can be used to make a positive identification However, most individuals have never had antemortem skeletal imaging, or the images may no longer be available. Some ME offices have installed computed tomography (CT) scanners that can provide images to compare with both conventional dental and medical radiographs along with antemortem CT images. The capability of a CT scan to provide multiplanar and reconstructed images of the skeleton can be very helpful in comparisons.

DNA

As with the other biometric methods of identification, DNA comparison relies on accessible antemortem data. However, unlike other modalities, familial relationship can be established even when antemortem data are not available. In addition, like ridgeology (fingerprints), large national databases are currently being established that can reduce the need for a presumptive identification, especially if the decedent has had contact with the justice system.

The best sources for DNA material are direct reference samples from the decedent during life. Direct reference samples are classified as primary and secondary. Primary direct DNA sources include blood, a tissue biopsy slide, a pap smear, tooth remnants, and a hair sample (with roots). Direct secondary DNA sources include a toothbrush, comb, bedding, or clothing. Indirect DNA reference samples are those from biological relatives. DNA testing requires more time, effort, specialized personnel, and higher cost than other identification methods. The degree to which human remains are fragmented or degraded determines the value of DNA analysis in the identification process. Intact, large body parts lend themselves to identification by less costly methods, such as dental, radiographic imaging, and fingerprints. However, DNA analysis may be the only viable method for identifying severely fragmented or degraded remains. The majority of forensic DNA tests are performed on nuclear DNA using polymerase chain reaction (PCR) amplification of the sample with short tandem repeat (STR) typing. Simultaneous analysis of mitochondrial DNA (mtDNA) may be necessary to improve the identification process.

STRs are particularly informative when using well-preserved soft tissue and bone samples and even on degraded tissue and bone fragments if the DNA extraction process is optimized. However, STRs alone are often not sufficient for identification when samples are severely compromised.

Forensic DNA analyses for human identification has seen a tremendous upsurge since the President's DNA Initiative Program that began in 2003. The program provided funding, training, and further financial assistance to ensure that forensic DNA would reach its full potential in identifying missing persons. From this program, the National Institute of Justice (NIJ) now provides funding to have DNA analyses performed on unidentified remains by the Center for Human Identification at the University of North Texas or the FBI. Once the analysis is complete, the profiles (if they are sufficient) are entered into the FBI's CODIS system (Combined DNA Index System) and uploaded into the National DNA Index System.

Dental

Dental identification is the most common biometric method for identifying burned, decomposed, skeletonized, and fragmented remains for multiple reasons.

1. Teeth survive; tooth enamel is the hardest biological substance in the human body, and posterior teeth are well protected by soft tissues (the tongue, facial musculature, and adipose tissue). Teeth survive prolonged immersion, decomposition, desiccation, extensive trauma, and direct heat in excess of 1000°F.
2. Tooth morphology; the presence or absence of teeth, tooth position, dental restorations,
3. Dental and oral pathology, bony anatomy, periodontium, maxillary and frontal sinus morphology, and many other features of the oral cavity and maxillofacial complex are available for comparison. No two individuals have the exact same dental features.
4. Many people have been to the dentist and have a dental chart and radiographs.

5. A postmortem dental examination (clinical and radiographic) can be done quickly and inexpensively.
6. Dental records of missing persons are kept in several national databases to compare with newly discovered remains.
7. In mass fatality incidents, it is often the most expedient method for identifying burned, fragmented, and decomposed human remains.

Since the complete adult human dentition consists of 32 teeth that may be virgin, missing, or restored on one or more of each tooth's five surfaces, a great many combinations of dental patterns exist that are helpful in making a dental identification. In addition, the postmortem radiographic appearance of the victim's teeth, restorations, bone, anomalies, and maxillary and frontal sinuses is essential when determining a dental identification.

COLLECTION AND PRESERVATION OF POSTMORTEM DENTAL EVIDENCE

Examination Procedures

The visual and radiographic examination and subsequent dental charting can be a relatively easy procedure or a difficult task, depending on the accessibility of the teeth and the condition of the remains.

The postmortem dental examination is usually conducted by the authority and request of the ME/C or his designee, typically a forensic pathologist. Thus, the protocol for the collection of postmortem dental evidence, particularly decisions to incise the facial tissues for access or to section the mandible, is subject to approval by the regional ME/C. The actual procedures to be followed in a dental identification case depend in large part on the condition of the remains.

Access the Oral Cavity

Complete, unrestricted access to the oral cavity is necessary to conduct a thorough clinical, radiographic, and photographic dental examination of the decedent. The forensic odontologist has both the legal and ethical obligation to perform a meticulous postmortem examination of the decedent. As this can only be accomplished with proper access to the oral structures, in some cases it may require surgical exposure of the oral cavity regardless of community or family wishes. The forensic odontologist must take all steps necessary to minimize the disfigurement of the body; however, if no other alternative can be found and surgical access is required, the exposure must be adequate to allow for the proper documentation of all structures of the oral cavity.

Viewable Remains

Restricted opening due to rigor may require: Intraoral incision of masticatory muscles, with or without fracture of the condyles.
Breaking the rigor with bilateral leverage on the jaws in the retromolar regions.
Waiting until the rigor subsides.
Inframandibular dissection with or without mandibular resection.
Removal of the larynx and tongue at autopsy may facilitate the visual examination of the teeth and/or placement of intraoral films. Again, the removal of these tissues should only be performed after the autopsy and with permission of the pathologist. These tissues should either be retained by the pathologist or replaced with the body.

Nonviewable Remains

Remains may be decomposed, incinerated, disfigured, or fragmented to the extent that they cannot (and should not) be viewed by family members or loved ones.
Jaw osteotomy/sectioning in such cases may facilitate dental charting and radiographic examination. Careful dissection of the incinerated head is required to preserve fragile tooth structure and jaws in situ. Photographs and radiographs should be made prior to manipulation of badly burned or fragile fragments. The use of a fixative agent to stabilize remains should be considered as necessary. Care should be taken to use stabilizing agents that will not degrade the remains and should only be utilized after any necessary DNA extraction occurs.

Surgical Exposure for Access to Oral Cavity

Although the surgical exposure of the hard and soft tissue of the maxilla and mandible via sectioning or resectioning may be necessary for full access to dental structures, this should only be performed with the approval of the ME/C and according to the autopsy protocols of the local municipality. Consideration of the fact that family members may wish to exercise their right to view even the most severely decomposed or fragmented remains requires that this procedure only be utilized when no other alternative is available.
If adequate justification is found, surgical access to the oral cavity should be performed in a manner that minimizes the extent of surgical intervention and with the goal, whenever possible, to attempt to return the tissues to their original location following the examination. In cases where this is not possible and in cases where the remains are not needed for additional examination, the resected section should be stored in the same human remains pouch as the rest of the remains.

Photography

Photographic documentation of dental evidence can be helpful in comparative dental identification and in documenting dental evidence, especially when there are unique dental features that would be difficult to describe. Photography can provide a double check for possible recording errors. Photographs, particularly those of the anterior teeth, may be useful for comparisons to antemortem photographs that show unusual features of these teeth. Photographs (with an accompanying scale) should be taken before and after appropriate cleansing. The ABFO No. 2 scale is recommended. The photographs should be in focus and clearly labeled with the case number/ name and date. All relevant photographic information should be documented.

Photographic Views

Full face, lips retracted
Close-up view of anterior teeth
Lateral views of teeth in slightly open position, and in occlusion
Occlusal views, upper and lower teeth
Special views, as required

Dental Radiographs

Every postmortem dental examination must include dental radiographs. An accurate dental examination without dental radiographs is not possible, since there are many conditions that are only detectable with them, i.e., endodontically treated teeth, retained roots, impacted teeth, etc. Dental radiographs are the documentation that will be needed to substantiate conclusions. People may make recording errors in a chart, but radiographs are the objective recordings of the dental characteristics/evidence. A thorough postmortem dental radiographic examination should include a complete series of periapical images of the available dental structures. Bitewing radiographs or projections should be included because they are the most common type found in antemortem dental records. Other dental-related postmortem radiographic images may include panoramic and occlusal imaging and CT imaging of the head. If postmortem cone beam computed tomography (CBCT) imaging technology could be done, the entire postmortem dental examination procedure would change with revolutionary results. CBCT imaging would allow for the reconstruction of standard dental radiographs from postmortem remains and allows for the possibility of three-

dimensional superimposition of antemortem and postmortem virtual data for matching and identification. CBCT records also allow for virtual archiving of specimens, tele-forensic techniques, and automated dental identification systems. The possibilities of CBCT imaging on decedents in a mass fatality incident are enormous and should be considered if funding considerations can be addressed. A single scan of the victim could later be compared to any possible variety of submitted antemortem dental images (i.e., bitewings, periapical, panoramic, occlusal, PA skull, Waters' view, etc.).

When making postmortem radiographs, the operator should be cognizant that the purpose of these images is for comparison to images taken when the decedent was alive. It is important that postmortem radiographs be properly angulated, exposed, processed, and digitally enhanced as necessary. Conventional (film) or digital dental bitewing and periapical radiographs of the anterior and posterior teeth should be made in a consistent manner on all decedents and living amnesiacs. A full mouth series of dental radiographs consisting of eighteen (18) radiographs should be made on adults with an intact dentition, which would include four (4) bitewing dental radiographs and fourteen (14) periapical dental radiographs. In lieu of conventional bitewings, a bitewing "projection" could be taken with the teeth out of occlusion using separate views of the upper and lower teeth with a horizontal bitewing angulation. Occlusal exposures may be used for objects larger than a periapical film and may be helpful in radiographic documentation of the deciduous dentition.

Although fewer radiographs may be taken when there are fewer teeth present or the dental evidence is fragmented, edentulous areas still need to be visualized. Edentulous areas or arches must be included in a radiographic exam as well as the empty alveolar sockets of teeth that have been lost postmortem. Since the quality of the antemortem and postmortem radiographs will affect the ability to make a positive dental identification, it is imperative that, whenever possible, high quality images are obtained. The original antemortem radiographic images should be requested from the missing person's dentist.

The Postmortem Dental Record

While most morgues will have the standard autopsy equipment, the forensic odontologist may wish to assemble a forensic odontology autopsy kit that may include mouth mirrors, explorers, camera equipment, anatomic dental charts, impression materials, mouth props, surgical access instruments, etc.

The postmortem dental examinations might utilize anatomic dental charts, photographs, radiographs, casts, tape recordings, and/or narrative descriptions. The data collected should be comprehensive in scope since antemortem records are commonly not discovered until days, weeks, or even years later.

Dental Examination

The universal tooth numbering system is currently used in the United States. The record should reflect any missing dental structures or jaw fragments as well as those present and available for evaluation. The chart should illustrate as graphically as possible the following:

Configuration of all dental restorations (including prostheses), caries, fractures, anomalies, abrasions, implants, erosions, or other features for all teeth.
Materials used in dental restorations and prosthetic devices, when known.
Periodontal conditions, calculus, stain.
Occlusal relationships, malposed teeth; anomalous, congenitally missing, and supernumerary teeth.
Intraoral photographs should be used to show anatomic details of teeth, restorations, periodontium, occlusion, lesions, etc.

Numbering Systems, Narrative Descriptors, and Nomenclature

The anatomic dental chart may be supplemented by a narrative description of the postmortem findings with particular emphasis on unusual or unique conditions. Standardized dental nomenclature should be used as described below and the tooth designation should be based on the anatomy of the tooth regardless of its location in the area of the mouth. This protocol should be utilized in cases of tooth numbering ambiguity regardless of the numbering system used.

Three-Dimensional Models

Three-dimensional models (study casts, working casts, 3-D digital models) are often a useful source of antemortem information. Direct comparison of antemortem and postmortem dental anatomy, rugae and occlusal relationships may also serve as an extremely useful tool for comparative dental identification.

Three-dimensional models may also be used to preserve evidence in identification cases, but due to the postmortem fragility of the teeth and the decomposition of the soft tissue, making impressions could alter the existing evidence. Preservation of dental cast evidence should be treated as any physical evidence. In addition, casts can now be digitized and stored in electronic form. The casts can also be recreated utilizing a 3-D printer.

Collection and Preservation of Antemortem Dental Evidence

A forensic odontologist should be retained to perform the examination of the antemortem dental chart and record the necessary information to assure that all recorded information is accurate and preserved in a report for potential comparisons. A complete visual inventory and written catalogue of all of the available antemortem dental evidence is critical to any forensic dental examination. The forensic dental chart of the antemortem condition (odontogram) should allow for adequate notations via either words and/or diagrams for all existing conditions. Charting designations for teeth should use a locally recognized numbering system. In the United States, this is the Universal Numbering System.

TYPES OF ANTEMORTEM INFORMATION

Antemortem dental records should be obtained from the most recent dental provider of the decedent as well as past providers as necessary. The antemortem dental records requested by the investigator should include the entire dental record: dental radiographs, written notes, odontograms, periodontal charts, treatment notes, photographs, three-dimensional models, (study casts, working casts, 3-D digital models), and dental laboratory prescriptions or notes. Medical imaging of the head and neck can be quite useful in comparison with the postmortem dental evidence and should be obtained if available. These might include CT scans, conventional head radiographs (lateral, lateral oblique, AP), Waters' view (occipitomental), odontoid, and others. Documented referrals to and from other providers can provide an additional source of antemortem data, including images and procedural information.

Collection of antemortem records is ordinarily the responsibility of the investigative agency that has access to missing persons reports at the local, state, or national level. The investigator is encouraged to check with local health departments, charity or interfaith dental clinics, for prior military service, regional dental specialists, chiropractic radiographs, dental schools, or even an email blast to all dental offices in the surrounding areas to find useful antemortem records.

Antemortem Radiographs

When antemortem digital radiographs are transmitted electronically, high-resolution single image radiographs should be sent along with a composite structured display (mounted film) image for location verification. Data transfer should follow American Dental Association (ADA) recommendations that include utilizing Digital Imaging and Communications in Medicine (DICOM) protocols. In cases where DICOM protocols cannot be utilized, the images should be properly annotated with the appropriate demographic data (name, date of birth, date of radiograph, etc.). A dental radiographic dot must be clearly visible on all images and special care should be exercised with some Phosphor Storage Plates imaging systems where image reversal is possible.

Panoramic Radiographs

This type of image provides a large single radiograph that reveals the maxilla and the mandible, the sinus cavities, nasal passages, lower portions of the orbits, and the angles of the mandible. They should be used for comparison to antemortem dental images cautiously if the antemortem images are of a different type. The individual teeth and supporting structures can be overlapped or distorted making comparison to other film types difficult.

Cone Beam Computed Tomography (CBCT)

CBCT is a medical imaging technique consisting of X-ray computed tomography (CT) where the X-rays are divergent forming a cone, not thin or fan-shaped such as that used in typical medical CT units. As a 3-D rendition, CBCT offers an undistorted view of the dentition that can accurately visualize both erupted and nonerupted teeth, tooth root orientation, and anomalous structures that conventional 2-D radiography cannot. CBCT has become increasingly important in treatment planning and diagnosis in implant dentistry, orthodontics, endodontics, oral surgery, and interventional radiology. The resolution of the images can range from 0.4 mm to as small as 0.125 mm in some units and the implications for forensic dental identification are enormous.

In addition to creating 3-D images of the bone and facial soft tissue, any intraoral or extraoral film image view can then be simulated from one scan with the ability of the operator to select the desired slice location and orientation. Thus, a panoramic image can be recreated with an adjustable thickness or zone of sharpness and there are no superimposed anatomical structures. There is no magnification and the images are 1:1 representations.

Medical Radiographs

These radiographs are made for orthodontic purposes or for diagnosis of head injuries, sinus problems, etc. They usually show the entire skull from a particular view or exposure. While anatomic features such as the sinuses, especially the frontal sinus in an anterior/posterior view or a Waters' view, can be depicted, the visualization of the teeth may be difficult due to overlapping of teeth, superimposition of the right and left sides of the arches, and other types of distortion. All of these factors can make comparison of specific dental features difficult. However, medical CT imaging of the head could be helpful when the scan includes the teeth and the jaws. These types of advanced images can allow visualization of the teeth and oral structures in the axial, coronal, and sagittal planes, 3-D reconstruction, and can mimic dental bitewing, periapical, and panoramic radiographs.

Preservation of Antemortem Dental Evidence

The antemortem dental record needs to be preserved once it has been used to make or exclude an identification. Even if exclusion was the result in the initial missing person case, the antemortem record should be saved to make comparisons to unknown decedents in the future. If it is exclusion, and policy allows, it should be inputted into a missing persons database (NamUs, NCIC, etc.) to be compared with unknown decedents in the future. All written, radiographic, and photographic records should be copied or scanned and digitized using appropriate techniques, and saved in the decedent's written or digital file if an identification has been made. The original records, after having been suitably copied or digitized, can be returned to the provider if requested, or stored.

RATIONALE FOR COMPARISON

All of the methods of human identification (visual, fingerprint, anthropologic/radiographic, DNA, and dental) involve the comparison of the antemortem data to postmortem evidence to establish a positive identification. The rationale for the forensic identification of deceased and living persons is based on the fact that each person has a unique phenotype and, along with the physical changes that occur during their lifetime, can be compared to biometric data of the unidentified person.

For dental structures, discernible physical differences between individuals as well as the physical alteration of the dentition by dental intervention can be visualized with a complete physical and radiographic exam. The stability of these changes over time and the known direction of change that typically occurs to these structures allow for the reliable dental comparison of biometric features and the identification of humans based on the uniqueness of these features.

Comparison

After all the postmortem data have been gathered, and antemortem dental records have been received and analyzed, a comparison of all the information can be completed. When comparing the antemortem records to the postmortem data it is important to stay as objective as possible, and state only what is certain based on the existing information. There is no place for speculation when performing a dental identification.

Most helpful to the examiner in the comparison process is to complete a side-by-side charting for each tooth, for both the antemortem records and the postmortem records. It is also prudent to keep in mind that while there are many charting methods one can utilize, choosing one consistent means at the outset will make your comparison review less complicated. The charting method most commonly used in the United States by forensic odontologists is WinID3.

Each tooth should be compared by the examiner. If information is missing from the antemortem (most often) record or postmortem record, then no comparison can be made for that tooth. When the information between the antemortem and postmortem data is the same for a tooth, then the finding is recorded as consistent. But what happens when the data are different between the antemortem charting and the postmortem charting? That depends on whether the difference is an "explainable" inconsistency or not. An explainable inconsistency is simply a difference that can be explained through the normal course of dental treatment. For example, in the antemortem record, tooth #19 has a large mesio-occlusal-distal amalgam and in the postmortem condition, tooth #19 has a crown. Put another way, an explainable inconsistency is a finding that is consistent with the natural progression of time in the "life-span" of a tooth. If an inconsistency cannot be explained by the natural course of time, such as a tooth missing in the antemortem record and is then present in the postmortem findings, the inconsistency is deemed unexplainable. Just one irreconcilable difference between the antemortem records and the postmortem records nullifies the identification. It is paramount that great care is taken in the comparison of the records to prevent a misidentification.

In the absence of dental restorations, tooth comparisons should take advantage of anatomical features of the tooth and surrounding structures including but not limited to crown and root morphology, shape of the pulp chamber, trabecular pattern of supporting bone, and the angulations of a tooth relative to the adjacent teeth. Additionally, any maxillofacial features seen in the records can be compared such as the size and shape of the maxillary sinuses, anterior nasal spine, foramen, and tori to name a few.

Additional Comparison Techniques

Evaluation of antemortem data is not limited to dental radiographs. Removable appliances can also be used for comparison including bleaching trays, night guards, sport guards, orthodontic appliances, removable partial dentures, and full dentures by simply placing the appliance in the decedent's mouth to confirm the fit.

When a decedent is found with a denture in place, it should be examined for any identifying information. Most states have laws and regulations mandating the dentures have identifying information embedded into the acrylic. Additionally, study models can also be compared and may have information that can be useful, such as capturing the palatal rugae for overlay comparison.

Sometimes antemortem dental records are not available. It is important to consider that other medical records can be used to make comparisons. Oftentimes there is valuable dental information found in head CT scans, skull X-rays, spinal X-rays, and the like. It is important when comparing a medical X-ray view to a dental X-ray that the examiner pays close attention to the orientation and angle of the X-ray and sometimes overlapping of the dental structures in the film, for example, when looking at a lateral skull X-ray.

While not as desirable as the abovementioned records for comparison, a close-up, full smile photograph of high resolution can be used for superimposition. In this technique, the examiner would use image processing software to create an overlay transparency to compare the anterior six upper teeth.

The fluorescence properties of composite resins and porcelain restorative materials often allow for the observation of esthetic tooth restorations that may be overlooked by conventional clinical examination. The light emitted from inexpensive UV flashlights in the 365–395 nm wavelengths will cause such restorative materials to fluoresce thus allowing for their observation and documentation. Advanced techniques using scanning electron microscopy to observe the microstructure of teeth and composite resins and the determination of the elemental composition of dental materials using either scanning electron microscopy–energy dispersive X-ray spectroscopy or X-ray fluorescence have been useful in the dental identification of human remains.

Direction of Change

As discussed in the preceding paragraphs, when there is an alteration in an individual's dental condition that direction of change is chronologically based in one direction. This was described by Lorton and Langley, "The direction of change of status of a tooth is fixed; that is, a tooth cannot have a filling on a surface and then proceed to a state in which there is no filling on that surface. It can only go from having no filling on a surface to a state in which there is one." Caution should be used when the comparison is between deciduous and succedaneous teeth. Likewise, once a tooth is extracted or otherwise deemed missing, it cannot subsequently be present. This change is significant during the verification process and must be considered during any comparison or search process. Again, care should be taken when the comparison is between deciduous and succedaneous teeth.

The forensic odontologist will evaluate and compare the postmortem evidence and the antemortem materials. It is their task to determine if the two records were made or could have been made from the same individual. Most will employ similar routines and techniques; however, there may be some variation in the way that this comparison is executed. For there to be a positive identification, all inconsistencies within the written records must be reconciled and distinguishing features must be demonstrable in the evidence.

It has been stated in forensic odontology literature that the comparison of dental features does not require any specific number or minimum number of concordant points to declare a positive dental identification. It is commonly believed that even a singular distinct feature may be enough in a particular instance to make an identification. However, there is little documented large-scale research to support this conclusion and the specific level of uniqueness of any specific feature has never been quantified.

As a rule, dental restorations have far more unique concordant features when compared to the number of unique morphological features on a natural tooth. Even a single restoration has multiple measurable metrics such as width, depth, and height, as well as shape. Shape, too, has multiple metrics including line angles, imperfections, and location relative to anatomical structures.

Some caution should be exercised when quantifying any of these biometric parameters since anatomical structures as well as the shape and size of a restoration can be altered by the angulation of the radiograph and the superimposition of adjacent structures.

Dental identification should rely solely on the weight of the dental evidence. The use of supporting contextual evidence, although important, should only be used by the ME/C in making a final determination if the dental evidence is insufficient to make a positive identification.

Categories and Terminology for Body Identification

The ABFO has defined the categories of terminology to describe the levels of certainty for a dental identification.

Positive Identification

The antemortem and postmortem data are concordant in sufficient detail to establish that they are from the same individual and there are no irreconcilable discrepancies.

Possible Identification

The antemortem and postmortem data have consistent features, but, due to the quality of either the postmortem remains or the antemortem evidence, it is not possible to confirm a dental identification.

Insufficient Evidence

The available information is insufficient to form a conclusion.

Exclusion

The antemortem and postmortem data are clearly irreconcilable. However, it should be understood that identification by exclusion is a valid technique in certain circumstances.

Since the forensic odontologist is not in a position to verify that the acquired antemortem records are correct with regard to name, date, etc., the report should state that the conclusions are based on records that are purported to represent a particular individual.

REPORT WRITING

It is customary that once the decedent's identity has been established, the odontologist submit a written report to detail their examination and findings. There is no standardized report for identification; however, there is basic information that should be included in every report.

- Name, address, and contact information
- Case identifier (number) provided by ME/C office and office contact information
- Introduction—individual or agency making the request
- Antemortem examination—identifies all material provided and agency or individual provided the material
- Postmortem examination—identifies the date you performed the dental autopsy, all of the things you did, and all the radiographs you took.
- Charting—side-by-side summary of the antemortem and postmortem data.
- Discussion of the findings
- Conclusion
- Signature

When it comes to an identification report, more information is better than less. A chart that compares each tooth, annotates its condition in the antemortem record and in the postmortem record, and then summarizes the consistent features for all teeth that had information and were compared by the examiner is not only practical but also a simple way to present the data in an unambiguous way.

We have all heard the expression "A picture is worth a thousand words." While it is not a requirement that images be part of a forensic dental report, the use of images in a dental identification report is a valuable visual tool. Showing side-by-side an antemortem radiograph to a postmortem radiograph with the same features seen in both is powerful. Remember, your report will be reviewed by professionals and nonprofessionals alike. Anyone who picks up your report should be able to "see" the reason for the positive identification.

Be sure to check and double check your report before sending it. Verify spelling of names; be sure that the dates and case number is correct; make sure there are no typos or grammatical errors. You will be held accountable for everything that is in your report.

TESTIFYING IN COURT IN A FORENSIC IDENTIFICATION CASE

There may be occasion when the forensic odontologist will be called upon to testify in court on the identification of an individual. Therefore it is important to understand how to prepare for your day in court, prior to taking the stand. Since most trials usually take place several years after you have performed the identification and written your report, it is crucial that the forensic odontologist maintain their files on cases in a detailed and organized fashion. Redundancy is an asset. A hard copy of your report, chain of custody forms, copies of antemortem records, and your handwritten notes may be old-fashioned, but it is also a very good idea. Be sure that you keep all your digital case files backed up, and in more than one place. Your computer can crash, your backup drive can be corrupt, any number of things can happen. You should be prepared for any and all of these occurrences. As stated before, when the request to testify in a case comes to you, it is likely much time has elapsed, you may not even remember doing the case until you have reviewed your files. Under these circumstances, the most important document will be your report This report will form the basis of your testimony. The better your report, the easier it is to prepare to testify.

Whether you are retained by the prosecutor or the defense, it is absolutely necessary that you have a pretrial conference to prepare with counsel, go over questions, review your CV, and the like. Remember, your job as an expert witness is to educate and inform the trier of fact and that starts with the lawyer that retained you.

It is essential that you prepare you own court exhibits, which will be based on your report. For the exhibit, arrange a computer slide presentation of your identification process, which should follow your report exactly but perhaps show slightly more detail. Foremost, your slides should have a side-by-side table of the antemortem and postmortem charting and clearly labeled side-by-side images of the antemortem and postmortem X-rays that can be explained in detail in court.

FORENSIC ODONTOLOGY SOFTWARE

One of the more difficult tasks for a forensic odontologist is the identification of unidentified remains when the investigators have no clue to the possible (presumptive) identity. With computer comparison programs, the antemortem and postmortem information can be entered into a database. Comparisons are made by generating a ranking list of possible candidates that can then be confirmed or rejected by visual comparison of the appropriate dental radiographs and/or other dental evidence.

Currently Used Software Packages

Numerous "search and match" software packages exist for dental data. Of these only three software packages are used within the US Government agencies including the US Military.

WinID3

WinID3 is a Windows-based software, written in Visual Basic 6/Microsoft Access. It was developed by Dr. James McGivney in the late 1990s. Designed to run either on a single PC or on a simple Workgroup network, it has been used extensively in the United States for numerous multiple fatality incidents, including the World Trade Center, Hurricane Katrina, and the Joplin Tornadoes. Postmortem or antemortem data are entered using primary codes similar to the NCIC dental coding system with optional secondary dental codes as well as free form comments. The user is given numerous sorting option choices to create a ranked list of likely matches. The forensic odontologist then scrolls through that list to visually determine matches by viewing both the antemortem and the postmortem odontograms. In 2014, the source code was assigned to the ABFO. WinID3 can be reviewed and downloaded on its website at http://www.abfo.org/winid/.

Unified Victim Identification System/UVIS Dental Identification Module

Following the September 11 World Trade Center attack, the Department of Homeland Security funded the Office of Chief Medical Examiner (OCME) of the City of New York to develop a web browser-based application to handle critical fatality management functions made necessary by a major disaster. UVIS (Unified Victim Identification System) is an enterprise-level application designed to manage and coordinate all of the activities related to victim identification and missing persons reporting. Numerous modules covering areas such as the call center, case management, family assistance center, field operations, disaster mortuary management, DVI, identification tracking, postmortem, and remains storage.

UDIM (UVIS Dental Identification Module) was developed by Dr. Kenneth Aschheim in conjunction with the forensic odontologists of OCME and the ICRA Sapphire Inc. As a Windows-based application, it is an integrated module in the UVIS—application. It utilizes a simple coding system as well as optional, user-editable, restoration codes, condition codes, and material codes, and unlimited image importation. UDIM utilizes a single sorting algorithm based on explainable and unexplainable discrepancies and has some built in coding correcting algorithms to compensate for the most common ambiguities.

In 2015, OCME released UDIM-Stand Alone (UDIM-SA), a standalone version of UDIM.

This version has all the features of UDIM/UVIS and UDIM-CMS but can be deployed on a single PC or within a simple workgroup. The UDIM application and source code is available from the Department of Homeland Security. The UVIS/UDIM system can be reviewed on its website at https://uvistraining.com/.

Disaster Victim Identification System International

The DVI System International is a product of Plass Data Software and is the official software application for most INTERPOL DVI teams as well as members of North Atlantic Treaty Organization (NATO). Like UVIS, it is an enterprise level application multiple fatality management package with an integrated dental module. It utilizes a three-letter mnemonically based coding system and is capable of displaying a detailed odontogram of even the most complex dental record. Complete integration of both paper and electronic data allows the system to work in any environment. As with the other two software applications described above, DVI International creates a ranking of possible matches based on a proprietary ranking algorithm. Unlike WinID and UDIM-SA, this is a paid commercial software package and does require a high level of expertise to install and operate. Information concerning the software and a trial package is available at http://www.plass.dlk.

OdontoSearch 3.0

In cases where antemortem radiographs are not available, comparative dental analysis comparisons can only be based on written notes and charts obtained from a missing individual's medical records. The problem with this data is that, unlike radiographs, the information cannot be exclusively correlated to a specific individual. Although absolute uniqueness cannot be determined, studies have shown that in large populations the frequency of certain restorative patterns is rarer than others. The OdontoSearch 3.0

computer program (http://www.odontosearch.com) provides an objective means of assessing the frequency of occurrence of these dental restoration patterns. By comparing an individual's pattern of missing, filled, and unrestored teeth to a large, representative sample of the US population, a likelihood of occurrence of this pattern (similar to mtDNAcomparisons) is calculated. Often, this information, when combined with contextual information, is sufficient to determine an identification, especially in non-fragmented cases.

MISSING AND UNIDENTIFIED PERSONS DATABASES

NamUs

National Missing and Unidentified Persons SystemThe National Missing and Unidentified Persons System (NamUs) database is an NIJ-funded program administered by the University of North Texas. NamUs consists of the unidentified persons, missing and unidentified persons (MUPs), and unclaimed persons databases that are cross-referenced, allowing advanced search and comparison protocols. The system is internet based and allows the uploading and reviewing of images (radiographs, dental records, photos, etc.). Law enforcement, ME/Cs, forensic specialists (odontologists, anthropologists, fingerprint examiners, etc.), and the public have various levels of access privilege to the system. It has been online since 2009 and has assisted hundreds of MUP identifications in the United States. More information is available at www.namus.gov.

NCIC

National Crime Information CenterThe FBI's National Crime Information Center, NCIC, contains approximately 13 million active records in 21 files to help criminal justice professionals apprehend fugitives, locate missing persons, recover stolen property, etc. https://www.fbi.gov/about-us/cjis/ncic Three of the files are Missing Person, Wanted Person, and Unidentified Person. Criminal justice agencies enter records into NCIC. Those records become accessible to law enforcement agencies nationwide. The system can cross-reference files and respond instantly. NCIC also contains images that can be associated with records to help agencies identify people and property items. The National Dental Image/Information Repository (NDIR) within NCIC permits law enforcement agencies to store, access, and supplement dental records, dental X-rays, photographs, etc., to help facilitate the identification of Missing, Unidentified, and Wanted persons (https://www.fbi.gov/foia/privacy-impact-assessments/ndir).

Others

There are other organizations and websites with missing and unidentified persons databases including the Doe Network (http://www.doenetwork.org), the Charley Project (http://www.charleyproject.org), and most individual states have online missing person clearinghouses/databases. These too should be consulted when appropriate.

CONCLUSION

The consequences of a misidentification have emotional and legal ramifications well beyond a specific case. Thus, using the proper methodology, procedures, and protocol for the determination of identification of human remains is of the utmost importance. Dental identification is the most common method of identifying human remains that are decomposed, skeletonized, burned, or fragmented. This method of identification is accomplished by conducting a thorough postmortem dental examination, the collection of antemortem dental and medical records, and the comparison of the postmortem evidence with the antemortem record. It is imperative that the proper procedures be followed and that meticulous attention is paid to the details of the postmortem examination and comparison to the antemortem dental record.

MOST COMMON PITFALLS IN FORENSIC ODONTOLOGY RADIOGRAPHY PRACTICES

Spatial Orientation of the Image/ Projection Geometry

Dental radiography in the process of human dental identification is a cornerstone in the techniques of establishing a positive comparison and, thus, the dental identification of a deceased individual. This is at the core of the tasks demanded in forensic odontology. In addition, the forensic dentist may provide the fastest and most economical means of accurate victim identification in this process. There are numerous benefits both emotionally and often financially to all concerned in carrying this process to fruition.

There are, however, several radiographic errors that are more likely to occur in a forensic dental setting when compared to routine dental practices and services. This begins with the unique orientation that often occurs in the forensic dental autopsy and the orientation of the dental structures and projection geometry relative to the beam, specimen, and image media (film/digital). In the case of injuries involving body fragmentation and/or resected maxillary and mandibular structures, unusual orientations not encountered in living patients can occur.

Fig. 3.1 represents typical fragmentation of a victim of a low-velocity aircraft crash producing severe blunt force trauma.

Fig. 3.2 illustrates a common forensic misalignment which could not occur in typical clinical radiography; that is, the receiving image film has been placed against the buccal bone of the fragmented specimen with the beam

FIGURE 3.1   Fragmentation remains of a victim of a low-velocity aircraft crash producing severe blunt force trauma.

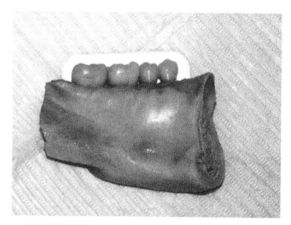

FIGURE 3.2   Common forensic radiographic error.

originating from the lingual direction. This will result in an image that is reversed spatially in terms of the image being exposed from the back side of the film even though there is no such indication from the film packet's lead foil and will confuse "left" from "right" structures. The beam must always be directed *from the buccal aspect* of the dental specimen.

A positive identification and subsequent death certificate is necessary to settle business and personal affairs. Disbursement of life insurance proceeds, estate transfer, settlement of probate, execution of wills, remarriage, and child custody issues can be delayed for years by legal proceedings if a positive scientific identification cannot be rendered.

MANUFACTURER'S INDICATORS OF DETERMINING LEFT AND RIGHT

All dental radiographs obtained via film-based systems may be viewed from either side when mounted on a light box. The bump orientation, however, will determine whether the teeth are being viewed from the facial or the lingual aspect. Film manufacturers have typically used a "raised bump" placed on the film to help orient the image properly and also determine left from right. A bump-up orientation is always assured when the bump is in either the lower-right or upper-left corners when the film is in a horizontal orientation.

A raised bump indicates that the teeth are being viewed from the facial, while a "depressed bump" indicates that the viewer has the image-oriented reading from the tongue or lingual. In addition, the image of the bump will be located in the lower right and upper left when the image is oriented bump up and in lower left and upper right when the image is bump down (Viewed from the lingual).as is seen in Fig. 3.3 (Gibson et al., 2003).

Many have described the same principle using the so-called "Seattle/Miami Rule" for obvious reasons. See Fig. 3.4. To reiterate, all film images will follow the Seattle—Miami Rule including *duplicated films* in which the bump is no longer physically palpable. See Fig. 3.5.

Note* Anterior films and vertical bitewings must always be oriented horizontally when using the Seattle—Miami rule.

SPATIAL ORIENTATION WHEN USING DIGITAL RADIOGRAPHIC SYSTEMS

Image orientation with direct digital X-ray sensors using charge-coupled devices is rarely an issue since the receiver has only one active surface available. Therefore, it is not possible to create images that are confusing as to patients' left and right.

However, systems utilizing photostimulable phosphor imaging plates may be exposed from either side of the plate and may not suitably indicate when the plate was placed in the reverse position by the resultant image alone. Therefore, care must be taken when exposures are made to

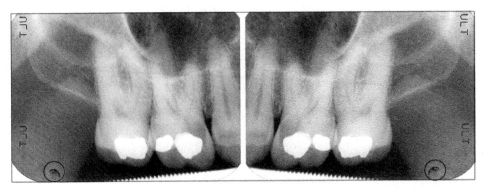

FIGURE 3.3 When a radiograph is viewed from the buccal when the bump is oriented in the upper left or lower right. (Seattle—Miami Rule) It is viewed from the lingual when the bump is in the upper right or lower left.

FIGURE 3.4 Seattle—Miami rule.

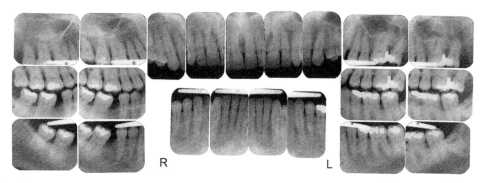

FIGURE 3.5 Anterior films and vertical bitewings must always be oriented horizontally when using the Seattle—Miami rule.

insure that the manufacturers' protocol for proper exposure is adhered to which phosphor surface is facing the beam.

Fig. 3.6 demonstrates the possible dilemma in which two exposures of a dental quadrant were captured with one plate surface oriented properly and the other incorrectly. There is no indication by observing the images alone. To limit this as an error, some offices affix a radiopaque marker (tape) to the back of the offices' supply of plates so that if the plate is then exposed backwards, a faint image of the tape

(A)   **(B)**

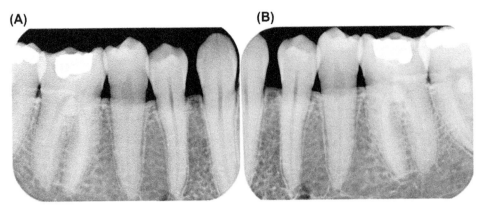

FIGURE 3.6   Radiographs demonstrating the possible dilemma in which two exposures of a dental quadrant were captured with one plate surface oriented properly and the other incorrectly.

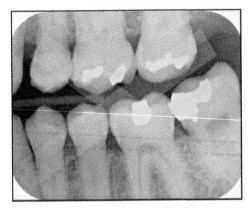

FIGURE 3.7   Radiograph illustrating benefit of use of radiopaque marker tape to identify improper exposure.

will be seen, thus mimicking the lead foil systems utilized in dental X-ray film packets. See Fig. 3.7.

Reference

Gibson, W.G., Aschheim, K.W., Consistent, A., 2003. Accurate method of interpretation of duplicate dental films in mass fatality incidents. In: Proceedings of the American Academy of Forensic Sciences (Chicago, IL).

Further Reading

Adams, B., 2003a. Establishing personal identification based on specific patterns of missing, filled, and unrestored teeth. Journal of Forensic Sciences 48 (3), 487–496.

Adams, B., 2003b. The diversity of adult dental patterns in the United States and the implications for personal identification. Journal of Forensic Sciences 48 (3), 497–503.

Almeida, M.A., Phillips, C., Kula, K., Tulloch, C., 1995. Stability of the palatal rugae as landmarks for analysis of dental casts. The Angle Orthodontist 65, 43–48.

American Board of Forensic Odontology, 2015. Diplomates Reference Manual. http://www.abfo.org.

Bonavilla, J.D., Bush, M.A., Bush, P.J., Pantera, E.A., 2008. Identification of incinerated root canal filling materials after exposure to high heat incineration. Journal of Forensic Sciences 53 (2), 412–418.

Botha, C.T., 1986. The dental identification of fire victims. The Journal of Forensic Odonto-Stomatology 4 (2), 67–75.

Bowers, C.M., 2004. Forensic Dental Evidence. Elsevier, Oxford, U.K.

Bowers, C.M., Bell, G.L., 1996. Manual of Forensic Odontology, third ed. American Society of Forensic Odontology, Saratoga Springs, NY.

Bush, M.A., Bush, P.J., Miller, R.G., 2006. Detection and classification of composite resins in Incinerated teeth for forensic purposes. Journal of Forensic Sciences 51 (3), 636–642.

Bush, M.A., Miller, R.G., 2011. The crash of Colgan Air flight 3407: advanced techniques in victim Identification. The Journal of the American Dental Association 142 (12), 1352–1356.

Bush, M.A., Miller, R.G., Norrlander, A.L., Bush, P.J., 2008. Analytical survey of restorative resins by SEM/EDS and XRF: databases for forensic purposes. Journal of Forensic Sciences 53 (2), 419–425.

Bush, M.A., Miller, R.G., Prutsman-Pfeiffer, J., Bush, P.J., 2007. Identification through XRF analysis of dental restorative resin materials: a comprehensive study of non-cremated, cremated, and processed cremated individuals. Journal of Forensic Sciences 52 (1), 157–165.

Caldas, I.C., Magalhaes, T., Afonso, A., 2007. Establishing identity using cheiloscopy and palatoscopy. Forensic Science International 165 (1), 1–9.

Committee on Identifying the Needs of the Forensic Sciences Community, National Research Council, 2009. Strengthening Forensic Science in the United States: A Path Forward. https://www.ncjrs.gov/pdffles1/nij/grants/228091.pdf.

Fridell, S., Ahlqvist, J., 2006. The use of dental radiographs for identification of children with unrestored dentitions. The Journal of Forensic Odonto-Stomatology 24 (2), 42–46.

Hemanth, M., Vidya, M., Shetty, N., Karkera, B.V., 2010. Identification of individuals using palatal rugae: computerized method. Journal of Forensic Dental Sciences 2, 86–90.

Harvey, W., 1971. Identification from dental data. British Dental Journal 131 (10), 432.

Hermanson, A.S., Bush, M.A., Miller, R.G., Bush, P.J., 2008. Ultraviolet illumination as an adjunctive aid in dental inspection. Journal of Forensic Sciences 53 (2), 408–411.

Herschaft, E.E., Alder, M.E., Ord, D.K., Rawson, R.D., Smith, E.S., 2006. Manual of Forensic Odontology, fourth ed. Impress, Albany, NY.

Jackowski, C., Lussi, A., Classens, M., Kilchoer, T., Bolliger, S., Aghayev, E., Criste, A., Dirnhofer, R., Thali, M.J., 2006. Extended CT scale overcomes restoration caused streak artifacts for dental identification in CT–3D color encoded automatic discrimination of dental restorations. Journal of Computer Assisted Tomography 30 (3), 510–513.

Khalid, K., Yousif, S., Satti, A., 2016. Discrimination potential of root canal treated tooth in forensic dentistry. The Journal of Forensic Odonto-Stomatology 1 (34), 19–26.

Kieser, J.A., Laing, W., Herbison, P., 2006. Lessons learned from large-scale comparative dental analysis following the South Asian tsunami of 2004. Journal of Forensic Sciences 51 (1), 109–112.

Keiser-Nielsen, S., 1980. Person Identification by Means of the Teeth: A Practical Guide. John Wright and Sons Ltd, Bristol, U.K.

Kogon, S.L., Peterson, K.B., Locke, J.W., et al., 1974. A computerized aid to dental identification in mass disasters. Forensic Science International.

Lorton, L., Langley, W.H., 1986. Decision making concepts in postmortem identification. Journal of Forensic Sciences 31 (1), 365–378.

Marella, G.L., Rossi, P., 1999. An approach to person identification by means of dental prostheses in a burnt corpse. The Journal of Forensic Odonto-Stomatology 17 (1), 16–19.

McGivney, J., Fixott, R.H., 2001. Computer-assisted dental identification. Dental Clinics of North America 45 (2), 309–325.

Merlati, G., Savio, C., Danesino, P., Fassina, G., Meghini, P., 2004. Further study of restored and un-restored teeth subjected to high temperatures. The Journal of Forensic Odonto-Stomatology 22 (2), 34–39.

Merlati, G., Savio, C., Danesino, P., Fassina, G., Osculati, A., Meghini, P., 2002. Observations on dental prostheses and restorations subjected to high temperatures: experimental studies to aid identification processes. The Journal of Forensic Odonto-Stomatology 20 (2), 17–24.

Muller, M., Berytrand, M.F., Quatrehomme, G., Bolla, M., Rocca, J.P., 1998. Macroscopic and microscopic aspects of incinerated teeth. The Journal of Forensic Odonto-Stomatology 16 (1), 1–7.

Narang, T., Arora, P., Randhawa, K., 2011. Cheiloscopy as an aid to forensic methodology. Indian Journal of Comprehensive Dental Care 1, 57–60.

Pretty, I.A., Addy, L.D., 2002. Dental postmortem profiles—additional findings of interest to investigators. Science & Justice: Journal of the Forensic Science Society 42 (2), 65–74.

Pretty, I.A., Sweet, D., 2001. A look at forensic dentistry—Part 1: the role of teeth in the determination of human identity. British Dental Journal 190 (7), 359–366.

Pretty, I.A., Webb, D.A., Sweet, D., 2001. The design and assessment of mock mass disasters for dental personnel. Journal of Forensic Sciences 46 (1), 74–79.

Senn, D.R., Stimson, P.G., 2010. Forensic Dentistry, second ed. CRC Press, Boca Raton, FL.

Senn, D.R., Weems, R., 2012. Manual of Forensic Odontology, fifth ed. CRC Press, Boca Raton, FL.

Sharma, P., Saxena, S., Rathod, V., 2009. Cheiloscopy: the study of lip prints in sex identification. Journal of Forensic Dental Sciences 1, 24–27.

Siegel, R., Sperber, N.D., 1977. Identification through the computerization of dental records. Journal of Forensic Sciences 22, 434–442.

Silver, W.E., Souviron, R.R., 2009. Dental Autopsy. CRC Press, Boca Raton, FL.

Smith, V.A., Christensen, A.M., Myers, S.W., 2010. The reliability of visually comparing small frontal sinuses. Journal of Forensic Sciences 55 (6), 1413–1415.

Stuart, L.S., Leonard, G., 2005. Forensic Application of Palatal Rugae in Dental Identification. Forensic Examiner Spring, Missouri, pp. 44–47.

Sweet, D., 2001. Why a dentist for identification? Dental Clinics of North America 45 (2), 237–251.

Sweet, D., DiZinno, J.A., 1996. Personal identification through dental evidence—tooth fragments to DNA. Journal of the California Dental Association 24 (5), 35–42.

Sweet, D., Hildebrand, D., Phillips, D., 1999. Identification of a skeleton using DNA from teeth and a PAP smear. Journal of Forensic Sciences 44 (3), 630–633.

Weeden, V.W., 1998. Postmortem identifications of remains. Clinics in Laboratory Medicine 18 (1), 115–137.

Weems, R., 2010. Forensic dental radiography. In: Senn, D.R., Stimson, P.G. (Eds.), Forensic Dentistry, second ed. CRC Press, Taylor & Francis Group, Boca Raton, FL, pp. 187–203.

Weems, R., Broome, J., Heaven, T.J., Yarbrough, R., 2004. Radiopacity of endodontic posts in dental identifications.

In: Proceedings of the Annual Meeting of the American Academy of Forensic Sciences.

Wood, R.E., Kirk, N.J., Sweet, D.J., 1999. Digital dental radiographic identification in the pediatric, mixed and permanent dentitions. Journal of Forensic Sciences 44 (5), 910–916.

Forensic Dental Photography

Mark L. Bernstein[1,2], Franklin D. Wright[3]

[1]Professor of Pathology and Oral Pathology, Dept. of Surgical and Hospital Dentistry, University of Louisville Dental School, Louisville, KY, United States; [2]Forensic Dental Consultant, Medical Examiner's Office, Louisville, KY, United States; [3]Forensic Odontology Consultant, Hamilton County Coroner's Office, Cincinnati, OH, United States

OUTLINE

Forensic Odontology
https://doi.org/10.1016/B978-0-12-805198-6.00004-9

INTRODUCTION

For the forensic dentist, collection, preservation, and accurate reproduction of visible evidence are paramount in identification of bitemark and abuse cases. Photography archives detailed information objectively. In identification cases, photographs corroborate written records and reports, help recall findings, and provide accountability Well-made forensic photographs may reveal details missed initially or undetectable by the unaided eye. In bitemark cases, photographs provide orientation views and working images upon which analysis and opinions are based.

Forensic dentists should be equipped with digital SLR or mirrorless cameras. Point and shoot cameras and cameras on smart phones typically cannot produce the types of images necessary for forensic purposes. In addition to the general instructions found in a camera owner's manual, a forensic odontologist needs a solid foundational knowledge of optical physics, lens function, and photography guidelines for evidence collection to produce optimal forensic photographs.

UNDERSTANDING THE BASICS OF PHOTOGRAPHY

How a Digital Camera Works

Although a digital camera appears similar to a film camera, they work differently. As in all cameras, when the button is depressed to take a picture, an aperture opens permitting light to pass through the lens and strike a light-sensitive senor. In digital cameras, the sensor captures the incoming light and converts it into electrical signals and this information is stored in a memory card.

Optical Physics

When incident light is transmitted through a transparent object of greater optical density (like a glass lens) it refracts, or bends the light toward an imaginary line perpendicular to the lens surface, called the "normal." As light exits, it bends away from the normal. Thus, a biconvex lens will bend parallel rays of light to a point known as the focal point (Fig. 4.1). This is where the camera sensor is positioned. The more

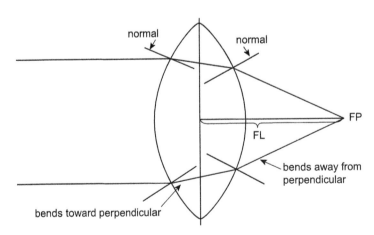

FIGURE 4.1   Diagram of light passing through a biconvex lens.

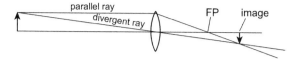

FIGURE 4.2 Diagram of divergent light rays focusing behind the lens' focal point.

biconvex the lens, the more the light is bent, and the closer the focal point is to the lens. The distance from the focal point to the center of the lens is termed the focal length (f.l.).

Physics of Image Formation

Light reflects from an object in all directions. A lens positioned at a great distance from an object will have access only to parallel rays of light. These incoming parallel light rays will be in sharp focus at the lens' focal point. As an object moves closer, the lens encounters divergent rays, having a greater angle of incidence to the lens surface and come into focus behind the lens' focal point (Fig. 4.2). This is problematic because the image sensor is fixed at the focal point. The human eye accommodates by increasing convexity of the eye's lens and thereby maintaining the image's focus on the retina. A camera cannot do this. To compensate, as the subject moves closer to the lens, the camera lens has to be extended away from the camera body to reestablish the focal point onto the sensor.

Lenses

The discussion in the section above describes the physics of light passing though a single piece of biconvex glass. In truth, such a lens would produce optical distortions and aberrations. A camera lens consists of multiple

elements designed to correct these errors. Lenses have iris diaphragms that open or constrict to let in more or less light through an opening much like the eye's iris. This opening is called the aperture and is measured in *f*-stops. *f*-stops are given numbers (1.4, 2, 2.8 up to 32 or 45). These numbers are not random and correspond to the powers of the square root of 2. As the *f*-stop number increases, the aperture opening becomes smaller with each progressive *f*-stop halving or doubling the amount of light permitted to pass through the lens and reach the sensor. Mathematically, the *f*-stop represents focal length divided by iris diameter. A 100-mm lens at *f*/4 has an opening of $100 \div 4 = 25$ mm; and a 50-mm lens at *f*/4 has a diameter of 12.5 mm. An aperture determines depth of field, or the distance between the nearest and furthest objects that produce an image judged to be in focus. Large apertures reduce the depth of field and produce the spherical aberration that reduces image clarity. Spherical aberration is an optical issue caused by the light rays refracting more at the lens periphery than they do at the lens center and thus not converging at the same focal point. Reducing the aperture size prevents light from passing through the lens periphery thereby increasing the depth of field and reducing the spherical aberration. However, as the aperture decreases, another law of physics, diffraction, degrades the image. Diffraction occurs when incident light strikes the edge of the lens' aperture diaphragm causing the light to be deflected. When the aperture is large, most of the light rays enter the lens in an uninterrupted straight line with only a small proportion of light rays deflecting off the edges of the iris diaphragm. Smaller apertures have a greater ratio of aperture edge to the area of the opening resulting in a higher percentage of deflected light passing through the lens and reducing image sharpness (Fig. 4.3). Since spherical aberration and diffraction occur at opposite extremes of lens openings, the sharpest acuity of most lenses occurs two *f*-stops smaller than their widest opening.

Types of Lenses

1. Wide angle lens: Extremely convex lenses that drastically bend light have a short focal length. These lenses capture light from 62 to 84 degrees, producing an image with a broad field of view (Fig. 4.4A). Objects within the

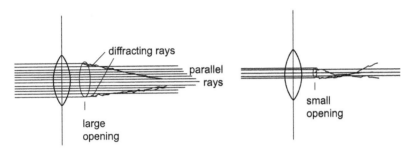

FIGURE 4.3   Diagram of diffracted light rays reducing image sharpness.

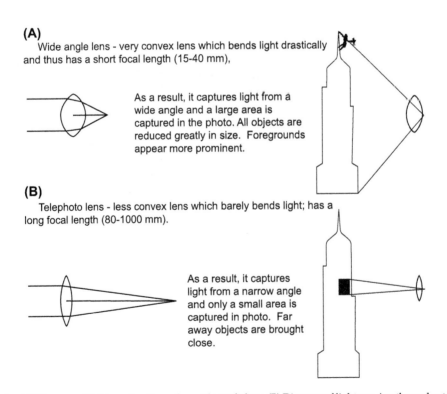

(A)
Wide angle lens - very convex lens which bends light drastically and thus has a short focal length (15-40 mm),

As a result, it captures light from a wide angle and a large area is captured in the photo. All objects are reduced greatly in size. Foregrounds appear more prominent.

(B)
Telephoto lens - less convex lens which barely bends light; has a long focal length (80-1000 mm).

As a result, it captures light from a narrow angle and only a small area is captured in photo. Far away objects are brought close.

FIGURE 4.4   (A) Diagram of light passing through a wide angle lens. (B) Diagram of light passing through a telephoto lens.

scene generally appear small and those closer to the lens appear disproportionately large.

2. Telephoto lens: Slightly convex lenses that have a long focal length making distant objects appear closer. These lenses bend light less and have a small field of view varying between 8 and 30 degree (Fig. 4.4B).
3. Zoom lenses: Complex lenses produce variable focal lengths and therefore photographs ranging from wide angle to telephoto.
4. Macro lens: Standard lenses typically do not permit close-up (macro) photography. A macro lens extends the physical portion of the lens further away from the camera body permitting focus upon closer objects. These lenses are more expensive because the optical quality must be improved to avoid distortion. Macro lenses used in forensic odontology can produce life-sized (1:1) images.

Perspective Distortion

When driving down a straight road you notice that the road appears wide close to you, while it seems to converge in the distance. Intellectually, you know that the entire road is the same width throughout and the sides are parallel. This is called normal perspective, and it occurs because the width of a subject closer to you takes up more of your visual field (Fig. 4.5). Normal perspective helps our brain perceive three dimensions even if we were to lose stereoscopic vision. The closer your eye moves to a subject, the more exaggerated the perspective. Some photographs show what is called "perspective distortion." Perspective distortion is not a true lens distortion; but merely, a point of view the human exe is unaccustomed and is caused exclusively by viewing an object at a distance not routinely experienced. When a photograph is taken at a normal viewing distance, the perspective seems natural. Wide angle lenses are "blamed" for causing perspective distortion but in truth a wide angle lens can view a scene from a closer point than the human eye can (Fig. 4.6). People are used to seeing the faces and bodies of other people from a distance of a few feet. Closing one eye and looking at someone's face from 6 inches away produces a similar "perspective distortion" as a wide angle lens—elongated faces with disproportionally large noses and lips and small ears. At this distance, the noses and lips are dramatically closer to the eye relative to the ears. This may be why people close their eyes when they kiss.

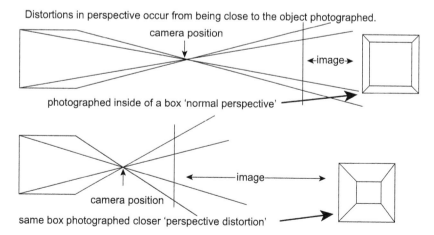

FIGURE 4.5 Diagram of a normal perspective image and a perspective distortion image of the inside of a box.

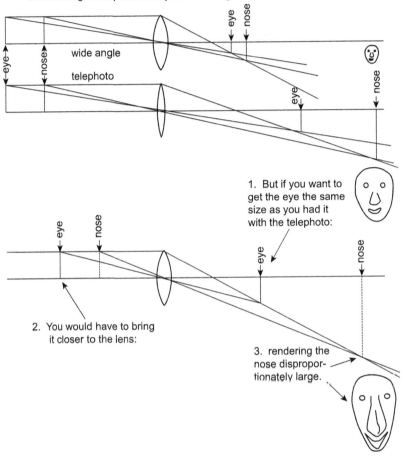

At a given object distance, wide angle and telephoto distort equally but the image size produced by the wide angle is smaller :

eye   nose

eye   nose

wide angle

telephoto

eye

nose

1. But if you want to get the eye the same size as you had it with the telephoto:

eye

nose

eye   nose

eye   nose

2. You would have to bring it closer to the lens:

3. rendering the nose dispropor- tionately large.

FIGURE 4.6   At a given object distance, wide angle and telephoto lenses distort equally.

Conversely, telephoto lenses cause the subject to appear flattened and wide. Perspective distortion does not occur with subjects having no dimensional depth, as long as the subject is perfectly parallel to the camera's sensor. If a flat subject is tilted relative to the plane of the sensor, perspective distortion occurs.

Depth of Field

No lens can focus a three-dimensional object on a two-dimensional flat sensor. The part of the object closest to the lens comes into focus behind the part that is further from the lens; therefore, only a single plane of the subject being imaged is in exquisitely sharp focus. However, the human eye has an area of "acceptable focus," which is a distance in front and behind the true focal point that is perceived to be in focus. The length of this range of acceptable focus is known as depth of field. When a camera lens aperture is made smaller, the incoming cone of light is constricted, elongating the range of visual acuity, and therefore increasing the depth of field

(Fig. 4.7). This rule of optical physics is not lens dependent. Another element that affects depth of field is distance—specifically the distance from the camera to the subject. As the camera is moved closer to the subject, the portion of the image remaining in focus gets smaller. Therefore, your aperture setting in conjunction with your distance from the subject affects how deep the range of focus will be.

Sensors

A sensor is the light-sensitive component upon which an image is formed. Examples include film, CCD/CMOS digital imagers, and even the retina of the eye. Prior to the development of digital sensors, 35-mm film was the most common photographic sensor measuring 24 × 36 mm

(1 × 1.5 inches). For macro, intraoral, and portraiture photography, a sensor of this size requires a 90–105 mm focal length lens. Today's sensors for digital cameras come with a variety of sensor sizes—some as large as 35-mm film and referred to as full frame sensors. Larger-sized sensors are capable of holding a greater number of pixels and thus producing images with high resolution and dynamic range. A higher pixel count on the sensor permits superior detail preservation during image enlargement. However, more pixels come with a price; images with high pixel counts produce larger file size, making storage and electronic transmission cumbersome and time-consuming. Most cameras use smaller sensors that crop the field of view by blocking light from the periphery and making the final image appear more "telephoto-like." Sensors are

No lens can focus a 3 dimentional object in a 2 dimentional plane of focus. The part of the object closest to the lens comes into focus behind the part that is further from the lens :

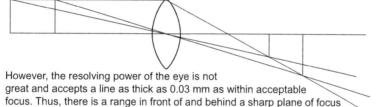

However, the resolving power of the eye is not great and accepts a line as thick as 0.03 mm as within acceptable focus. Thus, there is a range in front of and behind a sharp plane of focus which is acceptibly sharp to the human eye.

Depth of field can be increased by decreasing lens aperture (increasing f-stop). This restricts the operation of the lens to the central portion:

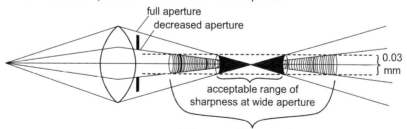

Incoming light rays enter at a more acute angle and achieve a 0.03 mm spot of light over a longer distance in front of and behind the focused object. Thus more foreground and background is within acceptable focus.

FIGURE 4.7 Small lens apertures constrict light, elongate visual acuity, thereby increasing depth of field.

designated with a "crop factor." This value when multiplied by the focal length of the lens provides the equivalent focal length with 35-mm film.

Various sensor sizes commonly used in DSLR cameras include as follows:

1. APS-C sensor—has a 1.5 or 1.6× crop factor, effectively converting a 50-mm lens into a 75- or 80-mm lens, by full frame standards.
2. APS-H—has a 1.3× crop factor.
3. A micro 4/3 has a 2× crop factor.

Despite size differences among sensors, most retain the same 2:3 rectangular aspect ratio of 35-mm film. Sensor size must be known to select the optimal focal length for a given task. A 60-mm lens with a sensor having a 1.5× crop factor is the equivalent of a 90-mm focal length. For the remainder of this chapter, suggested focal lengths will be referenced as full frame sensors. Users with different sensor sizes should multiply by the crop factor of their personal camera sensor to obtain the proper focal length.

In choosing a sensor size, the photographer must weigh options. A larger sensor containing more pixels provides a high resolution and the ability to enlarge images without loss of detail. These cameras will allow for selection of a reduced resolution when ultrafine resolution is not required. APS sensors are acceptable in most forensic work and permit the use of shorter, lighter, less expensive lenses.

Advantages of digital sensors over film:

1. Some sensors can exceed the resolution of film.
2. Color accuracy and contrast can be corrected to represent a better rendition of what the photographer saw.
3. Digital sensors are inherently more light-sensitive than film permitting a greater range of exposure time and aperture options.
4. Digital sensors can greatly exceed the dynamic light range of film, permitting greater capture of object detail in low- and high-light situations.
5. The spectral range of a back-illuminated CCD spans 200—1100 nm (from ultraviolet to near infrared). The inherent sensitivity of digital sensors to infrared is blocked by an IR cut filter or hot mirror (hot boot) in most cameras, but cameras that remove this filter can allow IR imaging that is especially useful in investigative forensic photography.
6. Unlike film, which can be used only once, digital sensors are used repeatedly and the images are stored and preserved on a memory card, permitting ease of storage and archival while eliminating the cost of film purchase and processing.
7. Real-time viewing. No longer does the photographer have to wait for film processing to know if the image was satisfactorily created. If the digital image is not optimal, it can be deleted and remade.
8. Copies of original images are easily made. Image enhancement is easily accomplished through the use of various software applications.
9. Film and film processing is no longer widely available.

When digital photography was first introduced, the forensic community had concerns regarding the ability to manipulate images. It is true that original digital images can be altered, but so can traditional film. Images taken with film can be enlarged and cropped, and the exposure, contrast, and color balance can be altered during printing. Alterations that improve or bring out detail already present in the image are acceptable. In addition to maintaining untouched original images, computers record and archive the history of all image enhancements and manipulations as proof against a claim of falsifying evidence.

Exposure Control

A photographed subject must be properly exposed, meaning that the image is neither too light nor too dark. Exposure is controlled by the amount of light activating the sensor. There are four exposure variables under the control of the photographer:

1. *Shutter speed*: This controls the amount of time a sensor is exposed to light. Since movement by either the subject or the camera can cause image blur, the faster the shutter speed the greater the ability to freeze motion. Shutter speeds are controlled manually or automatically by the camera body and are traditionally expressed in multiples of two (e.g., 1 second, $^1/_2$ second, and so forth, all the way to thousandths of a second). Each progressively halves or doubles the amount of light. As a rule of thumb, to prevent camera movement, one should not use a shutter speed slower than the reciprocal of the focal length of the lens unless using a tripod. For instance, a 60-mm lens should use 1/60 s as its slowest shutter speed. Blur from camera movement is magnified with the use of telephoto lenses and macro photography. Even speeds as fast as 1/125 s may be too slow to prevent blur in these situations. Most cameras today use image stabilization in the camera body or lens to reduce blur due to camera movement. Lenses are stabilized by a floating lens element, while camera bodies have a sensor that adjusts to movement or vibration. Image stabilization improves image sharpness when long exposure times, telephoto, or macro photography are desired. Blur remains a problem with fast moving subjects, as image stabilization is of no benefit. In these cases, shutter speeds of 1/125 s or faster are recommended depending on the focal length and speed of the subject. When using flash photography, the typical rules of shutter speed or image stabilization do not apply since the flash delivers a burst of light lasting 1/1000 s, fast enough to freeze motion and intense enough the sensor is "blinded" to ambient light even if the shutter remains open longer than the flash. Camera manuals specify which shutter speeds synchronize with the flash.

2. *Aperture*: Opening or closing the iris diaphragm changes the aperture and the volume of light to the sensor. As previously stated, smaller apertures increase depth of field, a characteristic often desirable in evidence photography when the entire depth of a three-dimensional object needs to be in acceptable focus. Macro photography is inherently plagued by shallow depth of field requiring the use of smaller apertures (f/16, 22, and 32) despite the effects of diffraction. Diffraction will be discussed in Macro (Close-up) Photography section.

3. *Sensor sensitivity*: The sensitivity of the sensor to light can be adjusted with ISO settings. Low ISO settings require the most light and provide the best detail. High ISO settings make the sensor extremely sensitive to light useful in low-light situations. The disadvantage in using high ISO settings is the added electronic "noise" that degrades the image quality.

4. *Light intensity*: Intense light allows the best exposure control because the photographer can optimize shutter speed, aperture, and sensor sensitivity. In particularly low-light situations, an electronic flash is used to add more illumination. A strong flash is especially useful to make sharp macro images of three-dimensional subjects because of the following reasons:
   a. It permits the use of smaller apertures increasing depth of field
   b. It permits the use of low ISO sensitivity
   c. It permits the use of fast bursts of light freezing movement.

One problem with flash photography is the creation of spectral highlights (glare) due to surface reflection from flash. Even if ambient light is used, flash should be considered as backup. Room lighting or shade may render undesirable color temperature or force the camera to select a suboptimal ISO, shutter speed, or aperture. With modern cameras, images can easily be made with and without flash. Most camera manufacturers have proprietary flash units that offer TTL (through the lens) exposure that automatically delivers the proper light intensity based on the selected aperture and ISO.

Macro (Close-Up) Photography

Close-up or macro photography can be defined as the production of an image that tightly frames an object. Macro photography, strictly speaking, is defined as producing images of objects larger than life-size, but for practical purposes, close-up and macro photography are used interchangeably in the literature.

As noted in an earlier section, when an object moves closer to a lens, its image comes into focus behind the sensor, necessitating the lens to extend forward and placing the focal point on the sensor. Optical physics dictates that when the object is further than two focal lengths from the lens, the image formed will be smaller than the actual object. When the object is exactly at two focal lengths from the lens, the resulting image will be the same size as the object and will focus at a point one focal length behind the sensor. This means that the lens has to extend one focal length to obtain image focus. To determine the required lens extension mathematically, we must first know the desired magnification. Either of the following formulas can be used: magnification = image distance ÷ subject distance or magnification = size of image ÷ size of object. A typical facial portrait is about 1/10th life-sized based on a full frame sensor. This records a 15-inch long face on a 1.5-inch sensor, expressed as a reproduction ratio (RR) as 1:10. A 1:2 RR is one-half life-sized and a 1:1 RR is life-sized. A 1:5 RR represents an image field of approximately 7.5 × 5 inches typically sufficient for making working images of a bitemark with an ABFO scale. A study model or excised maxilla measures about 3 inches and

is accommodated by a 1:3 RR. Details of individual teeth may require a 1:1 RR. The amount of lens extension required can be calculated by the formula: extension = RR × f.l. Thus one-half life-sized image using a 100-mm lens requires 50 mm of extension and a life-sized image with 100-mm f.l. requires 100 mm of extension (Fig. 4.8). Most macro lenses can extend to achieve a 1:1 RR.

Macro Photography Issues

When three-dimensional objects are very close to a lens, an uncomfortable camera-to-subject (working) distance can be created. Perspective distortion is increased and depth of field is very narrow. Field curvature also becomes an issue; all spherical lenses produce an image that is not actually flat but is a concave dish shape. Sensors, however, are flat, meaning that the image around the periphery will show softened focus. Macro lenses are designed as "flat field" lenses, correcting this problem.

Working distance and perspective distortion occur when a short focal length lens is used for close-ups. To achieve a 1:1 image, the object has to be placed at two times the focal distance from the lens optical center (see Fig. 4.8). For a 50-mm lens, this means 100 mm (4 in). Considering that the front of the lens is, perhaps, 25 mm from its optical center, the object is only 75 mm (3 in) from the front of the lens. Not only is this too close for comfort, but a flash attached to the lens also might be too intense or directed away from the object being photographed. A moderate telephoto lens will give a more comfortable working distance of about 175 mm from the front of the lens (7 in) and also reduce perspective distortion by giving the photographer a more familiar point of view of the subject.

Depth of field may be only a few millimeters in close-up views of three-dimensional subjects. The macro lens offers small f-stops up to f/32 to maximize depth of field. However, there is a trade-off. At full extension, a small f-stop is so far away from the sensor that incoming light is

In order to achieve reproduction ratios of 1:2 and 1:1, the object must be at 3x and 2x the focal distance respectively according to the formulas :

$$\frac{1}{\text{focal distance}} = \frac{1}{\text{object distance}} + \frac{1}{\text{image distance}} \quad \text{and}$$

$$\text{magnification(m)} = \frac{\text{size of image}}{\text{size of object}} \quad \text{or} \quad \frac{\text{distance image}}{\text{distance object}} \quad \text{thus:}$$

If my object is 25 mm (1 inch) tall and placed 3xfd. from a 50 mm. lens (150 mm)

$$\frac{1}{50} = \frac{1}{150} + \frac{1}{\text{image distance}} \quad \text{image distance = 75 mm.}$$

$$\frac{\text{image size}}{25} = \frac{75}{150} \quad \text{image size = 12.5 or 1/2 object size}$$

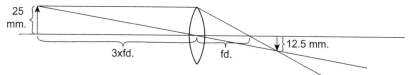

Since the film is placed at the fd. (50 mm) and the image is formed at 75 mm., the lens has to extend 25 mm.

If my object (25 mm.) is placed 2xfd. from a 50 mm lens (100 mm) :

$$\frac{1}{50} = \frac{1}{100} + \frac{1}{\text{image distance}} \quad \text{image distance = 100 mm}$$

$$\frac{\text{image size}}{25} = \frac{100}{100} \quad \text{image size = 25 mm or life size}$$

The image is formed at 100 mm. and the 50 mm lens must extend 50 mm.

FIGURE 4.8 Photographic reproduction ratio.

spread out and reduced, making the effective *f*-stop smaller than the set aperture according to the formula: effective aperture = aperture x (magnification + 1). With a set aperture of *f*/32 at 1:1 close-up, the effective aperture = 32 × 2 = 64. While maximizing depth of field, this may create unacceptable image softening due to diffraction. An aperture of *f*/16 usually optimizes depth of field and diffraction issues. A trick to maximize depth of field is to readjust the point of sharpest focus. If one was

photographing an anterior view of the dentition, focusing on maxillary central incisors would place them in perfect focus and lateral incisors behind them would also be an acceptable focus. But there is also a zone of acceptable focus in front of the maxillary incisors that are wasted because there is no subject there. To maximize depth of field, focusing on the canines permits a range of focus from the central incisors through the region. This is known as hyperfocal distance (Photo 4.1A and B).

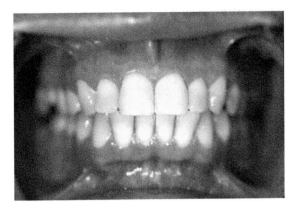

PHOTO 4.1A Photograph using a large lens aperture producing a narrow depth of field.

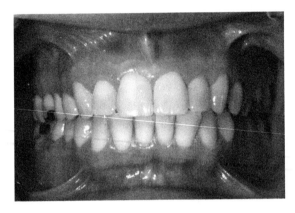

PHOTO 4.1B Photograph using a small lens aperture producing a wide depth of field.

ELECTROMAGNETIC SPECTRUM AND ITS APPLICATION IN FORENSIC PHOTOGRAPHY

The electromagnetic spectrum encompasses ultrashort wavelength gamma radiation through long wavelength radio waves (Fig. 4.9). Within that spectrum lies electromagnetic radiation that is visible to the unaided human eye known as "visible light." For recreational photography and most forensic casework, visible light photography is adequate. Most camera systems used in forensic photography are specially manufactured for the common consumer and optimized to capture only visible light. However, in forensics, nonvisible wavelengths can be especially useful in the photographic documentation of injuries in skin not readily visible to the naked eye. Infrared photography can reveal bruising patterns and some tattoos, while ultraviolet imaging reveals crisp surface detail and tissue changes associated with healed scars. These images are captured with special techniques and photographic equipment.

The ultraviolet spectrum spans from 100 nm to just under 400 nm (near the blue end of the visible spectrum) while the infrared spectrum is just outside the red end of the visible light spectrum with wavelengths spanning from just beyond 700 nm to nearly 1,000,000 nm. The use

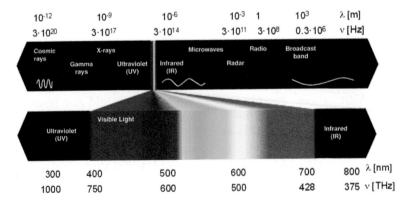

FIGURE 4.9 Spectrum of electromagnetic radiation highlighting visible light range.

of special photographic equipment is effective in capturing digital images in the near infrared spectrum ranging 700–1000 nm.

The use of full spectrum photography (from 100 to 1100 nm) allows a forensic investigator to record digital images in visible light, nonvisible ultraviolet, and near infrared, as well as narrow band visible blue light illumination. Each of these photographic techniques creates digital images of the same object with a slightly different appearance and detail. This chapter will discuss each of these photographic techniques and how best to apply them in forensic casework.

Four Effects of Electromagnetic Radiation on an Object

Before discussing the photographic techniques used in full spectrum photography, it is important to understand the four events that may occur when electromagnetic radiation strikes an object (Kochevar et al.).

1. *Reflection*: Incident light is reflected away from the object surface to the eye, and it is responsible for the perception of light intensity and color. When reflecting light is scattered, the object appears dull.
2. *Absorption*: Not all light energy that strikes an object is reflected; some is absorbed by the object. Light absorbed transforms into heat energy. It is not returned, and therefore, the object appears black.
3. *Transmission*: Transmission is the scattering of electromagnetic energy. In skin, the light is scattered throughout the successive cell layers until the light energy has been dissipated, and therefore, is not depicted in the image.
4. *Fluorescence*: When light energy strikes an object, there is a molecular excitation causing some of the light to be reflected at a longer wavelength than the incident light. This results in a faint glow, fluorescence. This fluorescent event is known as the Stokes Shift (Stokes, 1852) and lasts only a few

nanoseconds (10^{-8} s) (Eastman Kodak, 1972). Fluorescence seen in skin is dim and weak compared to surrounding ambient light and thus, not readily seen by the naked eye. However, when the skin is illuminated in a totally dark room with monochromatic light wavelengths of approximately 425 nm, special photographic techniques capture the fluorescent glow.

When light strikes skin, all four aforementioned events can occur simultaneously. By changing the incident light wavelength and the configuration of the camera, lenses, and filters, it is possible to photographically record any of the four dermal reactions to light energy. The specific technique and protocols for documenting injuries to human skin, in visible or nonvisible light, varies vastly depending upon the use of film or digital imaging equipment. The ability to create digital images using different wavelengths of light is particularly important when documenting injuries in skin (Fig. 4.10). Sharp surface details can be seen utilizing ultraviolet light, while detail up to 3 mm below the surface of the skin can be visualized using infrared light. Fluorescent photography frequently provides additional detail not normally seen with visual light photography.

VISIBLE LIGHT (CONVENTIONAL) PHOTOGRAPHY

Visible light photographs are the mainstay of forensic photography because they reproduce an image in the manner humans see and interpret reality. Most commercially available digital cameras are designed and manufactured to create quality digital images using only visible light. To prevent flash units from emitting, lenses from transmitting, and sensors from recording unwanted ultraviolet and infrared wavelengths, fluorite coverings and an infrared filter (hot boot) are used to permit only visible light to be

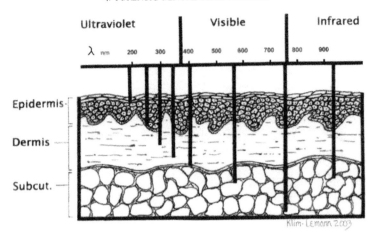

FIGURE 4.10   Skin penetration of various light wavelengths.

recorded by the camera's digital sensor. Therefore, almost all off-the-shelf modern cameras require very little altering of camera settings to create quality, well-focused digital images. However, there are component variables and quality issues that may significantly affect the resultant image.

High pixel count, uninterpolated sensors are better than those that interpolate the image captured to create higher resolution. The higher the native image resolution the better the image quality will be. High-resolution images offer the most versatility in terms of ability to enlarge and crop photographs and produce sharp images. A drawback to having large image resolution is that the file size is usually large making storage and electronic transmission cumbersome.

Internal camera programming and filtering can impact image quality. If the hot boot over the digital sensor is properly configured, only visible light can pass to the sensor. However, the hot boot sometimes permits bleed through (especially infrared light) contaminating image color and sharpness.

Additionally, lenses used by many point and shoot cameras do not have high-quality lenses thereby affecting image quality. High-quality properly focused glass lenses with fluorite coatings prohibit certain wavelengths of light to pass to the sensor improving image quality. Ideally, the lens should only permit visible light to pass.

Visible Light Photography Protocol (General Remarks)

The forensic photographer should create and follow a standard operating protocol and methodology to ensure complete photographic documentation of the case. This protocol should include demographic information (who contacted the photographer, when contacted, where the case originates, case subject matter, and how the photographic documentation was performed). Because all information will become a part of the case chain of evidence, detailed and accurate documentation is critical. The protocol involves careful and complete cataloging of all images taken, equipment used, and camera settings. Orientation images depicting the location of the evidence are made using visible light photography. The photographs are progressively taken closer to the subject until final macro images are made. Macro images should be taken with and without the use of an appropriate photographic scale. The scale is used for size reference and macro images without a scale permit the entire area of interest (injury) to be seen without obstruction. The camera should be programmed to the highest possible image resolution and the camera set in the "auto" mode. The "auto" mode setting defaults to the programmed image capture settings for aperture, exposure time, and often the amount of supplemental light (flash) necessary to create the image. The camera operator has very little ability to change programmable settings when the camera is operating in the "auto" mode. In most cases, using a camera in "auto" mode produces adequate visible light photographs.

These native images must be archived and copies be made for use in image enhancement, enlargement, and examination. The original images are NEVER used for enhancements. Any image enhancements are saved as new images, preserving the pristine unaltered files of the original images.

GUIDELINES FOR COLLECTING PHOTOGRAPHIC EVIDENCE IN IDENTIFICATION CASES

The objectives of photographic imaging for use in dental identifications are as follows:

1. Document visible case details.
2. Recall details of the dental findings long after archival of the case.
3. Verify the accuracy of reports.
4. Show subtle findings that might have been missed initially on visual inspection.
5. Aid in the determination of cause/manner of death (presence of trauma, mucosa discoloration, soot in airways, char patterns, etc.).
6. Illustrate why dental identification was required.

The following images are recommended:

1. Initial views of the body containing a case number label serve to indicate the general state of the body at the time of the examination. These views help recall the case, particularly if multiple bodies are to be examined and illustrate why a dental identification was needed. Wide angle lens may be used to image an entire body. This is especially useful when working distance is limited by the facility size. Depth of field is usually not a problem at longer distances; therefore, larger apertures (f/3.5 to f/5.6) may be used.
2. Appropriately labeled, in situ macro views of the exposed teeth are particularly valuable in char cases when removal of jaws might damage the dentition. If skeletal remains are being photographed, images of the skull and articulated mandible are helpful when traumatic injuries or deformities are noted (Photo 4.2).

PHOTO 4.2   Photograph of char injuries on human remains.

When jaws are resected, distracting soft tissue should be removed and teeth should be brushed free of debris. This permits a greater detail to be imaged and less likely considered inflammatory evidence if viewed in court. Better photographs are obtained when specimens are placed on a nonreflective, nontextured background. A moderate-value neutral gray color works best. Colored backgrounds can fool the camera's white balance meter causing color perversions. White or black backgrounds may alter exposure causing overexposed or underexposed teeth, respectively.

3. In fragmented cases, a complete set of close-up images can be made of each fragment. Images should include one labeled photograph containing all the dental evidence recovered. A close-up occlusal view of the maxilla and one of the mandible, serves to show any restorations, arch form, occlusal, and palatal anatomy. With teeth in occlusion (if possible), three close-up views, anterior, left, and right lateral, show labial and buccal restorations, occlusion, and gingival status. The anterior view in occlusion is valuable if antemortem smile photographs are available for comparison at a later date. These images should be framed with the occlusal line roughly parallel to the plane of the sensor or film (Photo 4.3A, B, C, D, and E).

4. Additional macro views may be required to document small or subtle details such as composite and lingual restorations, bone or dental fractures, anomalies, jaw fragments, and pathology. It may be difficult to include the case number in extremely close images, but, as long as other labeled images in the series can be linked to the macro images, the macro image can be labeled later using imaging software. Macro and extreme close-up images require flash photography and apertures between $f/11$ and $f/32$ to obtain the desired depth of field.

When there are multiple victims, an assembly line sequence of photography is most efficient. In these cases, all photographs should contain an identifying case number so that any stray image can be reunited with its respective case.

GUIDELINES FOR COLLECTING PHOTOGRAPHIC EVIDENCE OF PATTERNED INJURIES

Proper evidence photography for patterned injuries has been standardized for years. The objectives are as follows:

1. Document injury/injuries orientation on the body.
2. Create nondistorted, high-resolution, color-balanced, and properly exposed close-up (working) images that can be utilized to evaluate the patterned injury and compare to objects or instruments that may have created the pattern.
3. Produce images that record details not be seen by the unaided eye (infrared, ultraviolet, alternative light, or macro photography).

The following photographs are recommended following collection of trace evidence:

1. *Orientation views*: These show the position of the injury or injuries at a sufficient distance to evaluate their orientation on the body. The first images depict the body as the photographer found it, before any cleaning, touching, hair removal, or movement occurs. There are no labels on the body to demonstrate nothing was covered up (Photo 4.4A). This is followed by a second image of a similar view, which includes case identification.
2. *Macro photographs* (working): These images are intended to show injury details. After orientation photographs are taken, skin surfaces should be cleansed of dirt and blood

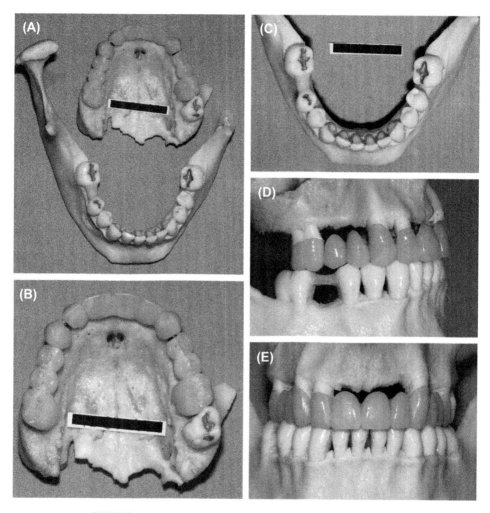

PHOTO 4.3   (A–E) Photographic series of an identification case.

and any hairs clipped. In decedents, the odontologist does not know the position of the body when the injury was inflicted; therefore, the injury should be photographed in throughout the range of possible positions. All images intended for determining the cause of the injury should be labeled with the case number. A scale, preferably an ABFO #2 scale, should be oriented near, but not touching, any portion of the injury, and placed as parallel as possible to the plane of the injury (Photo 4.4B). If an ABFO scale is unavailable, a nonflexible, nonreflective thin ruler and a perfectly circular object (like a quarter dollar) should be used. The injury and ruler is photographed with the lens extending perpendicular to the plane of the injury. A macro lens with a comfortable working distance of about 9 inches to 2 feet is most desirable. At this distance, a flat bitemark

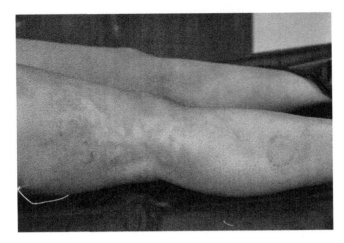

PHOTO 4.4A   Patterned injury orientation view.

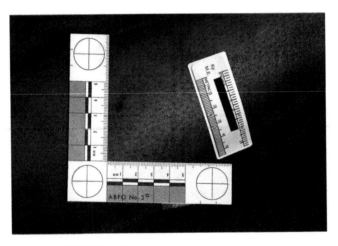

PHOTO 4.4B   Patterned injury macro view.

would normally not require the use of small lens apertures because depth of field is not a concern. However, if the film plane is not parallel to the subject, one portion of the injury will be closer to the lens than another. This may introduce both depth of field problems and perspective distortion. Additionally, if the ruler is not on the same plane as the injury, the measurement accuracy is compromised because the portion

closer to the lens will appear relatively larger than the portion located further away.

The circle on the scale permits anyone looking at the image to determine if the camera was not perpendicular relative to the plane of the injury/ ruler because perspective distortion will cause the circular scale to appear an oval. This problem can be corrected or rectified with software (Photo 4.5A, B, and C). This correction cannot be made on images where scale is not on the

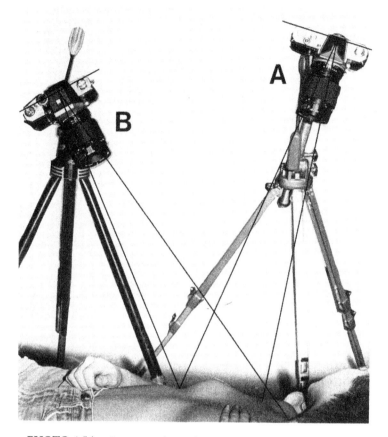

PHOTO 4.5A Camera angles to obtain images in Photo 4.5B and 4.5C.

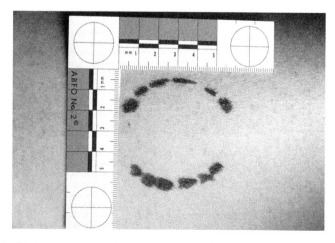

PHOTO 4.5B Photo of patterned injury with camera lens perpendicular to the injury/ruler.

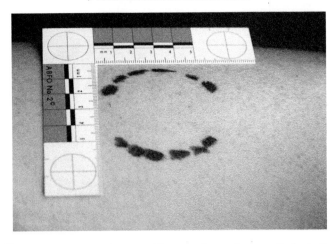

PHOTO 4.5C   Photo of patterned injury with camera lens not perpendicular to the injury/ruler.

same plane as the injury. If a patterned injury is located on a markedly curved surface, it will be necessary to photograph portions of the patterned injury independently. If a patterned injury is only moderately curved and the entire injury is visible within the camera viewfinder, then distortion due to surface curvature may be minimal and insignificant. In this case, the scale should be optimized and placed parallel to the overall injury.

Adjusting the position of flash lighting can accentuate topographical irregularities and reduce glare reflected from the flash. Since digital photography provides instant feedback and unsatisfactory images can be retaken, experimentation with flash angle and ambient light is encouraged.

The role of infrared, ultraviolet, and alternate light imaging in patterned injury documentation is discussed separately.

Written records and labeled sketches are valuable accompaniments to the photographic series. The narrative should include descriptions of the patterned injury, color, size, texture, anatomic position, and any possible problems such as tissue distortions or artifact due to postmortem changes or autopsy procedures.

GUIDELINES FOR COLLECTING PHOTOGRAPHIC EVIDENCE ON SUSPECTS

Before suspect photographs can be taken, informed consent or a court order must first be secured. This series of photographs may include full face and profile portraiture, the anterior dentition in centric and in protrusive relationship, maxillary and mandibular occlusal views, buccal views in occlusion, and a photograph with scale illustrating maximal opening.

1. *Portrait view*: The camera body is turned to take a vertical photograph with the individual's head and neck filling the viewfinder, leaving a small border on the periphery. To avoid perspective distortion, the photographer should be several feet from the subject, using a moderate telephoto lens with the plane of the face parallel to the sensor. If point flash is used, it should be directed from overhead. An aperture of $f/5.6$ or $f/8$ will provide adequate depth of field. Using hyperfocal distance, the closest distance at which a lens can be focused while keeping objects at infinity acceptably

sharp, will ensure that the nose and ears are within the depth of field.

2. *Profile view*: The same camera settings and orientation are used as in the portrait view photograph. In the viewfinder, the nose should be close to the edge of the vertical frame and the top of the head close to the upper horizontal frame. If point light is used, it is directed toward the face.

3. *Anterior view* (of the dentition): Cheek retractors are used to ensure that the buccal surfaces of the posterior teeth are visualized. The retractors pull the lips forward toward the lens, rather than backward toward the ears to protect the gingiva from injury and to give the best visualization of the teeth and gingiva. A medium length macro telephoto lens is used and an aperture setting between f/16 and *f*22 is recommended to optimize depth of field. The distal of the lateral incisors should be the point of focus to ensure that the centrals and posterior teeth are within the depth of field. Both centric occlusion and protrusive photographs should be taken keeping the facial midline in the center of the photograph and the camera sensor perpendicular to the occlusal plane (Photo 4.6A).

4. *Right and left buccal views*: These photographs are taken with the teeth in centric occlusion using a long, narrow buccal mirror.

5. *Occlusal view*: When an occlusal view photograph is taken, the cheeks are retracted and the subject opens as wide as possible with the occlusal mirror angled such that it touches the opposing arch. To avoid fogging, the mirror may be first placed in warm water and dried, or an air syringe can be used. The flash should be angled into the edge of the mirror. Remember that all mirror views reverse right and left orientation.

6. *Recorded maximal opening*: With a sterile ruler, the subject should be asked to open as wide as possible and the ruler placed on the front edge of the upper and lower central incisors to measure the interocclusal distance (Photo 4.6B).

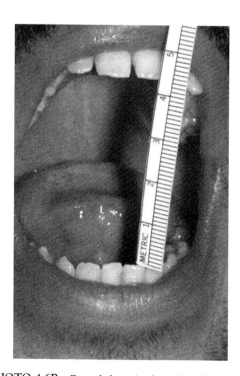

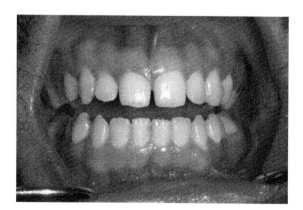

PHOTO 4.6A   Anterior photographic view of suspect dentition.

PHOTO 4.6B   Recorded maximal opening of a suspect.

PHOTOGRAPHIC DOCUMENTATION IN ABUSE CASES

When called to photograph suspected victims of abuse, the forensic dentist normally concentrates on injuries to the head and neck, including intraoral injuries. These injuries may include abrasions; contusions; lacerations; and patterned injuries such as slap marks, gag marks, grab marks, choke marks, black eyes, pinched or bruised ears, or burns. Intraoral injuries may include broken or discolored teeth, frenum tears, bizarre malocclusions, isolated soft palate injuries, palatal petechiae, or venereal warts. When called by a medico-legal agency, the photographs are made under the direction of the soliciting agent. When a private patient presents with suspicious injuries, most states permit taking of photographs to document these injuries without consent of the parent or caregiver.

Alternate Light Imaging

Alternate light imaging is a photographic technique that utilizes specific, narrow band wavelengths of light to enhance objects or injuries not readily seen with the human eye. It is also known as narrow band illumination or monochromatic light imaging.

Human skin fluoresces when exposed to visible light. The fluorescent glow is extremely faint and concealed by the rest of the ambient light. However, when only a wavelength of 415-nm light is used to illuminate skin, there is a molecular excitation of the uninjured skin. Light at a wavelength of 415 nm, is absorbed by the blood products and no molecular excitement. When the excited molecules of the uninjured skin return to the resting state, energy is reemitted as a faint fluorescent glow at a wavelength different than the incident light highlighting the injury and permitting imaging

(Forensic Light Source, 2016). This phenomenon is known as the Stokes Shift, named after the Irish physicist George G. Stokes, who first discovered and reported it in 1852 (Stokes, 1852).

When using alternate light to produce images of skin injuries, a special photographic technique is required. Most off-the-shelf cameras and lenses can be used because 415-nm light lies within the visible light spectrum. However, the light source must be rich in 415-nm light and a special yellow band pass (cut) filter placed on the front of the lens to allow only fluorescing light to pass to the camera sensor.

Because this technique images only the low energy fluorescence, all incoming light except 415 nm must be eliminated. Therefore, the room must be totally dark. Before photographing the injuries, yellow goggles are donned by the investigator and the alternate light is used to initially scan the entire body for injuries. By screening the entire body prior to imaging, the investigator will have the opportunity to see all the injuries on the body, often discovering some not readily seen in normal room lighting. The camera is mounted on a tripod because the exposure times are long. In the darkened room the light source is positioned to best highlight the injury, a yellow #15 filter is placed on the front of the lens, and the lens is focused (Wright and Golden, 2010). The f-stops are bracketed between f-16 to f-22 for greater depth of field. Exposure times are bracketed for $1/2$ s through 2 s at each f-stop, depending upon the camera's metering of light to determine optimal exposure (Table 4.1).

The resultant images may appear more "grainy" or fuzzy than typical unfiltered visible light images.

Uses of Alternate Light Imaging

The forensic uses of alternate light source imaging include (Spex Forensics, 2016):

- patterned injuries in human skin
- identification of gunshot residue
- questioned documents

TABLE 4.1 Summary Table for Full Spectrum Imaging

	UV	IR	ALI
Lens	Full spectrum quartz glass	Full spectrum quartz glass	Most standard off-the-shelf types
Filter	Baader Venus UV 2	Baader IR	#15 yellow gel
f-stop brackets	4.5–8	11–22	16–22
Exposure times	1/250–1 s	1/250–1 s	$^1/_2$ –2 s
Focus shift required	No	Yes	No

- latent fingerprint detection
- presence of hair and fibers
- detection of body fluids

AL CASE PRESENTATION

This is a child abuse homicide victim with a bitemark on the right deltoid. Note the indistinct patterns imaged in the visible light black and white image (Photo 4.7A) compared to the detail obtained in the digitally enhanced black and white ALI image (Photo 4.7B).

Infrared Photography

Infrared photography in forensic odontology utilizes near infrared (IR) light to selectively image pooled blood below the skin surface not be seen by the human eye. There are two IR properties permitting this to occur. First, IR light penetrates at least 3 mm below the skin surface and most of the light is reflected back resulting in an IR positive image. Second, blood absorbs IR light, rendering it IR negative. Therefore, in the photograph the skin appears bright and blood as a darkened area. As a result, contusions and patterned injuries may be enhanced. The near IR spectrum extends from 700 to 2000 nm with the deepest penetration of skin occurring between 1100 and 1250 nm. This technique can be used on living or deceased subjects.

A misconception of IR photography is that it images heat gradients—it does not. Thermography images heat gradients, which uses far IR (2000–15,000 nm). Near IR should simply be thought of as a "color" that humans cannot see because the wavelengths are just outside of the range of human visual acuity.

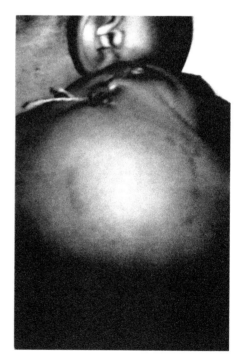

PHOTO 4.7A Visible light photograph of right deltoid region.

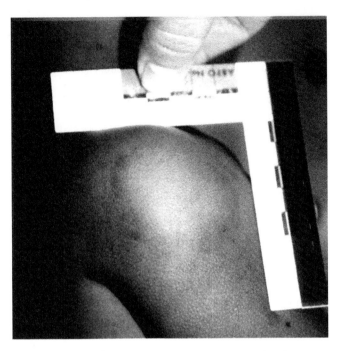

PHOTO 4.7B   ALI photograph of right deltoid region.

Making Infrared Images

Prior to digital sensors, special film with sensitivity to the near IR light spectrum had to be used. This technique required a lens filter permitting IR transmission while blocking all visible light. The IR filter was visibly opaque making it impossible to see the subject through the viewfinder; therefore, the subject had to remain motionless and the camera had to be mounted on a tripod. Composition and focusing was performed before the filter was placed over the lens. Exposure metering could not be performed and had to be bracketed with a range of apertures, in hopes of producing a useable image after film processing. Because only visible injuries were detected, any natural light discovered injuries were never photographed.

Digital sensors have replaced film. They are innately sensitive to IR, typically up to 1100 nm. This is a disadvantage in standard light photography because IR reflected from subjects distorts both color balance and exposure. It also fools a camera's autofocus since IR is focused at a different point (below the skin) than visible light. To mitigate unwanted IR, manufacturers affixed a hot mirror or IR cut filter in front of the camera sensor. For those wanting to make IR images, the advent of digital sensors made real-time IR imaging a reality. Initially, the market for this technology was in commercial surveillance video camera equipment that could covertly illuminate and record a subject at night. These cameras could also image subsurface blood below visible wounds. This added a new dimension—the ability to scan bodies searching for occult contusions in real time. Initially, IR video equipment was bulky and had to be wired to a separate monitor and recording device. Today, there are high-end integrated cameras manufactured that eliminate the IR cut filter and can image infrared as a still or video recording on a digital sensor.

Taking IR images with an IR compatible camera is similar to standard photography. An 87 IR gel filter or Baader IR glass filter is placed over the lens (Table 4.1). Any available strobe light or incandescent light (not fluorescent light) may be used. These sources are rich in infrared light. The image is easily previewed on an LCD screen or viewfinder and therefore can be composed and focused normally. Lighting, exposure, and aperture can be adjusted for best visualization of the area of interest. The body can also be scanned to discover unseen bruises. When making these photographs, the camera should be set to black and white mode to avoid recording IR as a false color. Such cameras overcome the cumbersome problems of IR film photography and videography while making both IR imaging and visible photography accessible and portable in a single unit. These cameras can theoretically be used for conventional photography if an IR blocking filter is placed over the lens. It is important to field test the filter because some leak IR wavelengths distorting color, focus, and exposure.

Results

1. Bruises located within the first few millimeters of skin appear as dark areas. Of course, those bruises that reach the surface will also be seen visually but the patterns may differ as the topography of blood beneath the surface is visualized. Acute bruises that have not yet "developed" may first be seen with IR imaging.
2. Blood in superficial veins is imaged by IR photography. Their branching anatomy will easily distinguish them from bruises. Blood within arteries is not seen as arteries are deeper, have a smaller diameter than corresponding veins, and are cloaked in a thicker vessel wall.
3. Abrasions overlying bruises will be de-emphasized. They may not disappear completely, but bruises concealed by abrasions may become more distinct.
4. Bruises concealed by all except darkly pigmented skin can be visualized with IR

photography because the thin, homogeneous layer of melanin confined to the single-celled basal layer of epithelium is relatively transparent in IR imaging. Similarly, fine surface hairs containing melanin will disappear or lighten.
5. The thin and homogeneous layer of blood in postmortem lividity is penetrated by IR light so that underlying bruises can be visualized.

False Negatives

1. If the blood volume within a bruise is insufficient, visualization may not be improved.
2. Bruising too deep for IR penetration will not be seen.
3. Contusion within adipose tissue is distributed into thin compartments between the fat lobules and may not be viewable.
4. IR may not penetrate the dense connective tissue of the galea preventing the visualization of underlying bruising.
5. Carboxyhemoglobin, occurring in smoke inhalation or in carbon monoxide poisoning may be IR negative.
6. Poor technique (lighting, aperture, exposure, improper equipment) may fail to image potentially recordable contusions.

False Positives

1. Although pigmented skin permits adequate IR photography, thicker and focal areas of melanin pigmentation (pigmented nevi, Mongolian spots, and darkly pigmented nipples) will image IR positive.
2. A blood-filled lesion such as a hemangioma will provide a false-positive image.
3. Some pigments in tattoos are IR positive. This is actually useful if decomposition has rendered an identifying tattoo illegible.
4. Atrophic skin overlying muscle may show diffuse IR positivity due to the myoglobin within muscle.
5. Uneven lighting may produce shadows misinterpreted as a bruise. Moving the light angle will change the shadow pattern.

Interpretation of the Infrared Image

Interpreting an IR image is not intuitive and requires education and experience. Five percent of IR radiation is reflected from the skin surface. The remainder penetrates below the surface at varying depths and scatters before being reflected back. The resulting image is uniformly light unless intervening blood absorbs the IR light, in which case, a dark area appears on the image. Pools of blood photograph as softly focused areas with diffuse edge detail due to the scattering of reflected light and the varying depths of IR reflection. Sometimes, IR images are disappointing, and the bruising is better visualized using standard photography. This should not be construed as a failure of IR, but rather, a superficial lesion with an inadequate volume of blood. Other times, a bruise is not well imaged due to poor lighting, improper exposure, or equipment. The camera filters and light source should always be field tested and optimized. This test can be easily accomplished by IR imaging superficial veins in the forearm (Medical Infrared Photography, 1973).

Because IR images of bruises are unseen or appear differently from what is visually seen with natural lighting, as a point of reference, a visible light image of the same subject area should always accompany an IR image.

When performed appropriately, IR imaging allows the photographer to visualize approximately 3 mm into the skin. The following diagrams illustrate the comparison between IR photography and visible light photography in selected situations:

CASE PRESENTATION 1

A victim of multiple blunt force injuries has a subtle dark area in between the indicator arrows (Photo 4.8A). The same location with infrared imaging shows a more intense dark area (Photo 4.8B). Incision of the dark area confirms a deep contusion (Photo 4.8C).

CASE PRESENTATION 2

A decedent with multiple abrasions and questionable contusions is illustrated with black and white photography (Photo 4.9A). The same location is photographed with infrared imaging and better visualizes the contusion pattern by minimizing surface abrasion (Photo 4.9B).

CASE PRESENTATION 3

A darkly pigmented African American child has a darkened ovoid pattern on the anterior thigh (Photo 4.10A). Infrared imaging enhances visualization of the contusion (Photo 4.10B).

Nonvisible Light Photography: Ultraviolet Technique

In contrast to infrared photography, ultraviolet (UV) photography uses 200—290 nm light as a source to highlight surface details of objects and injuries on the skin. The physical properties of the UV light are such that almost all of it is reflected from the surface with very little penetration into skin. The resultant images yield extremely sharp surface details. Selective absorption of UV light by melanin has the effect of accentuating subtle variations in skin pigmentation. In healed cutaneous injuries, postlesioned pigmentation can last for months or even years beyond when healing patterns are no longer visible to the eye. This sometimes permits old and healed patterned injuries to be visualized with UV photography.

UV light is not visible to the unaided human eye; therefore, cameras must be used to capture the image. Rarely are cameras manufactured to allow UV light to be captured. Camera manufacturers coat their flashes and lenses with a fluorite coating allowing only visible light to pass to the sensor. Additionally, the digital sensors have a "hot boot" and chip calibrated to only allow visible light to pass and be recorded by the sensor. Therefore, UV photography requires the use of

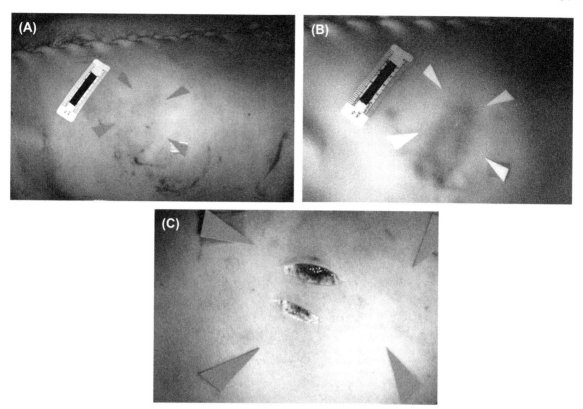

PHOTO 4.8 (A) A victim of multiple blunt force injuries has a subtle dark area in between the indicator arrows. (B) The same location in (A) with infrared imaging shows a more intense dark area. (C) Incision of the dark area confirms a deep contusion.

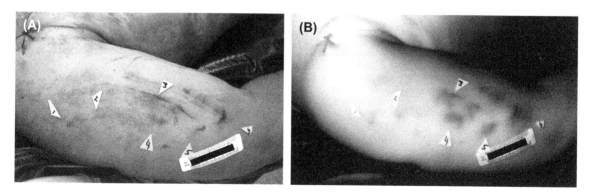

PHOTO 4.9 (A) A decedent with multiple abrasions and questionable contusions is illustrated with black and white photography. (B) The same location in (A) is photographed with infrared imaging and better visualizes the contusion pattern by minimizing surface abrasion.

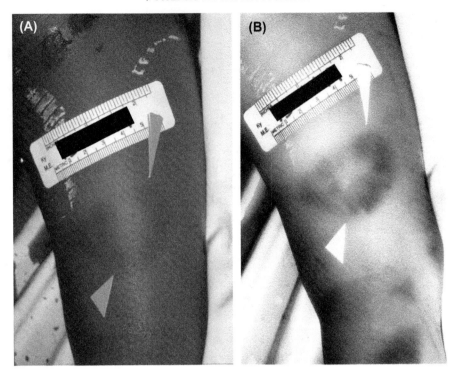

PHOTO 4.10 (A) A darkly pigmented African American child has a darkened ovoid pattern on the anterior thigh. (B) Infrared imaging enhances visualization of the contusion.

lenses that allow full spectrum light to pass, a full spectrum flash, and the camera sensor set to collect full spectrum electromagnetic radiation.

There are several after-market companies that can remove the "hot boot" filter from the sensor and recalibrate the sensor so it can capture full spectrum light (Table 4.2). Full spectrum lenses that permit the passage of visible, IR, and UV light are typically made of quartz glass and are usually very expensive. The Nikon Nikkor UV

TABLE 4.2 Full Spectrum Digital Camera, Lens, and Flash Units

Life Pixel (modification of camera to full spectrum digital camera)	Life Pixel Infrared 13024 Beverly Park Road Suite 101 Mukilteo, WA 98275	www.lifepixel.com
Jenoptik *Coastal Optic Systems* (full spectrum camera lenses—UV 105 lens)	Jenoptik Headquarters: Jena, Germany	www.jenoptik.com
Quantum Qflash (full spectrum flash systems)	Quantum Instruments A division of PromarkBRANDS 1268 Humbracht Circle Bartlett, IL 60103-1631 USA	www.qtm.com
Alpine Astronomical (Baader lens filters Venus UV, IR, non-UV/non-IR)	Alpine Astronomical Eagle, Idaho, USA	www.alpineastro.com

All information in the table above requires tripod mounted camera and an image sensor that is calibrated for the specific wavelengths of light for each technique.

105 lens was the first such lens that was manufactured. Although it is no longer made, there are other manufacturers that have manufactured similar lenses (Table 4.2).

A full spectrum flash unit is needed to create UV light in sufficient quantity to capture a UV image. There are companies that make full spectrum flash units that often come with their own cut filters permitting only specific wavelengths of light to pass (Table 4.2). These flashes emit very bright and intense light when fired without any filter in place; therefore, it is advisable to place a filter over the flash to prevent potential retinal damage to living individuals being photographed.

Additionally, a filter allowing only UV light to pass must be mounted on the front of the camera lens. Because the UV band-pass filter does not permit visible light to pass, the UV filter is placed only after focusing the lens on the object being imaged. Once focus is achieved, the lens set screw is tightened so the focus cannot change and the UV filter is placed on the front of the lens. There are several manufacturers of UV lens filters, but the Baader Venus UV2 is recommended (Fig. 4.11).

Since UV imaging captures only surface detail the required depth of field is narrow and a lens aperture of f5.6 is recommended. Under- and overexposure discrepancies are overcome by taking multiple images, bracketing the f-stop plus and minus one f-stop on either side of f5.6, and using exposure times between 1/250—1 s (Table 4.1).

When properly created UV photographs do not show any surface enhancement of the object being imaged, it does not necessarily mean there was a failure of the UV photography. The lack of surface enhancement may simply indicate there was no damage to the surface that the UV photography could enhance. Even in cases where there does not appear to be surface damage, especially in skin, it is still recommended that UV images are created. The human eye cannot see UV light; therefore it is impossible to know what UV light imaging will reveal.

One final comment about the Baader lens filters; Baader manufacturers use not only the IR and Venus UV 2 filters but another filter, the "non-UV/non-IR," which permits only visible light to pass. Using the Baader filters over a full spectrum lens, it's possible to not only capture UV and IR images, but when the "non-UV/non-IR" filter is used, the modified camera system returns to a typical visible light camera for every day recreational photography.

Ultraviolet Transmission Filters

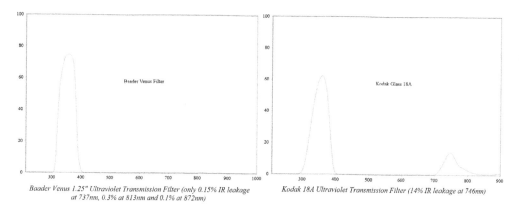

Baader Venus 1.25" Ultraviolet Transmission Filter (only 0.15% IR leakage at 737nm, 0.3% at 813nm and 0.1% at 872nm)

Kodak 18A Ultraviolet Transmission Filter (14% IR leakage at 746nm)

FIGURE 4.11   Comparison of Baader UV 2 filter and Kodak Wrattan 18A UV filter.

Uses for Ultraviolet Photography

Forensic dental application of UV photography generally covers two areas: patterned injuries in skin and the assisting in identification cases.

When a patterned injury in skin is believed to be a human bitemark, the use of full spectrum digital images is recommended (Wright and Golden, 2010). The image series include visible light, UV, IR, and alternate light images of each injury thereby obtaining and highlighting details for forensic evaluation and interpretation.

It may also assist a living victim's claim of having been bitten when no evidence of an injury remains. In these cases, the area can be photographed utilizing UV to search for invisible pigmentary patterns. UV photography can also assist in identification of remain through the detection of composite restorations not seen upon a visual examination.

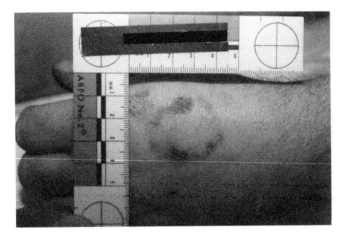

PHOTO 4.11A   B&W image of injury on back of hand.

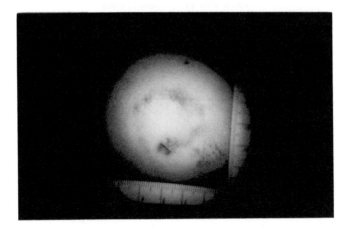

PHOTO 4.11B   ALI image of injury on back of hand.

CASE PRESENTATION 4

Defensive bitemark on the back of the hand of a murder victim—B&W, ALI, UV, and IR images shown. Note the difference in the appearance of the same injury photographed with different light sources and filters (Photo 4.11A, B, C, and D).

CASE PRESENTATION 5

A series of full spectrum images taken of one (1) out of thirty-seven (37) bites sustained by a victim. The injuries were photographed serially over twenty-eight (28) days (Photo 4.12A, B, C, D, and E). The results are as follows:

- IR images best at or near time of injury.
- Visible light and ALI images are best at or near time of injury but remain somewhat present at 1 week.
- UV images best from 7 to 9 days after the incident.

Application of photographic techniques other than for bitemarks:

CASE PRESENTATION 6

Decomposing homicide victim identified dentally and confirmed with IR image of tattoo on arm (Photo 4.13A and B).

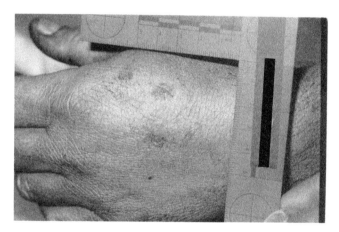

PHOTO 4.11C   UV image of injury on back of hand.

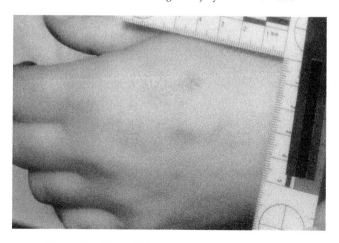

PHOTO 4.11D   IR image of injury on back of hand.

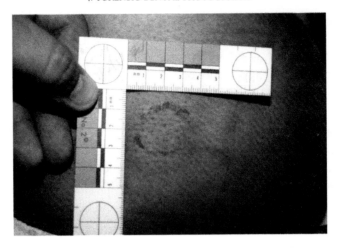

PHOTO 4.12A   Day 1, hip injury—color photograph.

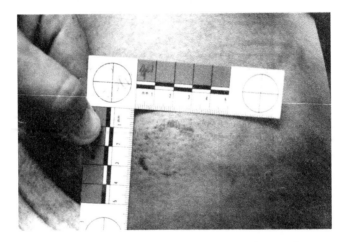

PHOTO 4.12B   Day 1, hip injury—B&W photograph.

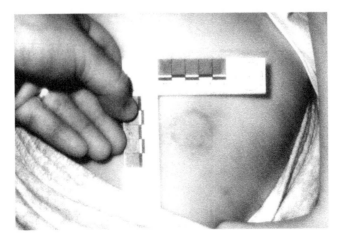

PHOTO 4.12C   Day 1, hip injury—IR photograph.

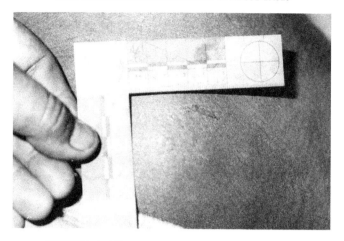

PHOTO 4.12D Day 1, hip injury—UV photograph.

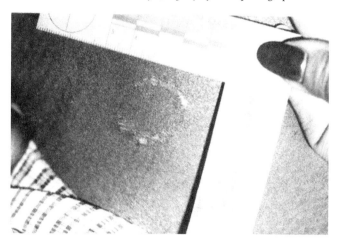

PHOTO 4.12E Day 8, hip injury—UV photograph.

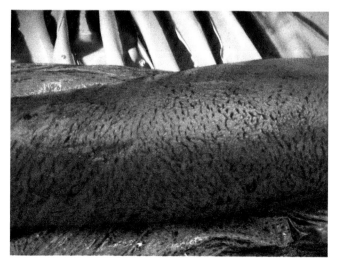

PHOTO 4.13A Color photograph of tattoo on decomposing arm.

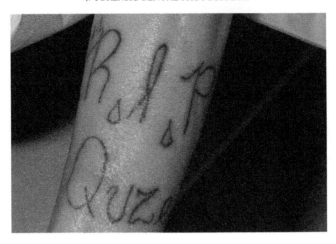

PHOTO 4.13B   IR photograph of tattoo on decomposing arm.

References

Eastman Kodak Company, 1972. Ultraviolet & Fluorescence Photography. A Kodak Technical Publication, M-27. Eastman Kodak Company, Rochester, NY, p. 12.

Forensic Light Source Applications: Wavelengths and Uses, May 17, 2016. From: http://www.horiba.com/fileadmin/uploads/Scientific/Documents/Forensics/fls.pdf.

Spex Forensics, May 17, 2016 from: https://spexforensics.com/applications.

Kochevar, I.E., Pathak, M.A., Parrish, J.A., 1993. Photophysics, Photochemistry and Photobiology. In: Fitzpatrick's Dermatology in General Medicine (Chapter 131), fourth ed. McGraw-Hill, New York. p. 1632.

Medical Infrared Photography, 1973. Kodak publication N-1, third ed. Eastman Kodak Co., Rochester, NY, p. 6.

Stokes, G.G., 1852. On the change of refrangibility of light. Philosophical Transactions of the Royal Society A 142, 385–396.

Wright, F.D., Golden, G.S., 2010. The use of full spectrum digital photograph for evidence collection and preservation in cases involving forensic odontology: Forensic Science International 201 (1–3), 59–67.

5

Disaster Victim Identification

Peter W. Loomis[1,2]

[1]Forensic Odontology Consultant, New Mexico Office of the Medical Investigator, Albuquerque, NM, United States; [2]Faculty - University of New Mexico School of Medicine, Albuquerque, NM, United States

OUTLINE

Forensic Odontology
http://dx.doi.org/10.1016/B978-0-12-805198-6.00005-0

DEFINITIONS AND TYPES OF DISASTERS

Disaster victim identification (DVI) is the term used for describing the identification process of human remains in a multiple fatality incident (MFI). The word "disaster," as defined by the International Red Cross Society is, *"a sudden, calamitous event that seriously disrupts the functioning of a community or society and causes human, material, and economic or environmental losses that exceed the community's or society's ability to cope using its own resources."* With respect to a disaster with multiple fatalities the definition can be paraphrased to, *an incident resulting in loss of life where there are more decedents that can be located, identified and processed by available resources.*

Disasters are classified according to the cause of the event as either natural, man-made unintentional and man-made intentional. Natural disasters include hurricanes, floods, tornadoes, volcanoes, wildfires, earthquakes, tsunamis, mudslides, epidemics, and pandemics. Man-made unintentional disasters include events such as transportation accidents, chemical spills, structural fires and structure collapse, explosions, and radiation accidents. Man-made intentional disasters include acts of terrorism, explosions, mass shootings, the destruction of aircraft, ships, subways, trains, chemical terrorism, biological terrorism, and radiological terrorism, which occur are all too often in the world community.

RESPONSE TO A MULTIPLE FATALITY INCIDENT

The local community or jurisdiction (city, county, parish, and state) has primary responsibility for the victim response, recovery and processing of an MFI. Federal assistance may be requested by the state, but it still remains the state's responsibility to recover process and identify victims of an MFI. Even though federal agencies (FBI, DHS, DOD, NTSB), may have the primary investigative responsibility of terrorist attacks or transportation accidents the local jurisdiction or state medical examiner or coroner (ME/C) is responsible for processing the victims.

The ME/C response to an MFI has five priorities:

1. Recovery of victims—Includes locating and recovering body fragments, scene documentation, and the transport of remains to the disaster morgue.
2. Decontamination—Neutralization (if indicated), of biologic or chemical contamination of the remains, which is usually done just prior to entering the morgue, or at the first station of the disaster morgue.
3. Examination—An assessment to determine cause and manner of death, which includes complete documentation of the remains and personal effects.

4. Identification and death certification—Identification should be made by a scientific method and not by visual or presumptive means.
5. Process remains for final disposition—The remains properly are prepared and returned to loved ones, usually through a mortuary service

It is imperative that there is the capable leadership to manage the incident, trained personnel to process the scene, recover remains, conduct family assistance operations, conduct morgue operations and the proper physical facilities to conduct the operations. Some of the requirements for MFI operations include preparation of morgue/autopsy facilities, establishing security and credentialing systems, coordination of transportation from scene to morgue, coordinating activities with family assistance center (FAC), establishment of communications and data management systems, establishment of fiscal and material requirements, identifying the deceased, issuing death certificates and establishing a system for disposition of the remains. Although many MFIs are characterized by initial confusion, disorganization, disinformation from various sources, a sense of urgency and a desire to help, these characteristics can be mitigated with proper preparation and leadership.

FEDERAL AUTHORITIES FOR DISASTER RESPONSE

In the United States, the Homeland Security Act of 2002 consolidated 22 federal departments and agencies and over 177,000 federal employees to create the Department of Homeland Security (DHS), an agency with a mandate to prevent or reduce the nation's vulnerability to terrorist attacks. The following year in February 2003, President George W. Bush signed the Homeland Security Presidential Directive 5 (HSPD-5) which mandated the Secretary of DHS to be responsible for the coordination of the federal preparations and response and recovery from terrorist attacks and major disasters. HSPD-5 directed the Secretary of DHS to create two specific documents: a National Incident Management System (NIMS) and a National Response Plan (NRP). The intent of these two documents was to provide a single, comprehensive national approach to incident management.

In 2008 the NRP was superseded by the National Response Framework (NRF). The National NRF is a guide that directs how the United States responds to all types of disasters and emergencies. It is built on scalable, flexible, and adaptable concepts identified in the NIMS to align key roles and responsibilities across the United States. This framework describes specific authorities and best practices for managing incidents that range from the purely local to large-scale terrorist attacks or catastrophic natural disasters. This framework is always in effect, and the structures, roles, and responsibilities in this framework can be partially or fully implemented in the context of a threat or hazard, in anticipation of a significant event, or in response to an incident. Selective implementation of NRF structures and procedures allows for a scaled response, delivery of the specific resources and capabilities, and a level of coordination that is appropriate to each incident. The response protocols and structures described in the NRF align with NIMS. The NIMS provides the incident management basis for the NRF and defines standard command and management structures. All of the components of the NIMS, including preparedness, communications and information management, resource management, and command and management, are intended to support response. The NRF outlines 15 emergency support functions and identifies the federal agency that is primarily responsible for the function during an emergency situation.

EMERGENCY SUPPORT FUNCTIONS

ESF #1—Transportation—DOT

ESF #2—CommunicationsDHS

ESF #3—Public Works and Engineering—DOD and Corps of Engineers

ESF #4—Firefighting—Department of Agriculture and Forest Service

ESF #5—Emergency Management—DHS, FEMA

ESF #6—Mass Care, Emergency Assistance, Housing and Human Services—DHS, FEMA

ESF #7—Logistics Management and Resource Support—GSA

ESF #8—Public Health and Medical Services—HHS

ESF #9—Search and Rescue—DHS, FEMA

ESF #10—Oil and Hazardous Materials Response—EPA

ESF #11—Agriculture and Natural Resources—Department of Agriculture

ESF #12—Energy—DOE

ESF #13— Public Safety and Security—DHS, FEMA

ESF #14—Long-Term Community Recovery—DHS

ESF #15—External Affairs—DHS, FEMA

EMERGENCY SUPPORT FUNCTION 8

The ESF #8 (Public Health and Medical Services), primary agency is the US Department of Health and Human Services (HHS). During a disaster event, when called upon, HHS is responsible for human and animal health and medical needs and mass fatality management.

1. Assessment of public health/medical needs
2. Health surveillance
3. Medical care personnel
4. Health/medical/veterinary equipment and supplies
5. Patient evacuation
6. Patient care
7. Safety and security of drugs, biologics, and medical devices
8. Blood and blood products
9. Food and agriculture safety and security.
10. All-hazard public health and medical consultation, technical assistance and support
11. Behavioral health care
12. Public health and medical information
13. Vector control
14. Potable water/wastewater and solid waste disposal
15. Mass fatality management, victim identification, and decontamination of remains.
16. Veterinary medical support

In a nutshell, when a disaster occurs, local and county (parish or borough) first-responders activate their disaster plan and resources to respond to the event. If the local resources are overwhelmed, a request for help is made from the county to state for additional assistance. If state resources are unable to cope with the event then a request may be made by the state to the federal government as additional resource needs are identified. From the authority of the Federal Stafford Act this is done by the Governor requesting a disaster declaration through the regional Federal Emergency Management Agency (FEMA) which proceeds to the FEMA Director and then to the President of the United States. The President, acting upon the recommendations from the Director and the Governor will sign a "Major Disaster Declaration," allowing for a Federal Coordination Officer to begin releasing federal assets and activating federal programs (NRF, NIMS and the ESFs), to respond, assist and mitigate the disaster.

Under ESF #8, (Health and Medical Services), the National Disaster Medical System (NDMS), as part of the Department of Health and Human Services, Office of Preparedness and Response, supports federal agencies in the management and coordination of the federal medical response to major emergencies and federally declared disasters.

It is the mission of the NDMS to temporarily supplement federal, tribal, state, and Local capabilities by funding, organizing, training, equipping, deploying and sustaining a specialized and focused range of public health and medical capabilities. NDMS has disaster response teams that consist of the following:

1. Disaster Medical Assistance Team (DMAT): A DMAT is a group of professional and paraprofessional medical personnel designed to provide medical care during a disaster or other event. DMATs are designed to supplement local medical care until other federal or contract resources can be mobilized, or the situation is resolved. DMATs deploy to disaster sites with sufficient supplies and equipment to sustain themselves for a period of 72 h while providing medical care at a fixed or temporary medical care site. The personnel are activated for a period of 2 weeks. In mass casualty incidents, their responsibilities may include triaging patients, providing high-quality medical care despite the adverse and austere environment often found at a disaster site, patient reception at staging facilities, and preparing patients for evacuation if necessary.

2. The International Medical Surgical Response Team (IMSURT) is a NDMS team of medical specialists who provide surgical and critical care during a disaster or public health emergency. Originally conceived to address the needs of US citizens injured overseas, the IMSURT role has expanded over the years to include domestic deployments as well.

3. National Veterinary Response Team (NVRT): The NVRTs are comprised of individuals with diverse expertise, including veterinarians, animal health technicians, epidemiologists, safety officers, logisticians, communications specialists, and other support personnel. During a response, the NVRT provides assessments, technical assistance, public health, and veterinary services under the guidance of state and/or local authorities. It is the primary federal resource for the treatment of injured or ill animals affected by disasters.

4. Disaster Mortuary Operational Response Team (DMORT): DMORTs are composed of personnel within a number of different fields of expertise to provide assistance to local authorities dealing with the remains of the deceased. DMORT personnel can also assist the local ME/C in the processing and identification of remains. When deployed to an emergency, DMORT personnel work under the guidance of local authorities (i.e., ME/C) to provide technical assistance and personnel to identify and process deceased victims with the ultimate goal of issuing a death certificate and returning the remains to loved ones. DMORTs provide temporary morgue facilities, victim identification, forensic odontology services, forensic anthropology services, DNA collection, processing, preparation, and disposition of remains.

The teams are composed of MEs, coroners, funeral directors, mortuary officers, photographers, medical records technicians/transcribers, forensic specialists (anthropologists, odontologists, and pathologists), logistics specialists, medicolegal death investigators, family assistance specialists, security specialists, and computer specialists. DMORT members are required to maintain appropriate certifications and licensure within their discipline. When members are activated, licensure and certification is recognized by all states, and the team members are compensated for their duty time by the federal government as intermittent federal employees. DMORT maintains three Disaster Portable

Morgue Units (DPMUs), staged at locations in California, Texas, and Maryland for immediate deployment in support of DMORT operations. The DPMU is a depository of equipment and supplies that can be deployed to a disaster site by truck, rail, plane, or ship. It contains a complete morgue with designated workstations and prepackaged equipment and supplies.

There are three specialty DMORTs: DMORT, Victim Information Center (VIC) team, and DMORT-All Hazards. The DPMU Team is a logistical team equipped to set up, operate, and maintain the DPMU. The standard DMORT can staff and operate either a DPMU or another established facility to examine remains. The VIC team can set up and operate in a FAC to assist state and local authorities collect antemortem data for victim identification. The DMORT-All Hazards is equipped for processing of human remains that have been contaminated with hazardous chemicals, radiation, or biological agents. The team can be deployed in response to a weapons of mass destruction (WMD) incident. Team composition is similar to a standard DMORT, except for the addition of hazardous materials/ weapons of mass destruction mitigation capability for remains. Unlike standard DMORTs, the DMORT-All Hazards maintains a specialized equipment cache and a number of support vehicles. Specific DMORT deployment configuration is based upon the particular needs of an incident.

The first DMORT deployment was for the Mississippi River flooding event in 1993 that caused cemetery disruptions in Hardin, Missouri with many caskets becoming disinterred. Other DMORT deployments included the Murrah Federal Building terrorist explosion in Oklahoma City in 1995, the Korean Airline crash in Guam in 1997, the 9/11 WTC disaster in New York City, the search and recovery effort for victims of the shuttle Columbia in Texas and Louisiana in 2003, the response to Hurricane Katrina in 2005, the Buffalo, New York aircraft

crash in 2009, the tornado in Joplin, Missouri, in 2011, and others.

Some states have incorporated their existing Forensic Dental Identification Team into their state Disaster Mortuary Team, such as in Michigan. The 27- year-old Michigan Dental Association Forensic Dental Identification Team is now a formal component of the Michigan Mortuary Operations Response Team.

Other states and even some major cities such as New York City, Miami, Toronto, and Chicago have separate forensic dental identification teams as well as separate mortuary operations response teams. The Armed Forces of the United States have DVI teams and the Dover Port Mortuary at Dover Air Force Base, Delaware, which is responsible for the identification and processing of the Nation's fallen combat veterans.

Another Department of Defense agency providing dental identifications is the former Armed Forces Central Identification Laboratory (CIL) in Hawaii, now known as the Defense POW/MIA Accounting Command (DPAA). Most of the remains accessioned into the DPAA are Americans from past conflicts who have been missing for decades. Dental comparison has been the most commonly used methodology for identifying these individuals at the CIL. As the advances in DNA continue, this may not be the case in the future.

INTERPOL is the world's largest international police organization with 188 member countries. Created in 1923, INTERPOL has a standing committee on DVI and published its first manual on DVI in 1984. The manual, which has been reviewed and revised numerous times, offers practical advice on the major issues of victim identification and encourages the compatibility of procedures across international boundaries, which is essential in disasters involving citizens of many different countries.

Two well-known private companies, Kenyon International Emergency Services and Blake Emergency Services are based in the United

Kingdom and have the capability of managing disaster operations including search and rescue and the identification and the return of human remains. They also can provide family assistance, counseling, telephone centers, and crisis communications, and work with aviation carriers, private business, and government entities.

DISASTER SITE MANAGEMENT

Notification and Assessment by Medical Examiners and Coroners

Disaster sites are usually managed in a manner similar to a crime scene. It is important that the proper chain of evidence and control of the scene is maintained and the site is secure. In a terrorist event, the Federal Bureau of Investigation (FBI) will likely oversee the investigation and the National Transportation Safety Board (NTSB) will investigate transportation accidents. However, as mentioned earlier in the chapter, it is the local ME/C that has jurisdiction and is in charge of processing and identifying the deceased. When a multiple fatality event occurs, notification is made to the county ME/C, the local emergency manager, the local emergency operations center, and the local public health officer. Upon notification, the ME assesses the following information: the type of incident, location of the incident, and the estimated number of fatalities. If the site is secure, the ME may visit the site to meet with the incident commander to determine if the incident is stabilized, the estimated number of fatalities, and the conditions of the bodies. If any bodies have been moved, the ME will inspect the location to which the bodies have been transported and determine whether it is appropriate to serve as a temporary morgue. Depending on the number of fatalities, the distance from the incident site to the ME's office and the ability of the local ME's office to absorb these additional fatalities, a decision may be made to establish a temporary morgue for the disaster victims.

Morgue Location

Certain parameters and considerations must be made in selecting a temporary morgue site. The ME, working with local officials including the local emergency operations center, the State Public Health Department, and any local or state Mortuary Operations Disaster Team should make the decision where to establish the site. It is strongly advised that the temporary morgue not be established at the current location of any public facility such as a recreation center, ice rink, or high school gymnasium. The temporary morgue should be set up in an area that can be secured for privacy from public and media intrusion. The following should be considered in selecting a temporary morgue site:

1. What infrastructure (water, sewer, electrical system, HVAC, truck access, storage space, telecommunications, etc.) is available at this location?
2. Can the facility be made secure with limited ingress and egress points and is the facility available for the time necessary to complete morgue operations?
3. Can the facility be retrofitted for necessities that are lacking and what is the cost?
4. Is the facility a weatherproof structure with concrete or nonporous floors?

The size of the temporary morgue will vary depending on the number of fatalities anticipated. The rule of thumb is: less than 100 fatalities, a structure of 6000 sq. ft., 101–200 fatalities, 8000 sq. ft; greater than 200 fatalities, 12,000 sq. ft.

Search and Recovery

Search and recovery operations occur as soon as the search and rescue operations have been completed. Individuals trained in the use of a grid system and/or a total station surveying device may be part of this team. The recovery operation must locate, document, and recover all artifacts involving human remains while maintaining respectful and ethical treatment of the deceased. Recovery of the victims is the first step in enabling the establishment of a personal identification of the individuals and the return of the deceased to their loved ones.

Before recovery operations begin, a thorough assessment of existing hazards must take place through consultation with fire and HAZMAT personnel. It is vitally important to maintain standards of personnel safety while still preserving evidence. The entire scene is documented before any recovery begins with still photography, video, and GPS readings. Boundaries and perimeters are established and the measured grids marked.

The recovery is done in a thorough and conscientious manner. However, "careful expediency" is important in recovering and transporting the remains to a mass fatality morgue, thus ensuring that the bodies are no longer exposed to the harsh weather conditions, decomposition, and public view. If body fragmentation has occurred, extra care must be taken so that the location of the body fragments is well documented and that commingling of separate individuals does not occur. If there is any doubt, a separate "victim number" may be assigned to each set of fragmented remains. Otherwise, improper commingling might preclude the identification of an individual victim.

The Search and Recovery Team is made up of three separate teams: the search team, the remains collection team, and the transportation team.

1. The search team is composed of at least four individuals. The team leader, who has overall responsibility for the team; two-team scribes are responsible for the documentation of location and condition of the remains; and the team photographer who will be photographing each body or fragment before and after a number is assigned.
2. The remains collection team is also made up of at least four individuals. The team leader, who is responsible for the team and three recovery specialists tasked to assist in placing the bodies and/or fragments into body bags or pouches. They also move the remains to the staging area. Forensic scientists, including dentists, should be at the disaster site to help with the determination as to whether recovered tissue fragments are human.
3. The transportation team is made up of at least three individuals, the team leader and two drivers. This team is responsible for the transportation of the bodies/fragments to the temporary morgue. A chain of evidence is maintained throughout these procedures.

Security and Safety

Security and safety at the disaster site and morgue are of paramount importance. Law enforcement must establish a perimeter around the site and control the access points. On-site fabrication of photographic ID and/or fingerprint scans aids in controlling both entry points and those areas that only authorized personnel may access. The security officers should be given an initial list of names of team members allowed on the site to streamline entry into team staging areas. The safety of the disaster team workers is one of the most important management aspects of a mass disaster site. A safety officer is assigned with the responsibility of working with HAZMAT team members to establish the safety of both the site and the temporary morgue area before responders enter the area. They are also responsible for establishing any needed decontamination of materials or individuals before leaving the controlled site. Universal precautions are also exercised at all times in both the disaster site and the morgue. Individuals should be paired while working on the recovery teams and in the morgue to affect a buddy system, which ensures that all responders remain safe or communicate a need to evacuate the area.

During the initial hours and days of a mass casualty incident, personnel often desire to work extended hours to achieve the goals of reuniting the deceased with their families. This enthusiasm may be to their (and the mission's) detriment if they do not take care to eat, hydrate, and get adequate rest. Skipping meals and working more than a 12 h shift is not conducive to peak performance of operations personnel. Eventually, personnel will begin to experience fatigue and become depressed. Responders should keep an eye on each other for signs of stress, depression, and emotional fatigue. The disaster team should have mental health workers present to monitor team members and conduct daily briefings and a final exit debriefing at the end of the individual's deployment, which are helpful in assessing and aiding the mental health of the responder.

Establishing a DVI Morgue Operation (DMORT Model)

The primary purpose of mortuary operations in a disaster is to provide the physical examination, identification, and disposition of deceased victims with sensitivity, dignity, and respect. Identification permits the deceased to be returned to their families, offering the family closure and the opportunity to grieve for their loved one according to their religious, cultural, or ethnic customs.

COMPONENTS OF MORTUARY OPERATIONS

Mortuary operational details are totally dependent upon the nature and size of the disaster. However, there are certain features and requirements within the morgue configuration that enhance mission success. As mentioned previously, all disaster morgues require the mandatory provision of clean water, sewer services, electricity, sufficient climate control/ventilation, and telecommunications. As an example, handling of remains in any form or fashion was not permitted at the DPMU East (Gulfport Mississippi) until sufficient fresh running water was available. Also, the only electrical generator available early in the operation was underpowered and on several occasions work in the morgue had to be curtailed when the electrical system failed.

The mortuary annex, as the temporary morgue is frequently called, is made up of separate examination workstations at which trained forensic scientists and other skilled personnel work diligently to provide scientific identification of the victim and proper disposition of the remains. These workstations include the following: decontamination, body registration, personal effects documentation, fingerprint collection, photography, full-body radiography, pathological/autopsy examination, anthropological examination, dental examination, DNA collection, embalming (if required), and the storage of remains until their release to funeral homes. All final documentation used to establish the identity of the victim is provided to the responsible local ME/C who signs the victim's death certificate.

Decontamination

The decontamination workstation is responsible for the removal of toxic or potentially harmful materials from the external surface of the remains. This task is typically completed by the WMD team. It is not possible to truly decontaminate a body, particularly one that has undergone decomposition; therefore, the purpose of this station is to remove contaminants from the surface of the remains that may be harmful to the mortuary workers. Harmful contaminants include organophosphates found in pesticides, petroleum products found in fossil fuels, toxic chemical substances such as ammonia or chlorine commonly used for industrial purposes, and radioactive contamination from a nuclear event or a dirty bomb. The decontamination station is only used when it is required.

Reception/Registration

The reception/registration workstation is responsible for a number of important duties. The initial task is to assign and catalog incoming remains with a unique numerical code specific to the disaster. In the 9/11 disaster, the first body received was assigned the number "DM01-00001." This indicated "Disaster-Manhattan" and the year "2001." This numerical system provided individual case numbers to approximately 19,000 recovered remains. It is good practice to utilize a numerical system that can over accommodate the anticipated volume of remains.

Next, the victim's personal effects are removed and photographed. The personal effects are catalogued and either secured for later distribution back to the family, or bagged and placed in the body pouch with the remains. Once the personal effects have been removed, an external examination is performed on the victim and photographs are taken for documentation (some MEs prefer that the clothing is not removed prior to autopsy). Special attention is placed on photographing any external feature that may aid in the identification. These features include scars, tattoos, birthmarks, piercings, or any physical developmental anomaly. The final duty of the reception station is to assign an "escort" for the remains. The escort accompanies the body as it progresses through the morgue, ensuring that the victim has been examined at each workstation, the documentation has been completed appropriately, and nothing gets displaced. The escort also ensures that the body is never left alone or set aside unattended from the time they are brought into the mortuary annex examination area until returned to the storage area. This establishes a chain of custody.

Fingerprint

The fingerprint collection workstation is typically staffed by law enforcement personnel trained and experienced in the collection of fingerprints. At times this will be local law enforcement crime lab personnel, and at other times members of a federal service such as the FBI. Fingerprint identification personnel are responsible for the accurate collection of fingerprints from the victims and coordinating the search, matching, and identification of the victims from the fingerprint data collected.

Radiography

The radiology workstation location is positioned among the other workstations as deemed appropriate by the ME. For example, it might be the very first if there is a possibility of live explosives on the victims. These workers are responsible for taking full-body radiographs, which are very useful in locating previous internal injuries not visible externally (i.e., healed bone fractures). Another important benefit of the radiographic exam is the detection of implanted medical devices such as pacemakers and artificial joints. These implanted devices have serial numbers that are linked to a specific patient and are recorded by the device manufacturer and the hospital, thereby providing an excellent lead in identification of the remains. The use of full-body radiographs assist in locating displaced dental fragments in traumatic incidents.

Pathology/Autopsy

At the pathology/autopsy workstation, the forensic pathologists perform autopsies and toxicological examination of the remains in a manner deemed appropriate for the specific case. In most disasters, the extent of the victim's autopsy and toxicology screening is done at the discretion of the local ME/C. However, the law requires that a complete autopsy is performed on crew members in transportation disasters to accurately determine cause and manner of death, rule out foul play, negligence, or malfeasance as contributing factors. Special attention is given to identifying scars, tattoos, piercings, and scarring indicative of past surgical procedures. The physicians staffing the pathology/autopsy workstation dissect and remove any implanted medical devices identified in the radiographic exam.

Anthropology

Anthropological examination provides important information in the identification of the deceased. After examining the skeletal structures, the forensic anthropologist often accurately determines the race, gender, stature, and approximate age of the victim, thereby narrowing the search parameters for the victim's identity. This examination is particularly important in the event of disinterred cemetery or skeletal remains.

Dental

The DMORT dental team members are divided into two distinct sections: postmortem and antemortem. In some cases, there is a third group responsible for the comparison/matching of the antemortem and postmortem data. However, this task is often performed by the antemortem team. The dental postmortem examination team is located in the mortuary annex and is responsible for collecting the postmortem dental data of each victim. The postmortem dental examination station is staffed by dentists and dental personnel trained in forensic odontology and who are familiar with the operation of the computer programs, digital radiography, digital photography, and other tools and equipment used in the collection of the dental identification data.

Using a computer-assisted patient identification program, WinID3, the postmortem examination team creates a digital dental record of the remains undergoing examination. The WinID3 software program activates the X-ray sensor, automatically assigning the remains identification number to the created radiographic image series thereby reducing clerical error. For over a decade, DMORT morgues have used the DEXIS Digital X-ray System (DEXIS Digital Diagnostic Imaging, LLC, 1910 North Penn Road, Hatfield, PA, 19,440). DEXIS captures the radiographic images, stores, and archives them in their original and unaltered format. The DEXIS software is capable of enhancing and optimizing the quality of the radiographic images. The radiographic images are exported to the WinID3 database where the files are stored and available for viewing.

After the postmortem radiographic examination has been performed, an intraoral examination is conducted, charting the victim's dentition using an odontogram contained within the WinID3 program. The charting and radiographic exams may be accessed by any individual with rights to the dental server. Each workstation has an individual assigned as the photographer and one to perform any required resections. Two additional team members are assigned the dental charting and the radiographic processes while a fifth individual operates a laptop computer, inputting the dental data and images.

The antemortem/comparison dental section is located in close proximity to the mortuary annex. This section collects and inputs antemortem dental data (biographical information, dental charting, and radiographs) from the victims' dental records into WinID3. Antemortem conventional film radiographs are digitally scanned on a digital flatbed scanner at 300 dots per-inch (dpi) resolution. The scanner is operated by DEXscan (DEXIS) software, which optimizes, stores, and archives the images. The images are then exported into the victim's

WinID record. All antemortem and postmortem data entered into WinID3 is stored on a server, which is networked to computer stations in both the morgue and the antemortem section. This permits information to be accessed in both areas. Victim identification is assisted by WinID's "best match" feature, which sorts all of the dental records in the system according to the number of matching dental features or "hits" the postmortem and antemortem records have in common. Confirmation is made using WinID's side-by-side record and image comparisons feature.

DNA

DNA samples are normally collected by law enforcement personnel (FBI DNA teams) trained in the collection and processing of DNA evidence. A variety of tissues can be used to obtain a DNA profile. Bone and teeth are reliable sources of DNA because of their durability. When the condition of the remains is favorable, blood and soft tissue can also be an adequate source of DNA.

Embalming/Casketing

After remains are positively identified and their condition warrants, embalming is performed, unless it is a culturally inappropriate practice for the victim. The prepared remains are stored until the remains are released and returned to the family for disposition in accordance to their personal, religious, or cultural customs.

Body Storage

In an MFI , the remains must be stored in a cooled, temperature-controlled environment to protect them from freezing in cold climates and slowing down the decomposition process in warm climates. Fifty-five foot refrigerated trailers with metal flooring are used if on-site refrigerated storage is not available.

Victim storage and logistical service is a vital component of the identification process and is termed "trailer management. Trailer management is performed by teams consisting of heavy equipment operators, funeral directors, and truck drivers who provide careful and respectful movement and storage of the decedents.

Clerical or Information Resource Center

The clerical area, or Information Resource Center, collects and stores the antemortem and postmortem records. In this area, observed postmortem physical attributes of the deceased (tattoos, personal effects, eye and hair color, or piercings) are compared to the physical attributes described by the victims' families in the FAC. Physical attributes are compared using the "Victim Identification Profile Program" (VIP), a computer-assisted identification program developed by Donald Bloom. This program is used by DMORT and many individual state disaster teams. Occasionally, work performed in this area results in identification; but more often, it provides important leads to the victim's identity. Additionally, Information Resource Center is responsible for the clerical needs of the legal authorities involved in the disaster. Working with the state or local ME, coroner or county attorney, and the command staff of the mortuary operation, they are responsible for required data entry, receiving, creation, and filing of the records, documents, and reports.

PROTOCOL FOR A LOCAL OR STATE DVI DENTAL SECTION

Morgue operation protocols should be established before an event occurs. This includes the formation, staffing, and operational development of the Dental Team. In 1994, the American

Dental Association passed resolution 1994:654. It states, "The American Dental Association urges all constituents to develop dental identification teams that can be mobilized at times of need."

Under the auspices of the state governmental agencies and/or local dental associations, many states presently have their own dental identification teams. Additional information regarding state DVI teams may be found at http://www.abfo.org/id_teams.htm. The ME/C with jurisdiction over a disaster scene will normally consult with the appropriate state, county, and/or municipal agencies to determine if the existing disaster plans are sufficient to meet the needs or whether additional external support is needed.

FORMATION OF A DENTAL IDENTIFICATION TEAM

Typically it is not difficult to identify and recruit willing volunteer dental personnel to serve on a "mass disaster dental identification team." However, without planning and training, this yields only a list of names, addresses, and telephone numbers. Details related to the function and operation of a dental identification team must be addressed *before* disaster strikes. Sadly, this is often not the case and the training deficiency becomes evident resulting in chaos and eventual plan failure. Unfavorable volunteer attrition rates in a prolonged DVI operation are well documented. A sufficient cache of required dental equipment, instruments, and supplies must be obtained prior to the event. This includes the selection and purchase of all software, computers, and server/network components. Personnel must have adequate time to train and develop the required computer and software skills. Governing agencies often do not realize that there are many systems and techniques used by a Dental ID team which are not

found in the typical dental office. Authorities need to consider if team members are to be volunteers or temporary employees and if compensation will be provided for travel, meals, and lodging. Provisions for workers compensation insurance in case of injury or death during the identification process must be made in advance. Complete planning is essential before a disaster occurs.

DENTAL SECTION TEAM LEADER

The dental team leader is responsible for complete team operations. There should be only one designated team section leader in command at any given time during an MFI. This person should have an active state dental license, be actively involved as a forensic odontologist and, if possible, be certified by the American Board of Forensic Odontology. He or she should be associated with a local ME/C's office within the jurisdiction and familiar with other agencies that will be involved in an MFI. The team leader is responsible for reviewing *all* dental identifications before forwarding to the ME. The ME should only accept a dental identification signed by two team members and the dental section leader.

When an incident occurs, the team leader is notified by the jurisdictional agency in charge. A "Go Team" consisting of individuals with disaster team leadership roles is notified and mobilized by the team leader. "Go Team" personnel are expected to be present for the entirety of the MFI. Once preliminary assessments and facility arrangements have been made at the disaster site by the "Go Team," the "Support Team" consisting of dentists and nondental administrative personnel are notified to mobilize. The dental identification process does not begin until after the support team arrives. Each team member is issued security identification.

The team leader provides orientation and daily team briefings. He/she is also responsible for monitoring stress, debriefing, and assigning counseling, as needed, during and at the end of the incident.

As mentioned previously, the odontology team is divided into three sections: postmortem, antemortem, and comparison. Each section will have a leader assigned by the dental team leader.

POSTMORTEM DENTAL SECTION

A disaster's scale determines personnel requirements. When digital postmortem systems are utilized and surgical access to the maxillofacial structures is required, there are normally five individuals assigned to the postmortem section team per shift. Postmortem team responsibility includes dental autopsy, a complete dental examination, a full mouth series of radiographs (bitewings and periapicals), charting of existing restorations and unique features present. To minimize error, it is standard practice for three members to examine and perform dental charting on each victim. One dentist examines the remains and a second verifies features present. A third member records the information on a postmortem information sheet or computer. The fourth and fifth team members obtain radiographic and photographic images for the postmortem dental record. Photography assists in identification when minimal antemortem records exist. The photographic record is performed at the direction of the team leader. When access to the dental tissues is restricted, a jaw resection may be required. This procedure is only performed with permission of the ME.

All fragments and resected tissues are placed in containers labeled with the appropriate case number. When dental DNA is requested, teeth are extracted, labeled, and stored for processing.

ANTEMORTEM DENTAL SECTION

The antemortem dental section consists of an experienced section leader, and three-member teams comprised of two dentists and an auxiliary or an additional dentist. Antemortem members may initially work independently compiling the dental records; however, they are paired for computer data entry and comparison of antemortem and postmortem records for identification. When sufficient staffing exists, a specialized team of individuals should be assigned the task of digitally scanning and importing the antemortem radiographs into WinID3, because this process is prone to numerous technical problems. Quality control protocols minimize mistakes that are not readily apparent and potentially result in long-term interference with the identification process. Antemortem records are rarely received immediately upon request. Obtaining antemortem dental records can be a daunting task which may take weeks. Transportation manifests and a list of potential victims should be requested. Often the dental records received are illegible, contain poor quality radiographs, and/or incomplete information. Furthermore, the dental professional of record can be reluctant to release the original records to authorities. WinId3 can interpolate data entry in either the Universal Numbering System or the Fédération Dentaire Internationale (FDI) system of dental charting. However, appropriate conversion tables are required when records are obtained using other systems. Once the antemortem dental information has been transcribed into WinId3, the section leader reviews all information for completeness and accuracy then sends the record to the Comparison section if an immediate identification cannot be made.

In 1996 the US Congress passed the Health Insurance Portability and Accountability Act (HIPAA) protecting the privacy of patients' medical and dental information. Exemptions were made to Law Enforcement and MEs and coroners allowing legal release of medical and dental records.

DENTAL COMPARISON SECTION

The comparison team consists of antemortem and postmortem team members whose primary responsibility is to make positive identification of the victims. Traditionally, each group within the team consists of three members, allowing redundancy in the review of each case. Computer-assisted systems improve efficiency allowing the team to be composed of two examiners with final review and approval being performed by the team leader.

Forensic dental software provides significant assistance in the identification process; however, the final determination of positive identification is always made by the forensic odontologist. Once the victim's identity is established, it is relayed to the ME or representative of the Information Resource Center. The chain of command and victim confidentiality must be respected at all times. It is *mandatory* that team members not speak with individuals outside of the operation and, in particular, the media without explicit permission from the commanding officer in charge of the entire DVI team. Failure to observe security and confidentiality protocols can result in immediate dismissal from the DVI team.

DENTAL EXAMINATION SUPPLIES

Dental section supplies required for DVI operations are similar to those used in dental offices for patient examination and treatments (mirrors, explorers, molt-style mouth props, cotton pliers, various hemostats and scissors). In addition, the postmortem dental examination stations require various scalpel blades and handles, Stryker saws, small Maglite flashlights to aid in illumination, and UV light sources (wavelength 395 nm) to aid in the recognition of

composite materials. Laptop computers with the WinID3 and the DEXIS Digital X-ray software, DEXIS digital X-ray sensors and holders, digital cameras, and portable X-ray generators are also required equipment. Disposable supplies include isopropyl alcohol, sodium hypochlorite, disinfecting solutions, cotton rolls, cotton gauze squares, cellophane wrap (clear plastic bags or head rest covers) for wrapping nonserializable equipment (table surfaces, X-ray generators, computer keyboards, etc.), digital sensor sleeves to protect the X-ray sensors, duct tape, sharps containers, examination gloves, and masks. When available, fiber optic headlamps have proven to be extremely useful in the examination process.

MORGUE SHIFTS

Each MFI is different and there is no definitive way to predetermine the precise number of forensic odontologists required, nor the length of each shift. Protocols established based upon noncomputerized systems of data collection are no longer valid. Today, when only one X-ray unit, digital X-ray sensor, laptop, and camera is available, there can only be one body processed at a time. In this case, having four to five forensic dentists in the morgue at one time is ideal. If there are two dental stations each having its own digital equipment, six to seven forensic odontologists are adequate because some duties can be performed by a single odontologist at both stations. Shift length will be dependent upon the number of deceased needing to be processed through the dental station and the availability of forensic odontologists available to work each shift. Shifts may vary from 3 to 4 h up to 12 h in length. In no circumstance should a shift be longer than 12 h. During each shift, it is important to require mandatory rest and meal breaks. A common DVI command mistake is the failure to realize that there are data entry and comparison duties remaining to be completed after the morgue shuts down for the day. This problem is exacerbated when there are an insufficient number of dental members assigned to the disaster.

PORTABLE DENTAL X-RAY GENERATOR

In recent years, a major breakthrough in obtaining postmortem radiographs was the advent of the NOMAD hand-held, battery-powered X-ray generator. In its first use in the disaster response to the tsunami disaster in Southeast Asia, the NOMAD, manufactured by Aribex (Aribex, Inc., Orem, UT 84,097), proved to be an extremely dependable and effective device. Its compact size and the utility of its battery-powered operation proved to be very useful in the relatively austere environment. Its first domestic use in a DVI morgue was by DMORT in the aftermath of Hurricane Katrina where, in conjunction with the DEXIS digital X-rays sensor, it performed admirably and provided the postmortem dental examination station with consistently high-quality dental radiographs.

Currently there are two models of the NOMAD. The classic NOMAD is the original version of the device. It weighs approximately eight pounds and is shielded in such a way as to essentially eliminate all leakage from the body of the device. This eliminated a common problem with previous X-ray devices, which required the operator to stand at least 6 ft. from the X-ray head when exposing a radiograph (Pittayapat et al., 2010). The NOMAD has a back-scatter shield that minimizes the amount of back-scatter radiation, thus creating a "zone of safety" behind the device for the operator to operate the device protected from the scatter (Turner et al., 2005). This zone is optimized, however, only when the scatter shield is placed at exposure end of the cone (position indicating device).

Due to significant radiation safety concerns, historically, the use of hand-held X-ray devices has previously been prohibited. However, independent research has provided overwhelming evidence of the NOMAD's safety to all members of the dental morgue team with exposure readings that are negligible, measuring well below the allowed annual maximum permissible doses (MPDs) (Hermsen et al., 2008; Danforth et al., 2009; NCRP, 2003, 2009). Therefore, no additional shielding of the operator or assistant is required unless one must be positioned within the primary beam.

The newest version is the NOMAD Pro. It has improved shielding to prevent radiation leakage and its smaller design weighs only five and one-half pounds. In addition to its smaller size, the "Pro" has incorporated a mechanism to lock the device, which prohibits its use by unauthorized personnel. At this point, both versions of the NOMAD have been approved for hand-held use in most, if not all, states (Herschaft et al., 2010).

Of course, radiation safety procedures must always be followed to comply with the ALARA principle (As Low As Reasonably Achievable). Using either model of the NOMAD does not dismiss the operator from responsibility for following accepted radiation safety procedures, which include never allowing auxiliary personnel to stand in direct line with the central beam, using the lowest exposure time setting possible, and maintaining as much space as possible between adjacent examination units. There is also a mounting stand available for the units, if so desired.

Another portable X-ray device that is effective in a dental morgue setting is the MinXray portable X-ray device (MinXray, Inc., 3611 Commercial Avenue, Northbrook, IL 60,062). Many morgue operations employ the MinXray medical system for obtaining full-body X-rays. There are two dental versions. The HF70DUL model is a high-frequency tubehead, weighs 10 pounds, and may be hand-held or mounted on a tripod stand (X100S). A back-scatter shield is an available option and should be purchased if the device is to be used in a hand-held manner. The P200D MK model weighs 18 pounds and must be operated on a tripod stand due to its weight. One critical factor with these units is that the configuration of the tripod stands for both units is without a horizontal supporting arm for the tubehead. The result is that they are best suited for patients in a seated or standing position as opposed to the supine positions in a morgue setting.

DIGITAL DENTAL RADIOGRAPHY SENSORS

Digital radiography was first utilized in a DVI setting after the crash of TWA Flight 800 on July 17, 1996, when 230 lives were lost. It has since become an indispensable part of victim identification. Digital radiography can be discussed along the same lines as digital photography. Both involve sensor technology that captures either the light spectrum for photography or the X-ray spectrum for radiology. Where photography uses mega pixels to define the resolution of the sensor, radiology uses line pairs per millimeter to do the same. For a digital sensor to be equal to conventional film radiograph resolution, it should approach 22 line pairs per millimeter. As an example, this will allow the examiner to easily distinguish the tip of a number 10 endodontic file.

Sensor design is important in forensic applications. The impermeable, nonflexible sensors can withstand the extreme conditions in which they are used. Sensors of different sizes have little advantage in the forensic field due to the fact that most postmortem radiologic examinations can be accomplished easier in deceased rather than living individuals. In practice, sensors with cables do pose some problems regarding breakage.

At this point both the Schick sensors and the DEXIS sensors have been used to the greatest extent in DVI morgues and have proven to be effective. Comparatively, one advantage of the DEXIS software is that it can function with either sensor and has a bridge to the WinID3 dental charting and matching software for a complete dental software package. Both sensors can be used in tandem with the hand-held NOMAD or MinXray X-ray systems to allow easy movement and access in the morgue setting.

The Schick sensor is thinner than the DEXIS sensor. This is because with the DEXIS sensor, the sensor electronics are located within a small dome on the back of the sensor. This increases the thickness of the sensor but also allows for the entire face of the sensor case to be available for radiation exposure. The Schick sensor is thinner but gains this by placing the sensor hardware around the outer edge of the sensor, thus reducing the exposure surface dimensions. The result is that DEXIS sensor is physically smaller than the Schick sensor, but the active exposure areas of the two are similarly sized.

In large operations it has been found that these sensors are capable of taking thousands of radiographs and then being packed up and stored for the next operation. Most sensors state their life in the 200,000 exposure range. Digital radiography also can increase the quality control of the operation. Once a digital image is captured it can be reviewed in real time. This means unacceptable angulation or exposures can be corrected and retaken on the spot. It has rarely been appreciated that this capability and the elimination of the film processing cycle has accounted for the savings of hundreds (perhaps thousands) of man-hours in the dental section over the course of recent DVI operation.

Digital scanners allow images or objects to be scanned and then digitized, transferred, and stored for later retrieval and review. In dental identification scenarios, scanners are usually located in the antemortem and comparison areas of the operation and allow antemortem information to be entered in a paperless digital system. All antemortem written records, photographs, conventional radiographs, and charting can be scanned into the digital record. Large format scanners can scan films all the way up to panoramic and cephalometric size films.

For several years after DMORT purchased the requested digital dental equipment, its dental teams conducted regional hands-on training with the entire digital package including DEXIS sensors and specimen, networked laptops loaded with WinID, scanners and the NOMAD device. The stated goal was to improve the dental workstation efficiency by using no paper or pencils, no film, and no film processor. When Katrina occurred, that goal was effectively met. It was, in fact, a bit shocking to witness that when the morgue generator occasionally failed at the DPMU East, the dental team was able to continue their work using flashlights, a battery-operated tubehead, and a laptop also running on battery power.

COMPUTER-ASSISTED DENTAL IDENTIFICATION SOFTWARE

Postmortem identification software has been used for many years by forensic odontologists. As computer applications were developed, the ability to simply list or catalogue cases evolved into "search and match" capabilities. The first dental application to do this was Computer-Assisted PostMortem Identification (CAPMI).

CAPMI was developed by Lorton, Langley, and Weed (programming specialist) in the late 1980s. It was used by the US Military on many mass disasters and soon by many forensic odontologists in the private sector. The CAPMI program was used in the bombing of the Alfred P. Murrah Federal Building in Oklahoma City, Oklahoma in 1995 and in the Crash of TWA Flight 800 off the coast of Long Island, New York in 1996. Subsequent disasters utilized windows-based computer systems.

WinID3

WinID was developed by Dr. James McGivney as a free, computer-assisted dental identification application, which has been used by forensic odontologists, pathologists, coroners, MEs, forensic anthropologists, law enforcement, and the criminal justice systems to identify the unknown. This Windows-based program has been used in numerous mass disasters including the terrorist attack on the World Trade Center, Hurricanes Katrina and Ike, and the EF 5 tornado in Joplin, Missouri in 2011.

WinID3 uses an intuitive algorithm that gives it the ability not only to sort for requested identifiers but also to compensate and not eliminate identifier changes that have occurred due to reasonable and explainable differences. For instance, a tooth that is reported as virgin or nonrestored in an antemortem record and shown as restored in a postmortem record will not be eliminated from consideration because the time lapse between the two allows for work to have been done on that particular tooth. Additionally, it will not exclude possible matches where an impossible treatment progression seems to have occurred. In doing so, it accounts for human error in data entry.

It also has numerous open categories outside of the dental section that can be used by other disciplines to sort and search for information. In this way, WinID3 can be used as a total package if desired by the disaster operational director or ME. WinID3 may be used in several languages and using metric versus English measurements and numbering systems. After 2001, Dr. McGivney's WinID3 developed a "bridge" with DEXIS (a digital radiography application for capture and management of dental radiographs and all other photographs and documents associated with a particular record). This allows WinID3 to combine dental charting with the radiographic/photographic record for a seamless integrated system of case review and comparison. In the postmortem arena, this allows radiographs and photographs to be captured and viewed in real time as the examiner's chart and view the decedents dental conditions.

WinID3 has also been used with touch screen tablets successfully in a morgue setting. The program is available as a freestanding application and may be used in a networked environment. WinID3 has been proven in the field and improved through various version changes. The program may be accessed through its website www.ABFO.org. A new version of WinID, termed "WinID for the Web" has recently been developed by Dr. John Melville, which incorporates most of the features of WinID3. WinID for the Web is a remote server based version of WinID with multiple upgrades over the original WinID that will be useful in an MFI. Antemortem data can be added remotely and comparisons of such data with the postmortem evidence can also be done remotely. WinID for the Web incorporates PhotoDocumentor, the image software that allows the system to capture, analyze, organize, and present forensic data. Like the original WinID3, this software is available at no cost from Dr. Melville and Business Casual Software at www.http://photodocumentor.com/.

DVI System International

DVI System International was developed by Plass Data Software and is used by INTERPOL for international disasters including the response to the 2004 Tsunami in Thailand. DVI is a total mass disaster program and the dental section is an integrated part of that system.

It can accomplish advanced searches for all entered data including DNA and dental findings. DVI has also been utilized in maintaining national missing and unidentified persons. The system has the capability to print all of its various disaster-related forms in English, French, Spanish, Norwegian, Dutch, Swedish, Danish, and German languages.

The dental section has good graphics for charting and works well in sorting for restorations and dental conditions. It allows dental radiographs to be entered into a template type section for later review, but depends on outside scanning of conventional radiographs or digital capture programs to obtain the images. This means an additional step for the dental identification team to insert images into the data base. The dental section is not available as a standalone program and thus, the entire DVI System International must be obtained to utilize the dental component. To obtain a DVI trial package visit its website at www.plass.dlk. The download and setup may take a considerable time to accomplish.

Unified Victim Identification System/UVIS Dental Identification Module

Unified Victim Identification System (UVIS) is a robust mass disaster management system that manages and coordinates all of the activities related to victim identification and missing persons reporting. Developed for the City of New York following the September 11 attack, it includes modules related to law enforcement's missing persons data, a centralized "call center," field operations, FAC, morgue operations, and data obtained in the victim identifications processes. UVIS Dental Identification Module (UDIM) is the dental recording/search component of the system. This dental module was developed by Dr. Kenneth Aschheim in consultation with the forensic odontologists of the NYC Office of the Chief ME and was released in 2007. It includes a self-correcting coding interface, a unique color-coded odontogram for rapid comparison and evaluation, partial jaw fragment management, linking and joining of specimens, and unlimited image importation. UVIS and the UDIM work as a complete unit. The UDIM has an intuitive algorithm to allow record comparisons. In addition to UDIM's color-coding odontogram, it also highlights both explainable and unexplainable discrepancies. The application is easy to use and works in a similar fashion to WinID3. UDIM reportedly now has a direct bridge with DEXIS to allow information to flow between the two programs. UVIS/UDIM is not designed to be used on a stand-alone laptop. It requires both a web server and SQL server as well as some expertise to get it installed and running. UVIS is evolving from a disaster response system into a complete morgue package for everyday use. The system is free of charge to law enforcement entities and government agencies. Multimillion dollar upgrades are in the works for future improvements to the package. These improvements include touch screen capabilities and the ability to switch from FDI to Universal dental coding. UVIS/UDIM can be reviewed on its website at https://uvistraining.com/.

In summary, the integration of a digital image system into or in association with a dental database application decreases the possibility of human error in managing digital information. Switching from application to application can create confusion and introduce mistakes. Being able to have seamless and direct access to a fully functional digital image enhancement application (e.g., DEXIS), along with automatic case or body number assignment from the computer-assisted comparison program to the imaging program is extremely valuable. Both can reduce or eliminate critical errors. As can be seen earlier, one system already uses this and another is developing this concept. The forensic odontologist is still responsible for the final decisions in comparing antemortem and postmortem records. However, these computer programs become invaluable in instances where the victim count runs into the hundreds or thousands. As the identification of human remains evolves and improves in efficiency, computer-assisted dental programs need to respond in kind. In looking to the future, user-friendly programs with the ability to integrate with similar programs used by other agencies and disciplines should be developed and will add to the tools available to the forensic odontology arsenal.

TECHNOLOGICAL ADVANCES IN DENTAL IDENTIFICATION/ FLIGHT 3407

Flight 3407 crashed in a suburb of Buffalo, New York, on February 12, 2009. Circumstances associated with the MFI were similar to other disasters involving airline accidents: incineration and fragmentation. Out of the 50 victims, 38 were identified through dental records. Of the 50, 3 were not dentally identified due to a lack of antemortem records. Eight were not dentally identified due to insufficient quality and quantity of postmortem evidence. Of the identified victims, the use of microscopy and analytical technology was instrumental in providing identifications that may have otherwise not been possible. Two cases will be presented where the use of analytical technology was used to the benefit of the forensic dental team and emphasize the importance of record-keeping. See Chapter 4 for further information regarding analysis methods.

In the first case, forensic archeological recovery provided the team with numerous fragments of disassociated dental remains including teeth, maxillary, and mandibular fragments. These fragments ranged in condition from calcined to charred and carbonized to relatively pristine. Radiographic and clinical evaluation of a majority of these teeth and fragments yielded little or no useful information. Some of the fragments did reveal the presence of endodontic and restorative treatment that necessitated further analysis.

A fragment was identified as a lower right mandibular segment containing teeth #30 and 31 without #32. This fragment was calcined and fragile and radiographic examination showed traces of possible root canal therapy #30. The clinical crowns had fractured and there was no evidence of restorative materials present. Two unidentified victims of the disaster had the profile suggested earlier. Morphological image comparison between the fragment and the antemortem radiograph was not conclusive for an identification based primarily on the postmortem damage to the incinerated specimen. The use of a stereomicroscope showed the root of #30 to contain small silver blebs that are suggestive of root canal sealer. Further analysis of this material through scanning electron microscope (SEM) and energy dispersive X-ray spectrography (EDS) showed the presence of elements that are unique to a particular brand of root canal sealer. The use of this sealer was clearly documented in the dental record of the presumed associated victim adding another level of certainty for a positive identification. This fragment was the only identifiable fragment establishing an identity of this victim.

Another lower right mandibular fragment was also recovered. This segment was not calcined but was more charred and carbonized demonstrating exposure to a decreased time and temperature exposure than the fragment discussed before. Radiographically and clinically the fragment did not appear to show evidence of restorative treatment even though the coronal portion of #31 was relatively intact. Upon further inspection with a stereomicroscope significant evidence was disclosed. A circular buccal preparation was noted along with a longitudinal preparation on the occlusal surface. These preparations were further analyzed using SEM–EDS. The elemental analysis confirmed the existence of a previous buccal amalgam and an occlusal composite resin restoration. The trace composite resin was entered into a dental material database incorporating elemental composition and filler particle size. The composite was identified as a particular brand and attempts were made to compare this information to the victim's dental record. The dental record was not complete as to brand name, and this lack of significant dental information precluded relationship of this fragment to a potential victim. This victim identification was established by other methods.

Advanced analytical techniques and accurate and complete dental records can add another level of evidentiary certainty under extreme conditions of incineration and fragmentation (Bush and Miller, 2011).

References

Bush, M.A., Miller, R.G., 2011. The crash of Colgan Air Flight 3407: advanced techniques in victim identification. Journal of the American Dental Association 142 (12), 1352–1356.

Danforth, R.A., Herschaft, E.E., Leonowich, J.A., 2009. Operator exposure to scatter radiation from a portable handheld dental radiation emitting device (Aribex NOMAD) while making 915 intraoral dental radiographs. Journal of Forensic Sciences 54 (2), 415–421.

Hermsen, K.P., Jaeger, S.S., Jaeger, M.A., 2008. Radiation safety for the NOMAD portable x-ray system in a temporary morgue setting. Journal of Forensic Sciences 53 (4), 917–921.

Herschaft, E.E., Hermsen, K.P., Danforth, R.A., McGiff, T.J., 2010. Current Radiation Safety Regulatory Policies and the Utilization Status in the United States of the Nomad Portable Hand-Held Dental Radiation Emitting Device. Paper presented at: AAFS Annual Meeting; Seattle, WA.

NCRP Report No. 145, 2003. Radiation Protection in Dentistry. National Council on Radiation Protection and Measurements, Bethesda, MD.

NCRP Report No. 160, 2009. Ionizing Radiation Exposure of the Population of the United States. National Council on Radiation Protection and Measurements, Bethesda, MD.

Pittayapat, P., Oliveira-Santos, C., Thevissen, P., Michielsen, K., Bergans, N., Willems, G., 2010. Image quality assessment and medical physics evaluation of different portable dental x-ray units. Forensic Science International 201, 112–117.

Turner, D.C., Kloos, D.K., Morton, R., 2005. Radiation Safety Characteristics of the NOMAD Portable X-ray System. Aribex Inc., Orem, UT.

Further Reading

ABFO Mass Fatality Guidelines: The Development of a Dental Identification Team, pp. 158–167. www.ABFO.org.

Bowers, M., Bell, G., 1997. ASFO Manual of Forensic Odontology, third ed. Manticore Publishers, AQ5, Grimsby, ON, Canada, pp. 158–167.

Kieser, J., Laing, W., Herbison, P., 2006. Lessons learned from large-scale comparative dental analysis following the South Asian Tsunami of 2004. Journal of Forensic Sciences 51 (1), 109–112.

U.S. Department of Health and Human Services, 2012. Disaster Mortuary Operational Response Teams (DMORTs). http://www.phe.gov/Preparedness/ressponders/ndms/teams/Pages/dmort.aspx.

6

Missing and Unidentified Persons

James P. Fancher[1,2,3,4], Peter Hampl[5,6,7,8,9]

[1]Forensic Odontology Consultant: Bexar County Medical Examiner's Office, San Antonio, TX, United States; [2]Central Texas Autopsy, Lockhart, TX, United States; [3]Forensic Anthropology Center at Texas State University, San Marcos, TX, United States; [4]Faculty — Forensic Dentistry Fellowship, Center for Education and Research in Forensics, The University of Texas Health Science Center at San Antonio, San Antonio, TX, United States; [5]Forensic Odontology Consultant: Pierce County Medical Examiner's Office, Tacoma, WA, United States; [6]Spokane County Medical Examiner's Office, Spokane, WA, United States; [7]Disaster Mortuary Operational Response Team (Region X), United States; [8]Blake Emergency Services, Combs, High Peak, England; [9]FBI's National Dental Image Repository (Review Panel), United States

OUTLINE

The Largest Ongoing Mass Fatality Disaster "The Silent Scream"

Dedication: *To the family and friends of the missing and unidentified.*

Show me the manner in which a nation or community cares for its dead and I will measure with mathematical exactness the tender sympathies of its people, their respect for the laws of the land and their loyalty to high ideals. **Sir William Gladstone**

INTRODUCTION

The problem of missing persons and unidentified human remains in the United States and around the world has existed for a very long time. Although significant progress has been made in recent years in some geographic regions, missing and unidentified persons are a persistent global problem. How big is the problem? As of January 1, 2016 in the United States, the National Missing and Unidentified Persons System (NamUs) has in its database 10,621 unidentified and 11,811 missing persons cases. The National Crime Information Center (NCIC) of the United States Federal Bureau of Investigation (FBI) also reports that as of December 31, 2015, their files contained 84,961 active missing persons records that have been accumulated since the inception of the NCIC Unidentified Person File in 1983 (N.C.I.C., 2016). There were also 8407 unidentified persons records in the NCIC File, with 850 new records entered in 2015. These new 2015 NCIC records are broken down as 626 (73.6%) deceased unidentified bodies, 5 (0.6%) unidentified catastrophe victims, and 219 (25.8%) living persons who could not ascertain their identity.

There are an estimated 40,000 unidentified human remains in the nation's medical examiners (MEs) and coroners offices (Ritter, 2007b); many have never been reported to the NamUs or the NCIC (Hickman et al., 2007). Additionally, there are many other underreported cases such as the suspected desert remains along the US southern border and the mass graves in the border counties in South Texas and Arizona that have been accumulating unreported human remains of undocumented border crossers for years (Anderson and Parks, 2008; Armendariz, 2013; Baker and Baker, 2008; Del Bosque, 2014; Ortiz, 2013). Additionally, outside of the United States are many thousands more missing and unidentified human remains that have accumulated over the past 100 years that have resulted from natural disasters, immigration tragedies, warfare, genocide, and criminal activity (Baraybar and Blackwell, 2014; Boric et al., 2011; Cappella et al., 2012; Carter, 2005; De Valck, 2006; Haglund et al., 2001; Hagopian et al., 2013; Hartman et al., 2011; Klinkner, 2012; Laczko et al., 2016; Marjanović et al., 2015; Shiroma, 2014).

The known numbers of missing and unidentified persons in the United States far exceed the mass fatality disasters of September 11, 2001 (2996 deaths) or Katrina and Rita hurricanes in 2005 (estimated 3000). What makes the missing and unidentified crisis so tragic is its ongoing nature, never-ending, and wide geographic range involving numerous local, state, federal, and non-US jurisdictions. There is a lack of awareness of the magnitude of the problem in the general public as well as the media, and it has multinational dimensions.

The phenomenon of missing and unidentified persons places a major strain on law enforcement resources, and it is complex and not well understood (Fyfe et al., 2015). The reasons for humans to go missing or to be found deceased and unidentified are summarized in the following quote:

"To go missing is not a crime. This apparently simple statement forms the basis of an exceedingly complex web of behaviors and responses that surround the phenomenon of missing persons. While it is not a crime to go missing, there may be factors relating to the criminal justice system, either underpinning the motives of the missing person or relating to the outcome of the missing person investigation. On the other hand, the explanation may be totally removed from any criminal dimension and could include social problems associated with mental health issues, alcohol use, child psychological abuse, child neglect or parental rejection of a child. It could be a combination of both criminal activities and social problems, for instance domestic violence, child sexual abuse, child physical abuse or illicit drug use. The reasons could be associated with problems at school or peer pressure. The incident may relate to child abduction by an estranged parent or a stranger. It could involve an older person with Alzheimer's disease or dementia. It may be a homicide or a suicide or it could be the result of an accident or misadventure. It could be because of displacement following a war or territorial conflict. The person could have gone missing from a foster home or an institution, or may have gone missing while travelling overseas. Their disappearance may have been reported to either the police or another search service. Their disappearance may not have been reported to anyone at all. The list is seemingly endless" (James et al., 2008).

A problem also exists in the manner used to report missing persons. Generally, reports for cases of missing persons, 18 years old and younger, must be taken by law enforcement, but reporting adult missing persons cases is voluntary because adults are considered to be independent, autonomous persons unless known to be physically or mentally incapacitated. It is estimated that up to 80% of individuals that are reported missing will return within 24 hours, often without police intervention (Fyfe et al., 2015). However, it is also reported that the mean time for return of missing adults is 66 days, with a median reported as 28 days (Shalev et al., 2009). Only a handful of states and/or countries have laws that require law enforcement agencies to prepare missing persons reports on adults.

The need to identify human remains is an important contribution to forensic pathology as well as civil and criminal law in all legal jurisdictions (Cappella et al., 2012). There are ethical reasons to make a positive identification in the death of any person, and the declaration of death reflects the common rights of human beings to be mourned according to local custom. It also allows the completion of many legal procedures that include civil inheritance and family law issues, business and property ownership, and criminal law concerns that may include establishing the identity of a murder victim to

investigate a potential crime. The investigation of missing individuals, unidentified deaths, and mass graves are also essential steps in the legal, moral, and ethical management of missing adults and children (Nazaryan, 2014), natural and man-made mass disasters (De Valck, 2006; Dadna Hartman et al., 2015; Hartman et al., 2011; Petju et al., 2007; Schuller-Götzburg and Suchanek, 2007), deaths due to armed conflicts (Boric et al., 2011; Klinkner, 2012; Marjanović et al., 2015; Policy on Child Identification Programs, 2010; Shiroma, 2014), serial murder cases (LePard et al., 2015), missing indigenous peoples (Kogon et al., 2010; Narine, 2015), civil and human rights cases (Kimmerle, 2014a, b), immigration and migration catastrophes (Anderson, 2008; Armendariz, 2013; Grant, 2011; Laczko et al., 2016; Reineke, 2013; Tise et al., 2014; Whitaker, 2009), transitional and restorative justice issues (Baraybar and Blackwell, 2014; Kontsevaia, 2013), and other circumstances of unidentified human remains (Andreev et al., 2008; Paulozzi et al., 2008).

Odontology has made a major contribution to solving the problem of missing persons and unidentified human remains. The greatest focus has been on unidentified human remains. Law enforcement and other investigative agencies have a responsibility to seek dental records and data for all persons that are reported missing, and a forensic dental examination should be part of all death investigations for unidentified remains. Both the NamUs and NCIC systems are set up to record dental data in a systematic fashion. NamUs allows an open system where dental data are available to large communities that include law enforcement, families, and other interested parties. The NCIC system is generally closed and allows access primarily to law enforcement agencies and other official parties with an interest in establishing identities, with a focus on solving crimes. In theory, information should be flowing into these systems within a few days or weeks of a reported missing persons case, and all unidentified remains cases should also be rapidly documented and reported to these central agencies.

Law Enforcement Agencies

If there is a weak link within the system of solving the missing and unidentified persons cases, it is the inconsistency of law enforcement jurisdictions as to how they react to the problem. When a family or friend feels an individual has gone missing, they often turn immediately to law enforcement. Law enforcement is basically providing a public service that no other agency, private or governmental entity, has jurisdiction over. Depending on the law enforcement agency contacted, the process of handling a "missing persons" case covers the gamut of a full, detailed investigation to no help at all.

Law enforcement is in a no-win situation when it comes to handling these cases. Understaffed, budget reductions, little training devoted to the subject, staff turnover, lack of interest, and low priority that is given to these cases are just a few of the factors that lead to the inconsistency in law enforcement agencies' response causing the "weak link" designation. A historical view of missing persons is that nearly all will eventually return home, and that the root causes of disappearances center around personal and family issues that law enforcement agencies are poorly equipped to solve (Stein, 1946). Key risk factors for going missing include mental health problems, alcohol and illicit drug use and abuse, domestic violence, child abduction, child abuse, underage runaways from home, financial problems, sexual orientation problems, history of suicide ideation or self-harm incidents, and possible victim of crime (James et al., 2008). It is reported that in the majority of missing persons reports in Great Britain, the individual is either found alive by a relative, public member, or the police or returns on their own in their own time and often returns without police intervention (Fyfe et al., 2015).

While it may be true that adult men and women have the freedom to vanish, few of the people that are listed in NamUs, NCIC, and other official worldwide records have arrived in these databases willingly (Nazaryan, 2014). The difficult task for law enforcement officials is to quickly identify missing persons reports that need priority attention and to shift their resources to support the demand (James et al., 2008). The challenge is to link the data of a missing persons report to a significant likelihood that the person is in danger of harm, and then respond with available resources. This is especially difficult when dealing with marginal or transient populations where investigating and tracking reports make it hard to identify evidence of foul play and illegal activities (LePard et al., 2015; Paulozzi et al., 2008).

Medical Examiners and Coroners

In June 2007, the Office of Justice Programs' (OJP) Bureau of Justice Statistics (BJS) confirmed that, in a typical year, medical examiners and coroners handle approximately 4400 unidentified human cases, approximately 1000 of which remain unidentified after 1 year (Hickman et al., 2007). It was estimated by this report that there are approximately 40,000 unidentified human remains in the offices of the nation's medical examiners and coroners. Many were buried or cremated before being identified (Ritter, 2007a). It is also estimated that a few hundred unidentified remains accumulate each year, making the 40,000 figure suspect and probably growing each and every year. BJS further identified the need to improve record retention policies. As of 2004, more than half (51 percent) of the nation's medical examiners' and coroners' offices had no policy for retaining records—such as X-rays, DNA, dental records, or fingerprints on unidentified human remains. BJS also noted, however, that more than 90 percent of offices servicing large jurisdictions did have such a policy (Hickman et al., 2007).

Three factors have been noted as making accurate characterization of unidentified decedents through large database creation difficult (Paulozzi et al., 2008). The first is that there is no standard manner of completing the name fields on death certificates of unidentified decedents, which hampers searching national death certificate databases. The second is that submission to databases is voluntary and passive, which includes reporting to the FBI's NCIC system and the National Association of Medical Examiners' Unidentified Decedent Registry. The final factor noted is that the number of unidentified decedents in most individual jurisdictions is small, which makes accumulating enough data at the lowest or local level difficult.

Paulozzi et al. (2008) also reported that over the 26 years studied (1979–2004), they found a total of 10,748 unidentified decedents filed in the United States for a rate of 16.1 per 10 million people and an average of 413 reported cases per year. Most of the decedents were male (80.6%), with nearly half (46.6%) estimated to be between the ages of 18 and 37 years old. Infants (less than 1 year old) accounted for 7.2%, and individuals aged 1–18 years old made up 1.2% of the decedents. Although 71% of the decedents were identified as white and 21% were identified as black, the unknown decedent rate was highest among black males at 46.2 per 10 million people. It must also be noted that the designation of "white" may have designated only Caucasian individuals, and probably included Hispanic groups that were not otherwise identified in the data. The leading cause of death (when known) was injury (82.7%), and more than one-fourth of these deaths were due to homicide. The causes of death (in descending order) following injury were circulatory (cardiovascular) disease, and digestive disease (primarily cirrhosis of the liver), and respiratory disease (primarily pneumonia). The rates of unidentified death were considered to be consistent with the higher rates of homelessness among males and individuals of African descent. Risk factors

identified were alcohol use, substance abuse, mental illness, and low socioeconomic status. All of these risk factors were somewhat associated with the margins of society and transient individuals. It is interesting to note that a study of unidentified decedents in Russia found many similar associations due to homelessness, social isolation, and marginalization of men due to economic crisis (Andreev et al., 2008).

Natural Disasters, Man-Made Disasters, and Armed Conflict

The concept of what constitutes a disaster is difficult to define because the scope, common measurements, impacts, and methods of response and mitigation are all viewed differently by various stakeholders such as the victims themselves, disaster managers, economists, politicians, health workers, first responders, and forensic experts (Rand, 2008). A simplified view of what constitutes a mass disaster is based on the concept that the victims themselves or the responders are overwhelmed to the point that outside assistance is required to meet the demands of the situation. The common denominator of mass disasters of concern for odontologists is that a large number of human individuals join the pool of missing and unidentified persons. This may be due to temporary or permanent geographical displacement of the living and possibly subsequent deceased status, or due to death as a direct result of the incident. If deceased, the missing individual may be dismembered, decomposed, or hidden for many years as a result of the disaster itself.

Disasters are commonly divided into natural and man-made groupings, including armed conflict (Edward Nathan and Sakthi, 2014; Rand, 2008). Natural disasters result primarily from the forces of nature and include weather and geographic/geologic phenomena such as tropical storms, extreme heat or cold, high winds, severe floods, earthquakes, landslides, and volcanic eruptions. Recent examples include Hurricane Katrina (approximately 3000 deceased); bushfires in Victoria, Australia (173 deceased) (Dadna Hartman et al., 2015; Hartman et al., 2011); and the South Asian Tsunamis of 2004 (230,000 deceased) (De Valck, 2006; Petju et al., 2007; Schuller-Götzburg and Suchanek, 2007). Man-made or human disasters are often associated with transportation and industrial accidents, collapse of buildings, release of hazardous materials, or large-scale changes in ecosystems leading to unstable natural environments (Rand, 2008). Examples include the sinking of the South Korean ferry MV Sewol in 2014 (304 deaths); the Bhopal gas tragedy in India in 1984 (2259 deaths); and the collapse of the I-35W Mississippi River Bridge in Minneapolis, Minnesota (13 deaths). Armed conflict and terrorist acts may be considered forms of man-made disaster, but the results often include thousands of missing and unidentified persons. Examples include US prisoners of war/missing in action (POW/MIA) for World War II, the Korean War, the Vietnam War, the Cold War, and Iraq and other Conflicts (total 82,756) ("Policy on Child Identification Programs," 2010; Shiroma, 2014); insurgent and terrorist acts in Iraq, Turkey, Israel, Europe, South America, and the United States; and mass graves in many global localities from conflicts in the last century, including Europe, Africa, Asia, Central and South America (Baraybar and Blackwell, 2014; Boric et al., 2011; Haglund et al., 2001; Hagopian et al., 2013; Kontsevaia, 2013; Marjanović et al., 2015; Skinner et al., 2010). Additionally, there is a new, contemporary class of migrant humans that may be subject to being declared as missing or unidentified persons. These peoples may be classified as economic, social, and/or political refugees or otherwise displaced individuals due to a myriad of natural, man-made, and criminal causes that may not fall neatly into the classifications listed above. Examples include migrants out of Africa and Asia intent on entering the European Union that are subject to disasters on land and sea (Grant, 2011; Guerette, 2007; Laczko et al., 2016; van

Houtum and Boedeltje, 2009) and undocumented border crossers in the Southern United States (Anderson, 2008; Reineke, 2013; Tise et al., 2014). Finally, missing and unidentified persons must also include those who have disappeared in North America and elsewhere due to inhumane acts, racial strife, maltreatment of disabled individuals, and seemingly powerless indigent peoples. Modern examples include open civil rights cases from the 1940s to 1970s and the excavation of unmarked burials in a Florida institution for boys (Kimmerle, 2014a, b), unmarked graves at Willard State Psychiatric Hospital, New York (Barry, 2014), and scores of missing aboriginal women in Canada (Carter, 2005; Kogon et al., 2010; Narine, 2015).

Finding the missing and identifying the dead, regardless of the cause, is based on the humanitarian principle that all people have the right to have their human status recognized and their identity confirmed. According to the Universal Declaration of Human Rights, 1948, everyone has the right to recognition everywhere as a person before the law; each member of the human family has an inherent dignity that gives an inherent value and distinctive worth that must be respected and nourished without exception (Hughes, 2011; MacKinnon and Fiala, 2015). Identification lends dignity not only to deceased victims but also families and humanity as well. Unfortunately, many victims of mass disasters cannot be identified due to lack of traditional antemortem records such as medical and dental records and fingerprints, the chaos of the event and long periods of intervening time between burial and excavation, and lack of resources to complete modern DNA analysis (De Valck, 2006; Djuric et al., 2007; Marjanović et al., 2015). Although the main objective of recoveries and exhumations may be stated as being able to identify individuals and return the remains to families, sometimes all that can be accomplished is establishment of the number of individuals or minimal number of individuals, creating a biological profile by anthropologists, and sometimes cause and manner of death (Boric et al., 2011).

Exhuming mass graves is a particularly difficult task where the aim of mass identifications alone is difficult to meet. Creating a historical record that will stand up to revisionists and exposure of atrocities that will perhaps deter future recurrences may be the cumulative effect of imparting stories from the grave (Haglund et al., 2001). Excavations and reburials in cases of mass murder, genocide, and ethnic cleansing may also be considered important processes in the commemoration of atrocities and the communal reconciliation of the victims and perpetrators (Kontsevaia, 2013). Obtaining detailed documentation of crimes and the biological facts associated with the victims at times is more important and more easily accomplished than individual identifications, and this can lead to serving the aims of justice to recognize and resolve gross violations of human rights and criminal activity (Klinkner, 2012). However, the absence of news from the missing and an increased likelihood of an individual's death can leave families in a state of limbo, clinging to the hope that the missing or disappeared person may return until a positive identification can be established.

Family and Friends

The family and friends of the missing are all too aware of this ongoing tragedy. The embodiment of emotions of grieving family and friends are often referred to as "The Silent Scream" (Fig. 6.1).

Where do they turn for help? The most important initial response is to contact local law enforcement as soon as possible. The family and friends know the missing person better than anyone. If something is amiss, they may have to convince law enforcement to start an investigation. Also keep in mind that if foul

FIGURE 6.1 Edvard Munch's "The Scream" (public domain).

play is suspected, a family or friend has to be cleared of any wrongdoing first. The family and friends should begin to look around the home and property in case your loved one is hiding, has fallen, or is hurt. Keep an eye out for any notes or clues. Contact family, friends, work, and/or school to verify if the person is actually missing. Keep a journal or notebook from the very beginning to include every phone conversation, names, dates, times, what was discussed, points of contacts, what has been done, searches conducted, family and friends involved, and anything that seems out of the ordinary or suspicious. A trusted family member or friend can help with these tasks.

File a missing persons report immediately (THERE IS NO 24 HOUR WAITING PERIOD IN US JURISDICTIONS)! The missing persons report should be filed by contacting the local, county, or state law enforcement agency, or call 9-1-1 and request assistance. If abroad, contact the local embassy, consulate, state department representative, or equivalent. It is important to be completely honest regarding the circumstances involving the missing person's disappearance. If the individual has been involved in illegal activities, drugs, etc., it is very important that investigators are provided with accurate circumstances surrounding their disappearance. Despite some public opinion, this does not make the case less important to detectives, and it may give clues for investigation. Keeping a copy of the case number and name/phone number of the investigator assigned to the case is extremely important for future reference. Request information to be entered into the NamUs and NCIC database and keep a copy of the NamUs and NCIC numbers. If out of the United States, find out what national or international databases are available and request that information be entered. (NOTE: Some law enforcement agencies are reluctant to give out the NCIC or other investigative numbers; just make sure the missing person has been entered). Provide law enforcement and investigators with a list of all known medical problems or assistive devices required by the missing person (Asthma, depression, glasses/contacts, hearing aids, heart problems, medications, disabilities, psychological problems, previous broken bones or fractures, etc.). Include as much personal information as possible, such as did they take any money, a purse/wallet, or extra clothing?

Contact local hospitals including psychiatric wards, drug rehabilitation centers, and short-term emergency clinics. Include surrounding county and city hospitals (especially the ones in larger cities around your area). Consider covering a 50 mile (80 km) radius. (Note, hospitals may not release patient information due to HIPAA laws, so consider faxing fliers to the hospital and request they put them in their emergency room).

Contact local jails or juvenile detention centers, homeless shelters, and area motels. Contact the state (and surrounding state) ME'soffice or coroner to inquire about any unidentified persons they may have. (Note: Some ME/Coroner's offices are too large to accept individual missing person's flyers so you may have to simply contact them periodically to inquire about unidentified persons). If the missing person's car is also missing, check with local towing yards and impound lots within a 50 mile (80 km) radius. Additionally, check the department of motor vehicles to see if tags have been turned in, any moving violations have occurred, and if the car is under a suspension.

In the case of a disaster scenario, contact the Red Cross or other agencies that may be establishing and managing shelter operations. Additionally, in the event there was an accident, the Red Cross or other agencies may have had contact with the missing person as they were processed at the scene. Contact the Salvation Army in the event the missing person has been known to stay in their shelters. Contact the local Search and Rescue (SAR) team, especially after a natural disaster. Depending upon the circumstances of disappearance, a human tracker can locate someone who may have left on foot. Such specialists should be one of the first on the scene as the scene is likely to become degraded as more people and dogs arrive.

Organize family, friends, and community to conduct searches that usually must be authorized and coordinated by law enforcement agencies. Drive and/or walk the areas the missing person frequents. If the missing person was driving, be on the lookout for areas that appear to be places where a car may have left the road as some vehicle accidents may be hidden by brush.

Make a list of contacts and other information to aid law enforcement. The list should include friends and places frequented by the missing person. Include full names, phone numbers, home addresses, and work numbers, and work addresses.

Gather recent photos of the missing person (head shots are best—smiling and not smiling, profiles, and frontal views). If recent photos are not available, be sure to clarify the year of the picture being used and what physical differences existed at the time of the disappearance. You can also obtain a copy of the missing person's driver's license or ID photo through your state's Departments of Public Safety or Licensing, but this can be a time-consuming task. You may also consider having an available photo age progressed to better represent what your loved one now looks like. This service may be provided by various missing persons' clearinghouses (LE or Project EDAN) at no charge.

Create flyers using the photos chosen. Write a description to include: the color of hair and eyes, height, weight, date of birth, race, and gender. Include identifiers such as eyeglasses, hair texture, braces, and easily identifiable blemishes, scars, marks, and tattoos (include description, color, location, and photos if available). You may also note piercings, any unusual characteristics, and clothing, shoe, and jewelry description when last seen. Include anything that sets the missing person apart from other missing persons within the same age group, physical characteristics, and time frame. (NOTE: DO NOT put your personal contact information, phone/home address on the flyer. This could put you in a vulnerable situation. Contact information should be addressed to the law enforcement agency in charge of the case). Post flyers in allowable, high-traffic public locations: homeless shelters, hospital emergency rooms, convenience stores, local coffee shops, grocery stores, gas stations, bus stations/taxi cab services, churches, social services office, drug and alcohol rehabilitation centers, local media (news stations and newspapers), tattoo parlors, salvation army, etc. E-mail the flyer to everyone in your e-mail address book. Ask friends and family to post and e-mail the flyer also. Use of social media is also encouraged (Facebook etc.).

Obtain medical and dental records that may aid in the missing person's identification, especially if they are missing under suspicious circumstances or for an extended period. Health care providers and facilities may be reluctant to provide you with records due to HIPAA regulations, but it is common for facilities to have

policies in place to allow cooperation with law enforcement and ME/coroner requests. You can provide law enforcement with the names of the missing person's physician, dentist, and other health care treatment facilities if they will not deal directly with you. As records are requested, verify that they have been picked up. Know which database medical and dental information will be kept in (i.e., NamUs, NCIC, CODIS, local law enforcement, ME/coroner, Interpol, etc.). Find out if fingerprints are available (and possibly footprints) and provide this information to investigators. These may be obtained from previous ID and Safety initiatives, military records, NamUs, and previous arrest records.

Contact your local media (newsprint, radio, television, and cable companies) and inquire about doing a public service announcement (PSA). Contact your local/county crime stoppers organization. There are numerous websites and agencies devoted to the issues of missing and unidentified persons that also may be contacted, but be sure to verify their legitimacy. Below is a partial list of some of these resources available to those interested in the issues related to the missing and unidentified crisis. It must be understood, however, that some organizations (especially private parties) spring up almost daily and no one monitors or verifies their legitimate qualifications or abilities. Although well meaning, they may muddy the water surrounding the already very complex issues related to the missing and unidentified person's dilemma.

Partial List of Public and Private Agencies to Assist Missing Persons Reports

Black & Missing Foundation http://www.blackandmissinginc.com/cdad/about.htm
Center for Missing Persons (CUE) http://www.ncmissingpersons.org/
Charley Project http://www.charleyproject.org/
Doe Network http://www.DoeNetwork.org

International Centre for missing & Exploited Children (ICMEC) http://www.icmec.org/
Interpol http://www.interpol.int/
Let's Bring Them Home http://lbth.org/
LOSTNMISSING, INC http://lostnmissing.org/
Missing Veterans http://www.missingveterans.com/
National Center for Missing & Exploited Children (NCMEC) http://www.missingkids.com/home
Project EDAN http://projectedan.us/
Project Jason (geared towards assisting families mostly) http://projectjason.org/
Polly Klaas Foundation http://www.pollyklaas.org/
Texas EquuSearch is also an excellent resource. Their website is www.texasequusearch.org.
Defrosting Cold Cases http://www.defrostingcoldcases.com

Missing Persons Checklist

1. Keep a journal
2. Contact local law enforcement and file a missing persons report
3. Make a list of contacts to aid law enforcement
4. Search local and familiar areas for the missing person
5. Contact family, friends, work site, and/or school site
6. Request information be entered into NamUs, NCIC, or other official databases
7. Contact local medical treatment facilities (hospitals and clinics) in at least a 50 mile (80 km) radius
8. Contact local justice centers (jails and detention facilities)
9. Check motor vehicle impounds and records of violations
10. Contact the Red Cross or other disaster relief organizations in cases of disasters
11. Contact the Salvation Army and other shelter providers, especially if the missing person is known to have stayed there before
12. Organize for authorized searches
13. Gather recent photos
14. Create and post flyers
15. Obtain medical and dental records
16. Get information on finger and footprints that are on file
17. Contact news media sources for PSAs
18. Contact official and volunteer organizations that are willing to help
19. If you are concerned about a missing person abroad, contact your State Department, Consulate, or Embassy

Forensic Odontology

Forensic odontologists are a relatively small but dedicated group of dental professionals who have not, as a whole, been as active as they could be regarding the missing and unidentified person issues. As noble a task as finding the missing is, it must be remembered that the function of the forensic dentist is not to find the missing. Rather, the primary tasks of an odontologist are to aid law enforcement agencies in inputting dental data into databases and to work to identify the over 40,000 unidentified human remains in the United States. Odontologists on an international scale also need to be available to assist identification of the many thousands outside the US borders (Skinner et al., 2010).

There are several ways to identify someone who has died. Visual identification is one way, but if there has been decomposition, burning, or trauma, very often, visual identification is not possible. Scars, marks, and tattoos can be helpful but are not considered a scientific means of identification, and these also will be altered due to postmortem changes in the remains. Antemortem fingerprints are excellent sources of identifications, but records are oftentimes not available or the individual has never been fingerprinted. DNA is a wonderful tool of forensic science but is time consuming and costly. Additionally, a single DNA test for identification may have a false positive even with astronomical statistical odds in its favor, and some experts strongly encourage the use of more than one identification method whenever possible rather than relying on DNA alone (Dadna Hartman et al., 2015; Hartman et al., 2011). For these reasons, dental records are often the fastest, most cost effective, scientific way to identify someone, and dental methods can certainly be used in concert with other identification methods to confirm a final identification.

Antemortem dental records are the driving force behind identification. The importance of dental record retention by the dental profession must be stressed. With the advent of digitalization in the dental office of both dental radiographs and charting, indefinite retention of these records will be less cumbersome. The accuracy of dental records of any age can prove useful for identifications as illustrated in the identification of a World War I US marine 92 years after he became missing in action in Saint-Mihiel, France, in September of 1918 (Shiroma, 2014).

The forensic dental community should take a more active role in the issues related to dental identification of the unidentified remains in the country's morgues, and there is a strong need for dentists throughout the world to be more active wherever unidentified human remains are found (Skinner et al., 2010). Drawing on experience and work on behalf of the United Nations High Commission for Human Rights, Physicians for Human Rights, and the International Commission on Missing Persons, and many other local commissions in Europe, Asia, and Africa, Skinner et al. (2010) found that dentists and oral biologists are poorly represented in humanitarian identification work. They also found that most dental data collection was done by medical pathologists and anthropologists, with results that were frequently inaccurate. Their main conclusion of reviewing over 6 years of work was that forensic odontologists have an ethical and moral obligation to become more involved with examination of mass grave victims because they are the experts in oral biology and pathology that is highly useful for identifications. Also needed is a stronger emphasis on searching for antemortem dental records to match with the postmortem examinations, especially since dental identification was used in 35% of cases reviewed. Extending these results and ethical responsibilities to the United States, there is certainly a need for odontologists to continue to assume the role of dental specialist for identifications in this domestic sphere.

Besides the work of identifications based on antemortem and postmortem dental comparisons, odontologists can interact with other forensic professionals in many ways. Age and ethnic assessments are two areas that are critical for the anthropologist to build a biological profile. Clues to both of these estimations are often present in the dentition. All trained and experienced odontologists should be well versed in a variety of age assessment techniques. The developing dentition from birth to 18 years of age is often cited as the most accurate source of age estimation data in the subadult human body (Buikstra and Ubelaker, 1994; Shirley et al., 2013; Uhl, 2013). Dental methods for adult age assessment are also available, but often must be tempered with variations in anatomy, pathology, and wear (Lewis and Senn, 2013). Nonetheless, dental age assessments are key contributions to the biological profile that helps narrow down the identification possibilities even when a definitive identification cannot be made.

There is also a growing body of work that is using dental trait characteristics to estimate ethnicity (Edgar, 2005, 2013; Hanihara, 2008; Pilloud et al., 2014). This is another part of the biological profile created by anthropologists that may need positive interaction from odontologists. Dental traits have been shown to be able to estimate the general ethnic groups of African-American, European

American, and Hispanics from southern Florida or New Mexico (Edgar, 2013). Tooth size measurements also can be used to differentiate between ethnic groups (Pilloud et al., 2014). Similar to age estimation, this will not establish conclusive identification, but can serve to narrow the possibilities among a pool of unknowns.

National and International Databases

There are numerous public and private sector databases and media sources throughout the world that are used to compile missing and unidentified person data that include the ability to compare antemortem and postmortem dental data (Kavanaugh and Filippi, 2013). The ones most widely used in the United States are the NamUs and NCIC databases, which are both sponsored by the US Department of Justice. Although the functions seemingly overlap, the sources of data and target audiences for each are different. NamUs is an online platform for missing and unidentified person data that is more open for public viewing, whereas NCIC is restricted to law enforcement agencies and other entities with a legal need to have access. Law enforcement also has access to a separate database known as the Violent Criminal Apprehension Program (ViCAP) that contains missing and unidentified person data as well, but it is aimed more at enhancing criminal investigations.

The DOE Network is an international volunteer organization that states that its mission is to give the nameless back their names and return the missing to their families. This is an online organization that has a team of volunteers that researches cases, works with media and families, finds potential matches, forms and maintains liaisons with law enforcement and governmental agencies. They provide support for solving current missing and unidentified cases as well as cold and/or mysterious cases.

Three major international groups that are active in working with missing and unidentified persons are the International Criminal Police Organization (INTERPOL), the International Centre for Missing and Exploited Children (ICMEC), and the International Federation of Red Cross and Red Crescent Societies (IFRC). These represent organizations that are active as intergovernmental and private bodies that can extend their support across many international borders with general support of sovereign governments, private and public institutions.

There is currently some debate about how detailed dental databases should be to best support missing unidentified person (MUP) identifications (Adams and Aschheim, 2016). Although most odontologists are familiar working with extremely detailed charting systems, a simplified system of only seven basic codes can be used to create an algorithm based on percentage of matches. Such matches cannot by themselves constitute an identification without further detailed verification, but can screen potential matching cases with less chance of error than a complex coding system. The use of statistical data can also be convincing in support of reported identifications, especially when associated with point-by-point comparisons of medical and dental records (Anderson, 2007; Steadman et al., 2006, 2007). This appears to have advantages for mass disaster—type scenarios and would likely apply to the present status of the world's thousands of unidentified persons.

Case Study #1

The mostly complete human remains of an unknown individual were recovered in October 2012 in a remote ranch situated in a South Texas county near the international border of Mexico and the United States. The circumstances of the discovery were highly suggestive of an undocumented border crosser who had died due to the extreme environmental conditions of the area while attempting to evade detection at a nearby US Immigration Services checkpoint. Unfortunately, there was no medicolegal investigation of the remains, which were buried in an unmarked grave in a local cemetery. In May 2013, the remains were legally exhumed for the purpose of possible identification by a team of anthropologists from Baylor University, Texas, and the University of Indianapolis, Indiana. The remains were brought to the Forensic Anthropology Center at Texas State University (FACTS) for a full forensic anthropological analysis following the law in the State of Texas (Code of Criminal Procedure. Title 1. Chapter 49. Inquests Upon Dead Bodies, 2005). The remains

were mostly skeletonized. Clothing items and other artifacts were documented, and an anthropological analysis was completed that consisted of estimations of sex, age, ancestry, and stature; evaluation for skeletal trauma; submission of a sample for DNA analysis; and postmortem dental documentation.

The postmortem dental exam consisted of comprehensive charting, photographs, and a full-mouth radiographic series. The dental exam found that most teeth were present with several having large, untreated carious lesions (#1, 5, 8, 9, and 18) (Fig. 6.2). An area of rarefaction of bone apical to the lingual of #18 suggested a chronic infection associated with this carious tooth, as well as possibly influenced by

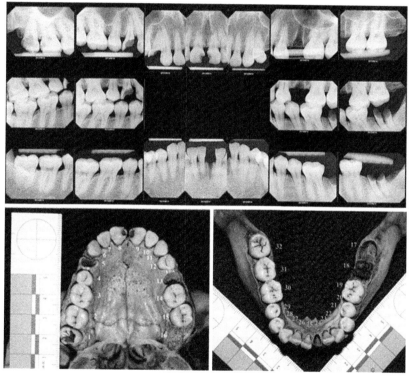

FIGURE 6.2   Full-mouth radiographic series, maxillary arch and mandibular arch photographs.

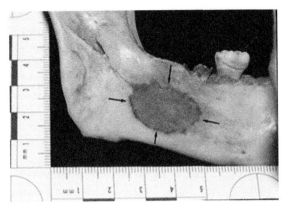

FIGURE 6.3 Left lingual mandible showing area of chronic infection.

the postmortem missing #17 (Fig. 6.3). Staining of the teeth, cervical calculus, and the lack of restorations all suggested that this individual had no recent dental treatment and it was unlikely that antemortem dental records would be present for an identification comparison. However, close examination of the dentition revealed that there were several traits that suggested a Maya heritage from Central America (Scherer, 2004; Scott & Turner II, 1997). In particular, there were cervical enamel projections noted in the facial furcations of #2 and 15; #5 and 12 appeared radiographically to have single roots; #7, 8, 9, and 10 have definite lingual shoveling; and #31 has five cusps with a Y-5 occlusal groove pattern. These dental data and conclusions were consistent with a metric analysis of the skull that placed this individual as being similar to the Hispanic reference sample in the FORDISC 3.1 program (Ousley and Jantz, 2005).

Additionally, an age estimation based on dental radiographs was completed using the method published by Kvaal et al. (1995). All the teeth were considered, with special emphasis placed on the six teeth #4, 7, 8, 21, 22, and 23. Based upon radiographic analysis of the evidence represented by this case, using the above stated published statistical data, the age was estimated to be 29.63 years plus or minus 8.6 years. The interval of possible ages for such a female was found to be 21.03–38.23 years based on the statistical standard error of the estimates in the data reported (Kvaal et al., 1995). However, even though caution was advised for overly strict interpretation of this conclusion because dental age estimation for adults can be highly variable due to ethnicity, disease, habits, and degree of professional care, this age estimation was very consistent with other anthropological techniques that used available osteological evidence that included the auricular surface of the os coxae (Meindl and Lovejoy, 1989) and fusion of the sacral segments (McKern and Stewart, 1957). The final age estimation agreed upon after considering all available data was 25–40 years.

The summary of forensic anthropological analysis, or biological profile, stated that this unidentified person is a female, aged 25–40 years, of Hispanic ancestry, stature of 4′10″ to 5′2″, with trauma limited to postmortem damage. All available data, including dental chart, radiographs, and summary photos, were entered into the NamUs database. Even though dental identification is an unknown variable, odontology input provided important data for the biological profile. A forensic artist was also engaged to create a two-dimensional sketch of the individual using cranial and dental landmarks (Fig. 6.4) (Taylor, 2001). Odontology documentation helped to create a primary and an alternate image with the person having a facial swelling from the probable chronic infection in the lower left mandible. The artist also chose to show the defects in the maxillary anterior teeth that may be key identifying traits. Identification will most likely require DNA analysis from members of a reference family source that can be narrowed down based on the biological profile and forensic sketch. There has been very significant odontology contribution to building this biological profile and refining the forensic sketch.

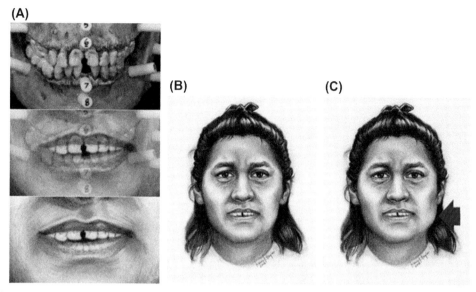

FIGURE 6.4 Facial reconstruction by a forensic artist (A) shows a sequence of constructing the oral structures around the existing teeth. The defects in the maxillary central incisors are displayed as potential identifying traits. Note generalized staining and calculus (B) is a final facial view using anatomical landmarks, plus anthropology and odontology data; (C) places emphasis on the left mandible that had signs of chronic infection and probable swelling. *Photo-reconstruction used by permission of Karen T. Taylor, Facial Images, and Lisa Sheppard, Dreamfly Creations.*

Case Study #2

On July 7, 2010, unidentified human female remains were discovered in a rural area.

(Fig. 6.5). On July 8, 2010, the local ME performed an autopsy. The cause of death was stated as blunt force trauma to the skull, and the manner of death as homicide. There was a distinctive tattoo of a "little red devil on the upper right leg/hip area" (Fig. 6.6). The consultant forensic dentist performed a postmortem dental examination with appropriate dental X-rays. On July 11, 2010, the local law enforcement agency entered the unidentified female **without** dental data into the state MUP database and NCIC. On July 24, 2010, Mary Carter (alias) was reported missing by her grandmother and was entered into the state MUP database and NCIC by a second law enforcement agency **without** dental data. This second law enforcement agency was over 250 miles from the discovery site of the unidentified human female remains found on July 7, 2010.

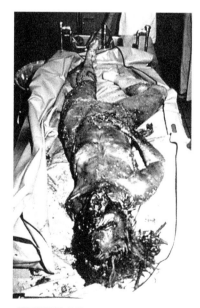

FIGURE 6.5 Unidentified female.

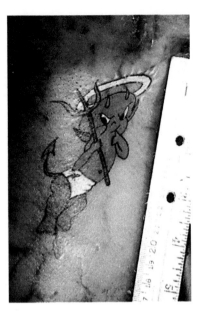

FIGURE 6.6   "Little red devil on the upper right area of the leg/hip.

On August 21, 2010, the postmortem dental data were entered into the state MUP database and NCIC. A search of the databases matching the unidentified female against the missing persons databases resulted in no "hits." On October 25, 2010, the antemortem dental data of Mary Clark were entered into the state MUP database and NCIC. A search of the databases comparing the unidentified female against the missing persons databases resulted in an immediate "hit." An examination of the antemortem versus postmortem dental evidence by the consultant forensic odontologist found no inconsistencies or unexplainable discrepancies between Mary Clark and the unidentified female discovered on July 7, 2010. They were one and the same individual based on the dental evidence. It is interesting to note that the tattoo of the "little red devil on the upper right leg/hip area" was never a factor in the identification. The grandmother who reported Mary Clark missing was unaware of the tattoo's existence. Therefore it was never part of the antemortem data.

SUMMARY

Never doubt that a small group of thoughtful, committed people can change the world. Indeed, It Is The Only Thing That Ever Has! *Margaret Mead*

There is a well-documented problem of many thousands of MUPs in the United States and around the world, and the list of individuals continues to grow every year. The efforts to control and reduce this number will require concerted efforts on the part of law enforcement agencies, governmental institutions, and many social and health care professionals. Dentists, in particular trained forensic odontologists, have an ethical, moral, and very practical obligation to be involved with inputting the data of missing and unidentified persons and working in any way possible on the teams of professionals that dedicate their time to resolve this humanitarian dilemma.

The United States Department of Agriculture can identify a single cow with "Mad Cow Disease" out of hundreds of thousands of cows? Maybe we should put the Department of Agriculture in charge of missing persons.

References

Adams, B.J., Aschheim, K.W., 2016. Computerized dental comparison: a critical review of dental coding and ranking algorithms used in victim identification. Journal of Forensic Sciences 61, 76–86.

Anderson, B.E., 2007. Statistical basis for positive identification in forensic anthropology. American Journal of Physical Anthropology 133, 741.

Anderson, B.E., 2008. Identifying the dead: methods utilized by the pima county (Arizona) office of the medical examiner for undocumented border crossers: 2001–2006. Journal of Forensic Sciences 53, 8–15.

Anderson, B.E., Parks, B.O., 2008. Symposium on border crossing deaths: introduction. Journal of Forensic Sciences 53, 6–7.

Andreev, E., Pridemore, W.A., Shkolnikov, V.M., Antonova, O.I., 2008. An investigation of the growing number of deaths of unidentified people in Russia. European Journal of Public Health 18, 252–257.

Armendariz, J., 2013. Unidentified Immigrant Body Count Remains Grave Issue in Brooks County. The Monitor, McAllen, TX.

Baker, L.E., Baker, E.J., 2008. Reuniting families: an online database to aid in the identification of undocumented immigrant remains. Journal of Forensic Sciences 53, 50–53.

Baraybar, J.P., Blackwell, R., 2014. Where are they? Missing, forensics, and memory. Annals of Anthropological Practice 38, 22–42.

Barry, D.A.N., 2014. Restoring lost names, recapturing lost dignity. New York Times 164, A1–A24.

Boric, I., Ljubkovic, J., Sutlovic, D., 2011. Discovering the 60 years old secret: identification of the World War II mass grave victims from the island of Daksa near Dubrovnik, Croatia. Croatian Medical Journal 52, 327–335.

Buikstra, J.E., Ubelaker, D.H., 1994. Standards for Data Collection from Human Skeletal Remains: Proceedings of a Seminar at the Field Museum of Natural History. Arkansas Archeological Research Series, Fayetteville.

Cappella, A., Magli, F., Porta, D., Cattaneo, C., 2012. The governmental Ri.Sc. Form for unidentified human remains and the role of forensic anthropology. Journal of Biological Research (1826–8838) 85, 347–349.

Carter, L., 2005. Where are Canada's Disappeared Women? Herizons 19, 20–46.

Code of Criminal Procedure. Title 1. Chapter 49. Inquests Upon Dead Bodies, 2005. Austin, Texas: State of Texas.

De Valck, E., 2006. Major incident response: collecting antemortem data. Forensic Science International 159, S15–S19.

Del Bosque, M., 2014. Saving lives in Brooks county. Texas Observer: A Journal of Free Voices 106, 8.

Djuric, M., Dunjic, D., Djonic, D., Skinner, M., 2007. Identification of victims from two mass-graves in Serbia: a critical evaluation of classical markers of identity. Forensic Science International 172, 125–129.

Edgar, H.J.H., 2005. Prediction of race using characteristics of dental morphology. Journal of Forinsic Sciences 50, 267–273.

Edgar, H.J.H., 2013. Estimation of ancestry using dental morphological characteristics. Journal of Forensic Sciences 58, S3–S8.

Edward Nathan, M.D., Sakthi, D.S., 2014. Dentistry and mass disaster – a review. Journal of Clinical & Diagnostic Research 8, 1–3.

Fyfe, N.R., Stevenson, O., Woolnough, P., 2015. Missing persons: the processes and challenges of police investigation. Policing & Society 25, 409–425.

Grant, S., 2011. Recording and identifying European frontier deaths. European Journal of Migration & Law 13, 135–156.

Guerette, R.T., 2007. Immigration policy, border security, and migrant deaths: an impact evaluation of life-saving efforts under the border safety initiative. Criminology & Public Policy 6, 245–266.

Haglund, W.D., Connor, M., Scott, D.D., 2001. The archaeology of contemporary mass graves. Historical Archaeology 35, 57–69.

Hagopian, A., Flaxman, A.D., Takaro, T.K., Esa Al Shatari, S.A., Rajaratnam, J., Becker, S., et al., 2013. Mortality in Iraq associated with the 2003–2011 war and occupation: findings from a national cluster sample survey by the university collaborative iraq mortality study. Plos Medicine 10, 1–15.

Hanihara, T., 2008. Morphological variation of major human populations based on nonmetric dental traits. American Journal of Physical Anthropology 136, 169–182.

Hartman, D., Benton, L., Spiden, M., Stock, A., 2015. The Victorian missing persons DNA database – two interesting case studies. Australian Journal of Forensic Sciences 47, 161–172.

Hartman, D., Drummer, O., Eckhoff, C., Scheffer, J.W., Stringer, P., 2011. The contribution of DNA to the disaster victim identification (DVI) effort. Forensic Science International 205, 52–58.

Hickman, J.J., Hughes, K.A., Strom, K.J., Ropero-Miller, J.D., 2007. Bureau of Justic Statistics Special Report: Medical Examiners and Coroners' Offices, 2004. United States Department of Justice.

Hughes, G., 2011. The concept of dignity in the universal declaration of human rights. Journal of Religious Ethics 39, 1–24.

James, M., Anderson, J., Putt, J., 2008. Missing Persons in Australia. Australian Institute of Crimonology Research and Public Policy Series, No. 86, Canberra.

Kavanaugh, S.A., Filippi, J.E., 2013. Missing and unidentified persons. In: Senn, D.R., Weems, R.A. (Eds.), Manual of Forensic Odontology. CRC Press, Boca Raton, FL, pp. 193–210.

Kimmerle, E.H., 2014a. Forensic anthropology in long-term investigations: 100 cold years. Annals of Anthropological Practice 38, 7–21.

Kimmerle, E.H., 2014b. Practicing forensic anthropology: a human rights approach to the global problem of missing and unidentified persons. Annals of Anthropological Practice 38, 1–6.

Klinkner, M., 2012. Psycho-social aspects surrounding criminal investigations into mass graves. International Criminal Law Review 12, 409–426.

Kogon, S., Arnold, J., Wood, R., Merner, L., 2010. Integrating dental data in missing persons and unidentified remains investigations: the Resolve Initiative and DIP3. Forensic Science International 197, e31–e35.

Kontsevaia, D.B., 2013. Mass graves and the politics of reconciliation: construction of memorial sites after the Srebrenica massacre. Totem: The University of Western Ontario Anthropology Journal 21, 15–31.

Kvaal, S.I., Kolltveit, K.M., Thomsen, I.O., Solheim, T., 1995. Age estimation of adults from dental radiographs. Forensic Science International 74, 175–185.

Laczko, F., Singleton, A., Brian, T., Rango, M., 2016. Migrant arrivals and deaths in the Mediterranean: what do the data really tell us? Forced Migration Review 30–31.

LePard, D., Demers, S., Langan, C., Kim Rossmo, D., 2015. Challenges in serial murder investigations involving missing persons. Police Practice & Research 16, 328–340.

Lewis, J.M., Senn, D.R., 2013. Dental age estimation. In: Senn, D.R., Weems, R.A. (Eds.), Manual of Forensic Odontology. CRC Press, Boca Raton, FL, pp. 211–256.

MacKinnon, B., Fiala, A., 2015. Ethics: Theory and Contemporary Issues, eighth ed. Cengage Learning, Stamford, CT.

Marjanović, D., Metjahić, N.H., Čakar, J., Džehverović, M., Dogan, S., Ferić, E., et al., 2015. Identification of human remains from the Second World War mass graves uncovered in Bosnia and Herzegovina. Croatian Medical Journal 56, 257–262.

McKern, T., Stewart, T., 1957. Skeletal Age Changes in Young American Males, Analyzed from the Standpoint of Age Identification. Headquarters Quartermaster Research and Development Command, Technical Report EP-45, Natick, MA.

Meindl, R., Lovejoy, C., 1989. Age changes in the pelvis: implications for paleodemography. In: Iscan, M. (Ed.), Age Markers in the Human Skeleton. Charles C. Thomas, Springfield, IL, pp. 137–168.

N.C.I.C., 2016. 2015 NCIC Missing Person and Unidentified Person Statistics. Federal Bureau of Investigation, National Crime Information Center, Washington, D.C.

Narine, S., 2015. Women continue to fall victim as debate rages on. Windspeaker 33, 6.

Nazaryan, A., 2014. Billy's gone. Newsweek Global 163, 34–41.

Ortiz, I., 2013. Activists Push DNA Testing for Immigrant Bodies in Falfurrias. The Monitor, McAllen, TX.

Ousley, D., Jantz, R., 2005. FORDISC 3.1: Personal Computer Forensic Discriminant Function. The University of Tennessee, Knoxville.

Paulozzi, L.J., Cox, C.S., Williams, D.D., Nolte, K.B., 2008. John and Jane doe: the epidemiology of unidentified decedents. Journal of Forensic Sciences (Wiley-Blackwell) 53, 922–927.

Petju, M., Suteerayongprasert, A., Thongpud, R., Hassiri, K., 2007. Importance of dental records for victim identification following the Indian Ocean tsunami disaster in Thailand. Public Health (Elsevier) 121, 251–257.

Pilloud, M.A., Hefner, J.T., Hanihara, T., Hayashi, A., 2014. The use of tooth crown measurements in the assessment of ancestry. Journal of Forensic Sciences 59, 1493–1501.

Policy on Child Identification Programs, 2010. Pediatric Dentistry 32, 27–28.

Rand, E.C. (Ed.), 2008. Public Health Guide for Emergencies. Johns Hopkins Bloomberg School of Public Health, Baltimore, MD.

Reineke, R., 2013. Lost in the system: unidentified bodies on the border. NACLA Report on the Americas 46, 50–53.

Ritter, N., 2007a. Identifying remains: lessons learned from 9/11. NIJ Journal 256, 20–26.

Ritter, N., 2007b. Missing persons and unidentified remains: the Nation's silent mass disaster. NIJ Journal 2–7.

Scherer, A.K., 2004. Dental Analysis of Classic Period Population Variability in the Maya Area. A&M University, Ann Arbor: Texas, p. 314.

Schuller-Götzburg, P., Suchanek, J., 2007. Forensic odontologists successfully identify tsunami victims in Phuket, Thailand. Forensic Science International 171, 204–207.

Scott, G.R., Turner II, C.G., 1997. The Anthropology of Modern Human Teeth. University of Cambridge, Cambridge, United Kingdom.

Shalev, K., Schaefer, M., Morgan, A., 2009. Investigating missing person cases: how can we learn where they go or how far they travel? International Journal of Police Science & Management 11, 123–129.

Shirley, N.R., Fazlollah, A.E., Tersigni-Tarrant, M.T.A., 2013. Age estimation methods. In: Tersigni-Tarrant, M.T.A., Shirley, N.R. (Eds.), Forensic Anthropology - AnIntroduction. CRC Press, Boca Raton, FL, pp. 161–180.

Shiroma, C.Y., 2014. The analysis of a world war I U.S. Service Member's dental remains recovered in France. Journal of Forensic Sciences (Wiley-Blackwell) 59, 1654–1657.

Skinner, M., Alempijevic, D., Stanojevic, A., 2010. In the absence of dental records, do we need forensic odontologists at mass grave sites? Forensic Science International 201, 22–26.

Steadman, D.W., Adams, B.J., Konigsberg, L.W., 2006. Statistical basis for positive identification in forensic anthropology. American Journal of Physical Anthropology 131, 15–26.

Steadman, D.W., Adams, B.J., Konigsberg, L.W., 2007. Statistical basis for positive identification in forensic anthropology: response to Anderson. American Journal of Physical Anthropology 133, 741–742.

Stein, J.G., 1946. How we find missing persons. Saturday Evening Post 219, 12–42.

Taylor, K.T., 2001. Forensic Art and Illustration. CRC Press, Boca Raton, Florida.

Tise, M.L., Kimmerle, E.H., Spradley, M.K., 2014. Craniometric variation of diverse populations in Florida: identification challenges within a border state. Annals of Anthropological Practice 38, 111–123.

Uhl, N.M., 2013. Age at death estimation. In: DiGangi, E.A., Moore, M.K. (Eds.), Research Methods in Human Skeletal Biology. Elsevier, New York, pp. 63–90.

van Houtum, H., Boedeltje, F., 2009. Europe's shame: death at the borders of the EU. Antipode 41, 226–230.

Whitaker, J., 2009. Mexican deaths in the Arizona desert: the culpability of migrants, humanitarian workers, governments, and businesses. Journal of Business Ethics 88, 365–376.

Domestic Violence

John D. Melville[1], John D. McDowell[2,3]

[1]Chief, Division of Child Abuse Pediatrics, Medical University of South Carolina, Charleston, SC, United States; [2]Distinguished Fellow of the American Academy of Forensic Sciences, Professor and Director Oral Medicine and Forensic Sciences, University of Colorado School of Dental Medicine, Aurora, CO, United States; [3]Professor, School of Medicine, Department of Family Medicine, University of Colorado Health Sciences Center, Aurora, CO, United States

O U T L I N E

ADULT AND ELDER ABUSE AND MALTREATMENT

(Perspectives from a Forensic Odontologist)

INTRODUCTION

We live in a society where individuals might try to accomplish their individual goals or to exert control over another individual through violent behavior. This violent behavior is often directed against family members or other individuals with whom the aggressor might have a relationship. In 2014, the United States Justice Bureau of Justice Statistics estimated that more than 3.5 million violent crimes were committed against family members. Physical evidence of this violent behavior is often manifested in the form of inflicted trauma resulting in injury patterns ranging from minor bruising to fractured bones and teeth. Frequently, this violent behavior results in permanent disability or death. Although this chapter is written to assist in recognizing the most common signs (i.e., physical evidence) of violence directed at the maxillofacial complex, it must be remembered that there might be symptoms (i.e., anxiety disorders, headaches, sleep and appetite disorders, depression, chronic pain, etc.) that manifest as a result of short-term or long-term violent behavior within a relationship.

Because of denial and inconsistent histories that are often given by victims of nonaccidental trauma within the family or other intimate relationship, it might be difficult to differentiate between accidental and nonaccidental trauma. Based on many years of experience in the emergency department and nonurgent health care setting, it has been this author's (JDM) experience that there are key features that can be very helpful in differentiating accidental injuries from inflicted injuries. The features often seen in nonaccidental trauma are: (1) Injuries at variance with history given or a denial history in the presence of pathognomonic evidence; (2) Injuries at

various stages of healing; (3) Bilateral injuries; (4) Defensive injuries to the hands and arms; (5) Difficulties relating to the history taker, the clinician, or ancillary personnel; and (6) Delayed presentation for care.

The National Institute of Justice has over the previous decades consistently reported that nearly one-third of homicide victims were killed by an intimate partner. Unfortunately, a female is nearly as likely to suffer violent or aggressive behaviors from a friend or family member as from a stranger. When presented with injury patterns that might suggest that the presenting injuries are inconsistent with the history given by the injured individual or the history given by the parties accompanying the injured individual, the treating doctor or investigator should consider that the traumatic injuries might not be accidental in origin. The health care provider or investigator should always keep intentionally inflicted trauma in the differential diagnosis.

To reduce the likelihood of a false negative (failing to recognize the victim of intentionally inflicted trauma), care providers and investigators must remember that all of the forms of familial and intimate partner violence are potentially interrelated. Whether it involves a child, adolescent, adult male or female, pregnant woman, or an elderly man or woman, disabled person, any person in a same-sex relationship or opposite-sex relationship, one form of violence cannot be completely separated from another form. Unfortunately, it is not uncommon for the sequelae of violence to directly or indirectly affect all age groups living together or any of the persons living in intimate relationships or in the initial dating process. Violent individuals living within the same household can cause trauma to anyone living in that household or to an "outside" individual (for example, law enforcement officers, a visiting nurse, a social worker, etc.) coming to that home. The health care provider or other investigator (the individual or individuals responsible for collection and potential analysis of evidence) should not exclusively focus his or her attention on the person (or persons) presenting with the injuries but must be aware that a battered child frequently has an abused mother. A child abused by a violent mother might also have an abused father or grandparent living in the same home. An older adult or a disabled person might be physically (including sexual abuse), emotionally, or financially abused. Additionally, the investigator or treatment provider should consider the possibility that spousal abuse can involve both the male or female partner living together and include domestic partners (for instance, a same-sex couple cohabitating together) living in a violent relationship.

RECORDS

Recorded data—whether in written or another means of capturing information—are invaluable for treating the victim and in the potential prosecution of the individual(s) responsible for the abuse or neglect. The diagnosis of causation for the presenting injuries can lead to more appropriate treatment plans with better outcomes. Law enforcement, protective services, or other agencies responsible for the collection and analysis of data will invariably have published protocols that investigators should follow. Following published protocols is especially important to forensic odontologists. If these protocols are available through professional organizations (i.e., The American Board of Forensic Odontology, ABFO), the data collected might become less valuable or even inadmissible in civil or criminal proceedings if these protocols are not followed precisely.

Whether it is in the form of a written record or part of the electronic health record, health care providers usually follow a treatment record protocol that has for many years been used effectively when collecting patient information. This protocol is identified by an acronym generally known as the SOAP format. When using this format, the letters S, O, A, and P represent a portion of the treatment record wherein specific information is recorded for potential later review and analysis. Information regarding the victim,

the history given regarding the injuries (also called the "chief complaint" or "history of present illness"), the examiner, treating doctor(s), ancillary personnel present, time, date, and place of examination, must be included in the record. If other persons are present in the examination area (i.e., the dental office or emergency department), it is also important to document any personnel present during the examination and treatment of the injured patient. An effective way to document those present is to share business cards so there are no questions that might arise later regarding who was present and what jurisdiction they were representing. If the examination is performed in the medical examiner or coroner's office, similar information should also be recorded.

When using the standard SOAP format, the letter S represents the subjective data collected from the patient, caregivers, guardian, or individuals bringing the patient for care including emergency transport personnel. The subjective data include a wide range of data including:

- Some form of patient-identifying data (name, age, gender, ethnicity, address, caregivers, etc.) including—if available—copies of a driver's license or other government photographic identification, insurance information, etc. As is well known to many health care providers, it is wise to assess the accuracy of the historian. False names and addresses might be used to reduce the ability to follow up with the victim or to have law enforcement or social services begin intervention on behalf of the victim.
- A record of the patient statement regarding the injured individual's chief complaint (why the individual presented for care). The chief complaint or history of present illness should be recorded in the patient's own words and not a summary recorded by the history taker. Some readers may be more familiar with a very similar term, "the history of present illness." In the history of present illness, information is gathered regarding the injury, especially when and how it happened.

Whenever possible, this information should be collected from the injured person. Collecting information from the injured person might be difficult when the person is very young, impaired, disabled, unconscious, unable to speak the same language as the caregiver, or otherwise noncommunicative. Careful attention should be paid to histories related to the injury given by others (spouse, intimate partner, parent, guardian, etc.) accompanying the injured party. The history of present illness should be taken in a private, quiet, supportive, nonaccusatory environment whenever possible. If the victim is the opposite gender from the examiner, it is not unwise to have one or more other individuals (preferably the same gender as the victim) present during the examination and history-taking process.

- A statement regarding the injured party's other pertinent medical and/or oral health care histories including any previous injuries, surgeries, and hospitalizations. Consistent with federal and insurance requirements, information should be recorded regarding previous illness or injuries, names, and locations of hospitalizations or doctors' office visits for similar or related injuries. Consistent with the Health Information Portability and Protection Act and as authorized by an appropriate person, this information can be provided electronically to other health care providers or other parties as deemed appropriate by the victim or consistent with federal law.
- A statement of relationship of the injured person to those presenting to the treatment facility with the injured person. If intentionally inflicted trauma is suspected, a statement from the injured person should include information about the potential source of the injury, any weapons that might have been used, or questions directly asked about the person responsible for the traumatic event. Some emergency department personnel are trained to ask, "Tell me again how you came to be injured?" or, "Do you feel safe in your home?" Some are trained to ask directly, "Who hit you?" or, in the case of suspected intimate partner violence, "What did he (or she) hit you with?" Again, these questions should be asked in a private, supportive environment to encourage truthful responses.
- When appropriate, a statement describing the family status or personal status of the injured person should also be included in the record.

The letter O in the SOAP format represents the objective data actually collected during the examination. The results of previous physical examinations, radiographs, or laboratory tests might be available for review during the instant examination. This is especially true if the injured party has been treated at the same facility. Objective information is the data that are visible, reliable, measureable, and quantifiable. Examples of objective data would be the vital signs, injury patterns (i.e., bruises, abrasions, bitemarks, fractured teeth, radiographic evidence of hard tissue injuries, etc.), or other forms of representative, reproducible data. Written records of the location of injuries and a description of the colors (potentially useful in aging the injuries) are also found in this section of the record. A record that states how trace evidence was collected, preserved, and transmitted to law enforcement or laboratory personnel should be recorded here.

The letter A in the SOAP format stands for the assessment of the injury patterns described during taking the patient history or discovered during the physical examination. For instance, in the situation when a child patient is incapable of providing a history, does an injury pattern suggest the source of the injury? By way of example, does the injury suggest a belt mark or blade injury? It is not unusual to encounter patterned injuries that suggest that the pattern is caused by the human dentition (bitemark). Although bitemark analysis is going through critical review (as well it should) as bitemarks apply to the justice system, evidence of suspected biting activity should definitely be recorded in great detail (including collecting trace salivary evidence from suspected bites). Additionally, in the case of an injury that might mimic a bitemark, it might be possible to make a record that the treating doctor or investigator believes that the source is something other than the human dentition.

The Assessment section of the patient record is also where the differential diagnosis and working diagnosis for the injuries is recorded. The differential diagnosis is the rank order of the most probable (most likely) diagnoses based on likelihood (probability) of the cause of the injury or injuries while taking into consideration the diagnostic imperative. The diagnostic imperative is the diagnosis that is so risky to the patient that it cannot be excluded. For instance, after reviewing the history and physical examination, is it likely (based on the history and physical examination) that the injury is caused by an accident or is it more likely that the injury was intentionally inflicted? If inflicted trauma is a probability, then it must be considered a first priority (the working diagnosis) in the treatment plan. Every investigator or health care provider should ask himself or herself, "Can I reasonably rule out the possibility that the injury patterns I am observing are the result of inflicted trauma?" If inflicted trauma cannot be reasonably ruled out, then further investigation designed to protect the victim from future or additional injuries should be initiated.

The final section of the SOAP format is the P section that represents the Plan. Not only does the Plan include the treatment plan (or plans) but the Plan section also includes what further tests are appropriate. For instance, are other diagnostic imaging techniques necessary to reach a definitive diagnosis? Or, if following the history review and the physical examination, in the best interest of the injured party is it appropriate to contact law enforcement officials or protective services personnel? Does the

written plan include the time and date that a law enforcement agency or protective services agency was contacted? Health care providers are reminded that it is mandatory to report a suspected case of inflicted trauma in a child, and depending on state law—that same health care provider might be a mandatory reporter of reasonably suspected inflicted trauma in an adult. Recording the actual treatment provided can also be valuable to law enforcement or human services personnel. For instance, did the facial injuries require assistance of an otolaryngologist, facial surgeon, or other medical or dental specialists? Did the injuries to the maxillofacial complex require removing teeth, splinting teeth, or intermaxillary fixation? Detailed notes on actual treatment should be recorded in the P section of the patient record.

Utilizing the SOAP format in record keeping is critically important to all of the various forms of abuse or neglect. The next section of this chapter will directly address the different types of abuse and neglect that might be encountered by the health care provider.

VIOLENT BEHAVIORS

Although the focus of this chapter is on the violent behaviors seen in the United States, North American, and Western society, violent behaviors are certainly not unique to those cultures. Violent behaviors directed against persons of all ages are seen in all developed or developing countries and in the urban, suburban, or rural environments. Violent behaviors and assaults can be found in all genders, religions, socioeconomic groups, races/ethnicities, and cultures. Although less frequently reported, violent behaviors can also occur within same-sex relationships. It should not be surprising to find that domestic violence and violence within the immediate or extended family—child abuse, spouse abuse, abuse/neglect of the disabled, and abuse of older persons—are far too common in but not isolated to Western society. Oral health care providers and all other investigators must be aware of the fact that intentionally inflicted trauma can result in injuries to the developing fetus, children, adolescents, adults, and the elderly—in fact, no age group is free from the potential for violent acts.

INTIMATE PARTNER VIOLENCE

Recent estimates from the Centers for Disease Control and Prevention (CDC) indicate that approximately 25% of women have been raped and/or physically assaulted by an intimate partner (Centers for Disease Control and Prevention[a]). Although women are predominantly the victims of violent behaviors by men, some researchers in the field of domestic violence report that men and women are nearly equally involved in assaults. Most reputable publications agree with the CDC that consistently issue reports that women experience more chronic injuries and assaults from men than men do from their female intimate partner (Centers for Disease Control and Prevention[a]). More than 40% of women who experience intimate partner sexual assaults (unapproved sexual relations within the intimate partner relationship—including within marriage) report that during the sexual assault they suffer some form of physical injury (Centers for Disease Control and Prevention[a]). These soft and hard tissue physical injuries can take the form of bruises, lacerations, contusions, blade injuries including thoracic and abdominal perforations, vaginal and rectal injuries, blunt object assaults, gunshot wounds, avulsed tissue injuries, broken bones (including the alveolar bone, jaws, and other bones of the maxillofacial complex), fractured, subluxated, and/or avulsed teeth, and bite injuries.

Intimate partner violence can take many forms to include psychological/emotional abuse (including isolation of the victim), verbal, physical, and sexual abuse. Intimate partner violence can begin in the dating relationship, while cohabiting, while married, when separated, or divorced and can continue into the later years of life. Unfortunately, the violence can often result in death, serious physical injury, disfigurement, and long-term, intergenerational, emotional problems.

Injuries associated with intimate partner violence include a wide range of injury patterns by location and severity. These soft and hard tissue injuries should be thoroughly documented in the treatment record (in the Objective findings section). While recognizing that emergency treatment takes priority, whenever possible, photographs should be made prior to treatment necessary to treat dental subluxations, remove nonrestorable teeth, intermaxillary fixation, suturing or removal of nonvital tissues. Orientation photographs and photographs with scales in place should be taken. Careful compliance with generally accepted techniques for photographic documentation of injuries must be followed. If serial photographs are indicated, then appointments should be made to record the changes that occur over time.

The investigator should also consider using multiple differing techniques to record physical injuries. Digital or film color photography using different lighting angles, camera aperture settings, and exposure times can be used to optimally record physical injuries. Making daily sequential photographs over a period of 1 week can be invaluable to capture injury patterns that might not be seen immediately after the assault. Many forensic odontologists are familiar with and have the equipment to use alternative light photography. If the health care provider or other recorder is not familiar with the techniques or does not have the proper equipment, assistance with alternative light source imaging techniques is often available through local, state, or federal law enforcement investigators or crime scene technicians. Since alternate light imaging might be invaluable to a prosecutor's or defense lawyer's case, if the health care provider is not familiar with these techniques or if the health care provider does not possess or have access to these technologies, then local, state, or federal agencies who have trained personnel knowledgeable in these techniques should be contacted.

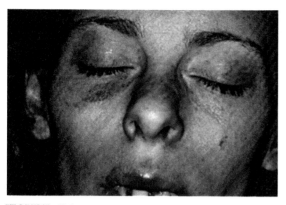

FIGURE 7.1 Photograph documenting facial injuries resulting from intentionally inflicted trauma in intimate partner abuse.

In addition to photographs (Fig. 7.1) and the written record, radiographs and other diagnostic images (i.e., orthopantomography, computed tomography with 3D imaging, medical computed tomography, and magnetic resonance imaging) of the facial bony structures, the jaws, or teeth are invaluable to document soft and hard tissue injuries to the maxillofacial complex. Examples might include fractured teeth, dental root fractures, alveolar fractures, mandibular or maxillary fractures, and other fractures of the facial bones (Fig. 7.2). Because healed and healing fractures

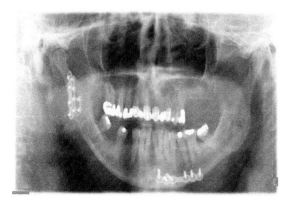

FIGURE 7.2 Orthopantomograph of woman presenting for treatment of dental injuries with evidence of previous mandibular right subcondylar fracture and left parasymphyseal fractures treated with fixation plates.

are frequently seen in domestic violence cases, careful attention must be paid to the possibility of recent and not so recent fractures when examining radiographic images. The patient history (for example, "I have trouble opening and closing my jaw." or, "I have difficulty chewing." or, "I have loose teeth." or, "My teeth do not fit together like they did before I was hit.") combined with the clinical examination will often reveal evidence of jaw fractures that indicate the need for specific radiographic images.

PHYSICAL INJURIES DURING ADOLESCENT/TEENAGE DATING RELATIONSHIP

Violence within an intimate relationship (to include dating) can begin at an early age (preteens 12 years of age and younger) and might involve adolescents (boys or girls having reached puberty but not yet reached full maturity) or teenage (ages 13 through 19) boys and girls. Dating violence (also termed Physical Dating Violence—PDV) has been defined as physical, or sexual violence, psychological/emotional abuse, or stalking within a dating relationship (Centers for Disease Control and Prevention[a]).

Dating violence can also take the form of sexually explicit texting or posting explicit photographs online through electronic and social media. The use of the term "sexting" was first used in the early 21st century and has been commonly used since approximately 2007. The term "sexting" can be applied to any image of a potentially sexual nature (to include nude or partially nude photographs), text messages of a sexual nature, or emails using mobile phones or other electronic devices (Rice et al., 2012; Centers for Disease Control and Prevention[b]). "Cyberbullying" is another recently evolving term that indicates an individual is bullied (threatened or intimidated) using electronic media. Cyberbullying and sexting can have serious sequelae to the victim of these actions including severe depression, suicidal ideations, suicide attempts, suicide, low self-esteem, poor academic performance, and participating in other risk-taking behaviors that can result in sexually transmitted infections and unwanted pregnancy (Rice et al., 2012; Centers for Disease Control and Prevention[b]).

A recently published study from the CDC reported that dating violence among students in grades 7−12 found that physical and psychological violence was 12% and 20% respectively (Centers for Disease Control and Prevention). Self-reports of violent behaviors indicated that there was hitting or scratching (see Fig. 7.3), slapping or some other form of physical harm during the dating period. Between 11 and 17 years of age, 22% of women and 15% of men first experienced some form of partner violence (Rice et al., 2012). Youth who are victims of dating violence are more likely to experience emotional symptoms like depression and anxiety and to engage in unhealthy behaviors like using alcohol, tobacco, use of illicit drugs, participation in antisocial behaviors, and to have suicidal ideations (Rice et al., 2012). In addition to the previously

described issues related to violence during dating, other forms of secondary risk associated with dating violence included rape or consensual sexual intercourse (protected and unprotected), attempted suicide, and physical fighting (Rice et al., 2012; Centers for Disease Control and Prevention[b]; Halpern et al., 2001).

Dating or acquaintance sexual assaults not only occur during the teenage years but can also extend into the college and postgraduate experience. A commonly reported figure is that 25% of female college students state that they have been the victim of sexual assault (The Costs of Intimate Partner) (Fig. 7.3 and Fig. 7.4). A survey recently conducted (from October 19 to November 16, 2015) on over 13,000 students at the University of Colorado−Boulder campus showed that 28% of female undergraduates said that they were sexually assaulted during their years in college (Krebs et al., 2007). An interesting finding in this same study found that 6% of undergraduate men reported being sexually assaulted while in college (Krebs et al., 2007). Another frightening finding was that 14% of undergraduate women and 7% of undergraduate men reported that they had experienced intimate partner abuse while on the Boulder campus (Krebs et al., 2007). These data are certainly of great concern to any parent sending a family member to college. While

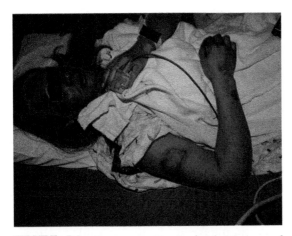

FIGURE 7.3 A young woman's facial injuries and patterned injury on upper right arm described by the victim as biting activity that occurred during a sexual assault. Note injury patterns suggestive of defensive injuries on right hand and forearm.

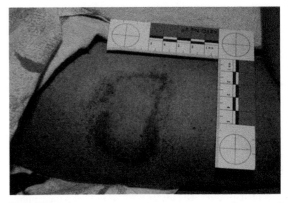

FIGURE 7.4 Photograph of patterned injury of suspected bitemark seen in Fig. 7.3.

maintaining the college student's sense of auton-omy, parents and family members should be aware of the common emotional or physical in-dicators of abuse in these young adults.

SPOUSE ABUSE (INTIMATE PARTNER VIOLENCE)

Spouse abuse (intimate partner violence) is a major cause of morbidity and mortality in the United States. The United States Bureau of Justice Statistics reported that although the overall rate of homicides has decreased significantly during the time period 1993–2011, nonfatal serious violence comprised more than a third of intimate partner violence against females and males during 2002–2011. That same Bureau of Justice Report estimated that two-thirds of female and male inti-mate partner victimization involved a physical attack (Full Report; Bureau of Justice Statistics).

The Federal Bureau of Investigation (FBI) Sup-plemental Homicide Reports, 1976–2004 report indicates that:

- Approximately one-third of female murder victims were killed by an intimate
- Approximately 3% of male murder victims were killed by an intimate
- Of all female murder victims, the proportion killed by an intimate declined slightly until 1995 when the proportion began increasing (most reports indicate that the rate has been stabilizing in recent years)
- Of male murder victims, the proportion killed by an intimate has dropped during the reporting period
- Annually, at least 1500 women were murder victims from domestic violence
- Approximately one-third of injuries presenting to the emergency department were nonaccidental—the result of deliberate, intentional acts of violence
- Approximately one-third of female homicide victims over the age of 15 are killed by their husbands, ex-husbands, or boyfriends

Further data on murder offenders available through the United States FBI show that the ma-jority of offenders are over the age of 21, and slightly more likely to be black than white (FBI). Suicide might also result if the murderer takes his or her life following the violent act resulting in the death of the intimate partner. It has been reported that 74% of all murder—suicides involved an intimate partner. Of these reported cases, 96% were females killed by their intimate partner, with 75% of these cases occur-ring within the home (Data Available).

Notwithstanding the physical injuries suf-fered during violent intimate partner relation-ships, there is also a significant financial burden placed upon families, community, state, and local agencies. Best estimates indicate that the annual medical expense associated with do-mestic violence is at least $3–5 billion. Busi-nesses are reported to lose another $100 million in lost wages, sick leave, absenteeism, and loss of productivity (Centers for Disease Control and Prevention[c]).

The costs of intimate partner violence are not limited to financial costs. Several different adverse health outcomes are also associated with intimate partner violence. Some of the adverse effects include bruises, knife wounds, broken bones, traumatic back injuries, head-aches, chronic pain syndromes, and bladder and kidney infections (Breiding et al., 2005).

Crandall, Nathens, and Rivara have reported that women who suffered blunt intentional trauma exhibited very different injury patterns than those hospitalized for motor vehicle acci-dents and falls. The risk for facial injury was much higher among the domestic violence vic-tims than was seen in other mechanisms of injury. Head injuries were also more common in female victims of intimate partner violence (Centers for Disease Control and Prevention[c]; Crandall et al., 2004).

The author's (JDM) published thesis (McDowell, 1993) also found that female inten-tional trauma victims were more likely than women who were victims of motor vehicle accidents to:

- present for care on a delayed basis (not presenting immediately after the incident causing the injuries associated with the chief complaint),
- have had a previous facial/dental injury,
- have had a previous emergency department visit for injuries associated with intimate partner violence.

Not surprisingly, multiple injuries have also been reported to be suggestive of intimate partner violence. A study available on Medscape indicated that 85% of intimate partner violence victims were found to have injuries on more than one area of the body (McDowell, 1993; Burnett, 2015). The most common sites for injury were the eye, side of the face, the throat and neck, the upper and lower arms, upper and lower legs, injury to the mouth, the outside of the hand, the back, the scalp (McDowell, 1993; Burnett, 2015). Injuries to the shoulder and back were less common in intimate partner violence cases than were injuries to the shoulder and back found in those cases known to be caused accidentally. Of importance to the dentist is that nearly 80% of the injuries were in areas clearly visible (injuries to the head and hands) during even a cursory physical examination (McDowell, 1993; Burnett, 2015). Very similar patterns of injuries and location were found in a study by Sheridan and Nash (2007).

ABUSE DURING PREGNANCY

A pregnant woman is not immune to intentionally inflicted trauma (Fig. 7.5). In fact, intimate partner violence is common in pregnancy and frequently has multiple associated serious sequelae (Coker et al., 2004; Chambliss, 2008; Sharps et al., 2007). Perinatal intimate partner violence (IPV) is a common term used to describe violence before, during, and after pregnancy and up to 1 year following (postpartum) delivery

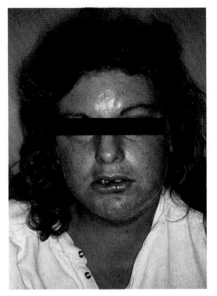

FIGURE 7.5 Lip and dental injuries from intentional blow to face of a pregnant woman.

(Sharps et al., 2007; Johnson et al., 2003). Important findings related to perinatal IPV developed from a metaanalysis study (Sharps et al., 2007) conducted from years 2001–06 include:

1. Increased risk for preterm delivery, low birthweight infants, and neonatal death.
2. Increased rates of vaginal bleeding over nonabused pregnant women.
3. Increased reporting rates for severe nausea and severe nausea with dehydration.
4. Increased rate of kidney infections, urinary tract infections, vaginal infections, and sexually transmissible infections.
5. Independent of insurance status (public or private), abused pregnant women are more likely to have preterm, low birthweight infants, and cesarean delivery.
6. IPV that occurs during a pregnancy is more likely to have an increased rate of premature rupture of the membranes over that which is seen in nonabused pregnant women.
7. Physiologic changes that include cardiac variability and higher than normal levels of maternal hormones.

A retrospective study at the University of Kentucky Medical Center reviewing the records of over 300 adult female intimate partner violence victims across the range of relationships (dating, cohabiting with, married, separated, divorced, pregnant, and not pregnant) who suffered facial trauma again demonstrated the importance that all health care providers (whether in their office or in the emergency department) need to be aware that battered women are more likely to have zygomaticomaxillary complex fractures, orbital blowout fractures, and intracranial injuries than women who were assaulted by unknown or unidentified assailants (Arosarena et al., 2009). In this study, female patients injured in falls had more nasal fractures, alveolar ridge fractures, and facial lacerations than female victims of intimate partner violence.

ELDER ABUSE AND NEGLECT

Most authorities on abuse of adults over the age of 65 (an arbitrary age at which the term "elderly" individual is generally used), define abusive behavior as intentional or neglectful acts that result in or may lead to harm of a vulnerable elderly individual. Although many organizations use similar terminology, the United States Health and Human Services Administration on Aging's National Center on Elder Abuse (NCEA) definitions are useful in investigations into elder abuse (The United States Department of Health and Human Services). The NCEA uses the below listed definitions for the various types of abuse and neglect. The investigator must remember that there can be significant overlap in the types of abuse and neglect that might be discovered in the course of an investigation. NCEA definitions are as follows:

Physical Abuse: Use of force to threaten or physically injure a vulnerable elder.

Emotional Abuse: Verbal attacks, threats, rejection, isolation, or belittling acts that cause or could cause mental anguish, pain, or distress to a senior.

Sexual abuse (many authors consider this a subset of physical abuse, but for their purposes, the NCEA chooses to consider sexual abuse separately from physical abuse): Sexual contact that is forced, tricked, threatened, or otherwise coerced upon a vulnerable elder, including anyone who is unable to grant consent.

Exploitation: Theft, fraud, misuse or neglect of authority, and use of undue influence as a lever to gain control over an older person's money or property.

Neglect: A caregiver's failure or refusal to provide for a vulnerable elder's safety, physical or emotional needs.

Abandonment: Desertion of a frail or vulnerable elder by anyone with a duty to care.

Self-neglect: An inability to understand the consequences of one's own actions or inaction, which leads to, or may lead to, harm or endangerment.

Some commonly referenced estimates by United States government agencies indicate that, at best, only one in six cases of elder abuse is reported. If we assume this statement to be representative of the problem, then it is easy to see why it is difficult to know the exact number of individuals over the age of 65 that are abused and neglected in the United States every year. Notwithstanding the challenges associated with establishing accurate estimates, the best available information from the NCEA (The United States Department of Health and Human Services, 2005 report) indicates the following:

- Between 1 and 2 million Americans aged 65 and older have been injured, exploited, or otherwise mistreated by someone upon whom they depended for care.
- The frequency of elder abuse range from 2% to 10% based on various surveys.
- For every case of elder abuse, neglect, exploitation, or self-neglect reported to authorities, about five go unreported.
- In the year 1996, nearly half a million adults aged 60 and over were abused and/or neglected in a domestic setting.

According to the NCEA (extensive information available at www.ncea.aoa.gov or by calling 1-800-677-1116), potential abusers include spouses, family members, adult children, personal acquaintances, professionals, or other persons in positions of trust or opportunistic strangers who prey on vulnerable older adults.

Many warning signs of physical abuse of an elderly individual might be confusing to a clinician or to an investigator because these injuries can appear to take on many different patterns (Zeitler, 2005; Wiseman, 2008). Because signs of the natural aging process, dermatologic conditions, or adverse reactions associated with medications can appear similar to the untrained individual and mistaken as inflicted trauma, special attention must be paid to the skin, muscles, and hard tissues of the head and neck complex during the investigation. If the investigator is not familiar with the soft and hard tissues of the head and neck, an individual (most often a physician) must be consulted to assess potential evidence of inflected trauma.

The reason that special attention must be paid to the head and neck complex during the initial stages of evidence collection is that the common signs of inflicted trauma can present in the head and neck complex. Some of the signs of nonaccidental (inflicted trauma) (Figs. 7.6 and 7.7) can

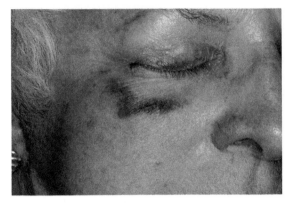

FIGURE 7.7 Facial bruising from zygomaticomaxillary complex fracture from blow to face.

include evidence of traumatic hair and tooth loss, rope or strap marks indicating physical restraint, multicolored bruises indicating injuries at various stages of healing, or injuries suggesting healing "by secondary intention." It must be remembered that evidence of delayed healing can indicate that there might be a purposeful denial of access to care for the vulnerable adult.

The National Committee for the Prevention of Elder Abuse (available at http://www.preventedlerabuse.org/elderabuse/) also reports that some of the indicators of elder abuse can include the following:

- Injuries that are unexplained or are implausible
- Family members provide different explanations of how injuries were sustained
- A history of similar injuries, and/or numerous hospitalizations
- Victims are brought to different medical facilities for treatment to prevent medical practitioners from observing a pattern of abuse
- Delay between onset of injury and seeking medical care

Not surprisingly, many of these indicators are very similar to those signs and symptoms of abuse/neglect seen in younger populations.

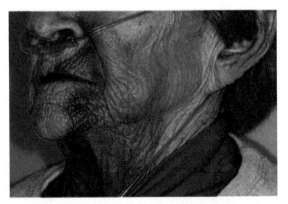

FIGURE 7.6 Example of facial bruising associated with mandibular body fracture in a case of elder abuse.

Several authors have reported that injuries to the head and neck area are not uncommon in elder abuse. Zeitler reported that approximately 30% of known elder abuse cases presented with neck and facial injuries. Injuries to the oral and perioral soft tissues, jaw fractures, and fractured or avulsed teeth have been reported to be indicators of elder abuse (Wiseman, 2008). Because many oral health care providers are aware that signs of intentional trauma are often seen in the orofacial structures, a dentist or otolaryngologist can be especially helpful during the investigation into a potential elder abuse case.

Whenever possible, the investigative process should utilize the skills of a multidisciplinary and/or interdisciplinary team. The clinician/ investigator should not hesitate to consult with medical radiologists, dentists (specifically oral and maxillofacial radiologists) who can be extremely helpful in diagnosing radiographic evidence of injuries that might be associated with the instant attack or discovering radiographic evidence of previous trauma. Differing diagnostic images (flat plane radiography, magnetic resonance imaging, computed tomography, and other imaging techniques) can be just as valuable as are photographs in the prosecution of individuals causing intentional trauma.

TECHNIQUES FOR RECORDING EVIDENCE OF TRAUMATIC INJURIES

A wide range of injury locations and patterns can occur as a result of all forms of intrafamily/ relationship violence. Initially, the most important step is to assure that proper medical/dental attention is directed to treating the injuries associated with the traumatic event. During or immediately after treatment has begun, priority should be given to seeking out emotional/psychosocial support for the victim. Unless photographs or video recordings can be made before or during treatment, evidence might be lost during the process of treating the injuries. During treatment in the emergency department or the dental treatment facility, it is necessary to assess neurologic status, maintain an airway, control bleeding, suture lacerations, stabilize fractures, or replace avulsed teeth prior to making photographs. If immediate intervention needs to be initiated to treat the injuries, treatment takes precedence over evidence collection. If sutures need to be placed, some evidence of trauma might be altered as tissues are replaced in physiologic position to control bleeding, reduce scarring, or reduce the possibility of tissue necrosis.

There are excellent references in the professional literature about the steps that need to be taken to assure the accuracy of the evidence collected (Golden and Wright, 2005; Wright and Golden, 2010). Independent of whether film or digital imaging are used, the general principles of accurate photography must be followed. A simple step-by-step procedure is as follows:

- First, make certain that there are orientation photographs made that clearly show the anatomic location of the injury or injuries. Date, time, and location of where the examination is being made should be included in the beginning photograph and the final photograph made.
- Following orientation photographs, photographs of the injury with a scale in place must be made. The ABFO scale is an excellent reference scale used by many dentists, medical examiners, and other investigators.
- If available, alternate light imaging (ALI) or/ or fluorescent image techniques might be utilized. Many regional crime labs or law enforcement agencies will have cameras or lighting systems that can be used upon request. If the photographer in the clinical setting is not familiar with the ALI techniques, a request for assistance often results in an offer to help.

If the clinician or investigator observes an injury pattern that is suspected as being a bite-mark injury, salivary evidence should be collected prior to cleaning, debriding, or disinfecting the area. As appropriate to the case, making impressions (molds) of the area should be performed prior to suturing lacerations or other breaks in the skin. Salivary evidence collection procedures should be followed precisely to ensure that there is no contamination of the area with the investigator's or the collector's genetic information.

When the assault results in death, it is essential to follow protocols established by the ABFO, the medical examiner's office, or the coroner's office. The basic steps for recording skin injuries should be followed identically as performed for a living victim. If indicated, tissues may be retained consistent with established protocols. Radiographic images are also essential to documenting fractured bones or teeth.

CONCLUSION

Violence is a widespread problem found in all countries and cultures. Analyses of prison populations reveal that many of those incarcerated are in penal institutions because of their witnessing as a child or later in life participating in some form of violent behavior. Much of this violent behavior witnessed or acted out occurred in the home or within intimate relationships. A review of the professional literature confirms what has been thought for many years—most of the injuries associated with inflicted trauma occur in the head, neck, and maxillofacial complex. Because these injuries are often clearly visible, any number of persons—including oral health care providers—might start the intervention process on behalf of the victim. Plans should be in place wherein intervention can appropriately begin on behalf of the suspected victim of violent behavior. The domestic violence hotline can be reached telephonically by calling 1-800-799-SAFE (7233).

Whether the suspected victim is a child, adult, or elderly individual, calling 9-1-1 is appropriate. For suspected elder abuse cases, the national Eldercare Locator's number is 1-800-6771116. The Eldercare locator can direct the caller to local Adult Protective Services agencies or direct the caller which agency to contact on behalf of the suspected victim. Specific state and local support can also be found online at: http://www.nccafv.org/state_elder_abuse_hotlines.htm.

Absent an action plan on behalf of the victim, an investigation cannot begin into the potential cause(s) of the injury patterns discovered. Without an investigation, intervention is not likely to begin on behalf of the victim. If interventional steps are not initiated, the assaults might increase in frequency and severity, potentially leading to serious sequelae including homicide (Johnson et al., 2003).

Clinicians and investigators must assure that they are adequately trained in recognizing the signs and symptoms most often associated with violent behaviors directed against persons [intentionally inflicted trauma] (Sharps et al., 2007; Johnson et al., 2003). They must further assure that the evidence they have collected is admissible in any criminal or civil proceeding. Each clinician or investigator must be able to testify that the evidence that was collected is a true and accurate representation of the injuries that were detected.

Every health care provider—especially oral health professionals—must be aware of the signs and symptoms associated with intentionally inflicted trauma. Without recognition, intervention on behalf of the victim cannot begin.

CHILD ABUSE AND MALTREATMENT

(Perspectives from a Child Abuse Pediatrician)
Since Henry Kempe's publication of "The battered child syndrome" (Kempe et al., 1962) over 50 years ago, child maltreatment has emerged on

the public consciousness as a prevalent and morbid (Felitti et al., 1998) threat to child and adult health. The first half-century of professional practice in child abuse has yielded robust knowledge on the prevention, recognition, and treatment of child abuse.

EPIDEMIOLOGY

One source of information regarding incidence of child abuse is the National Child Abuse and Neglect Data System (NCANDS) (US Department of Health and Human Services, Administration for Children and Families 2015). NCANDS receives reports of child abuse substantiated by state child welfare organizations. In 2014, about 3,188,000 children (4.92% of US children) were the subject of a report to a child protection agency. About 583, 000 (0.91% of US children) were the victims of substantiated abuse. Among children with substantiated abuse, 79.5% were neglected, 18.0% experienced physical abuse, 9.0% sexual abuse, and 8.7% psychological maltreatment.

NCANDS, however, underestimates the true incidence of abuse, as it includes only abuse that was reported to and substantiated by state authorities. The National Incidence Survey (NIS) (Sedlak et al., 2010) surveys professional observers (or sentinels) who have regular contact with children and who are trained to recognize abuse. Sentinels are recruited to obtain a sample representative of the population of the United States. NIS-4 estimates that 1.25 million children (1.7% of US children) experienced maltreatment in the 2005–2006 study year. Of these children, NIS estimates 771,700 (61%) were neglected, 323,000 (26%) were physically abused, 135,000 (11%) were sexually abused, and 148,500 (12%) experienced emotional abuse.

Rates of substantiated sexual abuse reported to NCANDS have been declining since the early 1990s. Despite initial concern that the decline might reflect stricter substantiation requirements and shrinking investigative budgets, many professionals (Finklehor and Jones, 2012) believe that at least part of the decline is explained by an actual decrease in the incidence of sexual abuse. Data regarding physical abuse are less clear. Reported and substantiated physical abuse have decreased, but two measures of severe physical abuse, hospitalizations, and deaths due to physical abuse have not declined over the same period.

RECOGNIZING ABUSE AND NEGLECT

The diagnosis of child abuse rests primarily on clinical suspicion and history taking, with smaller contributions from physical examination, radiology, and laboratory evaluation. In rare instances, more traditional forensic evidence, such as bitemarks, trace DNA, or patterned injuries are found. When present, forensic or other objective findings may strongly corroborate or refute a history given by the caregiver, the child, and others. An injury history that is internally inconsistent or is incompatible with objective findings is concerning for abuse. The comprehensive evaluation of a child who may have been physically (Christian, CW and the Committee on Child Abuse and Neglect, 2015) or sexually (Adams et al., 2015) abused is beyond the scope of this chapter. Many children's hospitals host child protection teams, often headed by a board-certified child abuse pediatrician (Block and Palusci, Child abuse pediatrics: a new pediatric subspecialty 2006), to complete these specialized evaluations.

Recognition of child abuse, in contrast, is an essential skill for all health care providers. Child abuse frequently occurs in private to children who are unable or unwilling to disclose their abuse. Perpetrators rarely confess to abusing the child when presenting with an injury. Health care providers' failure to recognize subtle signs of physical abuse has been associated with repeated injury (Sheets et al., 2013) and death (Jenny et al., 1999).

PHYSICAL ABUSE

The cardinal manifestation of physical abuse is an injury in a child that does not correspond to the reported mechanism, or a serious injury for which no mechanism is known. For example, bruises in any location are unusual before the child begins to walk along furniture at an age of 10 or 11 months (Sugar et al., 1999). Bruises to the trunk, ear, or neck in children under 4 years of age (mnemonic TEN-4) are also concerning for physical abuse (Pierce et al., 2010). A history of a young child with a serious and painful injury, such as a significant burn or fracture, but no history of a definite injury event should similarly be questioned.

An injury history is also indicative for abuse if it is inconsistently reported to various professionals. Caregivers of children who have been injured accidentally present remarkably consistent accounts of the child's injury whereas perpetrators of child abuse are looking for a story that arouses the least suspicion. Written documentation of the details of the account provided to each professional is essential in these cases.

Certain types of objects leave recognizable patterns (Kaczor et al., 2006). Slap marks (Fig. 7.8) typically outline the fingers, resulting in a characteristic pattern. A loop mark (Fig. 7.9) results when a flexible object is doubled over and the child is struck with the resulting loop. A child struck with a flexible object may also have bruises that wrap around the curvature of the body, which would not happen if the child fell against a rigid object. The analysis of bitemarks is discussed elsewhere in this book. Sometimes the object causing an injury will leave a recognizable pattern unique to that object (Fig. 7.10 A, B, and C).

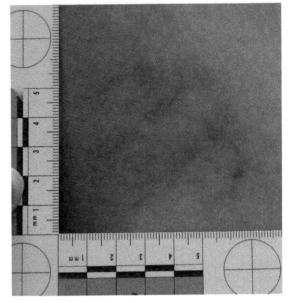

FIGURE 7.8   Facial slap marks.

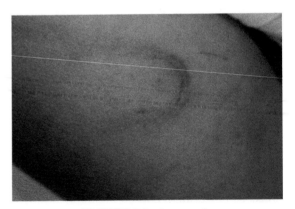

FIGURE 7.9   Loop mark.

Some specific findings of physical abuse can be noted in the head and neck (Kellogg and Committee on Child Abuse and Neglect, 2005a,b). Oral trauma may be the result of objects or caustic substances being forced into the mouth. Discolored teeth may suggest pulpal necrosis resulting from prior trauma. A torn frenulum appropriately raises concerns for abuse, but may also be the result of accidental injury (Maguire et al., 2007) (Starr et al., 2015).

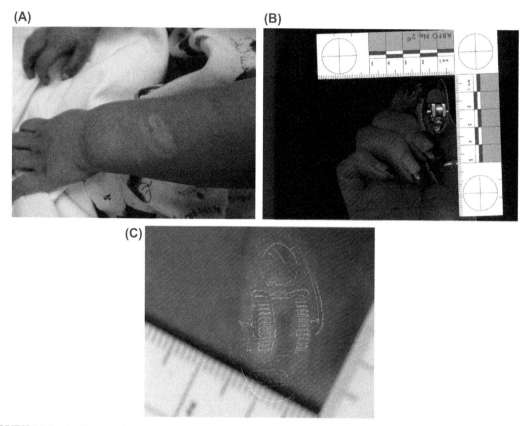

FIGURE 7.10   (A) Patterned injury on child's left forearm. (B) Bic lighter using American Board of Forensic Odontology No. 2 ruler for scale. (C) 1:1 overlay of lighter over patterned injury seen in (A).

ABUSIVE HEAD TRAUMA

Previously known as shaken baby syndrome, abusive head trauma (AHT) can occur via multiple mechanisms including vigorous shaking or impact to the head. AHT is the leading cause of infant death from injury and the leading cause of serious head injury in children (Keenan et al., 2003). In 2009, the American Academy of Pediatrics recommended the term "abusive head trauma" emphasizing that shaking is one of several mechanisms of inflicted neurotrauma in infants (Christian, Block and Committee on Child Abuse and Neglect, 2009).

The most common findings in the presentation of AHT is an acute neurologic injury associated with subdural hematomas or retinal hemorrhages (Levin, 2010). Other associated symptoms include apnea, seizures, long bone fractures, and rib fractures (Maguire et al., 2010). The differential diagnosis of subdural hemorrhage or retinal hemorrhage in an infant is broad, so AHT cannot be diagnosed mechanically based on a "triad" of findings. Despite this, AHT is the most common cause of neurotrauma in infants, and a careful evaluation for abuse is necessary.

Recently, a minority of practitioners have questioned the diagnosis of AHT(Tuerkheimer, 2009). A detailed description of data supporting the diagnosis of AHT (Narang, A Daubert analysis of abusive head trauma/shaken baby syndrome 2011) is beyond the scope of this chapter. Discredited explanations for severe neurotrauma in infants (Narang et al., 2013), such as ordinary household falls, CPR, or hypoxia, should not prevent practitioners from evaluating and reporting concerns for abuse.

NEGLECT

Child neglect is the failure of a parent or another responsible adult to provide necessary food, shelter, clothing, supervision, or medical care to a child. Many authors specifically exclude from the definition of neglect failures due to parent's poverty or other lack of resources.

In young children, the most frequent symptom of neglect is failure to thrive. Failure to thrive is difficult to define specifically and has a long list of differential diagnoses (Jaffe, 2011). An overwhelming majority of failure to thrive, however, is caused by inadequate nutrition. When a history and physical fails to reveal difficulties in feeding or absorption, a witnessed feeding trial is indicated (Block et al., 2005). A significant weight gain after several days, or better weeks, of appropriate feeding is sufficient for the diagnosis.

In older children neglect takes on a more varied presentation. The diagnosis of abuse will depend on history taking, possibly supplemented by a home visit by child protection authorities. Neglectful supervision results when a child is injured as a result of an accident the adult should have prevented. A variety of physical, emotional, or educational problems can result from parental inaction, each of which would require a careful evaluation for neglect.

Medical neglect occurs when a parent does not seek appropriate medical (Jenny and Committe on Child Abuse and Neglect, Recognzing and responding to medical neglect 2007) or dental (Kellogg and Committee on Child Abuse and Neglect, 2005a,b) care. Medical neglect includes both failure to seek care for clear need or failure to complete clearly indicated care recommended by a practitioner.

SEXUAL ABUSE

Sexual abuse occurs when "a child is engaged in sexual activities that he or she cannot comprehend, for which he or she is developmentally unprepared and cannot give consent, and/or that violate the law or social taboos of society." (Kellogg and Committee on Child Abuse and Neglect, 2005a,b) Sexual abuse most frequently attains professional attention after the child discloses abuse. Children who have been sexually abused will frequently have few or no behavioral or physical (Adams et al., 1994) (Kellogg, Menard and Santos, Genital anatomy in pregnant adolescents: "Normal" does not mean "nothing happened." 2004) signs that are specific to sexual abuse.

Frequently young, and often preverbal, children are presented to health care providers with behaviors that have raised concern for sexual abuse. Many parents are unaware of the range of normative sexual behaviors in children. Table 7.1 displays some common and less common sexual behaviors in children aged 2–6. (Kellogg and Committee on Child Abuse and Neglect, The evaluation of sexual behaviors in children 2009) Normative sexual behaviors in children generally are brief, playful, and are not preferred to other desirable activities.

Sexual abuse is rarely suspected due to positive STD tests or physical findings. Absent a clear history of vertical transmission, the identification of an STD in a prepubertal child should prompt an evaluation for sexual abuse, even in absence of a disclosure (Adams et al., 2015). Acute injuries of the genitals and anus can be indicative of physical or sexual abuse. However, anogenital erythema, anal dilation, and a vaginal opening that appears "too big" are complaints frequently noted in children with no history of sexual abuse.

As mentioned previously, sexual abuse is most frequently discovered because the child

TABLE 7.1   Normative and Concerning Sexual Behaviors in Preschool Children

Normative Behaviors Seen in Children With no History of Abuse	Behaviors Concerning for Sexual Abuse or Other Trauma
• Touches own genitals, possibly in public. • Rubs own genitals on objects. • Touches genitals or breasts of infants, peers, or adults. • Tries to look at peers or adults who are naked. • Crude mimicking of sexual acts.	• Asks another person to engage in a specific sexual act. • Inserting objects into genitals. • Explicitly simulates intercourse. • Sexual behaviors involving force, aggression, or coercion. • Sexual behaviors that result in emotional distress or physical pain.
• Intermittent • Spontaneous • Not preferred to other desired activities. • Stop when corrected by an adult.	• Frequent • Variety of sexual behaviors • Child becomes angry when distracted from sexual behaviors.

discloses abuse. The response a child receives to disclosure of sexual abuse may significantly impact the child (Melville et al., 2014). An adult to whom a child discloses sexual abuse should express belief in the disclosure and indicate willingness to help the child. While an unexpected disclosure of sexual abuse is most disconcerting for the adult, a child may perceive an adult's unease as a judgment of the child or disbelief in the disclosure. Professionals will be better prepared to respond to disclosures of abuse if they are familiar with child abuse reporting and response resources in their community.

TALKING TO CHILDREN ABOUT ABUSE

Often, the best way to find out what has happened to children is to ask them. In the proper environment, children as young as 3 years can provide reliable information about their experiences (Sjöberg and Lindblad, 2002) (Saywitz et al., 1991). Unfortunately, improper interview techniques can result in false disclosures of abuse (Garven et al., 1998). In the United States, forensic interviews for suspected abuse are best conducted by professionals with specific training in forensic interviewing (Newlin et al., 2015).

Conversely, some practitioners appear to believe that any conversation with an abused child should be deferred to a specialist. At times, real world urgencies—such as needing to provide for a child's immediate comfort, safety, or medical care—require an untrained professional to talk to a child about abuse. One such circumstance is when a child initially discloses abuse—a response that the child has disclosed to the "wrong" adult may discourage future disclosure. Such interviews should be limited to items that the child wished to disclose spontaneously or information for which there is a specific and immediate need.

When talking to children about abuse, it is essential to avoid leading or suggestive questions. A good rule of thumb is that a question requiring a "yes" or "no" answer is likely to be too leading. Requesting the child to provide a detail improves reliability significantly. The most reliable responses occur when the child recounts a narrative or many events in a sequence surrounding the abuse (Lamb et al., 1998).

Interviewers should also avoid reinforcing, positively or negatively, the child's disclosure or nondisclosure of abuse (Schriber et al., 2006). While the interviewer may acknowledge that disclosing abuse is difficult, the interviewer should not praise the child for disclosing abuse. Similarly, the interviewer should not scold the child for failing to disclose. A subtle, but perilous, form of negative reinforcement is repeating a question after an unexpected answer. A repeated question implies that the first response was somehow inappropriate.

MANDATED REPORTING

In the United States, many professionals are required to report suspected child abuse or neglect. Although state laws vary with regard to who must report abuse, federal law (42 USC 5100 et seq. n.d.) requires states to implement a mandated reporting system. Health care providers are mandated reporters in all 50 states (Child Welfare Information Gateway, 2014). State laws and the Health Insurance Portability and Accountability Act (Jenny and Committee on Child Abuse and Neglect, Policy statement—Child abuse, confidentiality, and the health insurance portability and accountability act 2010) each allow providers to disclose otherwise confidential information in the context of a mandated report.

Mandated reporters are required to report a "reasonable suspicion" (Narang and Melville, Legal issues in child maltreatment 2014) rather than knowledge of abuse. Health care practitioners need not, and generally should not, investigate or otherwise verify their concerns prior to reporting. Many physicians have difficulty recognizing and reporting suspicion of child abuse, especially when the diagnosis of abuse is unclear. In one survey (Levi and Brown, 2005), 40% of pediatricians indicated that the likelihood of child abuse would need to exceed 60% for the physician to report.

Perhaps the best legal definition (Narang and Melville, Legal issues in child maltreatment 2014) of reasonable suspicion comes from the US Supreme Court in Illinois v. Wardlow. (Illinois V Wardlow, 2000). In that case, the government needed to establish "reasonable suspicion" to justify a pat-down search of a suspected drug dealer. The court defined "reasonable suspicion" as "a minimal level of objective justification" and "more than an inchoate, unparticularized suspicion or hunch." Thus a professional who believed that child abuse likely did not occur could, nonetheless, have a duty to report a "minimal" level of concern for abuse.

Despite a low evidentiary burden and legal immunity for good faith reporting (Child Welfare Information Gateway, 2011), many professionals fail to report even significant concerns for child abuse (Flaherty et al., 2008). During a physician focus group on the topic (Flaherty et al., 2004), each physician described a single incident, positive or negative, that influenced that physician's attitude regarding mandated reporting. Disincentives to reporting abuse identified by the focus group included fear of upsetting the patient's family, lack of feedback from Child protective services (CPS) regarding the referral, prior reports having been unfounded by CPS, and a belief that the provider could help the family more effectively than CPS. Physicians also identified systemic barriers to reporting including time commitment, difficulty explaining why a skeletal survey is necessary, and difficulty obtaining insurance reimbursement for high-quality skeletal surveys. Another physician described an incident in which undetected child abuse lead to a critical injury as a strong motivator for future reporting.

CHILD ADVOCACY CENTERS

Responding to a report of child abuse requires the skill of many professionals including medical, law enforcement, child protection, and mental health. Independent responses by these agencies lead to repeated, duplicative interviews and poor coordination of services. In 1985, Madison County, Alabama instituted a joint response to allegations of child abuse including medical, mental health, law enforcement, and child protection professionals (National Children's Advocacy Center n.d.). This collaboration created the first child advocacy center (CAC) By 2015, 777 CACs had been accredited worldwide (National Children's Aliance n.d.a,b).

The CAC model benefits both the child and the participating partners (National Children's

Aliance n.d. a,b). Children seen at a CAC are more likely to receive medical exams (Walsh et al., 2007) and specialized mental health treatment (Smith et al., 2006). Communities that instituted CACs have seen significant increases in felony child abuse prosecutions (Miller and Rubin, 2009) and sentences assigned (Cross et al., 2008) in child abuse cases. Families of children thought to have been abused report greater satisfaction with interviews done at a CAC (Jones et al., 2007).

While CACs are as diverse as the communities they serve, accredited centers meet a common set of standards (National Children's Aliance, 2015a,b). A CAC must host a multidisciplinary team consisting of: law enforcement, CPS, prosecution, medical, mental health, and victim advocacy professionals. During regular multidisciplinary case reviews partners coordinate their response and track cases to ensure efficient transitions between the disciplines.

CACs maintain a child-focused environment that is designed to welcome children and put them at ease. An interview room allows the forensic interviewer to speak with the child alone while other team members observe from a separate room. As mentioned above, trained interviewers assist the child to make a complete disclosure without leading or suggesting responses to the child. Forensic interviews are recorded to reduce the need for repeated interviews.

In CACs that offer medical services on site, the medical examination is frequently scheduled immediately following the forensic interview. A comprehensive, head-to-toe evaluation serves to reassure patients and families that the child's body is normal and healthy. Injuries are photographed to facilitate follow up examinations, peer review, quality assurance, and legal testimony.

Other services may be provided before, during, or after the principal CAC evaluation. Victim advocates provide information about the CAC process and resources available to victims. Mental health therapists treat trauma symptoms and other psychological sequelae of child abuse. Child protection authorities work with the child's family or other caregivers to ensure ongoing safety for the child.

CONCLUSION

The first 50 years following Henry Kempe's "battered child syndrome" have seen a dramatic shift in how society views and responds to the very real problems of child abuse and neglect. A diagnosis once denied and ignored is now the subject of over 3 million official reports a year. Many jurisdictions have established multidisciplinary child protection teams that provide an effective and coordinated response to concerns for child abuse or neglect.

For professionals living in areas served by multidisciplinary teams, the remaining components of an effective child protection system are recognition and reporting of abuse. Recognition of abuse can be difficult, especially because there is no single observation or sign that is diagnostic for abuse. Careful vigilance and an appropriately low threshold for abuse reporting are the obligation of every health care professional.

References

42 USC 5100 et seq. n.d.

Adams, J.A., Harper, K., Knudson, S., Revilla, J., 1994. Examination findings in legally confirmed child sexual abuse: it's normal to be normal. Pediatrics 94 (3), 310–371.

Adams, J.A., et al., 2015. Updated guidelines for the medical assessment and care of children who may have been sexually abused. Journal of Pediatric and Adolescent Gynecology 1–7.

Arosarena, O.A., Fritsch, T.A., Hsueh, Y., Aynehchi, B., Haug, R., January/February 2009. Maxillofacial injuries and violence against women. Archives of Facial Plastic Surgery 11 (1), 48–52.

Block, R.W., Palusci, V.J., 2006. Child abuse pediatrics: a new pediatric subspecialty. The Journal of Pediatrics 148 (6), 711–712.

Block, R.W., Krebs, N.F., Committee on Child Abuse And Neglect, Committee on Nutrition, 2005. Failure to thrive as a manifestation of child neglect. Pediatrics 116 (5), 1234–1237.

Breiding, M.J., Black, M.C., Ryan, G.W., 2005. Chronic disease and health risk behaviors associated with intimate partner violence—18 U.S. states/territories. Annals of Epidemiology 2008 (18), 538—544.

Bureau of Justice Statistics, 1993-2011. Intimate partner violence: attributes of victimization. Available online at: http://www.bjs.gov/content/intimate/ipv.cfm.

Burnett, L.B., January 13, 2015. Domestic Violence. Updated. In: Brenner, B.E. (Ed.). Article available on Medscape at: http://emedicine.medscape.com/article/805546_clinical.

Centers for Disease Control and Prevention[a] Preventing Intimate Partner Violence, Sexual Violence and Child Maltreatment. pp. 1—7: Available online: cdc.gov/ncipc/pub-res/research_agenda/07_violence.

Centers for Disease Control and Prevention, 2014. Understanding Teen Dating Violence. Fact Sheet. National Center for Injury Prevention and Control, Division of Violence Prevention.

Centers for Disease Control and Prevention[c]: Intimate Partner Violence: Consequences. Available at: https://cdc.gov/violenceprevention/intimatepartnerviolence/consequences.html.

Chambliss, L.R., June 2008. Intimate partner violence and implication for pregnancy. Clinical Obstetrics and Gynecology 51 (2), 385—397.

Child Welfare Information Gateway, 2011. Immunity for Reporters of Child Abuse and Neglect. https://www.childwelfare.gov/pubPDFs/immunity.pdf.

Child Welfare Information Gateway, 2014. Mandatory Reporters of Child Abuse and Neglect. https://www.childwelfare.gov/pubPDFs/manda.pdf#page=1&view=Professionals. Required to Report.

Christian, C.W., the Committee on Child Abuse and Neglect, 2015. The evaluation of suspected child physical abuse. Pediatrics 135 (5), e1337—e1354.

Christian, C.W., Block, R., Committee on Child Abuse and Neglect, 2009. Abusive head trauma in infants and children. Pediatrics 123 (5), 1409—1411.

Coker, A.L., Sanderson, M., Dong, B., July 2004. Partner violence during pregnancy and adverse pregnancy outcomes. Paediatric and Perinatal Epidemiology 18 (4), 260—269.

Crandall, M.L., Nathens, A.B., Rivara, F.P., 2004. Injury patterns among female trauma patients. Recognizing intentional injury. Journal of Trauma — Injury, Infection and Critical Care 57, 42—45.

Cross, T.P, Jones, L.M., Walsh, W.A., Simone, M., Kolko, D., 2008. Evaluating children's advocacy center's response to child sexual abuse. Sociology Scholarship. Accessed 4 2015, 11. http://scholars.unh.edu/soc_facpub/106.

Felitti, V.J., et al., 1998. Relationship of childhood abuse and household dysfunction to many od the leading causes of death in adults. American Journal of Preventive Medicine 14 (4), 245—258.

Finklehor, D., Jones, L., 2012. Have sexual and physical abuse declined since the 1990's? Crimes Against Children Research Center. http://scholars.unh.edu/cgi/viewcontent.cgi?article=1060&context=ccrc.

Flaherty, E.G., Jones, R., Sege, R., The Child Abuse Recognition Experience Study Reserch Group, 2004. Telling their stories: primary care practitioner's experience evaluating and reporting injuries caused by child abuse. Child Abuse & Neglect 28, 939—945.

Flaherty, E.G., et al., 2008. From suspicion of physical; child abuse to reporting: primary care clinician decision-making. Pediatrics 122 (3), 611—619.

Garven, S., Wood, J.M., Malpass, R.S., Shaw, J.S., 1998. More than suggestion: the effect of interviewing techniques from the McMartin preschool case. Journal of Applied Psychology 83 (3), 347—359.

Golden, G., Wright, F., 2005. Photography: noninvasive analysis (Chapter 7). In: Dorion, R.B.J. (Ed.), Bitemark Evidence. Marcel Dekker publisher, pp. 169—182.

Halpern, C.T., Oslak, S.G., Young, M.I., Martin, S.I., Kupper, L.L., 2001. Partner violence among adolescents in opposite-sex romantic relationships: findings from the National Longitudinal Study of Adolescent Health. American Journal of Public Health 91, 1679—1685.

Jaffe, A.C., 2011. Failure to thrive: current clinical concepts. Pediatrics 32 (3), 100—107 in review.

Jenny, C., Committe on Child Abuse and Neglect, 2007. Recognzing and responding to medical neglect. Pediatrics 120 (6), 1385—1389.

Jenny, C., Committee on Child Abuse and Neglect, 2010. Policy statement — child abuse, confidentiality, and the health insurance portability and accountability act. Pediatrics 125 (1), 197—201.

Jenny, C., Hymel, K.P., Ritzen, A., Reinert, S.E., Hay, T.C., 1999. Analysis of missed cases of abusive head trauma. Journal of the American Medical Association 281 (7), 621—626.

Johnson, J.K., Haider, f, Ellis, K., Lindow, S.W., 2003. The prevalence of domestic violence in pregnant women. International Journal of Obstetrics and Gynecology 110 (3), 272—275.

Jones, L., Cross, T., Walsh, W.A., Simone, M., 2007. Do children's advocacy centers improve families' experiences of child sexual abuse investigations? Child Abuse & Neglect 31 (10), 1069—1085.

Kaczor, K., Clyde Pierce, M., Makoroff, K., Corey, T.S., 2006. Bruising and child physical abuse. Clinical Pediatric Emergency Medicine 7 (3), 153—160.

Keenan, H.T., Runyan, D.K., Marshall, S.W., Alice Nocera, M., Merten, D.F., 2003. A population-based study of inflicted traumatic brain injury in young children. Journal of the American Medical Association 290 (5), 621—626.

Kellogg, N.D., Committee on Child Abuse and Neglect, 2009. The evaluation of sexual behaviors in children. Pediatrics 124 (3), 992—998.

Kellogg, N.D., Committee on Child Abuse and Neglect, 2005a. Oral and dental aspects of child abuse and neglect. Pediatrics 116 (6), 1565—1568.

Kellogg, N., Committee on Child Abuse and Neglect, 2005b. The evaluation of sexual abuse in children. Pediatrics 116 (2), 506—512.

Kellogg, N.D., Menard, S.W., Santos, A., 2004. Genital anatomy in pregnant adolescents: "Normal" does not mean "nothing happened.". Pediatrics 113 (1), e-67—e69.

Kempe, C.H., Silverman, F.N., Steele, B.F., Droegemueller, W., Silver, H.K., 1962. The battered-child syndrome. Journal of the American Medical Association 181 (1), 17—24.

Krebs, C.P., Lindquist, C.H., Warner, T.D., Fisher, B.S., Martin, S.L., 2007. The Campus Sexual Assault Survey. Available through the National Institutes of Justice: https://www.ncjrs.gov/pdffiles1/nij/grants/221153.pdf.

Lamb, M.E., Sternberg, K.J., Esplin, P.W., 1998. Conducting investigative interviews of alleged sexual abuse victims. Child Abuse & Neglect 27 (8), 813—823.

Levi, B.H., Brown, G., 2005. Reasonable suspicion: a study of Pennsylvania pediatricians regarding child abuse. Pediatrics 116 (1), e5—e12.

Levin, A.V., 2010. Retinal hemorrhages in abusive head trauma. Pediatrics 128 (5), 961—970.

Maguire, S., Hunter, B., Hunter, L., 2007. Diagnosing Abuse: a systemic review of torn frenum and other intra-oral injuries. Archives of Diseases in Childhood 92, 1113—1117.

Maguire, S.A., Mary Kemp, A., Caroline Lumb, R., Farewell, D.M., 2010. Estimating the probability of abusive head trauma: a pooled analysis. Pediatrics 128 (3), e550—e564.

McDowell, J.D., 1993. A Comparison of Facial Fractures in Victims of Motor Vehicle Accidents and Battered Women (Master of Science thesis). The University of Texas Graduate School of Biomedical Science at San Antonio.

Melville, J.D., Kellogg, N.D., Perez, N., Lukefahr, J.L., 2014. Assessment for self-blame and trauma symptoms during the medical evaluation of suspected sexual abuse. Child Abuse & Neglect 38, 851—857.

Miller, A., Rubin, D., 2009. The contribution of children's advocacy centers to felony prosecutions of child sexual abuse. Child Abuse & Neglect 33 (1), 12—18.

Narang, S.K., 2011. A daubert analysis of abusive head trauma/shaken baby syndrome. Houston Journal of Health Law and Policy 11, 505.

Narang, S.K., Melville, J.D., 2014. Legal issues in child maltreatment. Pediatric Clinics of North America 61, 1049—1058.

Narang, S.K., Melville, J.D., Greeley, C.S., Anderst, J.D., Carpenter, S.L., Spivack, B., 2013. A Daubert analysis of abusive head trauma/shaken baby syndrome — part II: an examination of the differential diagnosis. Houston Journal of Health Law and Policy 13 (2), 203—327.

National Children's Advocacy Center. History. n.d. http://www.nationalcac.org/table/about/history/.

National Children's Alliance. NCA Policy Brief. n.d. http://www.nationalchildrensalliance.org/sites/default/files/download-files/15%20NCA%20Brief%20Editable_FINAL.pdf.

National Children's Alliance. Our Story. n.d. http://www.nationalchildrensalliance.org/our-story.

Newlin, C., et al., 2015. Child Forensic Interviewing: Best Practices. Office of Juvenile Justice and Delinquency Prevention.

Pierce, M.C., Kaczor, K., Aldridge, S., O'Flynn, J., Lorenz, D.J., 2010. Bruising characteristics discriminating physical child abuse from accidental trauma. Pediatrics 125 (1), 67—74.

Rice, E., Rhoades, H., Winetrobe, H., Sanchez, M., Montoya, J., Plant, K., October 2012. Sexually explicit phone messaging associated with sexual risk among adolescents. Pediatrics 130 (4), 667—673.

Saywitz, K.J., Goodman, G.S., Nicholas, E., Moan, S.F., 1991. Children's memories of a physical examination involving genital touch: Implications for reports of child sexual abuse. Journal of Consulting and Clinical Psychology 59 (5), 682—691.

Schriber, N., et al., 2006. Sugggestive interviewing in the McMartin Preschool and Kelly Michaels daycare abuse cases: a case study. Social Influence 1 (1), 16—47.

Sedlak, A.J., et al., 2010. Fourth National Incidence Study of Child Abuse and Neglect (NIS—4): Report to Congress. U.S. Department of Health and Human Services, Administration for Children. http://www.acf.hhs.gov/sites/default/files/opre/nis4_report_congress_full_pdf_jan2010.pdf.

Sharps, P.W., Laughon, K., Giangrade, S.K., April 2007. Intimate partner violence and the childbearing year: maternal and infant health consequences. Trauma, Violence & Abuse 8 (2), 105—116.

Sheets, L.K., Leach, M.E., Koszewski, I.J., Lessmeier, A.M., Nugent, M., Simpson, P., 2013. Sentinel injuries in infants evaluated for child physical abuse. Pediatrics 131 (4), 701—707.

Sheridan, D.J., Nash, K.R., July 2007. Acute injury patterns of intimate partner violence victims. Trauma, Violence & Abuse 8 (3), 281—289.

Sjöberg, R.L., Lindblad, F., 2002. Limited disclosure of sexual abuse in children whose experiences were documented by videotape. American Journal of Psychiatry 312—314.

Smith, D.W., Witte, T.H., Fricker-Elhai, A.E., 2006. Service outcomes in physical and sexual abuse cases: A comparison of child advocacy center-based and standard services. Child Maltreatment 11 (4), 354–460.

Starr, M., Klein, E.J., Sugar, N., 2015. A perplexing case of child abuse: oral injuries in abuse and physician reporting responsibilities. Pediatric Emergency Care 31 (8), 851–853.

Sugar, N.F., Taylor, J.A., Feldman, K.W., Puget Sound Research Network, 1999. Bruises in infants and toddlers: those who don't cruise rarely bruise. Archives of Pediatrics and Adolescent Medicine 153 (4), 399–403.

The Costs of Intimate Partner. United States Federal Bureau of Investigation. Reports and Publications. Campus Attacks. Targeted Violence Affecting Institutes of Higher Education. Available online at: https://www2.edu.gov/admins/lead/safety/campusattacks.pdf.

The United States Department of Health and Human Services, Administration on Aging, National Center on Elder Abuse available at http://www.ncea.aog.gov.Library/Data/index.aspx.

Tuerkheimer, D., 2009. The next innocence project: shaken baby syndrome and the criminal courts. Washington University Law Review 87 (1), 1–58.

US. Department of Health, Human Services, 2015. Administration for Children and Families. Child Maltreatment 2013. https://www.acf.hhs.gov/sites/default/files/cb/cm2013.pdf.

Walsh, W., Cross, T.P., Jones, L.M., Sione, M., Kolko, D.J., 2007. Which sexual abuse victims receive a forensic medical examination? The impact of children's advocacy centers. Child Abuse & Neglect 31 (10), 1053–1068.

Illinois V Wardlow, 2000. Us Supreme Court, pp. 98–1036.

Wiseman, M., October 2008. The role of the dentist in recognizing elder abuse. JCDA 74 (8), 715–720.

Wright, F., Golden, G., 2010 (Chapter 11). In: Senn, D.R., Stimson, P.G. (Eds.), Forensic Dental Photography. CRC Press, pp. 203–244.

Zeitler, D.L., 2005. Domestic violence. Journal of Oral and Maxillofacial Surgery 63 (8), 20–21.

Further Reading

Data available at https://www.fbi.gov/about-us/cjis/ucr/crime-in-the-u.s./2012.

Full report available at http://www.colorado.edu/studentsuccess.

Updated. FBI Supplementary Homicide Reports, June 29, 2015. Available at: https://fbi.gov/about-us/cjis/ucr/nibrs.

Federal Bureau of Investigation, 2012. Uniform Crime Reports. Crime in the United States (Expanded Homicide Data: Murder Offenders by Age, Sex and Race).

Assessment of Dental Age

James M. Lewis[1,2,3], Kathleen A. Kasper[4]

[1]Forensic Odontology Consultant, Alabama Department of Forensic Sciences, Madison, AL, United States;
[2]Assistant Professor, Department of General Dentistry, Forensic Dentistry Fellowship, The University of
Tennessee Graduate School of Medicine, Knoxville, TN, United States; [3]Adjunct Faculty, Center for
Education and Research in Forensics, The University of Texas Health Science Center at San Antonio, San
Antonio, TX, United States; [4]Forensic Odontology Consultant, Tarrant County Medical Examiner's
District, Fort Worth, TX, United States

INTRODUCTION

Forensic age assessment has been defined as the scientific process that estimates an individual's chronologic age by assessing skeletal and dental development and maturation. Over 2000 years ago, the Romans utilized molar eruption patterns to determine if a male individual had reached the age for military conscription (Müller, 1990). Within the modern legal system, the works of Dr. Edwin Saunders (Saunders, 1837) permitted the first application of forensic dental age assessment methodology. This method was utilized in the enforcement of the British child labor laws enacted in the early 1800s.

Despite a long historical use of age assessment methodology to answer medicolegal questions concerning chronologic age, forensic age assessment is, arguably, the most underutilized discipline within forensic odontology. The reason

Forensic Odontology
http://dx.doi.org/10.1016/B978-0-12-805198-6.00008-6

for its underutilization lies in both the forensic odontology and legal community's failure to fully understand how the science can be fully applied. In today's society, a commonly used application of dental age assessment is the determination of the estimated age at death and an associated parameter of minimum and maximum age range of the individual. When used in combination with sex and ancestral information, the search parameters are narrowed reducing the time required to make identification. This application is not only limited to the identification of missing and unidentified individuals within a medical examiner's office but may also be applied in mass disaster identification situations to differentiate clustered victims. It should be noted that the real benefit to the authorities in this application is not in the ability to accurately assess chronologic age. Instead, the benefit lies in providing the authorities a quick, inexpensive means to ascertain a reliable age interval in which to search. Age assessment may also assist in cases involving the living through the resolution of issues concerning legal age of license and legal age of majority for individuals that have undocumented or unreliable birth dates. This applies to those that have entered a country by means other than the legal route as well as legally immigrated individuals. The attainment of the legal age of license and majority is purely jurisdictional, and in the case of the legal age of majority, may also be dependent upon its exact application to the law. For example, in most countries, including the United States, the legal age of majority concerning disposition of undocumented immigrants that have entered the country illegally is 18—but not for all. In matters concerning contract law, age of legal majority varies greatly between countries, and even within the borders of the United States itself. While age 18 is the consensus for most states, there are three states and two territories that differ. The legal age is 19 in Alabama and Nebraska; age 21 in Mississippi and Puerto Rico; and 14 in the American Samoa (Lewis and Brumit, 2011). Occasionally, criminal and civil prosecution cases may require the assessment of age to determine if an individual is to be tried as an adult or juvenile. The US Supreme Court in the case of *Roper v. Simmons*, 2005 prevents capital punishment sentences against individuals under the age of 18. However, the prosecution of juveniles as adults remains possible. The minimum age limit and particular situation in which a juvenile may be tried as an adult will again vary among jurisdictions.

Inadvertent misrepresentation of an individual's chronologic age in age of license cases is short-lived and does not typically present dire consequences. However, cases of legal age of majority regarding legal status as an adult versus juvenile, whether in immigration, criminal or civil prosecution cases, errors may result in a severe change in the individual's disposition. Therefore in these situations, it is imperative that the forensic odontologist provides the trier of fact or governmental agency being consulted with the most accurate estimate of chronologic age and associated known rate of uncertainty possible. It is the responsibility of the investigating odontologist to remain unbiased and to present only the scientific information as best as it is understood permitting the responsible authority to make an informed decision.

Accuracy can only be accomplished through the understanding of the scientific rationale, statistical basis, and inherent limitations of the science. Classically, scientific rationale concerning dental age assessment is divided into three categories: (1) tooth formation and developmental growth changes; (2) postformation changes within the tooth; (3) biochemical changes.

Tooth formation and developmental growth changes are changes that occur through the progressive morphological development of the crown, root, and apex of any given tooth and/or its timed emergence and eruption sequence (Lewis and Senn, 2013). Techniques utilizing these criteria are those that estimate the age of infants, children, and adolescents. During human dental and skeletal development, techniques that utilize the dental morphological development criteria are the most reliable and accurate means to correlate growth and development to true chronologic age (Taylor and Blenkin, 2010). Although they will not be discussed within this text, it should be noted that there are anthropological methods that estimate age and that a prudent investigator will utilize multiple methods and disciplines to obtain the best estimate of age. Researchers have developed and described a multitude of staging systems in an attempt to correlate a specific interval of dental morphologic development to age. Each staging system typically has an associated diagram depicting each stage of development. However, when utilizing any staging system, the investigator must rely upon the written descriptors that fully describe the beginning and ending developmental aspects of each stage. Failing to do so will invariably result in inadvertent staging errors. It has been the experience of these authors that one of the more difficult aspects of dental age assessment is to teach accurate and consistent staging of dental development. Because knowledge of normal dental morphologic development is required, staging should be performed by trained dental professionals and anthropologists. Unfortunately, these staging systems cannot be cross-indexed. Therefore, odontologists and anthropologists need to become proficient utilizing numerous staging systems to apply various techniques and utilize population-specific data sets.

Adult dental age estimation techniques rely upon the assessment of postformation maturation changes. These maturation changes can be categorized as gross anatomical or histological changes. The traditional gross anatomical changes include occlusal or incisal attrition, the periodontal status of the tooth, apical root resorption, and pulp to tooth size ratio. Histological changes include secondary dentin apposition (a correlation to pulp to tooth size ratio), cementum apposition, dentin transparency, and cementum annuli. Some postformation maturation changes are better indicators of age than others.

Biochemical dental techniques utilize amino acid racemization within the tooth dentin and carbon 14 dating of the tooth enamel. When used in combination, it is possible to ascertain the age at death and for individuals born after 1943, the date of birth to ±3 years of age. An advantage of these techniques is that they can be utilized in all age groups. However, the disadvantage is that these techniques do require the sacrifice of dental tissue and are expensive lab procedures that require significant time to obtain results.

There are additional criteria that need to be considered in any scientific dental age assessment. Genetics is the primary factor that effects dental morphologic development, and some postformation maturation techniques have sex- and ancestry-specific data sets. Therefore the sex and ancestry of the individual must be considered. Traditionally an individual's ancestry has been considered to fall within the three anthropologic classifications: European, Asian, or African. In today's society, there is considerable ancestral admixture within the human race, thus necessitating that the forensic investigator understand its potential effects in a given case. Environmental factors have also been implicated as an influence on dental development and postformation changes. Some of the environmental factors include: disease, medical/dental treatments, climate, nutrition, addictions, habits, occupation, place of residence, as well as dental and skeletal abnormalities. In general, the expected effect of environmental stress is to retard dental development. However, unless the environmental factors experienced by the individual are extreme, the forensic dental age assessment will not be appreciably affected (Garn et al., 1965; Ryman, 1975), although there are exceptions. Diseases and disorders of the endocrine system have the potential to retard or accelerate skeletal, dental, and sexual development. Odontologists should avoid performing an age assessment on individuals with endocrine disorders.

Like other naturally occurring phenomena in nature, the random variation of human tooth morphologic development, histologic, and biochemical changes can be statistically described through a mathematical expression known as normal distribution (Lewis and Senn, 2015).

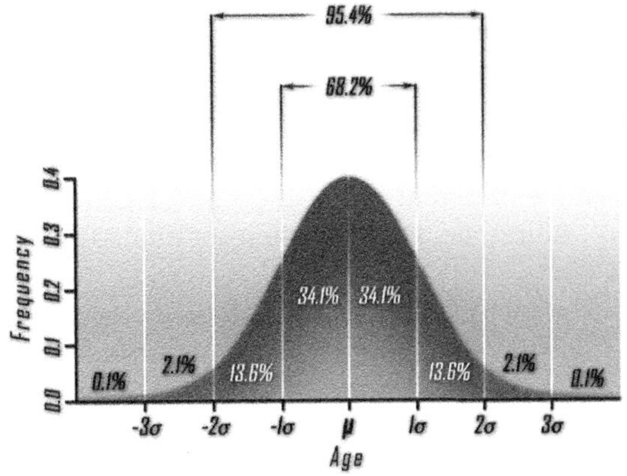

FIGURE 8.1 A normal distribution curve demonstrating the empirical rule.

Fig. 8.1 represents a typical normal distribution curve plotting the occurring frequency of a given stage of human tooth development to the age at which that stage of development is seen. Note that the curve is symmetrical with the majority of occurrences clustering towards the middle of the curve and that the frequency of occurrence decreases the further one moves away from the midline. The peak and center of the curve is marked by Mu (μ) and defines the statistical mean. Not all normal distribution curves have the same height and breadth. Standard deviation (SD) is the statistical expression that defines how tightly the data approximate the mean and therefore is a measure of a curves variability or risk. In Fig. 8.1, SD is indicated by sigma (σ). When the value of sigma is small, the curve will appear tall and narrow indicating that the measured stage of development occurs over a short period of time. Likewise, if the value of sigma is large, the curve is shorter and broader and the stage will occur over a longer period of time.

Normal distribution curves have two unique mathematical properties. First, each curve can be completely defined by two parameters—mean and SD. Knowing these values, allows for the probability of occurrence to be calculated at any given age. Second, every normal distribution curve follows the empirical rule which defines the dispersion of data. See Fig. 8.1. Specifically, the empirical rule states: (1) Approximately 68% of the data will fall between ±1 SD (±1σ) of the mean; (2) Approximately 95% of the data will fall between ±2 SD (±2σ) of the mean; and (3) Virtually all of the data will fall within ±3 SD (±3σ) of the mean.

As in all forensic sciences, forensic age estimation opinions must be derived from sound scientific methodology. The investigator needs to remain mindful that their opinions are estimates and should express a known error rate. The scientifically accepted threshold for error is 95% (Nawrocki, 2010) and is expressed in age estimation as the age interval containing 95% of the population. When an age interval cannot be provided at 95% confidence or the investigator elects to provide an age interval at a differing confidence percentage, the degree of error needs to be stated along with the age interval provided.

Some of the postformation techniques in adult age estimation evaluate multiple criteria within a single mathematical formula. In these cases, regression formulas are used to estimate age. The statistical measure of variability for regression formulas is standard error of estimate (SEE). SEE also follows the empirical rule whereby ±1 SEE provides an age interval containing 68% of the observed population and ±2 (SEE) contains 95% of the population.

Three independent studies concluded that technique selection is critical in ensuring accuracy in age assessment, and the technique(s) most suitable are dependent upon the specific circumstances of each case (Ritz-Timme et al., 2000; Willems, 2001; Soomer et al., 2003). Fig. 8.2 is a supplemental chart published by the American Board of Forensic Odontology (ABFO) intended to assist forensic age assessment investigators in best technique selection (ABFO website, 2016a). This chart subdivides techniques by scientific rationale and age categorization. It indicates methodology that is suitable in the living and/or deceased, radiographic requirements, and indicates when population-specific data are available.

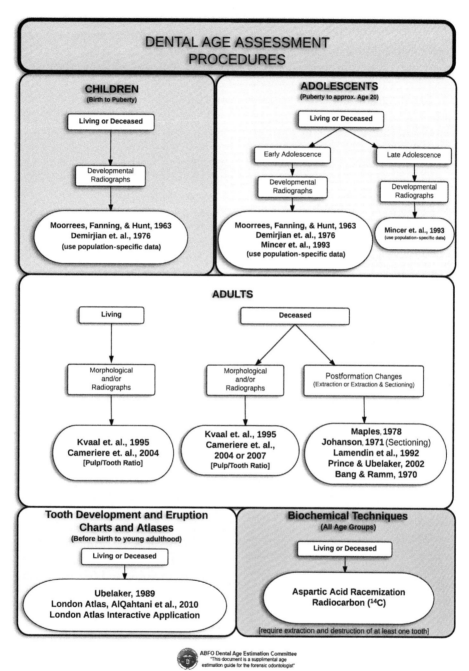

FIGURE 8.2 Dental age assessment procedures chart.

Although the ABFO techniques selection chart does an excellent job, there are some additional basic principles that the forensic odontologist should bear in mind. Large population–specific studies tend to provide more accurate results and should be utilized when appropriate. The odontologist should use sex and ancestrally specific studies and consider any environmental factors that may adversely affect the tooth development or maturation. All available methods should be considered and only normally developing teeth should be utilized in the assessment. A combination of techniques will improve the accuracy of the results (Lewis and Senn, 2013). Perhaps most important, it is critical for accurate age estimates that exact methodology described by the author is followed when a specific technique is performed.

INFANT/CHILD TECHNIQUES

The infant/child age interval is the interval in human dental development that includes the postnatal presence of the developing and resorbing primary dentition including the period of the mixed primary and secondary dentitions. Age assessment techniques utilized within this age interval rely upon evaluation of the maturation and development of the primary and permanent dentitions. Dental age assessment techniques have long been established as the most accurate indicators of chronologic age in subadults (Lewis and Senn, 2013). There are two categories of techniques available to perform age assessment in infants and children: Atlases and charts and techniques that require staging of individual developing teeth; both necessitate the use of good quality radiographs.

Atlases utilize diagrammatic representations of the morphologic developing tooth structures with their associated eruption pattern. Eruption is defined as the process of a tooth's migration from its initial position within its bony crypt until it establishes occlusion with the opposing dentition (Harris et al., 2010). This process is now more commonly termed emergence. Dental emergence can be further subcategorized into gingival emergence and alveolar emergence. Gingival emergence is a tooth's initial appearance through the gingival soft tissue. It is considered the least accurate means of estimating an individual's age because environmental factors such as premature tooth loss, caries, nutritional deficiencies, as well as genetic developmental disorders can affect the process. Alveolar emergence is defined as the moment the most coronal portion of a tooth makes its initial appearance through the alveolar bone (Harris et al., 2010). It is considered more accurate in dental age assessment of developing teeth than gingival emergence because it is less influenced by environmental and genetic factors. Atlas techniques are nonsex specific, have a limited number of population-specific data sets, which results in a higher degree of variability particularly in midchildhood through adolescence and are often derived from mixed ethnic data. Atlas techniques are particularly useful in mass victim identification and clustered victim situations due to their ability to rapidly segregate child, adolescent and adult remains into age intervals (ABFO Dental Age Assessment Standards and Guidelines). Atlases can also be useful in age assessment of the living.

Various charts utilize written descriptors spanning initial tooth mineralization to maturation. They are based on the specific tooth type and whether it is the primary or permanent dentitions with developmental intervals expressed in weeks, months, and/or years. Tooth mineralization is defined as the development of a tooth's hard tissues; it spans a much longer age interval, making it more broadly applicable than emergence (Harris et al., 2010). Most development of the primary dentition occurs in utero and the dental chart first created by Kraus and Jordan (1965) and later modified by Lunt and Law (1974) contains the most comprehensive data set for mineralization of the primary dentition

(Harris et al., 2010). Another commonly used chronological chart of human tooth development is that published in Wheeler's Dental Anatomy ninth edition (Nelson and Ash, 2010). Perhaps the biggest issue in using dental charts is the lack of distinguishable grades and the presence of gaps between stages (Harris et al., 2010).

Dental developmental atlases have been used by dentists and forensic odontologists for years to predict the chronologic age of infants and children. Historically, the dental developmental atlas that has been most popular within the dental community over the longest period of time was created by Schour and Masseler in 1941. This atlas was updated after 1941 as a standalone chart and published in the 1944 Journal of the American Dental Association. It has graphic representations of 21 dental developmental stages of the primary and permanent dentitions which define age through gingival emergence. The stages span from "in utero" to a fully developed adult dentition and include age ranges for each age period. This atlas has been criticized because the illustrations were created from a small sample population size of chronically ill or debilitated individuals, the methods of analysis and other pertinent information that led to its development is lacking or unclear (Smith, 2005; AlQahtani et al., 2014). The Schour and Masseler atlas is no longer used for age assessment in the forensic odontology community. Published atlases currently available that afford greater reliability include Ubelaker (1978, 1989) and AlQahtani et al. (2010).

Douglas Ubelaker in 1978 and again in 1989 developed an atlas similar to that of Schour and Masseler (1944) with important changes. These changes included a larger population size, (mainly skeletonized remains), stages of development with age range intervals based on numerous population studies, and he created nonstaged illustrations of dental development with tooth emergence through the gingiva. His population consisted mainly of the permanent developing dentitions of Native American Indians and the deciduous developing dentitions of nonIndians (predominantly United States' Caucasians). This atlas is best suited for use on individuals that are ages 5 months in utero through 15 years (ABFO Child and Adolescent Age Assessment Technique Chart). Like most dental developmental atlases, there is no differentiation for sex because there are few dental morphologic differences noted for sex in subadults (Lewis and Senn, 2013). Critics of this atlas state that the graphic diagrams of the representative developing teeth lack internal dental anatomy. Internal hard tissues of a developing tooth can help distinguish between developmental stages thus improving accuracy and reliability. Additionally, these same critics purport that there are an inadequate number of developmental stages as evidenced by gaps in the sequence of age categories between ages 12—15, ages 15—21, and ages 21—35 (AlQahtani et al., 2014). Smith (2005) states that both the Schour and Massler (1944) and the Ubelaker (1978, 1989) atlases performed equally well on age categories less than 6 years; however, both atlases' error intervals should be modified for sex differences between ages 6—14 when sex is known.

AlQahtani et al. (2010) developed the London Atlas of Human Tooth Development (https://atlas.dentistry.qmul.ac.uk/). This atlas corrects for several of the inadequacies present in the previously mentioned atlases and charts. The population sample size in this study is large, at n = 704; 176 skeletonized remains (Spitalfields Collection/London and Maurice Stack's Collection/England), and 528 living contemporary individuals (half Caucasian and half Bangladeshi). This atlas' graphic diagrams are defined by the Moorrees et al., (1963a,b) staging system of dental development; previous atlases had no such definitions. Each illustration, ages 1—23, show tooth development and eruption at the midpoint of the chronologic year. Internal hard tissue tooth anatomy is part of the developing tooth schematic and more representative of an actual developing tooth. Teeth are spaced to facilitate staging through direct visual or radiographic means. Emergence is defined through the alveolar bone. Gaps between dental developmental stages are minimized by increasing the total number of stages to 31; this includes three "in utero" developmental diagrams and one depicting birth. This atlas was tested against Schour and Massler (1941) and Ubelaker (1978) to assess the accuracy of estimating age from developing teeth by AlQahtani et al. (2014). The test sample size in this study was n = 1506, prenatal to 23.94 years. This group concluded that despite the high degree of age variation in tooth development, the London Atlas of Human Tooth Development is an improvement in estimating age, with individuals' ages 1 through 18 years, when compared to Schour and Massler (1941) and Ubelaker (1978). Like other atlases, the London Atlas of Human Tooth Development is also nonsex and nonancestry specific. The following link can be accessed for an interactive version of the London Atlas of Human Tooth Development; www.atlas.dentistry.qmul.ac.uk. Despite the fact that there are 31 different age categories, tooth emergence is defined through alveolar bone and a large contemporary study population was used; a weakness of the London Atlas is the lack of age ranges at each age category. Nonetheless, this atlas is an acceptable one for age assessment in children between the ages of 30 weeks in utero through 15.5 years (ABFO Child and Adolescent Age Assessment Technique Chart).

Atlases and charts can be useful for a quick and easy age assessment on infants and children for the aforementioned reasons; however, they are not ancestry or sex driven and as such afford less accuracy in reporting chronologic age estimation on individuals in this age category. Techniques that account for differences in sex, ancestry, morphologic development of individual teeth, and include a defined mean age and rate of uncertainty to include 95% of a given population will produce more accurate assessments of human dental chronologic age than those that do not (Smith, 2005; AlQahtani et al., 2014). Two methodologies commonly used today that meet these criteria, with both living and deceased infants/children, utilize radiographic techniques and include: The 1963a,b Moorrees, Fanning, and Hunt (MFH) and the 1976 Demirjian and Goldstein publications.

Moorrees et al. (1963a,b) studied a population of 380 predominantly healthy white children ages birth to 21 years from the Ohio and Boston areas of the United States. They developed a morphologic staging chart with graphic representations of progressive dental crown and root maturation and a corresponding chart with associated written descriptors. Moorrees felt that when one stages teeth using his scheme, the examiner should score the highest grade/stage that has been attained morphologically because it improves repeatability (Harris et al., 2010). These charts consist of 13 stages for single-rooted teeth and 14 stages for multirooted teeth. Multirooted teeth have the additional cleft stage. This technique can be used with developing primary mandibular canines and molars as well as developing permanent maxillary and mandibular incisors and developing permanent mandibular canines, premolars, and molars. There are data sets available for resorption of primary teeth (MFH, 1963a). The data sets for all teeth used with the Moorrees et al. (1963a,b) are sex and ancestry specific. When possible, multiple developing teeth should be included in the age estimation by averaging data sets, as this will improve accuracy. Tooth selection has a bearing in the accuracy of age estimation in that the developing crown will allow a more accurate assessment of age than the crown and developing root structure together (Lewis and Senn, 2013). This is due to the higher degree of variability in root formation. Those teeth that have completed root formation should **not** be used with this technique as no age can be assigned in age prediction when complete maturity is reached, because the subject has passed this transition by an unknown amount of time (Smith, 1991). In addition, teeth should not be utilized in this assessment of age if they have periapical pathology, extensive caries, are extensively restored, or exhibit dental morphologic abnormality. It should also be noted that use of the third molar with this technique should be avoided as there are other age assessment techniques that are better suited for developing third molars. The MFH technique process requires the odontologist to correctly identify the tooth, assess its proper stage of morphologic development, and to then read the associated mean age and SD from the sex-specific graph (Lewis and Senn, 2013). A problem in arriving at a mean age and SD using the original publication's data sets is that they are represented on difficult-to-read graphs. Thankfully, these graphs have been reverse engineered for simplification and ease of use on the deciduous dentition by Lewis and Senn (2013) and on the permanent dentition by Harris and Buck (2002). Ancestral specific studies have been published and should be used on the appropriate populations (Anderson et al., 1976; Harris and McKee, 1990; Haavikko, 1974; Mornstad et al., 1995; Liversidge, 2000).

Demirjian (Demirjian et al., 1973; Demirjian and Goldstein, 1976) studied a French-Canadian population of 2407 boys and 2349 girls, ages 2.5—17 years. They developed a dental morphologic staging system that consists of eight stages, A through H, and then added Stage 0 for no calcification. These stages are defined by initial crown mineralization through final apical root closure and are represented by both graphic diagrams and written descriptors. This technique requires staging all seven teeth on the mandibular left (teeth numbers 18—24 and excludes third molars). If one or all of these teeth are not available, then use the same tooth from contralateral side of mandible. The Demirjian and Goldstein (1976) technique also allows for use of four permanent teeth on the mandibular left in one of the following two

combinations: [M_2, M_1, PM_2 PM_1] or [M_2, PM_2, PM_1, I_1]. If one or all of these teeth are not available, then use the contralateral tooth. Teeth should not be utilized in this assessment of age if they have periapical pathology, extensive caries, extensively restored, or exhibit dental morphologic abnormality. Staging is performed using high-quality radiographs. The mandibular arch is used because of its clarity on dental radiographs and lack of obstructive anatomy. After all teeth have been staged, each tooth is assigned a "self-weighted score" based upon the stage selected and sex of the individual. Each of the seven or four teeth's "self-weighted scores," depending upon which technique within this Demirjian schematic you chose, will be added collectively. The resulting number is the "maturity score" and will be located on a dental maturity percentiles graph at the maturity score on the Y axis of the appropriate graph based on the number of teeth used and sex. Ages are determined by an intersecting line that crosses the 3rd, 10th, 50th, 90th, and 97th percentiles on the graph. The corresponding ages can then be expressed at the 94th percentile confidence interval. This technique is most useful with ages 2.5—14 years (ABFO Dental Age Assessment Child and Adolescent Technique Chart). The original graphs from the 1976 Demirjian and Goldstein publication are somewhat cumbersome to read due to a lack of detail. Fortunately, these graphs have been reverse-engineered by DAE Quicksheets creator Derek Draft, DDS in 2016. Quicksheets are Microsoft Excel spreadsheets that eliminate mathematical errors that can be associated with age estimation computations. These Quicksheets can be obtained at DAEquicksheets@gmail.com. The 1976 Demirjian technique is sex specific and there are multiple population-specific studies available. It is an excellent technique for age estimation in children. Limitations of this technique include the following: (1) it cannot be used in cases where there is an absence of appropriate teeth bilaterally; (2) fragmented remains or with malformed teeth; (3) the age range starts at 2.5 years versus at birth as in the Moorrees technique and the teeth used are weighted equally versus given tooth-specific data sets (Lewis and Senn, 2013).

ADOLESCENT TECHNIQUES

Adolescence may be defined as the period of time in human development that follows the onset of puberty through the time the individual attains adulthood. For the purposes of forensic age assessment, this equates to approximately age 12–20. In adolescence, the dental and skeletal structures continue to undergo morphologic development; and, therefore as in child techniques, methodology that evaluates these changes in growth is still utilized to assess chronologic age. However, during and after the onset of puberty, sexual dimorphism becomes more pronounced necessitating that the methodology utilized considers sex and ancestry of the individual. Therefore, population-specific data that most closely align with the individual's heritage should always be utilized. Since atlas techniques tend to not provide sex-specific information, their use to assess the age of individuals in early and late adolescence is questionable.

The Dental Age Assessment Procedures Chart (Fig. 8.2) subdivides adolescence into two categories: Early and Late Adolescence. The reasoning behind this division is that the third molars have been well documented as being among the most variable tooth in terms of morphologic development. Being highly variable implies that the SD values for staged third molars will be greater than those for the other teeth within the dentition—thus a greater rate of uncertainty. When teeth other than the third molars are still undergoing development, the odontologist should rely less on the third molar and more heavily on the remainder of the dentition in assessing age.

There are three (3) recommended early adolescent methods. Two of these, Moorrees

et al. (1963a,b) and Demirjian and Goldstein (1976) have been previously discussed. However, there are some important considerations that require noting when used on an adolescent individual. The Demirjian methods begin to lose their accuracy and therefore usefulness beginning around the age of 14. The Moorrees et al. method does provide statistical data through the full range of dental morphological development. However, the odontologist may want to consider avoiding the use of its third molar data because the Mincer et al. (1993) technique, a technique devoted solely for the third molar, provides a better estimate of age when appropriate population-specific data are utilized. Likewise, if teeth other than the third molar have not completed development, use of the Mincer et al. technique should be avoided.

In terms of forensic dental age estimation, late adolescence begins once the only human tooth continuing to undergo morphologic development is the third molar. Normally this occurs around the age of 14. During late adolescence there are anthropologic growth centers that can assist in the evaluation of chronological age. These include areas of the hand and wrist, clavicle, ribs, and cervical vertebrae (Hackman et al., 2010). The degree of third molar development variability has already been noted. Yet, the third molar remains the most reliable biologic indicator of age throughout adolescence (Harris et al., 2010). Because few teeth remain for evaluation and variability does exist, a multidisciplinary approach is recommended, especially in cases involving questions of legal age of majority.

The first study utilizing only the third molar for assessment of age was sanctioned by the ABFO and was performed and published by Mincer et al. (1993). The resulting data are statistically significant only for Americans of European descent. Mincer et al. utilized the Demirjian et al. (1973) system for staging the third molar radiographic morphological development. Fig. 8.3 is the Demirjian third molar developmental classification system modified

A			Cusp tips are mineralized but have not yet coalesced.	E			Formation of the interradicular bifurcation has begun. Root length is less than the crown length.
B			Mineralized cusps are united so the mature coronal morphology is well defined.	F			Root length is at least as great as crown length. Roots have funnel-shaped endings.
C			The crown is about 1/2 formed the pulp chamber is evident & dentinal depositon is occurring.	G			Root walls are parallel, but apices remain open.
D			Crown formation is complete to the dentinoenamel junction. The pulp chamber has a trapezoidal form.	H			Apical ends of the roots are completely closed, and the periodontal membrane has a uniform width around the root.

FIGURE 8.3 Demirjan third molar developmental stages. *Modified by from Kasper, K.A., Austin, D., Kvanli, A.H., Rios, T.R., Senn, D.R., 2009. Reliability of third molar development for age estimation in a Texas Hispanic population: a comparison study. Journal of Forensic Sciences 54 (3), 651–657.*

by Kasper to include example images of each stage (Kasper et al., 2009). The images depicting each stage are there to assist in the dental staging; however, the written descriptors are the official means by which each stage is differentiated. As with all radiographic staging systems, when the tooth exhibits unusual or abnormal morphology, substantial decay, periapical pathology, extensive dental restoration, the tooth orientation prevents visualization of the degree of morphologic development and/or anatomic structures prevent accurate staging, that tooth should not be staged and included within age assessment calculations. Otherwise, all third molars present should be utilized. The 1993 Mincer study revealed sexual dimorphism, bilateral symmetry within the arches, asymmetrical development between the maxillary and mandibular arches, and an empirical probability that an individual's third molar has reached complete morphologic development. Separate statistical data tables were produced for males and females providing the mean estimated chronological age, SD, and the empirical probability that the individual had attained age 18 for maxillary and mandibular third molars at Demirjian dental morphologic development stages "D" through "H."

Many late adolescent age estimation cases involve assisting authorities in answering legal age of majority questions regarding immigration and prosecution. Therefore, sound technique in the use of sex, ancestry, and population-specific data are essential. Fortunately, since 1993 many other third molar age estimation population studies have been performed. Table 8.1 lists currently available studies and their associated population specificity. Unfortunately, third molar age assessment studies do not have a uniformly standardized dental morphologic staging system. It is important that after selection of the appropriate population-specific study and data set, the forensic investigator utilizes the same dental morphologic staging system described within the study.

Regardless of dental morphologic staging system, calculating the average estimated age at which a tooth attains complete developmental maturation has historically been problematic. The goal is to estimate the average age in which a specific tooth's complete maturation is attained. Traditionally, researchers have arbitrarily set the upper age limit of the studied population's raw data set. However, collected data beyond the age at which a given tooth in all individuals within the studied population have

TABLE 8.1   Published Population-Specific Studies Using the Demirjian Technique

Population Specificity	Published Articles
Austrian	Meiln et al. (2007)
Bangladeshi	Liversidge H.M. (2008)
British (White)	Liversidge H.M. (2008)
Belgian	Gunst et al. (2003)
Brazilian	Soares et al. (2015)
Canadian	Anderson et al. (1976)
Chinese	Zeng et al. (2009)
Finnish	Nyström et al. (2007) and Haavikko (1970)
German	Olze et al. (2004) and Willershausen et al. (2001)
Indian	Bhat et al. (2007), Darji et al. (2011), and Mohammed et al. (2014)
Italian	De Salvia et al. (2004) and Cameriere et al. (2008)
Japanese	Olze et al. (2004) and Arany et al. (2004)
Korean	Choi et al. (1991) and Lee et al. (2009)
New Zealander	McGettigan et al. (2011)
Portuguese	Caldas et al. (2011)
Saudi Arabian	Ajamal et al. (2012) and Alshihri et al. (2014)
South African (Black)	Liversidge H.M. (2008) and Olze et al. (2004)
Spanish	Prieto et al. (2005) and Martin de las Heras et al. (2008)
Swiss	Kullman et al. (1992) and Knell et al. (2009)
Thai	Thevissen et al. (2009)
Turkish	Orhan et al. (2006) and Sisman et al. (2007)

TABLE 8.1   Published Population-Specific Studies Using the Demirjian Technique—cont'd

Population Specificity	Published Articles
United States (African American)	Blankenship et al. (2007), Lewis and Senn (2010), and Harris (2007)
United States (European)	Mincer et al. (1993), Morrees et al. (1963a,b), and Harris (2007)
United States (Hispanic)	Solari and Abramovitch (2002) and Kasper et al. (2009)

attained complete maturation should be excluded. Failing to exclude this data artificially inflates the average estimated age and associated rate of uncertainty. Likewise, if the raw data fail to include individuals up to the age where all the individuals have attained complete maturation, the calculated average estimated age of the terminal stage will be low. This process of eliminating extraneous raw data is known as "censoring" and was first described and applied in a study involving a British population (Boonpitaksathit et al., 2011). The age beyond which the remaining data should be censored is valued at three (3) SDs greater than the average estimated age of the stage prior to the terminal stage of development (i.e., In the Demirjian staging system, censoring begins at three (3) SDs beyond the calculated average estimated age for stage "G"). Very few of the third molar population—specific data sets have been censored. Of the US population studies, Kasper et al. (2009), Blankenship data modified by Lewis and Senn (2010) and the 1993, Mincer et al. have been censored (Moore et al., 2016). See Tables 8.2 and 8.3.

Originally, the third molar age assessment method was developed to estimate the age of late adolescents and to assist governmental agencies in the disposition of undocumented

TABLE 8.2 Censored Stage "H" Data for Kasper et al. (2009) and Blankenship Lewis and Senn (2010) as Reported by Moore et al. (2016)

	Male			Female		
	Mean Age (years)	Standard Deviation	Probability > 18	Mean Age (years)	Standard Deviation	Probability > 18
Kasper et al. (2009)						
Maxillary Arch	19.25	1.82	75.4%	*** Data not changed ***		
Mandibular Arch	19.52	1.56	83.5%	*** Data not changed ***		
Blankenship Lewis and Senn (2010)						
Maxillary Arch	20.00	1.34	93.2%	20.29	2.50	82.0%
Mandibular Arch	20.37	1.57	93.7%	20.64	2.37	86.7%

TABLE 8.3 Censored Stage "H" Data for Mincer et al. (1993) Calculated by Lewis

	Male			Female		
	Mean Age (years)	Standard Deviation	Probability > 18	Mean Age (years)	Standard Deviation	Probability > 18
Mincer et al. (1993)						
Maxillary Arch	19.49	1.56	83.1	20.55	1.89	91.2
Mandibular Arch	19.85	1.45	89.8	20.78	1.19	94

immigrants that had entered the United States illegally. Today's legal system has found other uses for this technique including, but not limited to, the assistance in determining age for human trafficking cases and cases involving criminal and civil prosecution. In these cases, legal council may ask for the forensic investigator to assess the age of an individual on the date of a crime, ask for the probability an individual has attained an age other than 18, or even to perform the current age assessment from radiographs known to have been taken of an individual years earlier. To provide the statistical information requested, the mathematics must be calculated by hand and cannot be read straight from the originally published data. Probability is calculated by using the continuous distribution function. For the lay person, think of this mathematical expression as a means to calculate the area under the normal distribution curve (probability) for any value along the x-axis (age). The only required known values to perform probability calculations are mean age and the SD. Most computer spreadsheet software will readily perform this calculation eliminating the potential for mathematical error. In Microsoft Excel, the function for determining probability from a continuous distribution function is:

NORMDIST(x, mean, standard deviation)

"x" is the value of the age in question for which probability is being calculated; "mean" is the assessed average mean age of the individual; and "SD" is the determined SD associated with the estimated average mean age of the individual.

ADULT TECHNIQUES

For the purposes of dental age assessments, the adult age range shall be defined as the interval in human dental development beyond which all teeth have completed crown/root development and the individual is therefore considered dentally mature. All dental development has ceased and postformation and maturational changes are all that remain to assess age in this category (Lewis and Senn, 2015). Adult dental age assessment techniques may utilize either radiographic or morphological evaluation or gross and microscopic observation of postformation changes within the dentition following the cessation of morphologic dental development. Although others have been described, there are six traditional postformation variables that have been utilized in the assessment of adult chronologic age. They are: root transparency, secondary dentin deposition, periodontal attachment, cementum apposition, attrition, and root resorption. Of these criteria, root transparency and secondary dentin deposition are the most useful and root resorption is the least valuable criterion (Maples, 1978). Another important note is that ancestry and sex minimally influence the progression of root translucency and secondary dentin. All postformation tooth variables can be affected by caries, restorations, malocclusion, traumatic occlusion, and endodontic treatment to some degree with the exception of root translucency. Therefore techniques that rely on the evaluation of nonrestored teeth in normal occlusion and utilize root translucency and secondary dentin formation as variables in the age assessment tend to be more accurate (Lewis and Senn, 2013). Ethical considerations may restrict the use of many adult age assessment methodologies in the living as well as the deceased due to the requirement of sacrificing tooth structure (ABFO Dental Age Assessment Standards and Guidelines). The American Board of Forensic Odontology has developed an adult technique chart intended to assist forensic odontologists in the selection and use of various adult dental age assessment techniques (ABFO, 2016d). Adult dental age estimation in this chapter will be separated into those techniques that are useful in the living and those techniques that are useful in the deceased.

Adult dental age assessment techniques that are successful predictors of chronologic age in the living include but are not limited to Kvaal et al. (1995) and Cameriere et al. (2004). These techniques assess dental age by evaluating morphologic degenerative changes to the pulp tissue due to secondary dentin deposition.

The Kvaal et al. (1995) adult dental age estimation technique utilizes radiographs of intact maxillary and mandibular single-rooted teeth. The study population size consisted of 100 individuals with full mouth dental radiographs taking into account ratios that measure tooth/root length, pulp/root length, pulp/tooth length and then pulp/root widths at three different levels. Lengths are assessed on the mesial aspect of each tooth. The ratios between the tooth and pulp measurements were calculated and used in the analysis, to reduce the effect of a possible variation in the magnification and angulation of radiographs (Kvaal et al., 1995). Once the aforementioned ratios are calculated then there are an additional nine measurements and eight calculations per tooth performed to arrive at an estimated age (Fig. 8.4). These measurements and calculations are cumbersome and can be accurately assessed and then processed through computer imaging software programs like Adobe Photoshop and Draft Age Estimation (DAE) Quicksheets (DAEquicksheets@gmail.com). The tooth selection hierarchy from best to least is as follows: maxillary teeth over mandibular teeth, maxillary centrals over maxillary laterals over maxillary second bicuspids, then mandibular laterals

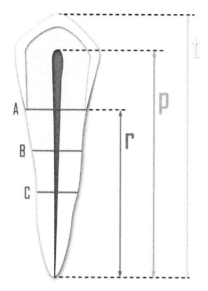

FIGURE 8.4   Illustration demonstrating the Kvaal et al. (1995) measurements made on each tooth.

over mandibular canines over mandibular first bicuspids. Utilizing multiple teeth produce a more accurate estimation of age. Teeth selected using this technique must be nonrestored, have no trauma, rotations, pathology, and be in normal occlusal function. This technique is non-sex and nonancestry specific unless using mandibular lateral incisors. If a mandibular lateral incisor is used in the age estimation, then sex is specific to the regression formula. Kvaal et al. (1995) is best suited for the age range of 20–87 years. The study population mean age was 42.6 years. The rate of uncertainty is mathematically expressed in the form of SEE and these values are presented for single teeth, three maxillary teeth or three mandibular teeth, and for six teeth from both jaws. Other advantages this technique offers include; it can be used successfully with archeological remains, it is noninvasive and nondestructive to teeth.

The Cameriere et al. (2004) adult dental age estimation technique utilizes radiographs of intact maxillary canines. Maxillary canines were selected because the size of the pulp chamber is such that it is more readily visible than other single-rooted or multirooted teeth and as such is more easily measured for analysis. Additionally, canines are less likely to be worn or restored. This study evaluated 100 Italian Caucasian individuals using dental panoramic radiographs. These radiographs were scanned and digitized then processed using a computer-aided drafting program (AutoCAD2000, Install Shield 3.0, 1997). Twenty points from each tooth outline and 10 points from each pulp outline were identified in the labio-lingual position and used to evaluate tooth and pulp volumes (Cameriere et al., 2004). Multiple morphologic tooth, root, and pulp variables were analyzed; however, the data suggest that only the pulp/ tooth area ratio (AR) and the pulp/root width at midroot (c) were statistically significant to estimate age using one of the appropriate regression formulas listed below:

$$Age = 86.53 - 457.15(AR) - 22.98(c)$$
Or
$$Age = 84.31 - 473.86(AR)$$

Both Formulas S.E.E. $= 5.35$ years

Using Draft Age Estimation (DAE) Quicksheets (DAEquicksheets@gmail.com) with this technique will eliminate the chance of human error performing the mathematical calculations. Computer imaging software programs like Adobe Photoshop can assist in accurate measurement of pulp and tooth volumes by using tools like the Magnetic Lasso/Lasso Tool and the Histogram which measures the pixel volume outlined.

Although Cameriere et al. (2004) lists using only the maxillary right canine, it is inferred that the left maxillary canine can be used as well due to morphologic symmetry of these teeth. Teeth selected for this technique must be nonrestored, have no trauma, rotations, pathology, and be in normal occlusal function. This technique is nonsex and nonancestry specific. The useful age range of the population studied is from 18 to 72 years. Disadvantages of this technique includes: (1) it depends on good radiographic images with little overlap; (2) requires special software for accurate measurements of pulp and tooth volumes; (3) it is not well defined how to take accurate measurements if a root is curved at the apex and; (4) one can only use the technique on maxillary canines. The biggest advantages are that this technique is noninvasive and it is nondestructive to teeth. This technique can also be used on archeological remains (Cameriere et al., 2007).

The next series of techniques that will be described include those that can be used on deceased individuals. These techniques can be subdivided into those that involve noninvasive dental age assessment using morphological changes and radiographs: Kvaal et al. (1995) and Cameriere et al. (2004) and those techniques that assess postformation changes with invasive methodology (extraction or extraction and sectioning): Cameriere et al. (2007), Bang and Ramm (1970), Johanson (1971), Maples (1978), Lamendin et al. (1992), and Prince and Ubelaker (2002).

Kvaal et al. (1995) and Cameriere et al. (2004) have been previously described in this chapter and need not be repeated because the technique and methodology is identical in living and deceased individuals. This leaves Cameriere et al. (2007). The basic study design mirrored that of the 2004 publication with the following differences; the study population increased to 200 (200) Caucasian male and females, the useful age range for dental age estimation is 20–79 years, **extracted** maxillary and mandibular canines were used, periapical radiographs in the labio-lingual and mesial orientations were evaluated, and regression formulas for all four maxillary and mandibular canines, only maxillary canine(s) or only mandibular canine(s) were created. The following regression formulas apply to this technique:

X_1 = Labio-Lingual (AR) = [pulp/tooth area ratio]; Maxillary Canine

X_2 = Mesial AR; Maxillary Canine

X_3 = Labio-Lingual (AR) = [pulp/tooth area ratio]; Mandibular Canine

X_4 = Mesial AR; Mandibular Canine

Age = $120.737 - 337.112(X_1) - 79.709(X_2) - 364.534(X_3) - 65.655(X_4) + 1531.918(X_1)(X_3)$
(Maxillary and Mandibular Canines) S.E.E. = 3.62 years

Age = $111.75 - 373.78(X_1) - 182.92(X_2)$
(Maxillary Canines only) S.E.E. = 4.74 years

Age = $102.09 - 318.25(X_3) - 117.89(X_4)$
(Mandibular Canines only) S.E.E. = 4.47 years

The disadvantages of this technique are the same as the Cameriere et al. (2004) with the addition of the requirement that teeth must be sacrificed or extracted from the deceased. The advantages include that all canines (both maxillary and mandibular) can be potentially assessed if available, which consequently gives a more accurate estimate of an individual's chronologic age. Furthermore, adding the labio-lingual and mesial projections of each canine radiographically can yield a larger amount of information and thus a more accurate age estimate (Cameriere et al., 2007).

The following set of adult dental age assessment techniques involves analysis of extracted and sectioned teeth.

The first technique is Johanson, 1971. This study evaluated 162 extracted teeth from 31 males and 15 females. After the tooth is sectioned buccal-lingually to 0.25 mm, there are six different morphologic variables that are assessed. These are attrition (A), periodontosis (P), secondary dentin formation (S), cementum apposition(C), root resorption(R), and root translucency (T). The grading of each variable is based upon the Gustafson (1950) four-point tooth charts; however, Johanson felt staging would be more accurately represented if a seven-point grading system was implemented. This grading system stages each variable previously listed; 0, 0.5, 1.0, 1.5, 2.0, 2.5, 3.0. The graded variables are next put into the following regression formula and the age estimate is calculated:

recommends examination of the dental occlusion noting the number of teeth present, location, and potential habits of the individual. Teeth utilized should be vital and not be in traumatic occlusion or have evidence of previous trauma (including extensive caries or restorations). This technique is nonsex and nonancestry specific with a useful age range between 23 and 79 years. The disadvantages of the Johanson (1971) technique include having the appropriate training and equipment available to section a tooth and view all six morphologic variables, accurately grading each tooth variable, and most importantly having to sacrifice a tooth rendering it useless for other methods of analysis. Advantages include a favorable rate of error in the assessment of adult chronologic age.

The next technique that also involves sectioning of teeth is Maples 1978. In this study 355 teeth were longitudinally sectioned to a thickness of 250–350 µm. The study population consisted of 267 individuals from Caucasian and African-American ancestry. The same six tooth variables used in Johanson (1971) were also evaluated in this study. Maples found that root resorption is by far the worst variable to assess age out of the six. He also felt that root transparency is the best indicator of dental age followed by secondary dentin apposition, attrition, periodontosis, and cementum apposition (Maples, 1978). Grading these six variables follows those described by Gustafson (1950) using values of 0–3 and using 0.5 increment

$$Age = 11.02 + 5.14(A) + 2.30(S) + 4.14(P) + 3.71(C) + 5.57(R) + 8.98(T)$$

1 Standard deviation(SD) = 5.16 when using multiple teeth

1 Standard deviation(SD) = 8.00 when using a single tooth

When making the decision to assess dental age using this technique, use multiple single-rooted teeth (Incisors and Bicuspids) from both maxillary and mandibular arches. This method

grades when necessary for borderline evaluations (Maples, 1976). Maples also found that tooth position regression formulas gave more accurate assessments of adult chronologic age.

The Position Regression formulas correspond to specific teeth; Position 1 = Central Incisor, Position 2 = Lateral Incisor, Position 3 = Canine, Position 4 = first Bicuspid, Position 5 = second bicuspid, Position 6 = first Molar, Position 7 = second Molar (**This is the BEST tooth for the most accurate assessment of age using this technique**), and Position 8 = Third Molar (**Do NOT use the third molar for this technique**). These authors will only state regression formulas for this technique using Secondary Dentin Apposition and Root Transparency (ST) values since they are the variables which gave the best results in this study.

reducing operator error in calculating age and that tooth position regression formulas afford more precise estimates of age (Maples, 1978).

Bang and Ramm (1970) developed a method of adult age estimation using only one of the six tooth variables previously mentioned, root transparency. The study sample consisted of 265 individuals (158 males and 107 females) and a total of 926 extracted teeth. Teeth studied were both intact and sectioned. Longitudinal sections were accomplished by cutting each tooth to a thickness of 400μ in the labio-lingual dimension. In both cases the total root length (RL) was measured from the labial surface

Central Incisor/Position 1:	Age $= 3.89(S) + 14.23(T) + 15.28$	S.E.E. $= 9.1$ years
Lateral Incisor/Position 2:	Age $= 6.51(S) + 12.55(T) = 25.16$	S.E.E. $= 9.6$ years
Canine/Position 3:	Age $= 18.67(S) + 11.72(T) + 21.94$	S.E.E. $= 11.0$ years
First Bicuspid/Position 4:	Age $= 2.82(S) + 15.25(T) + 19.65$	S.E.E. $= 12.2$ years
Second Bicuspid/Position 5:	Age $= 4.79(S) + 15.53(T) + 17.99$	S.E.E. $= 7.6$ years
First Molar/Position 6:	Age $= 11.28(S) + 5.32(T) + 10.86$	S.E.E. $= 11.1$ years
Second Molar/Position 7:	Age $= 6.99(S) + 10.86(T) + 19.31$	S.E.E. $= 6.8$ years
Third Molar/Position 8:	Age $= 4.71(S) + 12.30(T) + 24.57$	S.E.E. $= 12.0$ years

This method recommends examination of the dental occlusion noting the number of teeth present, location, and potential habits of the individual. Teeth utilized should be vital and not in traumatic occlusion nor have evidence of previous trauma (including extensive caries or restorations). The technique is nonsex and nonancestry specific with a useful age range between 10 and 90 years. Disadvantages of this technique include having the appropriate training and equipment available to section a tooth, accurately grading each tooth variable, and most importantly sacrificing a tooth rendering it useless for other methods of analysis. Advantages of this technique over Johanson (1971) include a reduction from six to two tooth variables potentially

from the cemento-enamel junction (CEJ) to the apex. The root transparency (T) was measured from the apex of the root in a coronal direction to the border of transparent and opaque dentin boundary. If this junction was not represented evenly on the facial and the lingual surfaces of the root, then both measurements were recorded and the mean measurement was used. If this junction was even, then only one measurement was recorded (Bang and Ramm, 1970). There is an apparent slowing of root transparency by age 70 and as a result two separate regression formulas were created for this technique (Lewis and Senn, 2013). The first involves root translucency zones ≤9 mm for intact and sectioned teeth and the second involves root translucency zones >9 mm for intact and sectioned teeth. The regression formulas are as follows:

Translucency zone ≤ 9 mm:

$$Age = B_0 + B_1(X) + B_2(X)^2$$

Translucency zone > 9 mm:

$$Age = B_0 + B_1(X)$$

B_0, B_1, and B_2 are tooth-specific regression coefficients and X is measured length of root translucency in millimeters.

Teeth available for selection include maxillary and mandibular single-rooted teeth numbers 4 through 13 and 20 through 29. The mesial and distal roots of teeth numbers 3, 14, 19, and 30 may also be utilized. Transparency is measured on the labial surface. Teeth selected can be restored or nonrestored and have pathology or trauma associated with them. Because root translucency has not shown appreciable ancestral and sex variation, and is minimally affected by other external factors, this method has been widely applied in cases where the volume of skeletal remains is small and the sex and ancestry are unknown (Lewis and Senn, 2013). The useful age range of this technique is 25–75 years. The rate of uncertainty is provided in SD and is tooth specific. Disadvantages of this technique include: obtaining accurate measurements for zones of translucency as these zones are not always clearly discernible (Tang et al., 2014), determining what light source to use to make the zone of translucency visible, (These authors believe visibility of the transparency zone can be enhanced by keeping the teeth hydrated in water then using a light source like a film radiograph view box or white light emitting diode (LED) light.), according to Tang et al. (2014) this technique is not as accurate in prediction of age in archeological material and should be used mainly on contemporary populations, and lastly the teeth used in this method may be sacrificed rendering them useless for other methods of analysis. The advantages to this technique include that only one morphologic variable is required; root transparency and thus regression formulas for age estimation are simplistic and easy to use, radiographs are not required, and there is no specialized equipment or training required.

Lamendin et al. (1992) developed an adult dental age estimation technique reducing the morphologic variables evaluated to periodontosis and root transparency on single-rooted teeth. The sample included 208 individuals; consisting of 135 males, 73 females; 198 Caucasians; 10 Blacks with a total of 306 single-rooted teeth harvested for study. Periodontosis (gingival recession) is measured on the labial surface of each tooth and defined as the degeneration of the soft tissues surrounding the tooth progressing from the CEJ to the apex of the root. It is the maximum distance between the CEJ and the line of soft tissues attachment. Root Transparency is the physiologic feature that appears after age 20 and is due to deposition of hydroxyapatite crystals within the dentinal tubules. The Lamendin technique measures translucency on the labial surface between the apex and the maximum height of translucency. Root height is that distance measured between the root apex and the CEJ (Lamendin et al., 1992). After these measurements have been recorded, then the following regression equations will be calculated:

$$Age = (0.18 \times P) + (0.42 \times T) + 25.53$$

Where P and T are defined as: P = (measured periodontal recession height $\times$ 100)/measured root height; T = (measured root transparence height $\times$ 100)/measured root height; RH = distance measured between the root apex and the CEJ.

Lamendin et al. (1992) published sample error rates in mean error (ME) and subdivided the error rates by decade of life yielding an average mean error of approximately 10 years. The teeth utilized in this technique are intact single-rooted incisors with maxillary centrals providing the best results. For more precise estimation of age, multiple teeth should be used and average the results. Teeth selected may have minimal restorations; however, there should be no periapical pathology. This technique is nonsex specific, should be used predominantly on Caucasian populations with a useful age range of 40–80 years. The disadvantages to this technique include: difficulty in measuring periodontosis and root translucency, inability to use this technique on individuals less than 40 years due to the inaccuracy, extraction of tooth required, and poor oral hygiene, a diet high in sugars, and periodontal soft tissue surgeries can all influence accuracy of the periodontosis measurements. Advantages to this technique include use of only two morphologic variables, root transparency and periodontosis, simplifying regression formula calculations; radiographs are not required and there is no specialized equipment or training that is needed.

The last adult dental age assessment technique described in this chapter is Prince and Ubelaker (2002). Like Lamendin et al. (1992), this technique utilizes two morphologic variables, periodontosis and root transparency, to assess age at death. The population sample included 359 individuals; 98 Black males, 94 Black females, 95 Caucasian males, and 72 Caucasian females. The teeth studied were taken from the Terry Collection housed at the National Museum of Natural History in Washington, DC. This collection has over 1600 individuals from the time period 1900–65, of known sex, ancestry, age at death, and cause of death. Prince and Ubelaker tested the Lamendin adult dental age estimation technique looking specifically at how ancestry and sex would affect age prediction. They concluded that ancestry does not have an effect on age estimation using the Lamendin technique and that sex alone does have an effect on the use of the Lamendin technique. They also concluded that the mean error rate is decreased when both sex and ancestry are included even though ancestry plays a lesser role in the new regression formulas. As a result, regression formulas were created and are listed as follows:

Male African Ancestry

$$\text{Age} = 1.04(\mathbf{RH}) + 0.31(\mathbf{P}) + 0.47(\mathbf{T}) + 1.70 \qquad 1 \text{ standard deviation} = 4.97 \text{ years}$$

Male European Ancestry

$$\text{Age} = 0.15(\mathbf{RH}) + 0.29(\mathbf{P}) + 0.39(\mathbf{T}) + 23.17 \qquad 1 \text{ standard deviation} = 5.92 \text{ years}$$

Female African Ancestry

$$\text{Age} = 1.63(\mathbf{RH}) + 0.48(\mathbf{P}) + 0.48(\mathbf{T}) + (-8.41) \qquad 1 \text{ standard deviation} = 7.17 \text{ years}$$

Female European Ancestry

$$\text{Age} = 1.10(\mathbf{RH}) + 0.31(\mathbf{P}) + 0.39(\mathbf{T}) + 11.82 \qquad 1 \text{ standard deviation} = 6.21 \text{ years}$$

The new regression formulas incorporated root height (RH) into the equation and calculated the variables "**P**" and "**T**" in the same manner as Lamendin et al.

This technique requires selection of single-rooted teeth. The hierarchy of best tooth selection is as follows; maxillary centrals over maxillary laterals, mandibular incisors over mandibular canines over mandibular bicuspids. The labial surface is used for all measurements. Teeth selected can have minimal restorations; however, there should be no periapical pathology. This technique is sex specific and is ancestry specific for European Americans and African-Americans. Results of the Gonzalez-Comenares study (Gonzalez-Comenares et al., 2007) demonstrated that the original Prince and Ubelaker method and the modified method provided better results than the Lamendin method confirming the need to create sex-differentiated population-specific data (Lewis and Senn, 2013). The useful age range of this technique is 30–69 years. Disadvantages of this technique include: poor oral hygiene, a diet high in sugars, and periodontal soft tissue surgeries, which can all influence accuracy of the periodontosis measurements; there is a learning curve involved in measuring periodontosis and root translucency, and lastly the teeth must be extracted.

The advantages of this technique include the use of only two morphologic variables, root transparency and periodontosis, simplifying regression formula calculations; radiographs are not required and there is no specialized equipment or training that is needed.

It should be emphasized that all of the aforementioned adult dental age estimation techniques tend to overestimate the ages of young adults less than 35 years and underestimate older adults greater than 80 years. Therefore when performing age assessment in the adult, the odontologist is wise to incorporate multiple age assessment modalities before the final age estimation is reported, including those skeletal indicators of age that a forensic anthropologist can provide. All age assessment methods have advantages and shortcomings, and are dependent upon the availability or existence of suitable population-specific reference data.

BIOCHEMICAL TECHNIQUES

Biochemical and histological dental age assessment techniques can be utilized in any age group and provide a high degree of accuracy. However, these techniques have disadvantages. The procedures are time intensive, expensive, require the use of specialized equipment, and the sacrifice of tooth structure. As a result, the use of these techniques can only ethically be performed on deceased individuals or in special situations in the living where tooth extraction is necessary for medical reasons.

Enantiomers, also known as stereoisomers, are two asymmetrical geometric mirror image forms of the same molecule. Enantiomers of a compound are either designated as the "L" or "D" forms based upon their optical characteristic to bend polarized light. Racemization is the spontaneous process in which one enantiomer of a compound converts to the other enantiomer. This process continues between forms eventually resulting in a solution of equal 1:1 enantiomeric mixture. In nature, the L-form of all amino acids is the biologically active form of the molecule and present at birth (Arany and Ohtani, 2010). Therefore an assay of the degree of amino acid racemization that has occurred within bradytrophic tissues is an indicator of chronologic age. Aspartic acid has the fastest racemization rate among the amino acids and thus the best for assessment of age (George et al., 1999). Bradytrophic tissues rich in aspartic acid include: vertebral discs, lens of the eye, portions of the brain, and tooth dentin (Riz-Timme and Collins, 2002). Because dental tissues have a high degree of durability, are protected from many extrinsic environmental factors, and survive the process of decomposition at death, dentin is an excellent source of aspartic acid for age assessment using the racemization technique. Tooth dentin aspartic acid racemization (AAR) has resulted in rates of uncertainty estimating the age at death as low as ± 3 years (Ohtani and Yamamoto, 2010).

Although use of radioactive ^{14}C has been utilized as an archeological tool since the mid-1900s, its use as a forensic application has only recently been realized. ^{14}C is naturally occurring, produced by cosmic rays interacting with atmospheric nitrogen, and had a stable atmospheric concentration for thousands of years. In the years between 1955 and 1963, aboveground nuclear testing produced and released large volumes of ^{14}C into the atmosphere. Following the Test Ban Treaty of 1963, atmospheric ^{14}C has declined due to radioactive decay and its incorporation into marine and terrestrial carbon reservoirs (Buchholz, 2007). Metabolically active plant and animal tissues reflect the atmospheric ^{14}C levels at the time of their development. Knowing the measured atmospheric levels of ^{14}C during its release and understanding the decay rate of ^{14}C, date of birth can be estimated from biologic tissues that are inert and biologically inactive. One source rich in carbon that is metabolically inactive is tooth enamel. An uncertainty rate of ±1.6 years has been reported by Spaulding et al. in assessing the date of birth in humans using radiocarbon enamel analysis. However, this technique is limited to the age assessment of individuals that were undergoing tooth development in 1955 or after. Therefore, when considering that the last tooth to undergo morphologic development is the third molar and that this tooth completes crown formation approximately at age 12, the earliest date of birth that can possibly be estimated is 1943 (Spalding et al., 2005).

Combining the techniques of AAR dentin analysis with ^{14}C enamel analysis can significantly improve the ability of investigators to identify unknown decedents by providing an estimate of the decedent's date of birth (^{14}C), age at death (AAR), and date of death—calculated by comparison of the results of the two techniques (Lewis and Senn, 2013).

Recent research has described the unification of a combination of techniques providing new information possibilities derived from human teeth. When used in combination, AAR, ^{14}C, ^{13}C, ^{18}O, and DNA analysis techniques have produced a genetic and geographic profile of individuals that include information indicating an individual's sex, assessed year of birth, assessed year of death, DNA profile, and information regarding the geographic region where the individual lived (Alkass et al., 2013).

GUIDELINES AND STANDARDS

There are a number of organizations throughout the world that create and publish lists of guidelines and standards meant to establish forensic protocols in performing age assessment. Two of the most prominent organizations that do so are the ABFO and the International Organization for Forensic Odonto-Stomatology (IOFOS). Published guidelines and standards from these two organizations can be found on their respective websites. The National Institute of Standards and Technology is currently working with the forensic science community and has established the Organization for Scientific Area Committees (OSACs). It is the charge of the OSAC to coordinate and develop standards and guidelines in an effort to improve quality and consistency of work within the forensic community.

Guidelines are intended to help direct procedures. They are recommended but are not compulsory. Standards establish required protocol and methodology of practice that has met the scrutiny of scientific study. The guidelines and standards listed below are a compilation of the efforts of the ABFO and IOFOS. It is expected that OSAC will produce a similar practice protocol.

Forensic Dental Age Assessment Guidelines

The forensic investigator should record:

1. Case identification data:

This information includes but is not limited to case number, referring agency, name of the examiner(s), date of the examination, the individual's name, and stated date of birth (if known), and any other pertinent informational data.

2. Biographical information of the individual (when known):

This information includes but is not limited to ancestry and geographic population specificity, sex, nutritional health, current and prior systemic diseases, socioeconomic status, habits, and addiction that may affect heath or the dentition, and any other environmental factors that may affect morphologic or postformation dental and skeletal development.

3. Dental evidence observed, collected, and measured:

This information includes but is not limited to specific teeth utilized in the evaluation, age assessment criteria (morphologic developmental staging, eruption pattern, root translucency, secondary dentin apposition, attrition, periodontal health, or any other measured dental developmental, or postformation characteristics), occlusion, oral hygiene, pathology, photographs, and radiographs.

The forensic report should include:

1. An introduction including case identification data and biographical information regarding the individual; an inventory of evidence received and/or collected; method(s) of analysis; and conclusion stating the expert's results, assessment of age, and error rate.

2. A disclaimer statement indicating that the opinion is subject to review and/or modification if additional information or evidence becomes available.

Forensic Dental Age Assessment Standards

1. The odontologist is to provide the best and most accurate assessment of true chronologic age of the individual utilizing scientific methodology.

2. The odontologist is responsible for being familiar with and will utilize current age assessment methodology.

3. All available information, including sex, ancestry, population specificity, biological information, and environmental factors is to be considered.

4. The most appropriate statistical data shall be utilized and applied in the assessment of an individual's chronologic age.

5. When practical, use multiple independent statistical methodologies.

6. Results of each independent statistical method applied are to be reported.

7. When utilizing an age assessment technique and its associated data to assess chronologic age, the specific methodology outlined within the study must be followed precisely. This will include but is not limited to morphologic staging and criteria measurements.

8. A list of dentition, anatomic structures analyzed, and specific technique(s), and/or the published study where statistical data were obtained shall be included within the body of the final forensic report.

9. The final age assessment is a matter of the dental provider's expert judgment by synthesizing all available information. However, conclusion statements specific to each methodology employed shall include estimated age and an associated uncertainty rate or age interval. When the information is available, the uncertainty rate should include statistically 95% of the considered specific population, or two SDs. If a peer-reviewed published scientific study(s) utilized to assess chronologic age does not provide a statistical rate of uncertainty of 95%, then, the rate of uncertainty as defined by that study shall be clearly stated in the forensic report

10. Immigration and legal age of majority cases shall include a probability statement that the individual has attained the age in question.

There are two supplemental guides published by the ABFO that can greatly assist the forensic odontologist in technique selection and utilization: the Child and Adolescent DAE Technique Chart and the Adult Dental Age Technique Assessment Chart. Copies of these supplemental guides can be found on the ABFO website (http://www.abfo.org). These charts list for a variety of methodologies, the age range of individuals included within the study, whether the technique utilized intact teeth or requires sectioning, measurements required to perform the method, best teeth to use for optimal results, tooth selection restrictions, and whether sex- and population-specific data are available.

References

AlQahtani, S.J., Hector, M.P., Liversidge, H.M., 2010. Brief communication: the London atlas of human tooth development and eruption. American Journal of Physical Anthropology 142, 481–490.

AlQahtani, S.J., Hector, M.P., Liversidge, H.M., 2014. Accuracy of dental age estimation charts: Schour and Massler, Ubelaker and the London atlas. American Journal of Physical Anthropology 154, 70–78.

Ajamal, M., Assiri, K.I., Al-Ameer, K.Y., Assiri, A.M., Lugman, M., 2012. Age estimation using third molar teeth: a study on southern Saudi population. Journal of Forensic Dental Sciences 4 (2), 63–65.

Alkass, K., Saitoh, H., Buchholz, B.A., Bernard, S., Homlund, G., Senn, D.R., Spaulding, K.L., Druid, H., 2013. Analysis of radiocarbon, stable isotopes and DNA in teeth to facilitate identification of unknown decedents. Plos One 8 (7), e69597.

Alshihri, A.M., Kruger, E., Tennant, M., 2014. Western Saudi adolescent age estimation utilising third molar development. European Journal of Dentistry 8 (3), 296–301.

American Board of Forensic Odontology, 2016a. Dental Age Estimation Procedures Chart. http://www.abfo.org.

American Board of Forensic Odontology, 2016b. Dental Age Assessment Guidelines and Standards. ABFO Reference Manual. http://www.abfo.org.

American Board of Forensic Odontology, 2016c. Adult Dental Age Estimation Technique Chart. http://www.abfo.org.

American Board of Forensic Odontology, 2016d. Child and Adolescent DAE Technique Chart. http://www.abfo.org.

Anderson, D.L., Thompson, G.W., Popovich, F., 1976. Age of attainment of mineralization stages of the permanent dentition. Journal of Forensic Sciences 21, 191–200.

Arany, S., Iino, M., Yoshioka, N., 2004. Radiographic survey of third molar development in relation to chronological age among Japanese juveniles. Journal of Forensic Sciences 49 (3), 1–5.

Arany, S., Ohtani, S., 2010. Age estimation by racemization method in teeth: application of aspartic acid, glutamate and alanine. Journal of Forensic Sciences 55 (3), 701–705.

Bang, G., Ramm, E., 1970. Determination of age in humans from root dentin transparency. Acta Odontologica Scandinavica 56, 238–244.

Bhat, et al., 2007. Age estimation from root development of mandibular third molars in comparison with skeletal age of wrist joint. The American Journal of Forensic Medicine and Pathology 28 (3), 238–241.

Blankenship, J.A., Mincer, H.H., Anderson, K.M., Woods, M.A., Burton, E.L., 2007. Third molar development in the estimation of chronologic age in American Blacks as compared with Whites. Journal of Forensic Sciences 52 (2), 428–433.

Boonpitaksathit, T., Hunt, N., Roberts, G.J., Petrie, A., Lucas, V.S., 2011. Dental age assessment of adolescents and emerging adults in United Kingdom Caucasians using censored data for stage H of third molar roots. European Journal of Orthodontics 33, 503–508.

Buchholz, B.A., 2007. Carbon-14 Bomb-pulse Dating. Wiley Encyclopedia of Forensic Science. John Wiley & Sons, Ltd., Chichester.

Burns, K.R., Maples, W.R., 1976. Estimation of age from individual adult teeth. Journal of Forensic Sciences 21, 343–356.

Caldas, M.I., Júlio, P., Simões, J.R., Matos, E., Afonso, A., Magalhães, T., 2011. Chronological age estimation based on third molar development in a Portuguese population. International Journal of Legal Medicine 125 (2), 235–243.

Cameriere, R., Ferrante, L., Belcastro, M.G., Bonfiglioli, B., Rastrelli, E., Cingolani, M., 2007. Age estimation by pulp/tooth ratio in canines by mesial and vesicular peri-apical x-rays. Journal of Forensic Sciences 52 (No 5), 1151–1155.

Cameriere, R., Ferrante, L., Cingolani, M., 2004. Precision and reliability of pulp/tooth area ration (RA) of second molar as indicator of adult age. Journal of Forensic Sciences 49, 1319–1323.

Cameriere, R., Ferrante, L., De Angelis, D., Scarpino, F., Galli, F., 2008. The comparison between measurement of open apices of third molars and Demirjian stage to test chronological age over 18 year old living subjects. International Journal of Legal Medicine 122, 493–497.

Choi, J.H., Kim, C.Y., 1991. A study of correlation between the development of the third molar and second molar as an aid in age determination [in Korean]. Korean Academy of Oral and Maxillofacial 16, 121–134.

Darji, J.A., Govekar, G., Kalele, S.D., Hariyani, H., 2011. Age estimation from third molar development a radiological study. Journal Indian Academy of Forensic Medicine 33 (2), 130–134.

Demirjian, A., Goldstein, H., 1976. New systems for dental maturity based on seven and four teeth. Annuals of Human Biology 3, 411–421.

Demirjian, A., Goldstein, H., Tanner, J.M., 1973. A new system of dental age assessment. Human Biology 45, 211–227.

Draft Age Estimation Quicksheets™ (Assists the odontologist in calculating age, age range and rate of uncertainty using Excel Spreadsheets): DAEQuicksheets@gmail.com, 2017.

Di Salvia, A., Clzetta, C., Orrico, M., De Leo, D., 2004. Third mandibular molar radiological development as an indicator of chronological age in a European population. Forensic Science International 166 (S), S9–S12.

Garn, S.M., Lewis, A.B., Kerewsky, R.S., 1965. Genetic, nutritional and maturational correlatives of dental development. Journal of Dental Research 44, 228–241.

George, J.C., Bada, J., Zeh, J., Scot, L., Brown, S.E., O'Hara, T., Suydam, R., 1999. Age and growth estimates of bowhead whales via aspartic acid racemization. Canadian Journal of Zoology 77, 571–580.

Gonzalez-Comenares, G., Botella-Lopez, M.C., Moreno-Rueda, G., Fernandez-Cardente, J.R., 2007. Age estimation by a dental method: a comparison of Lamendin's and Prince & Ubelaker's technique. Journal of Forensic Sciences 52 (5), 1156–1160.

Gunst, K., Mesotten, K., Carbonez, A., Willems, G., 2003. Third molar root development in relation to chronological age: a large sample sized retrospective study. Forensic Science International 136, 52–57.

Gustafson, G., 1950. Age determination on teeth. Journal American Dental Association 41, 45–54.

Haavikko, K., 1970. The formation and the alveolar and clinical eruption of the permanent teeth; an orthopantomographic study. Suomen Hammaslaakariseuran Toimituksia 66, 104–170.

Hackman, S.L., Buck, A., Black, S., 2010. Age evaluation from the skeleton. In: Black, S., Aggrawal, A., Payne-James, J. (Eds.), Age Estimation in the Living. Wiley-Blackwell, West Sussex, U.K., pp. 202–235

Haavikko, K., 1974. Tooth formation age estimate on a few selected teeth: a simple method for clinical use. Proceedings Of The Finnish Dental Society 70, 15–19.

Harris, E.F., 2007. Mineralization of the mandibular thirdmolar: a study of American Blacks and Whites. American Journal of Physical Anthropology 132, 98–109.

Harris, E.F., McKee, J.H., 1990. Tooth mineralization standards for blacks and whites from the middle southern United States. Journal of Forensic Sciences 35, 859–872.

Harris, E.G., Buck, A., 2002. Tooth mineralization: a technical note on the Moorrees-Fanning-Hunt standards. Dental Anthropol 16, 15–20.

Harris, E.F., Mincer, H.H., Anderson, K.M., Senn, D.R., 2010. Age estimation from oral and dental structures. In: Senn, D.R., Stimson, P.G. (Eds.), Forensic Dentistry, second ed. Taylor and Frances Group, Boca Raton, FL, pp. 263–303.

Johanson, G., 1971. Age determinations from human teeth: a critical evaluation with special consideration of changes after fourteen years of age. Odontologisk Revy 22, 1–126.

Kasper, K.A., Austin, D., Kvanli, A.H., Rios, T.R., Senn, D.R., 2009. Reliability of third molar development for age estimation in a Texas Hispanic population: a comparison study. Journal of Forensic Sciences 54 (3), 651–657.

Knell, R., Ruhstaller, R., Prieels, F., Schmeling, A., 2009. Dental age diagnostics by means of radiographical evaluation of the growth stages of lower wisdom teeth. International Journal of Legal Medicine 123, 465–469.

Kraus, B.S., Jordan, R.E., 1965. The Human Dentition Before Birth. Lea & Febiger, Philadelphia.

Kullman, et al., 1992. Root development of the lower third molar and its relation to chronological age. Swedish Dental Journal 16, 161–167.

Kvaal, S.I., Kolltveit, K.M., Thomsen, Ib O., Solheim, T., 1995. Age estimation of adults from dental radiographs. Forensic Science International 74, 175–185.

Lamendin, H., et al., 1992. A simple technique for age estimation in adult corpses: the two criteria dental method. Journal of Forensic Sciences 37 (5), 1373–1379.

Lee, S.H., Lee, J.Y., Park, H.K., Kim, Y.K., 2009. Development of third molars in Korean juveniles and adolescents. Forensic Science International 188, 107–111.

Lewis, J.M., Brumit, P.C., 2011. Dental age estimation and determination of the probability an individual has reached the legal age of majority. In: Paper Presented at the Annual American Academy of Forensic Sciences Meeting, February 21–26, Chicago, IL.

Lewis, J.M., Senn, D.R., 2010. Dental age estimation utilizing third molar development: a review of principles, methods, and population studies used in the United States. Forensic Science International 201, 79–83.

Lewis, J.M., Senn, D.R., 2013. Dental age estimation. In: Senn, D.R., Weems, R.A. (Eds.), Manual of Forensic Odontology, fifth ed. Taylor and Francis Group, Boca Raton, FL, pp. 221–255.

Lewis, J.M., Senn, D.R., 2015. Forensic dental age estimation: an overview. California Dental Association Journal 43 (6), 315–319.

Liversidge, H.M., 2008. Timing of human mandibular third molar formation. Annals of Human Biology 35 (3), 294–321.

Liversidge, H.M., 2000. Crown formation times of human permanent anterior teeth. Archives of Oral Biology 45, 713–721.

Lunt, R.C., Law, D.B., 1974. A review of the chronology of calcification of deciduous teeth. The Journal of the American Dental Association 89, 599–606.

Maples, W.R., 1978. An improved technique using dental histology for estimation of adult age. Journal of Forensic Sciences 23 (4), 764–770.

Martin-de las Heras, S., Garcia-Fortea, P., Ortega, A., Zodocovich, S., Valenzuela, A., 2008. Third molar development according to chronological age in populations from Spanish and Magrebian origin. Forensic Science International 174, 47–53.

McGettigan, et al., 2011. Wisdom tooth formation as a method of estimating age in a New Zealand population. Dental Anthropology 24, 33–41.

Meiln, A., Tangl, S., Huber, C., Maurer, B., Watzek, G., 2007. The chronology of third molar mineralization in the Austrian population – a contribution to forensic age estimation. Forensic Science International 169, 161–167.

Mincer, H.H., Harris, E.F., Berryman, H.E., 1993. The A.B.F.O. study of the third molar development and it use as an estimator of chronological age. Journal of Forensic Sciences 38 (2), 379–390.

Mohammed, R.V., Koganti, R., Kalyan, S.V., Tircouveluri, S., Singh, J.R., Srinivasulu, E., 2014. Digital radiographic evaluation of mandibular third molar for age estimation in young adults and adolescents of South Indian population using modified Demirjian's method. Journal Forensic Dental Sciences 6 (3), 191–196.

Moore, J.A., Lewis, J.M., Senn, D.R., 2016. Third molar age estimation: appropriately censoring stage "H" using the data from two previously published studies. Blankenship et al. (2007) & Kasper, et al. (2009). In: Presented at the Annual American Academy of Forensic Sciences Meeting, February 22–27, Las Vegas.

Moorrees, C.F.A., Fanning, E.A., Hunt Jr., E.E., 1963a. Formation and resorption of three deciduous teeth in children. American Journal of Physical Anthropology 21, 205–213.

Moorrees, C.F.A., Fanning, E.A., Hunt Jr., E.E., 1963b. Age variation of formation stages for ten permanent teeth. Journal of Dental Research 42, 1490–1502.

Mornstad, H., Reventlid, M., Teivens, A., 1995. The validity of four methods for age determination by teeth in Swedish children: a multicentre study. Swedish Dental Journal 19, 121–130.

Müller, N., 1990. Zur altersbestimmung beim menschen unter besonderer berückschtigung der weisheitszähne (MD thesis). University of Erlangen-Nürnberg, Erlangen, Germany.

Nawrocki, S.P., 2010. The nature and sources of error in the estimation of age at death from the skeleton. In: Latham, K.E., Finnegan, M. (Eds.), Age Estimation of the Human Skeleton. Charles C. Thomas, Publisher, Springfield, U.K., pp. 92–101

Nelson, S.J., Ash, M.M., 2010. Development and eruption of the teeth. In: Wheeler's Dental Anatomy, Physiology, and Occlusion, ninth ed. Saunders Elsevier, St. Louis, pp. 21–44.

Nyström, M., Ranta, H.M., Peltola, S., Kataja, J.M., 2007. Timing of developmental stages in permanent mandibular teeth of Finns from birth to age 25. Acta Odontologica Scandinavica 65, 36–43.

Ohtani, S., Yamamoto, T., 2010. Age estimation by amino acid racemization in human teeth. Journal Forensic Science 55 (6), 1630–1633.

Olze, A., Taniguchi, M., Schmeling, A., Zhu, B., Yamada, Y., Maeda, H., Geserick, G., 2004. Comparative study on the chronology of third molar mineralization in a Japanese and German population. Legal Medicine (Tokyo) 5 (1), S256–S260.

Orhan, K., Ozer, L., Orhan, A.I., Dogan, S., Paksoy, C.S., 2006. Radiographic evaluation of third molar development in relation to chronological age among Turkish children and youth. Forensic Science International 165, 46–51.

Prince, D.A., Ubelaker, D.H., 2002. Application of Lamendin's adult ageing technique to a diverse skeletal sample. Journal of Forensic Sciences 47 (1), 107–116.

Prieto, J.L., Barberia, E., Ortega, R., Magana, C., 2005. Evaluation of chronological age based on third molar development in the Spanish population. International Journal of Legal Medicine 119, 349–354.

Ritz-Timme, S., Cattaneo, C., Collins, M.J., Waite, E.R., Schutz, H.W., Kattsch, H.J., Borrman, H.I.M., 2000. Age estimation: the state of the art in relation to the specific demands of forensic practice. International Journal of Legal Medicine 113, 129–136.

Ritz-Timme, S., Collins, M.J., 2002. Racemization of aspartic acid in human proteins. Ageing Research Reviews 1, 43–59.

Ryman, N., 1975. A genetic analysis of the normal body weight growth and dental development in man. Annals of Human Genetics 39, 163–171.

Saunders, E., 1837. The Teeth, a Test of Age, Considered with Reference to the Factory Children: Addressed to the Members of Both Houses of Parliament. Renshaw, UK, London.

Schour, I., Massler, M., 1941. The development of the human dentition. Journal of the American Dental Association 28, 1153–1160.

Schour, I., Massler, M., 1944. The Development of the Human Dentition Chart, second ed. American Dental Association, Chicago.

Sisman, Y., Uysal, T., Yagmur, F., Ramoglu, S.I., 2007. Third molar development in relation to chronological age in Turkish children and young adults. Angle Orthodontics 77, 1040−1045.

Smith, B.H., 1991. Standards of human tooth formation and dental age assessment. In: Kelly, M.A., Larsen, C.S. (Eds.), Advances in Dental Anthropology. Wiley-Liss, New York, pp. 143−168.

Smith, E.L., 2005. A Test of Ubelaker's Method of Estimating Subadult Age from the Dentition (Master's thesis). University of Indianapolis.

Soares, et al., 2015. Evaluation of third molar development in the estimation of chronological age. Forensic Science International 254, 13−17.

Solari, A.C., Abromovitch, K., 2002. The accuracy and precision of third molar development as an indicator of chronological age in Hispanics. Journal of Forensic Sciences 47 (3), 531−535.

Spalding, K.L., Buchholz, B.A., Bergman, L.E., Druid, H., Friesen, J., 2005. Age written in teeth by nuclear tests. Nature 437, 333.

Soomer, H., Ranta, M., Lincoln, A., Penttilla, A., Leibur, E., 2003. Reliabiliity and validity of eight dental estimation methods for adults. Journal of Forensic Science 48 (1), 149−152.

Tang, N., Antoine, D., Hillson, S., 2014. Application of the Bang and Ramm age at death estimation method to two known-age archeological assemblages. American Journal of Physical Anthroplogy 155, 332−351.

Taylor, J., Blenkin, M., 2010. Age evaluation and odontology in the living. In: Black, A., Aggrawal, A., Payne-James, J. (Eds.), Age Estimation in the Living. Wiley-Blackwell, West Sussex, U.K., pp. 176−201

Thevissen, P.W., Pittayapat, P., Fieuws, S., Willems, G., 2009. Estimating age of majority on third molars developmental stages in young adults from Thailand using a modified scoring technique. Journal of Forensic Sciences 54 (2), 428−432.

Ubelaker, D.H., 1978. Human Skeletal Remains, Excavation Analysis, Interpretation, first ed. Taraxacum, Washington D.C.

Ubelaker, D.H., 1989. Human Skeletal Remains, Excavation Analysis, Interpretation, second ed. Taraxacum, Washington D.C.

Willems, G., 2001. A review of the most commonly used dental age estimation techniques. Journal of Forensic Odontostomatol 19, 9−17.

Willerhausen, B., Loffler, N., Schulze, R., 2001. Analysis of 1202 orthopantograms to evaluate the potential of forensic age determination based on third molar developmental stages. European Journal of Medical Research 6, 337−384.

Zeng, D.L., Wu, Z.L., Cui, M.Y., 2009. Chronological age estimation of third molar mineralization of Han in southern China. International Journal of Legal Medicine 124, 119−123.

Patterned Injury Analysis and Bitemark Comparison

Thomas J. David[1,2], James M. Lewis[3,4,5]

[1]Forensic Odontology Consultant, Georgia Bureau of Investigation, Division of Forensic Sciences, Decatur, GA, United States; [2]Clinical Assistant Professor, Department of General Dentistry, Forensic Dentistry Fellowship, The University of Tennessee Graduate School of Medicine, Knoxville, TN, United States; [3]Forensic Odontology Consultant, Alabama Department of Forensic Sciences, Madison, AL, United States; [4]Assistant Professor, Department of General Dentistry, Forensic Dentistry Fellowship, The University of Tennessee Graduate School of Medicine, Knoxville, TN, United States; [5]Adjunct Faculty, Center for Education and Research in Forensics, The University of Texas Health Science Center at San Antonio, San Antonio, TX, United States

OUTLINE

Forensic Odontology
https://doi.org/10.1016/B978-0-12-805198-6.00009-8

HISTORY OF BITEMARK EVIDENCE

Early Reports Concerning Biting and Bitemark

Although the history of dental identification dates to ancient times, the use of bitemark evidence is much more contemporary. There are several incidents involving biting and bitemarks beginning with William I (the Conqueror) (1066–87). There are no written records to corroborate these stories, but folktales claim that William I used his distinctive teeth to bite into the Seal of England as a means of authenticating his correspondence (Lerner, 2006). There are also largely unsubstantiated reports of biting during the time of the Salem Witch Trials in 1692. The Reverend George Burroughs is alleged to have bitten either those he was trying to induce into witchcraft or those who refused to sign their names in his book. Regardless of the circumstances surrounding these alleged biting incidents, George Burroughs was in prison during the times of the alleged attacks. The first use of bitemark evidence in a court of law in the United States occurred in 1870 in Mansfield, Ohio. Ansil Robinson was accused of the murder of his mistress, Mary Lunsford. She was found with "imprints of teeth" on her arm. During Robinson's trial, there was testimony concerning the bitemark evidence by Dr. Jonathan Taft, who later became the first Dean of the University of Michigan School of Dentistry. Ultimately,

Mr. Robinson was acquitted and therefore the admissibility of bitemark evidence was not reported or tested on the appellate level.

20th-Century Reports of Bitemark Evidence

A burglary case involving a bitemark in a piece of cheese took place in 1906 in County Cumberland in northern England. The teeth of one of the two alleged burglars were determined to "fit" the bitemark in the cheese, which led to a conviction (Harvey, 1976). This is one of the few reported bitemark cases in the first half of the century. However, the second half of this century saw a dramatic increase in the number of reported cases involving the use of bitemark evidence (Pitluck, 2000). One of the more noteworthy cases involving the use of bitemark evidence occurred in 1954 in Aspermont, Texas (Doyle v State, 1954). Under remarkably similar circumstances as the burglary case in England in 1906, there was a burglary of a grocery store and a piece of cheese was recovered, which contained a bitemark. An individual was later arrested for the burglary and while in custody, he was asked to bite into another piece of cheese. He complied with this request and the two pieces of cheese were later compared by a toolmark examiner as well as a dentist. Both individuals agreed that the same person had made both bites. Doyle was convicted at trial and later appealed his conviction. This is the first reported bitemark case in the United States. However, the appeal concerned violation of his fourth and fifth Amendment rights against self-incrimination and illegal search and seizure, but not the admissibility of the bitemark evidence itself. The Court ultimately denies his appeal on both issues (Doyle v State, 1954). Therefore, the issue of legal admissibility of bitemark evidence would be addressed later. Although there were several other cases of note in the 1950's and 1960's, there are many noteworthy cases from the 1970's (*Illinois v. Johnson, 1972; California v. Marx (1975), Illinois v. Milone (1976); Florida v. Bundy (1979, 1980); Florida v. Stewart (1979)*).

Admissibility of Bitemark Evidence

From 1923 until 1993, the standard for the admissibility of any expert witness testimony (including bitemark evidence) was *Frye v. United States*. Under the Frye standard or "general acceptance test," expert opinion based on a scientific technique is admissible only when the technique is generally accepted as reliable in the relevant scientific community. However, in 1993 the Daubert ruling (*Daubert v. Merrill Dow Pharmaceuticals*) modified the standard for the admissibility of expert witness testimony. Under the Daubert standard the Court determined that Rule 702 of the Federal Rules of Evidence (FRE) did not incorporate the Frye general acceptance test, but rather a flexible reliability standard. This standard was further refined in 1997 by the *General Electric Co. v. Joiner* case. This decision allowed district court judges to exclude expert testimony if there are gaps between the evidence relied on by an expert and his conclusion. The final refinement of the Daubert standard occurred in 1999 with *Kumho Tire v. Carmichael*. This decision clarified that a judge's gatekeeping function in Daubert applied to all expert testimony, including that which is nonscientific. However, the Daubert standard was only mandated in Federal courts,

although some states have adopted the Daubert standard as well.

Exonerations Involving the Use of Bitemark Evidence

Beginning in 2000, a number of exonerations in cases that included bitemark testimony began to occur. Most, but not all, of these exonerations were based on the use of DNA evidence and these cases have continued up to the present time. Needless to say, these cases have generated increased scrutiny concerning the use of bitemark evidence. Additional scrutiny was also generated by the NAS report in 2009 (Strengthening Forensic Science, 2009). While excellent bitemark casework has been and continues to be done, these exoneration cases (The Innocence Project) have led to increased criticism of its use by the defense bar. The problem with much of the criticism is that rather than focusing on correcting the problems identified by the exonerations, the focus has been on elimination of its use completely. This "scorched earth" philosophy is counter-productive to resolving some of the problems identified by the NAS report concerning the use of bitemark evidence.

BITEMARK CASES OF NOTE

As mentioned earlier, the second half of the 20th century saw a dramatic increase of the use of bitemark evidence in criminal cases. It also resulted in an increased level of appellate review of many of these same cases, thereby resulting in them being "reported." The vast majority of "reported" cases are the result of an appeal and subsequent review by state or national appellate courts or supreme courts. The most comprehensive list of appellate cases involving the use of bitemark evidence has been compiled by Pitluck and others (Pitluck, 2000). This list is chronologic and includes more than 300 cases beginning with Doyle v State, 1954.

Doyle v State, 1954, 159 Tex. C.R. 310, 263 S.W. 2d 779

The Doyle case is noteworthy because, as mentioned earlier, it is the first reported case involving the use of bitemark evidence in the United States. This case also included an appellate review, although the admissibility of the bitemark evidence was not part of the appellate review. Nevertheless, it became the precedent cited by many attorneys for the admissibility of bitemark evidence in other states.

Fredrik Fasting Torgersen (Norway), 1958

Although this case began with the murder of Rigmor Johnsen in 1957, it is still debated today. The most recent discussion of this case occurred at the American Academy of Forensic Sciences (AAFS) Meeting in New Orleans in February of 2017. After the discovery of her body on December 7, 1957, it was determined that she had been strangled, sexually assaulted, and also had a bitemark on her left breast. A forensic dentist from the University of Oslo, Professor Ferdinand Strom collected the bitemark evidence. He and another dentist linked the bitemark evidence to the teeth of Torgersen in the original trial in 1958. Torgersen was convicted of murder and sentenced to life in prison. An appeal, later that year, affirmed his conviction. He was released from prison in 1974 after serving 16 years. Despite his release from prison, Torgersen continued to maintain his innocence and repeatedly sought a new trial. Eventually, the Norwegian court agreed to reexamine the case. Professors Gordon MacDonald and David Whittaker of Scotland and Wales, respectively, reviewed the evidence in 1999 and 2000. Their reports supported the earlier conclusions. In February, Dr. David Senn traveled to Oslo to review the remaining materials. He reviewed all these materials, including the preserved breast of Rigmor Johnsen. All these materials were duplicated or photographed. These materials were examined and tested and later shown independently to three other forensic odontologists who reviewed case materials that were anonymous and blinded. All three wrote independent reports that excluded the alleged biter. These reports along with the report of Dr. Senn, who also excluded Torgersen, were sent to Norway and in 2001, the Supreme Court of Norway held a special hearing to review the evidence. Drs. MacDonald and Whittaker testified for the prosecutor and Dr. Senn testified for the defense. The Supreme Court denied Torgersen a new trial. Later, Torgersen's defense succeeded in getting a new hearing. Dr. Whittaker again testified for the prosecutor and Dr. Senn testified for the defense. Once again, Torgersen was denied a new trial. Nevertheless, although it has been more than 50 years since the original conviction, there is still an active effort to obtain a new trial.

Crown v. Hay (Scotland), 1967

The body of 15-year-old Linda Peacock was discovered on August 6, 1967, in a cemetery in Biggar, Scotland. She had been strangled and there was a bitemark on her right breast. The investigation focused on residents at a nearby minimum security school for troubled boys—the Loaningdale School. Drs. Warren Harvey and Keith Simpson conducted a detailed analysis of many of the local residents, including the boys at the Loaningdale School. The list of potential suspects was narrowed from 29 to 5 based on dental models that were collected. Additional evidence was collected from those five and eventually one of the boys at the school, Gordon Hay, was identified based on unusual pitting in the cusp tips of his right canine teeth. Hay was tried and found guilty. However, because he was a minor, he was sentenced to serve an undetermined term characterized as "at Her Majesty's pleasure" (Harvey et al., 1968).

People v. Johnson, 1972, 8 Ill. App.3d 457, 289 N.E.2d 772

This was the first US case involving a bitemark on human skin. The defendant was accused of rape and aggravated battery. There was a bitemark on the breast of the victim. Dr. Paul Green testified that the teeth of the defendant were similar to the bite pattern on the breast of the victim. Johnson was convicted of rape and aggravated battery. His appeal was denied.

People v. Marx, 1975, 54 Cal. App.3d 100, 126 Cal. Rptr. 350

This was the first bitemark case in California. Walter Marx was charged with the murder of Lovey Benovsky and the bitemark was the only physical evidence linking the defendant to the victim. At autopsy, "an elliptical laceration of the nose" was noted and later thought to be a bitemark. The defendant was jailed for refusing to provide his dental impressions for comparative purposes. He later complied with the court order and the victim was exhumed to document the bitemark on her nose. All this material was sent to Los Angeles where the crime occurred. This was the first time a team of three forensic dentists (Vale et al.) worked on a bitemark case together. This case also included the use of a three-dimensional model of the nose, as well as scanning electron microscopy. The three-dimensional features noted in the bitemark are unusual, even by today's standards. All three dentists testified at trial that the teeth of Walter Marx made the bitemark on Lovey Benovsky. Marx was convicted of voluntary manslaughter and his conviction was upheld on appeal.

People v. Milone, 1976, 43 Ill. App.3d 385, 356 N.E.2d 531

In 1972, Sally Kandel was murdered and had a bitemark on her inner right thigh, which some believe may have been inflicted after death. Richard Milone was charged with her murder and initially tried in 1976. At the initial trial, three forensic dentists testified for the prosecution and four testified for the defense. This case was considered by many as the first "battle of the experts" in forensic odontology. Milone was ultimately convicted and there were several appeals, all of which were denied. An executive clemency petition prompted the Governor to request a review of the evidence. Therefore, three different forensic odontologists who were not involved in the initial trial provided a joint opinion that Richard Milone made the bitemark on the leg of Sally Kandel. The defense later offered the testimony of another forensic odontologist to support the claim of their client's innocence to no avail. In all, there were 11 different forensic odontologists who opined in this case, 6 stating that he made the bitemark and 5 stating that he did not. This case was complicated even more after a convicted serial killer confessed to killing Sally Kandel. This case is noteworthy for the large number of experts who were involved in the case and the extreme range of their opinions, as well as the confusion created by confession of a different convicted killer.

Bundy v. State, 1984, 455 So.2d 330 (Fla. 1984), 349

In January of 1978, two women who were asleep in their beds at the Chi Omega Sorority House at Florida State University were attacked and bludgeoned to death. At autopsy, a bitemark was discovered on one of the homicide victims. This evidence was excised and preserved in formalin. After analysis, it was determined to be a bitemark and it was suggested that the biter had crooked teeth. The suspect in the case was a suspected serial killer from the state of Washington who was an escapee from a Colorado prison. Fortunately for the prosecution, they were able to find a scaled photograph of the bitemark for comparative purposes at trial. In all, three experts testified on behalf of the prosecution and one for the defense. Ted Bundy, who acted as his own attorney, was convicted of the murders of the two women who were killed and sentenced to death. He was ultimately executed for the murder of another victim, Kimberly Leach. This case received national media coverage because of Bundy's notoriety as a suspected serial killer. It also brought the use of bitemark evidence to national prominence.

Stewart v. Florida, 1982, 420 So.2d 862

Margaret Hazlip, a 77-year-old woman, was sexually assaulted and murdered in February of 1979. There were teeth marks found on the hip of Ms. Hazlip and a piece of bitten bologna was also found at the crime scene. The forensic odontologist for the prosecution indicated that the bitemarks in the bologna were not made by Ms. Hazlip and the bitemark on her hip was made by someone with a large space (diastema) between the upper two central incisors. Roy Stewart was later arrested and charged with the murder of Ms. Hazlip. Mr. Stewart did have a large diastema between his upper central incisors. This trial took place in the same courthouse and during jury selection for the Bundy trial. Mr. Bundy's defense team all attended the prosecution forensic dental expert's testimony. They took notes for later use in challenging his testimony in the Bundy trial. Mr. Stewart was convicted and sentenced to death. After numerous failed appeals, he was executed in 1994.

All later bitemark cases of note are discussed in this chapter under **Wrongful Convictions Involving Bitemark Evidence** (Description of Bitemark Exonerations, 2017).

RATIONALE FOR THE USE OF PATTERNED INJURY EVIDENCE

Introduction

Before discussing the rationale for the use of patterned injury evidence, it is essential to understand the definition of a patterned injury, an injury in tissue with distinctive configuration and features indicating the characteristics of the contacting surfaces of the object or objects that made the injury (ABFO, 2017). These injuries are often important pieces of evidence in criminal investigations. They may be instrumental in determining what object caused the injury and possibly lead to the object itself and perhaps who was in control of that object at the time the injury was inflicted. Because of the nature of these injuries, violent encounters are inherently associated with these investigations. In some cases, it is possible to profile the source of a patterned injury and sometimes it is not. Therefore, only cases where a profile of the patterned injury is deemed potentially identifiable progress beyond initial investigation. In other words, not all patterned injuries are useful for evidentiary purposes.

Human bitemarks are a specific subset of patterned injuries that are made by teeth, which can differ in arrangement, size, and surface configuration. Bitemarks are most often found on human skin, but may also be found on inanimate objects such as foodstuffs or chewing gum. The impressions left by teeth in inanimate objects are frequently more definitive than those left in skin, a less than ideal impression medium. Nevertheless, in some cases, there may be sufficient injury patterns that permit an analysis of the patterned injury in question. In these cases, it is possible to make a determination as to whether the injury represents a human bitemark and only then proceed beyond an initial investigation. This is an important point of clarification to make for those who are not forensic odontologists and may not be familiar with the analytic procedures that precede any comparison of bitemark evidence. Many individuals mistakenly believe that all patterned injuries suspected of being human bitemarks are compared with the dentitions of suspected biters. This is not true. Most cases never get beyond the initial phase of analysis. However, the small number of cases that proceed beyond the initial phase of the patterned injury analysis to determine if the injury is indeed a bitemark can produce valuable information for those conducting an investigation into the circumstances surrounding a violent encounter. Irrespective of any other violence, a bitemark (on skin) is indicative of a violent encounter. To produce a bitemark on skin, there must be sufficient force to cause blood vessels to hemorrhage and cause bruising, scraping, or cutting of the skin. This is a painful event for the person who is bitten and these injuries may provide important clues concerning the size, shape, and arrangement of the teeth of the biter. Sometimes these features are not particularly distinctive and may, under those circumstances, not be especially useful. However, if there are distinctive features in a human bitemark, this can be helpful in eliminating those individuals who do not have these distinctive features. This is especially useful in cases where the number of suspected biters is defined. Therefore, the rationale for the use of patterned injury evidence is its ability to, under certain circumstances, provide valuable evidence for those charged with conducting an investigation into the particular circumstances surrounding a violent encounter. It can help to determine who may be involved and who can be eliminated as participants in the event(s) in question.

Analysis of Patterned Injury Evidence

Patterned injuries may be caused by any number of objects other than teeth, including watches, necklace pendants, catheter tubes, and EKG pads (Figs. 9.1–9.4). Therefore, the first determination that must be made by a forensic odontologist is whether the patterned injury in question is a bitemark. The second question to be answered is whether the injury is a human bitemark, as opposed to an animal bite. Recognition of class characteristics is helpful in making this determination. The American Board of

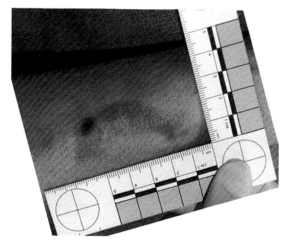

FIGURE 9.1 Patterned injury on the wrist of a decedent taken at autopsy after clothing and personal effects were removed. This patterned injury appears as though it may be a human bitemark.

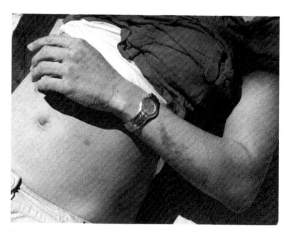

FIGURE 9.2 Another photograph of the decedent taken before autopsy with clothing and personal effects not removed. A watch is seen on the same wrist as the patterned injury in Fig. 9.1. Now it appears much less likely that this patterned injury is a human bitemark.

Forensic Odontology (ABFO) Manual defines a class characteristic as "A feature, trait, shape or array that tends to distinguish a bitemark from other patterns or patterned injury, an expected finding within a group" (ABFO, 2017). If it

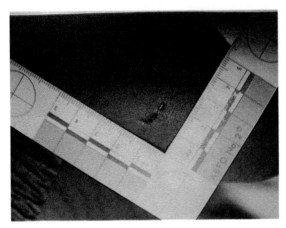

FIGURE 9.3 Patterned injury on the back of the hand. This patterned injury appears as though it may be one arch partial human bitemark.

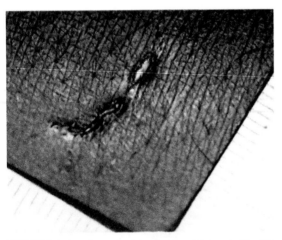

FIGURE 9.4 Close up of the patterned injury in Fig. 9.3. Note the curvature of the mark in the center of the pattern. Incisal edges of human anterior teeth are not curved. This patterned injury is not a human bitemark.

is determined not to be an animal or human bitemark, then the analysis goes no further. The ABFO guidelines, concerning the degree of confidence that an injury is a human bitemark, recommends the following terminology: (1) human bitemark; (2) not a human bitemark; and (3) inconclusive (ABFO, 2017). To determine

whether an injury is a bitemark, it is important to define a bitemark. "A bitemark is a patterned injury in skin or a pattern in an object caused by the biting surfaces of human or animal teeth" (Senn and Souviron, 2010). Although part of the analytic process involves measurement of various quantitative pieces of information, the indispensable part of the analysis is the ability of humans to recognize patterns. "Pattern recognition describes a cognitive process that matches information from a stimulus with information retrieved from memory. Pattern recognition does not occur instantly, although it does happen automatically and spontaneously. Pattern recognition is an innate ability of animals" (Pattern recognition (psychology), 2016). However, some humans are better at recognition of patterns than others. Therefore, the investigative component of the analysis must be combined with the qualitative ability to recognize patterns and patterned injuries. In other words, there is an element to the analysis that is much more intuitive and cannot be quantified. Even the quantitative part of the analysis cannot definitively determine whether a patterned injury is a bitemark. There is no formula for determination of whether a patterned injury is a human bitemark. Rather, it is a complex interpretive process based on analytic principles of medicine and dentistry. That is why this determination is called an opinion and bitemark analysis is not a bench science (White, 2016) as are toxicology or DNA analysis. Opinions concerning analysis of bitemarks are similar in many ways to determinations made by medical examiners as to cause and manner of death—they both are based on investigative principles founded on the basis of education, training, and experience to reach an interpretive conclusion after evaluation of all evidence.

All bitemarks are patterned injuries, but not all patterned injuries are bitemarks. If a patterned injury is a human bitemark, there are certain criteria that are usually present. The ABFO Manual describes a bitemark as follows:

"(1) a curvilinear pattern or patterned injury consisting of two opposing arches, often, but not always, separated at their bases by unmarked space; sometimes only one arch is clearly visible; (2) individual marks, abrasions, contusions, or lacerations from specific teeth may be found near the periphery of each arch; (3) a central area of contusion may or may not be present; (4) in more severe human bitemarks material may be forcefully removed from the medium bitten; (5) the marks present should reflect the size, shape, arrangement, and distribution of the contacting surfaces of the human teeth; (6) the size and shape of each arch conforms to the varying ranges of size and shape of the human dentition" (ABFO, 2017). In addition to the pattern described above, there may be additional individual patterns within the overall patterned injury that can help to determine whether it is a bitemark. Some of these individual patterns are quantitative and some are qualitative. However, there are several important factors that are essential to the determination of whether a patterned injury is a bitemark. These factors include the following: (1) Which is the maxillary (upper arch) and which is the mandibular (lower arch)? (2) Can the midline be identified? (3) Are there any individual tooth markings? (4) Can the mesio-distal width of any teeth be measured? If the forensic odontologist cannot determine which arch is which and where the midline is located, it will be difficult to say with any degree of certainty that the injury in question is a bitemark. These two pieces of information are critical if an analysis is to proceed beyond an initial phase of investigation. Any additional information (items 3 and 4 above) helps to support the determination that this injury is a bitemark and may warrant further analysis.

As stated earlier, if a patterned injury is determined not to be a human bitemark or there is insufficient information to make that determination, then the analysis does not proceed any further. However, even if the patterned injury is determined to be a bitemark, it still may not be suitable for further analysis. Oftentimes, there is insufficient evidentiary value for comparative purposes. Therefore, only a limited number of patterned injuries are ever compared to dentitions of suspected biters (ABFO, 2017) (Fig. 9.5).

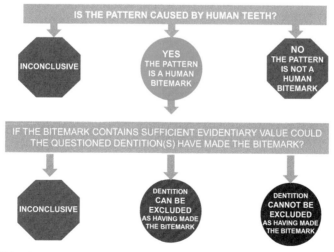

FIGURE 9.5   ABFO bitemark analysis and comparison Flowchart, 2017.

Comparison of Bitemark Evidence With Suspected Biters

If a patterned injury is determined to be a human bitemark and it has sufficient evidentiary value for comparative purposes, then and only then are suspected biter's dentitions compared with the bitemark in question. At some point during the investigation, dental impressions of suspected biters are taken and casts fabricated for possible comparative purposes. The individual who collects this evidence should not be the forensic odontologist who conducts the analysis and comparison of the evidence. This would introduce potential bias into the analytic process. When the actual number of suspects is low, there may be a "dental line-up" added to the pool of dental casts used for comparison. This dental line-up should include the dental casts of the person of interest and several randomly selected dental casts of other individuals all of which are labeled anonymously. All casts should be similar in appearance and marked with only numbers and/or letters. The individuals who correspond with these numbers or letters should only be known by the person who collected the evidence and the attorney in charge of the investigation. Therefore, the analyst is blinded as to the identity of suspects whose dentitions are compared to the bitemark(s) in question. There are numerous methods for comparison of bitemark(s) to dental casts recommended by the ABFO Manual (ABFO, 2017). These techniques include both direct and indirect methods of comparison, including digital enhancement of bitemark photographs and casts, digital overlay production, computer generated superimposition of casts over the bitemark(s), test bites, comparison of exemplars of the casts with 1:1 photographs of bitemark(s), video superimposition, and scanning electron microscopy. After all comparisons are completed, the forensic odontologist should state their opinion(s) relating the various dentitions to the bitemark(s) in question. The ABFO recommends the following terminology

(Senn and Souviron, 2010): (1) **excluded as having made the bitemark**—criteria: the bitemark demonstrates class and/or individual characteristics that could not have been created by the dentition in question; (2) **not excluded as having made the bitemark**—by definition this conclusion means that the dentition in question cannot be eliminated from having produced the bitemark and therefore is included within the population of dentitions that could have created the bitemark; (3) **inconclusive**—criteria: although the analyst has concluded that the pattern is a human bitemark, there is missing, incomplete, or otherwise insufficient information to support the formation of an opinion as to whether the bitemark in question could have been made by a specific individual's dentition. A linkage opinion should be provided for each suspected biter according to the aforementioned guidelines. If any of the linkage opinions are inconclusive, the forensic odontologist should state whether any additional evidence may be helpful in reaching a definitive conclusion. Once the analysis and comparison are complete, the forensic odontologist should produce a written report that summarizes their findings. The report should state how many patterned injuries were analyzed and whether each of the patterned injuries in question is determined to be a human bitemark. It should include how many of the patterned injuries determined to be bitemarks were compared to dentitions of suspected biters and it should state how many suspected biter's dentitions were compared to the patterned injuries determined to be bitemarks. Finally, there should be a linkage opinion for each suspect's dentition compared biter to the bitemark(s) in question.

Evidentiary Value of Bitemark Evidence

What is the evidentiary value of bitemark evidence? The answer depends upon whom you ask. The best answer to that question is—it varies. From an investigative and analytic perspective, sometimes bitemark evidence has little to no value and sometimes it can have tremendous value, depending on the evidentiary value of the patterned injury in question and the individual characteristics of the suspect dentitions. Although expert witness opinions (concerning the evidentiary value of bitemark evidence) are intended to be unbiased, our adversarial legal system inevitably makes them contentious. Therefore, the evidentiary value of bitemark evidence (or any other piece of evidence) is often dependent on whom you ask. If a prosecution expert believes that bitemark evidence has sufficient evidentiary value to render a definitive opinion, invariably the defense will attempt to find an expert who will say just the opposite. Recently, many pattern recognition forensic disciplines (including bitemark analysis and comparison) have come under fire and have been characterized as nonscientific. Most of these criticisms have been brought by the defense bar, in general, and the Innocence Project, in particular. Aside from their arguments concerning the scientific basis of bitemark analysis and comparison, considerable time is spent arguing whether a particular individual can be included within the population of individuals who could have made the bitemark in question. Often, a great deal of time is spent discussing how large that "included" population may be and whether the evidence is distinctive enough to narrow the pool of those who are included. Nevertheless, in many ways, the inherent value of bitemark evidence lies in its ability to exclude, rather than to include suspected biters in a given case. As a matter of fact, part of the process of comparison of dentitions to bitemark injuries includes a deliberate effort to exclude each dentition. On an analytic basis, it is more difficult to exclude someone than to include them in a pool of suspected biters. If someone is not excluded, then by definition, they are included. Inclusion means that the forensic odontologist cannot find evidence to exclude them. Therefore, the argument about how large the population of

suspected biters may be and whether that number can be reduced based on additional distinctive features found in the bitemark continues ad nauseam. However, if an individual is excluded, the argument concerning whether they made the bitemark in question is effectively concluded.

The practical difference between including and excluding someone as a suspected biter lies in understanding the significance of the presence or absence of markings in a bitemark. If a suspected biter has all of their anterior teeth, but the bitemark in question contains no marking in the position of tooth #7 (upper right lateral incisor), this finding does not necessarily exclude the suspect. There are a variety of reasons that a tooth that is present may not mark, including a bite through clothing, orientation of victim in relation to the biter, and the arrangement of teeth within the dentition. On the other hand, if the bitemark in question reveals that tooth #7 is marking, but the suspected biter's dentition does not contain tooth #7, that finding will exclude the individual as having made the bitemark. In summary, the absence of marking where a tooth is present does not necessarily exclude the dentition of a suspected biter, but the presence of marking where a tooth is absent does exclude a suspected biter as having made the bitemark with their dentition. In these authors' opinion (David & Lewis), exclusion is more powerful than inclusion because it requires a positive finding to demonstrate exclusion. It has the potential to eliminate a suspected biter early in an investigation and prevent the possibility of a wrongful conviction. This type of scenario has actually occurred in a child abuse investigation. The boyfriend of a woman who ran a babysitting service in her home was arrested as a suspected biter based in part on his previous criminal record. One of the children kept at the home had numerous injuries consistent with bitemarks discovered on the child's body when the parent came to get them at the end of the day. Analysis of the patterned injuries determined that they were human bitemarks. The bitemarks in question were then compared with the adult male suspect in custody. That individual's dentition was excluded as having made the bitemarks in question. This exclusion was based on lingual cusp marking on the lower arch of the bitemark in question. The adult male in custody did not have lingual cusp registration on the lower arch (Fig. 9.6). Further investigation revealed that one of the other children present in the home created the bitemarks in question. This child still had a complete primary dentition including lower primary molars with lingual cusp registration. All these events took place shortly before Christmas and as a result of the bitemark investigation, the adult male suspect was released from custody before Christmas. This is a practical example of the power of exclusion. Previous comments concerning the value of bitemark evidence summarize its significance best of all—"Bitemark evidence is too valuable to the investigation and adjudication of certain crimes to be abandoned, discounted, or overlooked. The use of bitemark analysis to exclude suspects is powerful and important" (Senn and Souviron, 2010).

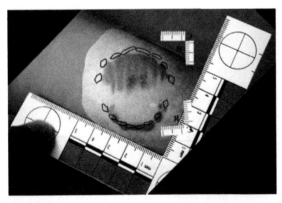

FIGURE 9.6 Overlay of suspect's bite pattern superimposed over bitemark in question. Note lack of lingual cusp registration in suspect overlay where marking is demonstrated by *arrow*. This suspect is excluded as having created this bitemark.

WRONGFUL CONVICTIONS INVOLVING BITEMARK EVIDENCE

Wrongful convictions are human tragedies and shine a dubious light on the judicial system. However, wrongful convictions are not necessarily the same as actual innocence. Not everyone wrongfully convicted is actually or completely innocent (Findley, 2007). There is a distinct difference between being legally innocent, but perhaps factually guilty. Nonetheless, the vast majority of the criticisms brought by the defense bar concerning the use of bitemark evidence are based on exonerations of previously convicted individuals, whose trials included bitemark testimony. Most of these exonerations are based on the use of DNA evidence. As of this writing, 350 individuals have been exonerated based on the use of DNA evidence (The Innocence Project). However, only a small number of those exonerations involve the use of bitemark evidence (Description of Bite Mark Exonerations, 2017). While these cases may demonstrate improper use of bitemark evidence, the use of bitemark evidence as a whole should not be branded as "junk science." Nevertheless, the Innocence Project seems determined to paint bitemark evidence as "the poster child of unreliable forensic science" (Chris Fabricant, Director of Strategic Litigation at the New York–based Innocence Project, as cited in Meyers, 2013) and "contrary to the overwhelming consensus of the scientific community" (Chris Fabricant, Director of Strategic Litigation at the New York based Innocence Project, as cited in Hansen, 2013). The vast majority of forensic odontologists who perform bitemark analysis and comparison readily acknowledge the past misapplications of bitemark evidence. As a matter of fact, the ABFO has recently enacted numerous measures to address prior misapplications of the use of bitemark evidence (ABFO, 2017). The Innocence Project reports that there are twenty-eight (28) exoneration cases that included the use of bitemark evidence (See Appendix). However, not all these cases were wrongful convictions and not all the exonerations were based on the use of DNA evidence. Six (6) of the twenty-eight (28) reported cases involve two (2) defendants (Description of Bite Mark Exonerations, 2017) and therefore there are actually twenty-five (25) cases involving twenty-eight (28) defendants. In the six (6) cases involving two (2) defendants there are a number of unusual circumstances, which will be discussed in more detail (Description of Bite Mark Exonerations, 2017). In the Williams & Washington case, the bitemark testimony indicated that Williams' dentition was "consistent" with the bitemark and Washington was excluded as the source of the bitemark in question. Therefore, the bitemark testimony does not appear to have played a critical role in the conviction of these defendants—one was excluded and the other was only linked as a possible source of the bitemark. Additionally, although Washington was exonerated by DNA testing in 2000, Williams' conviction was set aside for other reasons in 1992. In the Cristini & Moldowan case, two (2) forensic odontologists testified that the bitemarks in question were made by both defendants to the exclusion of all others and both men were convicted. After the conviction, an investigator found a witness whose eyewitness statement contradicted the victim's testimony. Subsequently, one (1) of the forensic odontologists recanted her testimony. Later, the court granted a new trial based on new eyewitness evidence, the recantation of the forensic odontologist and stronger alibi evidence. Ultimately, both defendants were acquitted in retrials. Therefore, the "exonerations" in this case were not based on DNA testing, but rather contradictory eyewitness testimony and controversial bitemark testimony. It is debatable exactly what role the bitemark testimony played in the outcome of the case. In the Hill & Young case, a forensic odontologist testified at trial

that the defendant's teeth were "similar to" or "consistent with" the bitemark in question. While DNA testing later excluded these defendants, the linkage opinion of the forensic odontologist did not contradict the DNA findings. "Similar to" or "consistent with" does not preclude the possibility of someone else making the bitemark in question. Twenty-one (21) of the twenty-eight (28) reported cases are exonerations from convictions, while the other seven (7) cases are arrests or indictments that ultimately resulted in the release of these suspects (Description of Bite Mark Exonerations, 2017). Therefore, of the twenty-eight (28) reported cases, only twenty-one (21) are actual convictions, while the charges against the other seven (7) defendants resulted in dismissal of charges without a trial. Some may argue that these individuals should not have been charged. However, the investigative process in these cases resulted in charges being dropped and ultimately these cases never went to trial. In the seven (7) wrongful indictment/arrest cases, DNA testing played a critical role in charges being dropped in six (6) of the cases, while charges were dropped in the remaining case due to problems with previous eyewitness statements. Of the twenty-one (21) actual conviction cases, seven (7) of those exonerations did not involve DNA testing (Description of Bite Mark Exonerations, 2017). In these authors' opinions (David & Lewis), only DNA exoneration is considered convincing proof of innocence. If you eliminate the cases that did not involve convictions (7) or DNA testing (7), there are fourteen (14) cases that involve DNA testing where bitemark testimony played a role in that conviction. When that number (14) is compared with the total number of DNA exonerations (350), the percentage of DNA exonerations involving bitemark testimony is **4.0%** (14/350). There will be more discussion of the importance of that percentage later.

Other important considerations in cases involving wrongful convictions and bitemark testimony include: (1) other evidence in these cases; (2) the linkage opinions of the forensic odontologists that testified; (3) whether there was opposing bitemark testimony in any of these cases. In the fourteen (14) cases that include bitemark testimony and subsequent exoneration by means of DNA testing, only three (3) of those cases had no other evidence. The remaining eleven (11) cases all included other evidence, which may have also played a role in the convictions. The Innocence Project agrees with this assessment and states that "most wrongful convictions involve more than one contributing cause" (The Innocence Project). The other evidence in these cases included the following: (1) blood evidence; (2) snitch testimony; probable Brady violations; (3) hair evidence; (4) footprint evidence; (5) eyewitness identification; (6) personal effects; (7) serology evidence; (8) possession of stolen items related to the crime; (9) confessions; (10) testimony of other witnesses. Many of the other forms of evidence listed above are associated with higher rates of wrongful convictions, including other forensic disciplines. If the cases that involve other evidence are eliminated, then only three (3) cases remain that demonstrate a clear association between the use of bitemark evidence and the wrongful conviction. Under these circumstances, the percentage of DNA exonerations that involve bitemark evidence is **0.8%** (3/350). The linkage opinions of the forensic odontologists who testified must also be considered. Any linkage opinions that are not definitive, do not contradict the possibility that someone else may have made the bitemark in question. The term "probable" means that it is more than 50% likely that the defendant made the bitemark. The term "possible" means the suspects' dentition may or may not have made the bitemark (i.e., teeth similar to the suspects could be expected to create a mark like the one examined but so could other dentitions) (ABFO, 2005). The terms "consistent with" and "cannot exclude" mean that the defendant is in the subset of the population that could have made the bitemark. Only the terms reasonable scientific, medical, or dental certainty or "the biter" are definitive and indicate a degree of confidence that is much higher and would contradict a DNA-based exoneration. However, even those terms do not indicate absolute certainty. The ABFO Bitemark Standards, which were revised in 2005, state that "terms ensuring unconditional identification of a perpetrator, or identification 'without doubt,' are not sanctioned as a final conclusions in an open population case" (ABFO, 2017). In the fourteen (14) cases under consideration, seven (7) of the bitemark linkage opinions provided by the forensic odontologist for the prosecution at the original trial were equivocal (less than definitive) and do not contradict a subsequent DNA exoneration (Description of Bite Mark Exonerations, 2017). Therefore, when only definitive opinions are considered, seven (7) of the fourteen (14) cases remain and the percentage of DNA exonerations that involve bitemark evidence is **2.0%** (7/350). Consideration of opposing testimony is important in the context of the adversarial legal system in the United States. In other words, did the defendant offer opposing bitemark testimony to challenge the opinions of the prosecution expert? If there was opposing testimony, then the defendant cannot argue that the opinions of the prosecution expert went unchallenged. Under these circumstances, the judge and/or jury was able to consider all perspectives concerning the bitemark testimony offered at trial. Of the fourteen (14) cases involving DNA exonerations that included bitemark testimony, six (6) of those cases had opposing bitemark testimony by the defense at trial (Description of Bite Mark Exonerations, 2017). Therefore, when only cases with no opposing testimony are considered (8), the percentage of DNA exonerations that involve the use of bitemark evidence is **2.3%** (8/350). In addition to opposing testimony at trial, many of these fourteen (14) cases had opposing opinions during the appellate review process (after conviction). In all, eleven (11) of these fourteen (14) cases included opposing opinions during appellate review (Description of Bite Mark Exonerations, 2017).

In this discussion of wrongful convictions involving bitemark evidence, consideration was given to the following factors: (1) How many exonerations involved actual convictions as opposed to arrests or indictments that later were dismissed prior to trial? (2) How many exoneration cases involved multiple defendants? (3) How many exonerations were based on DNA testing? (4) How many exonerations were based on cases with no other evidence to consider? (5) How many exonerations were based on a definitive linkage opinion of the forensic odontologist? (6) How many exonerations were based on cases with no opposing testimony at trial? After consideration of all these factors, the original twenty-eight (28) individuals on the list were narrowed down to single digits in many cases. When cases that did not involve convictions were eliminated, the list was narrowed to twenty-one (21). When cases that did not involve

DNA testing were eliminated, the list was again narrowed to fourteen (14). The list was further narrowed when other evidence, linkage opinions, and opposing testimony were considered. Therefore, the original exoneration rate of cases involving bitemark evidence, which started at **8.0%** (28/350), was reduced to **6%** (21/350) and later **4.0%** (14/350) when non-DNA exonerations were eliminated. This decrease in the percentage is based on consideration of the first three (3) factors listed above. The final reductions in the percentage of wrongful convictions were based on consideration of the final three (3) factors listed above and ranged from **2.3%** to **0.8%** (8/350 and 3/350). Regardless of what percentage is considered, it seems apparent that the percentage of wrongful convictions involving bitemark evidence is very small when compared with other forensic disciplines (Fig. 9.7). This is especially relevant when comparing these percentages with the amount of media attention devoted to criticism of the use of bitemark evidence from the defense bar. In addition, it is noteworthy that when

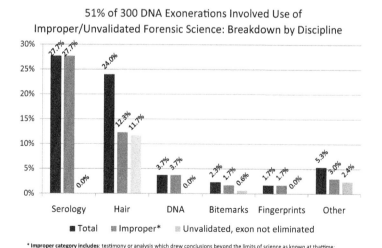

FIGURE 9.7 DNA exonerations involving various forensic disciplines as reported by the Innocence Project and found on their website on July 26, 2015.

comparing DNA exonerations among the different forensic disciplines, bitemark evidence is the second lowest of all disciplines. Only fingerprint evidence has a lower rate of wrongful convictions and DNA has a higher rate of wrongful convictions. This is especially ironic since the "gold standard" for measuring the rate of wrongful convictions is based on the use of DNA evidence!

Although erroneous forensic testimony is often cited by the defense bar as a culprit for many wrongful convictions, there are numerous other causes of erroneous convictions. In 2012, Dr. John Gould published a comprehensive study on the causes of erroneous convictions (Gould et al., 2012). This study includes a list of factors that correlate with erroneous convictions. Although forensic error is included in the list, there are nine (9) other factors discussed, which have nothing to do with forensic disciplines. Interestingly, the forensic error discussion does not include bitemark evidence. The take home message from this study is that forensic errors play only a small part in wrongful convictions, despite the pervasive comments in the media to the contrary.

IS PATTERNED INJURY ANALYSIS A SCIENCE?

According to Dorland's Medical Dictionary, "Science" is defined as the systematic observation of natural phenomena for the purpose of discovering laws governing those phenomena. Opponents of pattern analysis (i.e., bitemark, ballistics, fingerprint, etc.) argue that this form of evidence does not have measurable results producing error rates and therefore is unscientific. The fallacy in this statement lies in the fact that these opponents try to hold all the forensic disciplines to the standard of the bench sciences.

Bench sciences are performed in controlled laboratory settings using and testing nonhuman subjects. The logic employed in bench science is primarily one of deduction. Deductive reasoning allows the hypothesis to be tested resulting in specific data that confirms or rejects the original theory (see Fig. 9.8). The intent of deductive reasoning is to provide a guarantee of the truth based upon the conclusion provided. Therefore, a deductive argument provides such support for a premise that it would be impossible for the conclusion to be false (Butte College). Bench sciences rely upon strict adherence to definitions, mathematics, and formal logic producing statistical error rates and thereby validating the conclusions. Examples of forensic bench science utilizing deductive reasoning include DNA and toxicology analyses.

Obviously, pattern analysis does not meet the definition of a bench science. It is a nonbench science utilizing observation, measurement, and comparison to detect patterns and regularities (or irregularities) to formulate hypotheses that

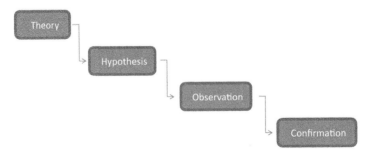

FIGURE 9.8   Schematic of deductive approach.

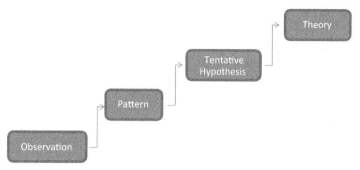

FIGURE 9.9   Schematic of inductive approach.

ultimately develop and produce general conclusions (see Fig. 9.9). This method of thinking is known as inductive reasoning. Inductive reasoning produce opinions or judgments based upon the argument that if the premise is true, it is unlikely that the conclusion is false (Butte College). An important distinction between inductive and deductive reasoning is that inductive reasoning can be affected by the acquisition of new evidence but deductive reasoning cannot. Therefore, conclusions resulting from inductive reasoning are in degrees of strength. William R. Oliver, MD, has published articles describing the ability of pathologists to interpret patterned injuries on human skin (Oliver and Fang, 2016; Oliver, 2016, 2017). The results demonstrate the importance of history and context in the medical diagnosis of patterned injuries. Similarly in bitemark analysis, it is imperative for the investigator to gather best evidence and to receive all the evidence associated with a patterned injury (orientation photographs, properly oriented photographs with scale, alternate light photographs, crime scene photographs, etc.).

Aristotle was the first to describe the difference in deductive and inductive arguments. Simply put, the difference is in the intentions of the observer or the investigator. If the investigator believes that the evidence definitely establishes the truth of the conclusion, then the argument is deductive. When the investigator believes that the evidence provides only good reason(s) to believe that the conclusion is most likely true, the argument is inductive. So, is pattern analysis a science? Absolutely! It is science that uses inductive reasoning to form an opinion or judgment following careful evaluation, testing, analysis, and comparison. When one evaluates the quality of a conclusion, the question is: How well does the evidence support conclusion? And thus, is the conclusion inductively strong, or is it weak?

To take this argument a step further, one needs to understand that pathologists and forensic odontologists are in a special category of investigators. They are clinicians. As clinicians, they are trained in the skill of differential diagnosis that relies upon the education, experience, and some testing to give the best opinion or judgment to identify an underling disease or pathological process. And as pathologists and forensic odontologists, they utilize this same differential diagnosis approach in the evaluation of patterned injuries on skin (or objects). Specifically, in the case of patterned injuries investigated as potential bitemarks, the forensic odontologist utilizes checklists to ensure the collection of appropriate evidence, and criteria and tests to assist in the development of sound inductive conclusions. For example, checklists are used to ensure proper evidence collection of the patterned injury and from dentitions of individuals of interest. Checklists have also been developed to assist in independent verification (second opinions) of the primary investigator's case evaluation, analysis, comparison, and conclusion(s). Criteria assist the investigator in analyzing the patterned injury to ascertain if the injury was created by teeth, and tests are performed to permit comparison and carefully developed conclusions.

For completeness, a third form of reasoning should be discussed—abductive reasoning. Abductive reasoning produces a most likely explanation or conclusion when the information available is incomplete (Butte College). Health care providers often utilize this form of reasoning to produce a medical diagnosis even if the diagnosis fails to explain all the symptoms present or absent, or the doctors are limited in their ability to obtain a complete medical history. This type of reasoning is also used by jurors in a trial to reach a verdict. Jurors are often provided incomplete evidence or must consider which argument provides the best explanation regarding the evidence in the case. Expert witnesses cannot always provide the jurors with simple "yes" or "no" answers; at times the best answer is "sometimes" or "maybe." Yet, jurors come to a verdict ("guilty" or "not guilty") based upon what they know and not necessarily all of the facts. It should be noted that a conclusion can be derived from one, a combination of any two, or all three forms of reasoning.

It is the most important to note that in bitemark analysis, there are two separate and independent conclusion processes. The first utilizes observation, measurement, and analysis of the patterned injury to determine if the injury meets the criteria specific to it having been made by teeth (a bitemark). If and only if this patterned injury is definitively judged to be a bitemark, does the investigative process proceed to performing tests and comparisons between suspect dentitions and the bitemark injury(s) in question to ascertain if a linkage cannot or can be made to an individual's dentition. There are only three conclusion and opinion statements currently sanctioned by the ABFO in their Standards and Guidelines for Pattern, Patterned Injury, and Bitemark Evidence regarding linkage between a bitemark and a dentition (ABFO, 2017). They are Inconclusive, Dentition Excluded as Having Made the Bitemark, and Dentition Not Excluded as Having Made the Bitemark. When there is insufficient detail (low evidentiary value) in the bitemark or suspect dentition(s), the evidence is "Insufficient" to draw a conclusion of exclusion or inclusion. The real value and power of bitemark analysis lies in the ability of the investigator to identify unexplained marks, abrasions, contusions, etc. (or lack thereof) within the pattern or patterned injury permitting the elimination of a particular dentition as having made the bitemark, thereby "Excluding" an individual. It is these authors' opinion (David & Lewis) that in comparison of dentitions to bitemark injuries, the duty of the forensic odontologist is to purposely attempt to exclude each dentition. When there is sufficient evidentiary value; and through analysis, testing, and comparison, no unexplainable discrepancies between the patterned injury and a dentition can be found, through inductive reasoning the conclusion of the investigator will be that the Dentition is Not Excluded as Having Made the Bitemark. By definition this conclusion means that the dentition in question cannot be eliminated from having produced the bitemark and therefore is included within the population of dentitions that could have created the bitemark.

MINIMIZING BIAS

To the lay person, bias can be defined as a strong inclination of the mind or a preconceived opinion resulting in an action supporting or opposing a particular person or thing in an unfair manner. Black's Law Dictionary Online, second edition, describes and applies the word bias in a legal context:

> Inclination; bent; prepossession: a preconceived opinion; a predisposition to decide a cause or an issue in a certain way, which does not leave the mind perfectly open to conviction. Maddox v. State, 32 Ga. 5S7, 79 A.m. Dec. 307; Pierson v. State, 18 Tex. App. 55S; Hinkle v. State, 94 Ga. 595, 21 S. E. 601. This term is not synonymous with "prejudice." By the use of this word in a statute declaring disqualification of jurors, the legislature intended to describe another and somewhat different ground of disqualification. A man cannot be prejudiced against another without being biased against him; but he may be biased without being prejudiced. Bias is "a particular influential power, which sways the judgment; the inclination of the mind towards a particular object."

A duty of a forensic expert is to form a judgment or opinion without themselves becoming prejudiced and in turn, inadvertently creating bias toward the trier of fact's cognitive process of reaching a verdict. There is potential for prejudice beginning with the first and continuing with subsequent contact between law enforcement and crime scene investigators requesting assistance from a forensic odontologist in the evaluation of a patterned injury. Often the investigators are more than eager to offer information or evidence pertaining to the situation or person(s) of interest that is inflammatory. The odontologist must resist the temptation to permit this information from being provided to them.

The Totalitarian Ego is a process where the ego fabricates and revises information or justifies a conclusion through cognitive biases (Senn and Souviron, 2010). Greenwald, 1980 described three cognitive means by which human behavior and ego are affected.

1. *Egocentricity*: the self-perceives itself more central to events than it truly is.
2. *Beneffectance*: the acceptance of credit for positive acts or outcomes and the denial of undesired results.

3. *Conservatism*: the selective acceptance of information or evidence that supports their judgment or conclusion and the reluctance to acknowledge information or evidence that is contradictory. This results in a resistance to cognitive change and is problematic for the identification sciences.

Senn and Souviron, 2010 commented on the effects of Totalitarian Ego and concluded that:

> Forensic odontologists must learn to deal with these (Totalitarian Ego inserted by author) effects before the consequences appear in their work. They must recognize personal signs of ego-related hazards, and take draconian steps to reduce expectation or confirmation bias. This can be greatly facilitated by continuing the development and positive modification of guidelines and protocols designed to minimize those effects.

In bitemark and patterned injury analysis, there are several ways that the forensic odontologist can consciously minimize the potential for inadvertent prejudice. The ABFO Standards and Guidelines for Pattern, Patterned Injury, and Bitemark Evidence should be consulted and reviewed for changes and edits and these standards and guidelines should be followed by all forensic odontology bitemark investigators.

Blinding

In patterned injury analysis, blinding is the process whereby the identifying information is masked or concealed from the investigator until all evaluation, analysis, testing, and comparison have been performed, and the resulting conclusions and opinions have been made. This does not imply that an investigator is not permitted to amend or change an opinion(s) if additional information is later provided. Forms of blinding that should be practiced by the forensic odontologist in the performance of patterned injury analysis include as follows:

1. Collection of Evidence Protocol: An odontologist performing testing and comparison of dentitions to the bitemark in question should not collect evidence from both the persons having injuries suspected as being bitemarks, and in addition, the evidence from individuals who potentially could have created the bitemark. It is these authors' (David & Lewis) personal opinion that it is best for the forensic odontologist performing the analysis of the patterned injury, testing, and comparison to avoid contact with and collection of evidence from any person of interest who may have created the bitemark.

2. All evidence should be similarly produced, devised, and constructed to prevent the disclosing of any information, including but not limited to identifiers who could produce bias. This particularly pertains to labeling of casts, photographs, and other evidence that may identify a person of interest. Blinding must be maintained until after all evaluation, analyses, comparisons, and opinions have been formulated by the investigator.

3. Dental lineup: The forensic odontologist performing the evaluation and analysis of the patterned injury, testing, and comparison should utilize dental casts from multiple individuals when performing bitemark analysis. This deflects bias away from any one individual. When there are several individuals who had opportunity, a natural lineup is created. However, when only a single individual is the person of interest, the forensic odontologist should request that a "dental line-up" is created by another dentist. This dental line-up should include the dental casts of the person of interest and several additional randomly selected dental casts of other individuals all of which are labeled in a manner providing anonymity.

Independent Verification (Second Opinion)

In bitemark analysis, independent verification or second opinion is an internal process whereby the primary investigator of a patterned injury case provides all case information to another forensic odontologist for evaluation, testing, analysis, and comparison to confirm that there is agreement in conclusion(s) and that the ABFO Standards and Guidelines for Pattern, Patterned Injury, and Bitemark Evidence has been followed. It is common practice for other pattern sciences to use independent verification (i.e., Fingerprint analysis). However, in bitemark analysis, this practice was first encouraged by the ABFO in 2011 as a voluntary technical review to determine if the analysis and the report adhered to the ABFO bitemark standards, guidelines, methodology, and terminology. Since that time, independent verification has become an ABFO bitemark and patterned injury guideline. This guideline should be followed by all forensic odontologists. It states that before submission of a final report excluding or including a dentition as having made a bitemark, forensic odontologists should seek independent verification in the form of a second opinion from a minimum of one other ABFO Diplomate. Although non-ABFO diplomates are not required to utilize ABFO Diplomates as a source of a second opinion, these authors strongly encourage their use because the utilization of a certified competent forensic odontologist only strengthens the verification of the opinion(s). The ABFO guideline on independent verification further states that the forensic odontologist performing the second opinion should be blinded to the original conclusions or the referring odontologist, as well as to the information that could reveal identifying information regarding persons of interest or otherwise introduce bias.

Following Patterned Injury Analysis Methodology

In any patterned injury case, the established methodology should be followed in every facet of evaluation, analysis, and comparison. The intent of methodological protocols is to provide an objective, standardized approach to pattern and patterned injury analysis to improve results and strengthen inductive conclusions. Following established methodology encourages the investigator to stick to the facts thereby limiting cognitive bias.

Conservative Opinion Statements

Despite the fact hearings and trials are designed to be unbiased assessments of the facts of a case, prejudice can be introduced to unfairly sway the trier of fact. As an expert witness, the forensic odontologist should form an opinion, write a report, and express in court that opinion pertaining to a patterned injury in which *"eventus apte apta conclusio,"* the results appropriately fit the conclusion. There should be no embellishment of the conclusion(s) linking an individual to a bitemark. The ABFO Standards and Guidelines for Pattern, Patterned Injury, and Bitemark Evidence terms for relating or linking an individual's dentition to a bitemark only provide the odontologist three options: "Excluded as Having Made the Bitemark"; "Not Excluded as Having Made the Bitemark"; or "Inconclusive." The definitions are simple and the mathematics is elementary. "Inconclusive" means that the available information is insufficient to support a formation of an opinion as to if the bitemark could have been created by a specific individual's dentition. "Excluded" means the bitemark demonstrates characteristics that could not have been made by a specific individual's dentition. In the case of the opinion of "Not Excluded," the bitemark demonstrates characteristics that could have been made by a specific individual's dentition,

and there are no unexplainable discrepancies between the features of the bitemark and that dentition. Therefore, the conclusion is that the individual's dentition is included in the population of dentitions that could have created the bitemark. In other words, the mathematics is only in terms of sets and identifying subsets. The expert needs to keep in mind that pattern and patterned analysis is a nonbench science that produces a judgmental conclusion through the process of inductive thought. Therefore, a statistical error rate will *never* be available to validate the opinion. Our opinion or judgment is NOT scientific fact but rather is our best understanding of the circumstances and our belief at that particular time. It is the trier of fact that will place weight on the evidence, not the expert.

The 2009 National Academy of Sciences Report, "Strengthening Forensic Science in the United States: A Path Forward," did conclude that forensic scientists are susceptible to cognitive and contextual bias. Although there is always a danger of misconduct, cognitive bias is most often unintentional and unconscious. The very nature of bitemark analysis results in the investigator's exposure to powerful and disturbing images and events. Awareness, training, and good intent will not provide immunity to cognitive bias. As a forensic investigator, the odontologist should attempt to improve their judgment and decision-making by reducing the potential for bias and error. This may in part be accomplished through the use of blinding techniques to prevent exposure to potentially bias producing information that is irrelevant to the investigative process. Following the patterned injury methodological protocols will assist in the development of strong inductive conclusions; conclusions that need to remain accurate and conservative without prejudice. And the utilization of independent verification will provide a pathway for quality control and error management.

APPENDIX

Description of 28 bitemark exoneration cases as reported by the Innocence Project.

INNOCENCE PROJECT

DESCRIPTION OF BITE MARK EXONERATIONS

1. **Keith Allen Harward:** Keith Harward was convicted of the September 1982 murder of a man and the rape of his wife. The assailant, who was dressed as a sailor, bit the rape victim's legs multiple times during the commission of the rape. Because of the assailant's uniform, the investigation focused on the sailors aboard a Navy ship dry-docked near the victims' Newport News, Virginia, home. Dentists aboard the ship ran visual screens of the dental records and teeth of between 1,000 and 3,000 officers aboard the ship; though Harward's dentition was initially highlighted for additional screening, a forensic dentist later excluded Harward as the source of the bites. The crime went unsolved for six months, until detectives were notified that Harward was accused of biting his then-girlfriend in a dispute. The Commonwealth then re-submitted wax impressions and dental molds of Harward's dentition to two ABFO board-certified Diplomates, Drs. Lowell Levine and Alvin Kagey, who both concluded that Harward was the source of bite marks on the rape victim. Although the naval and local dentists who conducted the initial screenings had excluded Harward as the source of the bites, in the wake of the ABFO Diplomates' identifications they both changed their opinions. Harward's defense attorneys also sought opinions from two additional forensic dentists prior to his trials, but those experts also concluded that Harward inflicted the bites; in total, six forensic dentists falsely identified Harward as the biter.

   At Harward's second trial, Dr. Levine testified there was "a very, very, very high degree or probability"—so high that it would be a "[p]ractical impossibility"—that anyone other than Harward inflicted the bites on the victim. Similarly, Dr. Kagey testified that Harward was the biter "with all medical certainty" and "that there is just not anyone else that would have this unique dentition." Post-conviction DNA evidence, however, excluded Harward as the source of all biological evidence collected from the victim and the crime scene and identified the true perpetrator, a sailor who was stationed on Harward's ship at the time of the crime. That man died in an Ohio prison in 2006 while serving time for abduction. On April 7, 2016, Harward was declared innocent by the Virginia Supreme Court, and he walked out of prison the next day, following 33 years of wrongful imprisonment.[1]

2. **Robert Lee Stinson:** Robert Lee Stinson served over 23 years in a Wisconsin prison for the brutal rape and murder of 63-year-old victim Ione Cychosz. The only physical evidence against Stinson at his 1985 trial was the bite mark testimony of two board-certified ABFO Diplomates, Drs. Lowell Thomas

---

[1] *The Innocence Project – Know the Cases: Browse Profiles: Keith Harward*, http://www.innocenceproject.org/cases/keith-allen-harward/.

Johnson and Raymond Rawson. Dr. Johnson concluded that the bite marks "had to have been made by teeth identical" to Stinson's and claimed that there was "no margin for error" in his conclusion. Dr. Rawson, the chairman of the Bite Mark Standards Committee of the ABFO, testified that the bite mark evidence was "high quality" and "overwhelming." Both experts testified "to a reasonable degree of scientific certainty" that the bite marks on the victim had been inflicted at or near the time of death, and that Stinson was the only person who could have inflicted the wounds. After examining Dr. Johnson's workup, Dr. Rawson stated that the methods Dr. Johnson used in gathering the evidence complied with the "standards of the American Board of Forensic Odontology."

The Wisconsin Innocence Project accepted Stinson's case in 2005 and sought DNA testing of saliva and blood-stains on the victim's sweater, which ultimately excluded Stinson. On January 30, 2009, Stinson, then 44, was freed and his conviction was vacated.[2]

3. **Gerard Richardson:** On December 17, 2013, Gerard Richardson was exonerated after post-conviction DNA testing proved his innocence in a 1994 murder case. He spent nearly 20 years in prison for a crime he did not commit. At Richardson's 1995 trial, ABFO board-certified Diplomate Dr. Ira Titunik testified that a bite mark found on the victim's back "was made by Gerard Richardson . . . there was no question in my mind," and the prosecutor argued that the bite mark was indisputably made by Richardson: "Mr. Richardson, in effect, left a calling card. . . . It's as if he left a note that said, 'I was here,' and signed it because the mark on her back was made by no one else's teeth." There was no other physical evidence tying Richardson to the crime. He was sentenced to 30 years in prison without the possibility of parole. More than 19 years after Monica Reyes was murdered, new evidence demonstrated that Richardson was innocent.[3]

4. **Willie Jackson:** On May 26, 2006, Willie Jackson was exonerated after post-conviction DNA testing proved his innocence in a 1986 sexual assault case. He had spent 17 years in prison for a crime he did not commit. At Jackson's trial, Dr. Robert Barsley, past president of the American Board of Forensic Odontology (ABFO), told the jury that the bite marks on the victim matched Jackson: "My conclusion is that Mr. Jackson is the person who bit this lady." Ultimately, DNA evidence showed that it was Willie Jackson's brother, Milton Jackson, who

---

[2] *The Innocence Project – Know the Cases: Browse Profiles: Robert Lee Stinson*, *http://www.innocenceproject.org/cases/robert-lee-stinson/*; *State v. Stinson*, 134 Wis. 2d 224, 397 N.W.2d 136 (Ct. App. 1986).

[3] *The Innocence Project – Know the Cases: Browse Profiles: Gerard Richardson*, http://www.innocenceproject.org/cases/gerard-richardson/; *see also* http://www.innocenceproject.org/docs/Richardson_Final_Motion_to_Vacate_091713.pdf.

attacked and raped the victim.[4]

5. **Roy Brown:** In January 2007, Roy Brown was exonerated of stabbing and strangling Sabina Kulakowski after spending 15 years in prison. He was convicted of her murder in January 1992 based on bite mark evidence that was the centerpiece of the prosecution's case against Brown. Kulakowski's body had been discovered with multiple bite marks on her back, arm, and thigh, all of which board-certified ABFO Diplomate Dr. Edward Mofson[5] claimed were a match to Brown's teeth. Mofson testified to a "reasonable degree of dental certainty" that Brown's dentition was "entirely consistent" and "completely consistent" with all of the bite marks, noting that the bite marks depicted the absence of the same two teeth Brown was missing.

Fifteen years after the conviction, however, DNA testing performed on saliva stains left by the perpetrator excluded Brown and matched another suspect, Barry Bench. Nevertheless, citing the prosecution's bite mark evidence at the original trial, which the jury asked to review during deliberations, the judge in the case initially refused to release Brown. Ultimately, in January 2007, the district attorney acknowledged Brown's innocence, and he was exonerated after spending 15 years in prison for a murder he did not commit.[6]

6. **Ray Krone:** On December 31, 1991, Ray Krone was arrested and charged with the murder, kidnapping, and sexual assault of a woman who worked at a bar he frequented. Police had a Styrofoam impression made of Krone's teeth for comparison to bite marks found on the victim's body and, thereafter, he became known in the media as the "Snaggle Tooth Killer" due to his crooked teeth. Dr. Raymond Rawson, a board-certified ABFO Diplomate, testified that the bite marks found on the victim's body matched Krone's teeth. Based on this testimony, Krone was convicted of murder and kidnapping and sentenced to death.

---

[4] *The Innocence Project – Know the Cases: Browse Profiles: Willie Jackson,* http://www.innocenceproject.org/cases/willie-jackson/; *Jackson v. Day,* No. Civ. A. 95-1224, 1996 WL 225021, at *1 (E.D. La. May 2, 1996), *rev'd,* 121 F.3d 705 (5th Cir. 1997); Barsley 1989 trial court testimony, *transcript available at* http://www.law.virginia.edu/pdf/faculty/garrett/innocence/jackson.pdf.

[5] All representations that the dentists at issue in this appendix were "board-certified ABFO Diplomates" are based on the *American Board of Forensic Odontology Diplomate Information, available at* http://www.abfo.org/wp-content/uploads/2013/02/ABFO-Diplomate-Information-revised-9-29-2015.pdf.

[6] Fernando Santos, *In Quest for a Killer, an Inmate Finds Vindication,* N.Y. Times, Dec. 21, 2006, http://www.nytimes.com/2006/12/21/nyregion/21brown.html?pagewanted=all&_r=1; *The Innocence Project - Know the Cases: Browse Profiles: Roy Brown,* http://www.innocenceproject.org/cases/roy-brown/; Brandon L. Garrett, *Convicting the Innocent: Where Criminal Prosecutions Go Wrong* 108-09 (Harvard University Press 2011); Mofson 1992 trial court testimony, *transcript available at* http://www.law.virginia.edu/pdf/faculty/garrett/innocence/brown1.pdf; David Lohr, *Quest for Freedom: The True Story of Roy Brown, available at* http://www.trutv.com/library/crime/criminal_mind/forensics/ff311_roy_brown/5.html.

In 1996, Krone won a new trial on appeal, but was convicted again based mainly on the state's supposed expert bite mark testimony. This time, however, the judge sentenced him to life in prison, citing doubts about whether or not Krone was the true killer. It was not until 2002, after Krone had served more than 10 years in prison, that DNA testing proved his innocence.[7]

7. **Calvin Washington &**
8. **Joe Sidney Williams:** Calvin Washington was convicted of capital murder in 1987 after a woman was found beaten, raped, and murdered in Waco, Texas. It was alleged that Washington and Williams murdered and sexually assaulted the victim in the course of committing a burglary. A forensic dentist and former president of the American Academy of Forensic Sciences, Dr. Homer Campbell, testified that a bite mark found on the victim was "consistent with" Williams' dentition. While Campbell excluded Washington as the source of the bite mark, his bite mark testimony about Williams (which was given at Washington's trial) tied Washington to the crime.

   After serving more than 13 years of his sentence, Washington was finally exonerated in 2000 when DNA testing showed that blood on a shirt found in Washington's home did not come from the victim, as previously asserted; testing conducted a year later pointed to another man as the perpetrator.[8] Prior to Washington's exoneration, the Texas Court of Criminal Appeals had set aside Williams' conviction in 1992 and the charges against him were dismissed on June 30, 1993.

9. **James O'Donnell:** James O'Donnell was convicted in 1998 of attempted sodomy and second-degree assault. Board-certified ABFO Diplomate Dr. Harvey Silverstein opined that a bite mark on the victim's hand was consistent with O'Donnell's dentition. Based on an eyewitness' identification and the bite mark evidence, and despite testimony from O'Donnell's wife and son that he had been at home with them when the crime occurred, the jury convicted O'Donnell. He was sentenced to three-and-a-half to seven years in prison.

   In 2000, after DNA samples from a rape kit excluded O'Donnell as the source of the semen found on the victim, his conviction was formally vacated.[9]

---

[7] *The Innocence Project – Know the Cases: Browse Profiles: Ray Krone*, http://www.innocenceproject.org/cases/ray-krone/.

[8] *The Innocence Project – Know the Cases: Browse Profiles: Calvin Washington*, http://www.innocenceproject.org/cases/calvin-washington/; Michael Hall, *The Exonerated*, Texas Monthly, Nov. 2008, *available at* http://www.texasmonthly.com/articles/the-exonerated/.

[9] *The Innocence Project – News: Cases Where DNA Revealed That Bite Mark Analysis Led to Wrongful Arrests and Convictions*, http://www.innocenceproject.org/cases-where-dna-revealed-that-bite-mark-

10. **Levon Brooks:** Levon Brooks spent 16 years in prison for the rape and murder of a three-year-old girl that he did not commit. Forensic dentist Dr. Michael West claimed that the marks on the victim's body were human bite marks and he testified at Brooks' trial that, of 13 suspects whose dentitions he had compared to the wounds on the victim's body, Brooks' teeth "matched" the marks on the victim. As he explained, "it could be no one but Levon Brooks that bit this girl's arm." Based on this, Brooks was convicted of capital murder and sentenced to life in prison.

In 2001, DNA testing and a subsequent confession revealed that Justin Albert Johnson committed the murder. Johnson had been one of the 12 other suspects whose dental impressions Dr. West had determined did not match the bite marks on the victim's body. Following Johnson's confession, Brooks was freed on February 15, 2008.[10]

11. **Kennedy Brewer:** In 1992, Kennedy Brewer was arrested in Mississippi and accused of killing his girlfriend's three-year-old daughter. The medical examiner who conducted the autopsy, Dr. Steven Hayne, testified that he had found several marks on the victim's body that he believed to be bite marks. Hayne called in Dr. West to analyze the marks, and Dr. West concluded that 19 marks found on the victim's body were "indeed and without a doubt" inflicted by Brewer. Brewer was convicted of capital murder and sexual battery on March 24, 1995, and sentenced to death. His conviction was based almost entirely on the bite mark evidence.

In 2001, DNA tests proved that Justin Albert Johnson, not Kennedy Brewer, committed the crime; Johnson was the same perpetrator responsible for murdering the child in the Levon Brooks case. As a result of the DNA testing, Brewer's conviction was overturned. He had served seven years on death row and one year in jail awaiting trial.[11]

12. **Bennie Starks:** Bennie Starks was convicted of raping and assaulting a 69-year-old woman in 1986, based, in part, on testimony by two forensic dentists, Drs. Russell Schneider and Carl Hagstrom. Both dentists testified that a bite mark on the victim's shoulder matched Starks' dentition. Starks spent 20 years in prison before an appeals court ordered a new trial, after DNA testing on semen recovered from the victim excluded Starks. On January 7, 2013, the state's attorney

---

analysis-led-to-wrongful-arrests-and-convictions/; Silverstein 1998 trial court testimony, *transcript available at* http://www.law.virginia.edu/pdf/faculty/garrett/innocence/odonnell.pdf.

[10] *The Innocence Project – Know the Cases: Browse Profiles: Levon Brooks*, http://www.innocenceproject.org/cases/levon-brooks/.

[11] *The Innocence Project – Know the Cases: Browse Profiles: Kennedy Brewer*, http://www.innocenceproject.org/cases/kennedy-brewer/.

dismissed all charges against Starks.[12]

13. Michael Cristini &

14. Jeffrey Moldowan: In 1991, Michael Cristini and Jeffrey Moldowan were convicted of the rape, kidnapping, and attempted murder of Moldowan's ex-girlfriend, Maureen Fournier. At trial, two board-certified ABFO Diplomates, Drs. Allan Warnick and Pamela Hammel, testified that bite marks on the victim's body had to have come from both defendants, to the exclusion of all others. Both men were convicted. Cristini was sentenced to 44 to 60 years, and Moldowan to 60 to 90 years.

After the conviction, an investigator hired by the Moldowan family found a witness who said he had seen four black men standing around a naked woman at the scene of the crime. The witness' story contradicted Fournier's, as Cristini and Moldowan are both white. Dr. Hammel then recanted her testimony, saying that she had been uncertain that either defendant had in fact been responsible for the bite marks. According to Dr. Hammel, she had agreed to testify only when Dr. Warnick had assured her that a third odontologist had also confirmed that the bite marks could be matched to Cristini and Moldowan to the exclusion of all others.

On October 20, 2003, the Macomb County Circuit Court granted Cristini a new trial, citing the new eyewitness evidence, Dr. Hammel's recantation, and stronger alibi evidence. Cristini was acquitted by a jury on April 8, 2004, after having served 13 years in prison. Later, Cristini filed wrongful conviction lawsuits against the City of Warren, Macomb County, and Dr. Warnick. The suit against Dr. Warnick was settled quickly for an undisclosed amount.

In 2002, the Michigan Supreme Court reversed Moldowan's conviction. On retrial, in February 2003, Moldowan was acquitted of all charges and released, having served nearly twelve years in prison. Moldowan's lawsuit was settled for $2.8 million in 2011.[13]

---

[12] *The Innocence Project – Innocence Blog*: *Bennie Starks Exonerated After 25 Year Struggle to Clear His Name*, http://www.innocenceproject.org/bennie-starks-exonerated-after-25-year-struggle-to-clear-his-name/; Lisa Black, *Exonerated Man's Ordeal Ends: 'I Am Overwhelmed with Joy',* Chicago Tribune, Jan. 7, 2013, http://articles.chicagotribune.com/2013-01-07/news/chi-bennie-starks-lake-county-charges-dropped_1_bennie-starks-mike-nerheim-ordeal-ends; Donna Domino, *Dentists Sue Over Bite Mark Testimony*, http://www.drbicuspid.com/index.aspx?sec=nws&sub=rad&pag=dis&ItemID=309572.

[13] *People v. Moldowan*, 466 Mich. 862, 643 N.W.2d 570 (2002); *Moldowan v. City of Warren*, 578 F.3d 351 (6th Cir. 2009); Ed White, *Warren Settles Rape Case Lawsuit for $2.8 Million – Falsely Imprisoned Man Sued for Violation of His Civil Rights*, Detroit Legal News, Oct. 19, 2011, http://www.legalnews.com/detroit/1109085; Jameson Cook, *Michael Cristini Wants Bigger Settlement than Jeffrey Moldowan*, Macomb Daily, Dec. 25, 2012, http://www.macombdaily.com/article/20121225/NEWS01/121229769/michael-cristini-wants-bigger-settlement-than-jeffrey-moldowan#full_story; Michael S. Perry, *Exoneration Case Detail: Michael Cristini*,

15. Anthony Keko: Anthony Keko was convicted in 1994 for the 1991 murder of his estranged wife, Louise Keko. Dr. Michael West testified that a bite mark on the victim's shoulder matched Anthony Keko's dentition. Dr. West's testimony was the only direct evidence linking Keko to the crime, and prosecutors conceded that without the bite mark evidence there was no case. Keko was found guilty and sentenced to life in prison. In December 1994, however, the trial judge became aware of previously undisclosed disciplinary proceedings against Dr. West. The judge began to express doubts regarding West's forensic abilities and ultimately reversed Keko's conviction.[14]

16. Harold Hill &

17. Dan Young, Jr.: Harold Hill was 16 when he and his codefendant, Dan Young, Jr., were convicted of the rape and murder of 39-year-old Kathy Morgan in 1990. Both men would end up spending 15 years in prison for a crime they did not commit. At trial, board-certified ABFO Diplomate Dr. John Kenney linked a bruise and a bite mark on the victim's body to Hill and Young. Both were found guilty and sentenced to life in prison without parole. It wasn't until 2004 that DNA tests excluded both Hill and Young as the source of DNA evidence found on the victim. In 2005, prosecutors finally dismissed the charges against both men. Dr. Kenney later said that the prosecution pushed him to exaggerate his results.[15]

18. Greg Wilhoit: Greg Wilhoit's wife, Kathy, was murdered in Tulsa, Oklahoma, in June 1985. Wilhoit was left to raise his two daughters—a 4-month-old and a 1-year-old. A year later, he was arrested and charged with the murder based on the opinions of two forensic odontologists that his dentition matched a bite mark on his wife's body. Wilhoit was found guilty and sentenced to death.

During his appeal, other forensic odontologists examined the bite mark evidence and independently concluded that the bite mark could not be matched to Wilhoit. He was released on bail for two years, and when a retrial was finally held in 1993, the judge issued a directed innocence verdict. In total, Wilhoit dealt with this

---

Nat'l Registry of Exonerations, http://www.law.umich.edu/special/exoneration/Pages/casedetail.aspx?caseid=3133; Hans Sherrer, *Prosecutor Indicted For Bribery After Two Men Exonerated of Kidnapping and Rape*, Justice: Denied, 2005, at 10, *available at* http://www.justicedenied.org/issue/issue_27/Moldowan_cristini_exonerated.html.

[14] *A Dentist Takes The Stand*, Newsweek, Aug. 19, 2001, http://www.newsweek.com/dentist-takes-stand-151357; Mark Hansen, *Out of the Blue*, ABA J., Feb. 1996, *available at* http://www.abajournal.com/magazine/article/out_of_the_blue/print/.

[15] Ctr. on Wrongful Convictions, *Exoneration Case Detail: Harold Hill*, Nat'l Registry of Exonerations, http://www.law.umich.edu/special/exoneration/Pages/casedetail.aspx?caseid=3296.

tragedy for 8 years, fighting a case built entirely on bite mark analysis. Wilhoit's story was documented by John Grisham in "The Innocent Man."[16]

19. **Crystal Weimer:** A Fayette County, Pennsylvania, jury convicted Crystal Weimer of third-degree murder in 2006 for the beating death of Curtis Haith. Apart from a jailhouse informant, the only evidence placing Weimer at the scene was the testimony of forensic odontologist Dr. Constantine Karazulas, who concluded that a bite mark on the victim's hand was a "match" with Weimar's dentition. After the National Academy of Science's landmark 2009 report, *Strengthening Forensic Science in the United States: A Path Forward*, criticized the lack of scientific support for bite mark analysis, Dr. Karazulas undertook an independent review of the "science" of bite mark and his testimony. He concluded that bite marks cannot be used for conclusive matches to an individual. On the basis of Dr. Karazulas' recantation, as well as a recantation from the informant, Weimer's conviction was vacated in October 2015, and the underlying indictment was dismissed in June 2016.[17]

20. **Steven Mark Chaney:** Steven Chaney was convicted of the murder of John Sweek, a Dallas-area cocaine dealer, in 1987; Sweek's wife was also killed. Although nine alibi witnesses accounted for Chaney's whereabouts on the day the crime occurred, the state's case relied largely on the testimony of two ABFO board-certified forensic dentists, Drs. Jim Hales and Homer Campbell. At trial, Dr. Hales purported to match a bite mark on the victim's arm to Chaney and claimed that there was a "one to a million" chance that someone other than Chaney was the biter. Similarly, Dr. Campbell opined to a reasonable degree of dental certainty that Chaney left the bite mark. Decades after Chaney's conviction, Dr. Hales admitted that his matching testimony exceeded the limits of the science and that, in contrast to his claims at trial, there was no basis for his statistical testimony in the "scientific literature." In light of the change in the scientific understanding of bite mark evidence since 1987 and Dr. Hales's recantation, the Dallas County District Attorney's Office agreed to vacate Mr. Chaney's conviction pursuant to Texas's "junk science writ," which provides an avenue for post-conviction relief where the science used at trial is subsequently discredited. In October 2015, Chaney was released after 28 years of wrongful

---

[16] Journey of Hope, *Greg Wilhoit*, *available at* https://www.journeyofhope.org/who-we-are/exonerated-from-death-row/greg-wilhoit/; Witness to Innocence, *Exonerees: Greg Wilhoit, 1954-2014*, *available at* http://www.witnesstoinnocence.org/exonerees/greg-wilhoit.html.

[17] Joe Mandak, *Bite-mark backtrack helps toss verdict*, The Boston Globe, Oct. 2, 2015, available at https://www.bostonglobe.com/news/nation/2015/10/01/woman-conviction-tossed-junk-science-bite-mark-case/Dgi1n45ib85uqdW1u2yqNO/story.html; Associated Press, *Judge dismisses charges in bite-mark conviction*, June 29, 2016, *available at* https://www.indianagazette.com/news/police-courts/judge-dismisses-charges-in-bitemark-conviction,24491656/.

incarceration; his case is currently pending before the Texas Court of Criminal Appeals, which has final authority in Texas over all habeas determinations.[18]

21. **William Joseph Richards:** In 1997, Bill Richards was convicted of the 1993 murder of his estranged wife. On the night of her murder, Richards returned home from the graveyard shift at his job and discovered his wife bludgeoned to death. The crime scene evidence revealed a violent struggle, and an autopsy of the victim uncovered a crescent-shaped lesion on her hand. To analyze that wound, the prosecution contacted Dr. Norman Sperber, an ABFO Diplomate, who examined a photograph of the lesion and opined that the wound was a human bite mark. At Richards' fourth trial—the first three attempts to try Richards did not include bite mark evidence and ended in mistrials—Dr. Sperber testified that his comparison of Richards' dentition to the photograph of the purported bite mark yielded a "pretty good alignment," and that Richards' teeth were consistent with the lesion. Dr. Sperber also testified that one facet of Richards' dentition was relatively rare. Richards presented an alibi defense based on the time of death, and he presented testimony from another ABFO board-certified forensic odontologist, Dr. Gregory Golden, who opined that although he could not eliminate Richards as the source of the bite, five out of fifteen sample dental molds from his clients in private practice also matched the lesion. With the introduction of the bite mark testimony, Richards was convicted and given a 25-year-to-life sentence.

In 2007, Dr. Sperber recanted his bite mark testimony at a post-conviction evidentiary hearing, but the California Supreme Court ultimately ruled against Richards in 2012, finding that recanted expert testimony does not constitute "false evidence." In response to the Court's decision, the California state legislature amended the habeas corpus statute the following year to explicitly deem expert recantations false evidence, and Richards filed a successive habeas petition shortly thereafter. In May 2016, the California Supreme Court finally granted his habeas petition and vacated his conviction.[19] In June 2016, the district attorney dismissed all charges against Richards.[20]

---

[18] Jennifer Emily, *Dallas County man freed after serving 25 years for murder over faulty science of bite marks*, The Dallas Morning News, Oct. 12, 2015, http://crimeblog.dallasnews.com/2015/10/dallas-county-man-freed-after-serving-25-years-for-murder-over-faulty-science-of-bite-marks.html/.

[19] *In re Richards*, 63 Cal. 4th 291, 371 P.3d 195 (2016).

[20] Jordan Smith, *After 23 years and four trials, prosecutors finally dismiss charges against Bill Richards*, The Intercept, June 28, 2016, *available at* https://theintercept.com/2016/06/28/after-23-years-and-four-trials-prosecutors-finally-dismiss-charges-against-bill-richards/.

DESCRIPTIONS OF WRONGFUL INDICTMENTS
BASED ON BITE MARK EVIDENCE

1. **Dale Morris, Jr.:** In 1997, Dale Morris, Jr., was arrested based on bite mark analysis matching his dentition to a mark found on a nine-year-old murder victim, Sharra Ferger. Morris was a neighbor to the little girl, who had been found stabbed, sexually assaulted, and bitten in a field near her Florida home. Board-certified ABFO Diplomates Dr. Richard Souviron and Dr. Kenneth Martin agreed that the bite marks on the girl were a probable match to Morris. Morris spent four months in jail until DNA tests proved his innocence. Highlighting the importance of the bite mark evidence to the police's decision to arrest Morris, Detective John Corbin said that Morris "was probably one of our least likely suspects in the neighborhood, but through the forensics that we conducted in the investigation he was linked to the crime."[21]

2. **James Earl Gates:** In April 1997, prosecutors from Humphreys County, Mississippi, arrested James Earl Gates for the capital murder of his then-girlfriend. Gates' indictment rested solely on the purported match between a bite mark found on the victim and Gates' teeth. Dr. Steven Hayne claimed to have found bite marks on the victim while conducting an autopsy, and forensic odontologist Dr. Michael West confirmed the marks were bites and concluded that they matched Gates' dentition. Gates spent several months in jail awaiting trial before nascent DNA technology excluded him from a profile obtained from scrapings from the victim's fingernails. Prosecutors subsequently dismissed the case. In 2012, the Mississippi Crime Lab, at the request of Humphreys County law enforcement, engaged in additional DNA testing of the biological material collected at the murder scene. Because of advancements in technology, the subsequent testing yielded an identifiable profile of an individual who had, in the initial stages of investigation, been a prime suspect. That individual had since been convicted of another homicide. [22]

3. **Edmund Burke**: In 1998, Edmund Burke was arrested for raping and murdering a 75-year-old woman. The victim had bite marks on her breasts, and board-certified ABFO Diplomate Dr. Lowell Levine "formed an initial opinion that Burke could not be excluded as the source of the bite marks," but asked to see

---

[21] Ian James & Geoff Dougherty, *Suspect in Girl's Murder Freed after Four Months*, St. Petersburg Times, Feb. 28, 1998, at 1.A, *available at* http://www.wearethehope.org/pdf/times_02_28_1998.pdf; *Innocence Project - Cases Where DNA Revealed That Bite Mark Analysis Led to Wrongful Arrests and Convictions*, *supra* n.9; Flynn McRoberts & Steve Mills, *From the Start, a Faulty Science*, Chic. Trib., Oct. 19, 2004, http://www.chicagotribune.com/news/watchdog/chi-041019forensics,0,7597688.story.

[22] Radley Balko, *Solving Kathy Mabry's Murder: Brutal 15-Year-Old Crime Highlights Decades-Long Mississippi Scandal*, Huffington Post, Nov. 7, 2013, http://www.huffingtonpost.com/2013/01/17/kathy-mabry-murder-steven-hayne-michael-west_n_2456970.html.

enhanced photos before rendering a final opinion. After examining the enhanced photos, Dr. Levine concluded that Burke's teeth matched the bite mark on the victim's left breast to a "reasonable degree of scientific certainty." DNA testing on saliva taken from the bite mark site excluded Burke as the source of the DNA, however, and prosecutors dropped the case against him. The true killer was later identified when DNA from the bite mark was matched to a profile in the national DNA database. Dr. Levine remains one of the few full-time forensic odontologists in the nation, and is regarded as one of the field's top practitioners.[23]

4. **Anthony Otero:** In 1994, Anthony Otero was charged with larceny and the first-degree murder and rape of a 60-year-old woman, Virginia Airasolo, in Detroit, Michigan. A warrant for Otero's arrest was issued after ABFO Diplomate Dr. Allan Warnick claimed to have matched the bite marks on the victim's body to Otero's dentition. At the preliminary hearing on December 13, 1994, Dr. Warnick testified that Otero was "the only person in the world" who could have caused the bite marks on Airasolo's body.

   In January 1995, DNA testing excluded Otero as the source of the DNA found on the victim and he was released in April, after spending five months in jail. Following Otero's release, a second forensic odontologist, ABFO Diplomate Dr. Richard Souviron, concluded that the marks on the victim were consistent with human bite marks, but were too indistinct to be used to identify a suspect. Ultimately, the charges against Otero were dismissed.[24]

5. **Johnny Bourn:** In 1992, Johnny Bourn was arrested for the rape and murder of an elderly Mississippi woman after Dr. Michael West matched a bite mark on the victim to Bourn. Bourn was imprisoned for 18 months, despite hair and fingerprint evidence pointing to another suspect. Ultimately, Bourn was released when he was excluded as a suspect by DNA testing performed on fingernail scrapings from the victim, but not before he had spent about one and a half years in jail awaiting trial.[25]

6. **Dane Collins:** In 1989, Dane Collins was arrested and charged with the rape and murder of his 22-year-old stepdaughter, based largely on bite mark comparison evidence. The Sante Fe, New Mexico, District Attorney declared his intent to seek the death penalty. Despite evidence that Collins could not produce sperm and therefore could not have been the perpetrator, the DA gave several public

---

[23] *Burke v. Town of Walpole*, 405 F.3d 66, 73 (1st Cir. 2005).

[24] *Innocence Project - Cases Where DNA Revealed That Bite Mark Analysis Led to Wrongful Arrests and Convictions, supra* n.9; *Otero v. Warnick*, 614 N.W.2d 177 (Mich. Ct. App. 2000).

[25] Hansen, *supra* n.14; *Michael West Responds*, Part 167, The Agitator, March 1, 2009, http://www.theagitator.com/2009/03/01/michael-west-responds/; Paul C. Giannelli & Kevin C. McMunigal, *Prosecutors, Ethics, and Expert Witnesses*, 76 Fordham L. Rev. 1493 (2007).

interviews stating that while there was not enough evidence to try the case, he believed Collins was guilty of the crime. Fifteen years later, a man named Chris McClendon was matched to DNA found on the victim. He pled "no contest" to the crime in exchange for describing how he had committed the rape and murder. (McClendon was already serving life in prison after he was convicted of kidnapping and raping a 24-year-old woman.)[26]

7. **Ricky Amolsch:** Ricky Amolsch's girlfriend, Jane Marie Fray, was found dead on August 23, 1994. She had been stabbed 22 times and had an electrical cord wrapped around her neck. The arrest warrant for Amolsch was based on a finding by Dr. Allan Warnick that a bite mark that had been found on the victim's left ear was "highly consistent" with Amolsch's dentition. Charges were not dropped until 10 months later when the eyewitness who had identified Amolsch's van at the crime scene was himself arrested for raping another woman in the same trailer park. Amolsch was jailed for 10 months until his trial. During that time, he lost his home, savings, and children.[27]

---

[26] Jeremy Pawloski, *Plea in '89 Slaying Eases Parents' Pain*, Albuquerque J., Aug. 14, 2005, http://abqjournal.com/news/state/380765nm08-14-05.htm.

[27] *Forensics Under Fire: Bite Mark Evidence,* Jim Fisher, The Official Website, http://jimfisher.edinboro.edu/forensics/fire/mark.html; Katherine Ramsland, *Bite Marks as Evidence to Convict – Whose Bite Mark is it, Anyway?*, Crime Library, TruTV.com, http://www.trutv.com/library/crime/criminal_mind/forensics/bitemarks/5.html (last visited Apr. 12, 2013).

References

ABFO Diplomates Reference Manual, 2005. ABFO Standards and Guidelines for Pattern, Patterned Injury, and Bitemark Evidence.

ABFO Diplomates Reference Manual, Section 4 — Standards, Guidelines, 2017. ABFO Standards and Guidelines for Pattern, Patterned Injury, and Bitemark Evidence.

Daubert v Merrill Dow Pharmaceuticals, 509 U.S., 579, 113 S.Ct. 2786, 125 L.Ed2d 469. 1993.

The Innocence Project, 2017 Description of Bite Mark Exonerations, June 4, 2017. https://www.innocenceproject.org/wp-content/uploads/2017/01/Description-of-bite-mark-exonerations-and-statistical-analysis_final.pdf.

Dorland's Medical Dictionary, twenty second ed. W.B. Saunders Co, Philadelphia.

Doyle v State, 1954, 159 Tex. C.R. 310, 263 S.W. 2d 779.

Findley, K.A., 2007. "Wrongful Conviction." Encyclopedia of Psychology and Law. SAGE Publications. http://www.sagereference.com/psychologylaw/Article_n353.html.

Frye v United States, 293 F. 1013 (D.C. Cir. 1923).

General Electric Co. v Joiner, 522 U.S. 136, 118 S.Ct. 512, 139 L.Ed.2d 508. 1997.

Gould, J.B., Carrano, J., Leo, R., Young, J., Dec. 2012. Predicting Erroneous Convictions: A Social Science Approach to Miscarriages of Justice. https://www.ncjrs.gov/pdffiles1/nij/grants/241389.pdf.

Greenwald, A.G., 1980. The totalitarian ego: fabrication and revision of personal history. American Psychologist 35, 603—618.

Hansen, M., 2013. Crimes in the Lab: a string of shoddy, suspect and fraudulent results has put forensic labs under the microscope. ABA Journal 99 (9), 44—51.

Harvey, W., 1976. "Dental Identification and Forensic Odontology", xii. Kimpton, London.

Harvey, et al., 1968. The Biggar Murder. Dental, medical, police and legal aspects of a case in some ways unique, difficult and puzzling. Journal of the Forensic Science Society 8, 157—219.

Kumho Tire v Carmichael, 526 U.S. 137, 119 S.Ct. 1167, 143 L.Ed.2d 238, 1999.

Lerner, K.L.B., 2006. "Odontology, Historical Cases", World of Forensic Science.

Meyers, A.L., June 16, 2013. Bites Derided as Unreliable in Court: AP Impact.

Oliver, W.R., 2016. Reasons for lack of consensus in forensic pathologist interpretation of photographs for patterns of injury of the skin. Journal of Forensic Sciences 62 (3), 674—680.

Oliver, W.R., 2017. Effect of history and context on forensic pathologist interpretation of photographs of patterned injury of the skin. Journal of Forensic Sciences. https://doi.org/10.1111/1556-4029.13449 (Epub ahead of print).

Oliver, W.R., Fang, X., 2016. Forensic Pathologist consensus in the interpretation of photographs of patterned injuries of the skin. Journal of Forensic Sciences 61 (4), 972—978.

Pattern Recognition (Psychology): Wikipedia, Dec. 2016. https://en.wikipedia.org/wiki/Pattern_recognition.

Pitluck, H.M., 2000. Bitemark Case Citations, Bitemark Management and Legal Update. Las Vegas; S.W. 2d.

Senn, D.R., Souviron, R.R., 2010. Bitemarks. In: Senn, D.R., Stimson, P.G. (Eds.), Forensic Dentistry, second ed. Taylor and Francis Group, Boca Raton, FL, pp. 305—368.

Strengthening Forensic Science in the United States: A Path Forward, 2009, ISBN 0-309-13131-6. https://www.ncjrs.gov/pdffiles1/nij/grants/228091.pdf.

Vale, G., Gerald Felando, Reidar Sognnaes, The team of forensic dentists that worked together.

Further Reading

Butte College. Deductive, Inductive, and Abductive Reasoning, May 2017. https://www.butte.edu/departments/cas/tipsheets/thinking/reasoning.html.

Black's Law Dictionary Online Legal Dictionary, second ed., May 2017 http://thelawdictionary.org/.

The Innocence Project, June 4, 2017. www.innocenceproject.org.

10

United States Jurisprudence

Robert E. Barsley[1,2,3], Haskell M. Pitluck[4]

[1]Professor, Department of Diagnostic Sciences, LSUHSC School of Dentistry, New Orleans, LA, United States; [2]Chief Forensic Odontologist, Jefferson Parish Coroner, New Orleans, LA, United States; [3]New Orleans Forensic Center, Orleans Parish Coroner, New Orleans, LA, United States; [4]Retired Circuit Court Judge, State of Illinois, 19th Judicial Circuit, Crystal Lake, IL, United States

OUTLINE

INTRODUCTION

Many forensic dentists assume that once the identification or other action is finished and a final report is delivered to the requesting authority that their work is complete. Although sometimes that is the case, quite often much more is required. The ultimate consumer of forensic dental output is the legal system—a criminal case can hinge upon the conclusions of a dental identification, a bitemark analysis, or the conclusion reached in a case of physical abuse. Mass fatality incidents and resulting dental identifications may play an important role in criminal and civil matters arising from the incidents. Dental standard of care cases require expert opinion(s).

Therefore a forensic dentist should have a basic understanding of the law and legal system in the country in which his or her work is performed. In the United States, one should also be able to appreciate the differences in the laws and legal systems between states and have a basic understanding of the rules of evidence and courtroom proceedings in the state or states in which they routinely operate. This chapter is designed to assist the reader in that task. The legal system and courts in the United States of America have at their heart many basic principles.

SYSTEMS OF LAW

The court systems are enshrined in constitutions, which form the basis for a governing authority. The federal courts derive their powers and duties from the US Constitution, and similarly each of the state court systems is established by its respective state constitution. Legislative acts (laws) passed by the associated legislatures regulate the particulars of each court system. Generally, one can find three levels of courts. Most numerous are the district courts—these are the courts in which testimony and evidence are presented to a jury and/or judge. District courts are usually found at a county level and may be situated according to population and in some states are further subdivided according to subject matter. More populous states and regions of states are likely to have more courtrooms and more judges. In some states each court has a specific judge and in other states several judges may share the same courtroom at different times. Some state systems may further subdivide these courts by jurisdictional methods—specific courts and judges for criminal matters; others for civil matters; and even some for family/juvenile matters such as divorce, custody, wills and probate, for example. The federal court system also has district courts in every state (and territory). The federal courts in some large or more populous states are divided into several districts, while other states have a single federal district encompassing the entire state.

Regardless of whether the case is federal or state, the district court level is the court in which a forensic dentist will be called upon to testify. Although there are many differences between federal and state courts that are very important to the attorneys involved, for a witness the experience can be remarkably similar. One of the major differences is that all federal judges are appointed for life without any specified retirement age. In the various state systems the judges may be elected or appointed (but for specific terms, not for life) and many states enforce a strict retirement age. Some states require that candidates for judicial office be licensed attorneys with a specified minimum number of years in practice to qualify for office.

In the federal and state systems other "entry-level" courts exist. These are often for a specific purpose; for example, there are the federal bankruptcy and tax courts. In state systems there are often administrative courts to rule on issues such as zoning or professional licensing as examples. For each of these specialized courts, a losing defendant can escalate the case to the proper "district" court. Another feature that distinguishes some "lesser" courts from district courts is a limitation of their jurisdiction (or reach) to only matters that are considered misdemeanors as opposed to felonies. Although there are some variations between the states, a felony is usually defined as a crime for which a guilty party can be sentenced to prison or "hard time" for terms of more than 1 year (including up to a life sentence or the death penalty in some states). Most misdemeanors have as penalties only fines and jail time of 1 year or less.

The second level of courts is known as appeals or appellate courts. Appeals courts are composed of many judges and appeals courts do not hear testimony from witnesses. Rather, a panel of judges is tasked with deciding whether or not the judicial proceedings in the lower court were conducted according to law. To do so, one of the parties in the matter at hand files an appeal in the proper appellate court. In criminal cases, only a convicted defendant may appeal—an unsuccessful criminal prosecution cannot be appealed in the United States in either federal or any state court. (The prosecution may choose to appeal the length of sentence/amount of fine levied, however.) In some countries, the prosecution can appeal a criminal verdict of not guilty (jury or judge pronounced). However, in noncriminal cases, either side, "winning" or "losing," can appeal—issues such as negligence or liability, amount of award, or other terms of the decision are commonly appealed. Appellate courts are divided into "circuits," which exercise jurisdiction over specific geographical groups of district/lower courts. For example, in Louisiana, the 42 judicial districts that house all of the lower courts are assigned to one of the five Circuit Courts of Appeal. In the federal system, the 89 federal district courts (94 if including US Territories) are assigned to one of the 11 US Circuit Courts of Appeal. For example, all federal district courts in the nine federal districts that comprise Texas, Louisiana, and Mississippi are under the jurisdiction of the Fifth US Circuit Court of Appeals whose primary location is New Orleans, Louisiana. Decisions rendered by the Fifth US Circuit are binding on all federal courts within the circuit and also on cases involving United States law and/or federal constitutional questions in state courts within Texas, Louisiana, and Mississippi.

There are basic rules that apply in federal and state courts of appeal. An attorney appealing the decision must file a notice of appeal within a certain time frame and the opposing party(s) is notified in order that their attorneys can respond in a timely fashion. Generally, new issues that were not raised at trial cannot be introduced, only issues upon which testimony was provided at trial, or in which testimony was expressly denied at trial, or other errors alleged to have been made by the presiding judge can be the basis for an appeal. The vast majority of appeals argue points of law and whether or not the trial judge applied or interpreted the law correctly. Attorneys prepare detailed written briefs supporting their issues and arguments and are usually allowed a limited appearance (known as oral argument) before the panel to present their case and/or answer questions posed by the judges. Appellate courts do not hear testimony or question witnesses. In most systems, including the federal system, all parties have a right to an initial appeal. The appellate court will issue a

decision that may take several forms, the simplest being the original verdict is upheld in all respects. In some cases, the original verdict is reversed in whole or in part. Or the case may be remanded back to the lower court with specific findings, instructions, or questions. Remands and partial reverses often result in new trials or hearings on specific issues. In civil cases, a remand or partial reversal may result in a settlement between the parties. Similarly, in criminal cases, a reversal or remand may result in a new trial, a reduction in sentence, a settlement or negotiated plea or, in some cases, an election by the prosecutor not to continue with prosecution.

Appellate cases form the basis for what many people consider the "law." One of the bedrock principles of American law is a concept known as *stare decisis*—or the concept that once a case has been decided at the appellate level, all similar cases—cases that are "on point"—that have similar facts and circumstances will result in the same decision. This concept is also known as precedent and applies in criminal and noncriminal matters. The "law books" that attorneys used to line the libraries of their office with were filled with the decisions handed down by various appellate courts, and unless a particular case could be distinguished as sufficiently different from those previous cases, the result could often be predicted. In today's world, the digitization and instant communication of appellate decisions coupled with powerful search engine technology has in many ways revolutionized the practice of law. For example, it is now a simple matter of a couple of clicks on a computer to discover a multitude of information about a topic, expert witnesses who have testified on the topic, and even cases in which a particular expert has testified.

The final appellate level is commonly referred to as the "supreme court." In the federal system (and in the vast majority of the states) that body is actually called the Supreme Court of the United States or the Supreme Court of Louisiana (or other state). A few states style their intermediate appellate courts as the "supreme" court and use a version of "superior" or "appeals" courts for the ultimate appellate level; for example, the highest appellate court in the state of New York is the Court of Appeals. A few states divide the appellate process for civil and criminal cases with some specialized courts of appeal hearing only criminal matters and others hearing only civil matters. An example is Texas, whose constitution authorizes a Supreme Court and a Court of Criminal Appeals (each with members elected statewide).

In the federal and most state systems, unlike the intermediate courts of appeal, no automatic right to appeal exists concerning the supreme courts, except in special circumstances. An attorney may petition the Supreme Court to accept an appeal by filing a brief (a written statement supporting the basis of the appeal), but the court is not obligated to accept the appeal or hear an oral argument. Most supreme courts refuse the majority of appeals. The US Supreme Court accepts only a handful of cases each year, now usually less than 100. It is important to realize that each state's court system is sovereign, meaning a decision reached in one state has no legal bearing on cases in other states (although other states must honor judgments from any state). In fact, a case arising in federal court that does not involve purely federal law will be decided based upon the laws of the state in which it arose.

There are in a general sense three types of legal cases—civil matters, criminal matters, and administrative matters. As a practicing dentist, one is most likely to be involved in administrative matters—zoning (how many parking places must a dental office provide); tax disputes at the local, state, or federal level; or disputes with government programs such as Social Security, unemployment claims, tax issues just to name a few. Disputes that cannot be settled in negotiation or other informal methods are first heard by administrative law judges who specialize in the interpretation and administration of the laws and regulations governing that area. Some of these cases can have criminal components (tax evasion or Medicare/Medicaid fraud) as well as civil (noncriminal) monetary penalties. The burden of proof falls to the state in most administrative cases—the government must prove its case by a preponderance of the evidence (just over 50%) or by a somewhat higher standard of "clear and convincing" evidence, which is more than preponderance but less than the much higher standard "beyond a reasonable doubt." An unfavorable decision at the administrative level can be "appealed" to a district (lower level trial) court in most jurisdictions. If so, in some cases the battle begins anew (de novo) and in others the decision of the administrative judge forms the basis for the case. The burden of proof generally remains the same.

Civil law matters include divorce, custody, sales, contracts, probate, and torts (which includes negligence and malpractice). In contrast to criminal cases, these are cases brought by private parties against each other. Dentists are most likely to be involved professionally in a tort case—perhaps as a defendant in a malpractice claim alleging negligence in the treatment (or more likely alleged mistreatment) of a patient. A claim for damages is made—damages are often measured in monetary value. A claim may be made for compensatory damages (designed to make the prevailing party "whole" again), which might include awards for remedial treatment, pain and suffering, loss of earnings, loss of affection; or punitive (or exemplary) damages may be awarded in some jurisdictions, which are designed to deter the defendant and others from performing similar acts. The burden of proof in a civil matter is a preponderance of the evidence—that is, the party making the allegations must present evidence, the majority (just over 50%) of which is found by the trier of fact to favor the prevailing party.

Criminal cases are brought by the government (the "People" or the "State") against a citizen for alleged violation(s) of the criminal statutes (criminal code). The statutes define the illegal actions—the elements of the crime as well as the specific penalties or sanctions the state can enforce against defendants who are found guilty. The prosecution must prove through the presentation of evidence to the court that the accused defendant violated each element. The burden of proof is on the prosecutor to prove to the trier of fact beyond a reasonable doubt that the defendant committed the crime. The trier of fact is usually a jury—citizens empaneled by the court to hear and judge the case. Each jurisdiction has specific rules for how juries are chosen, how many jurors are required to hear the case (usually 12, but at least 6), and whether their decision must be unanimous or not (Louisiana and one other state allow a less than unanimous verdict in criminal cases). The trier of fact can be the judge alone—a defendant may have the right to forgo a jury trial if he or she desires. As mentioned above, criminal matters are divided into misdemeanors and felonies. Defendants accused of misdemeanors may not be afforded the opportunity for a jury trial in some jurisdictions. No matter the type of criminal charge or whether heard by a jury or by a judge alone, the burden of proof is much more formidable. The state must prove its case "beyond a reasonable doubt." While not proof to a virtual certainty, this is considered to be proof to the extent that no reasonable juror could conceive of any other explanation beyond that presented by the prosecution. At the conclusion of the case, before the jury begins its deliberations, the judge will "charge" the jury and explain their duties. If the judge does not believe that the prosecution has met that threshold of proof through the evidence presented, the judge may order the trial ended and find the defendant not guilty by a process known as a directed verdict.

The American judicial system embraces two foundational principles not always present in other countries' systems. First, a verdict of "not guilty" in a criminal case cannot be appealed by the prosecution—a person cannot be tried twice for the same crime (if having once been found not guilty). This concept is also known a double jeopardy. The second is that our system is an adversarial one—the parties (especially the defendant in a criminal case) have an absolute right to be represented by an attorney. In a felony criminal case, a public defender may be appointed at no cost to the defendant. It is the attorney's sworn duty to zealously guard the rights and privileges of his or her client(s). One essential method of accomplishing that task is through vigorous cross-examination during trial. In criminal cases, it is not the prosecutor's duty to convict the accused defendant, the prosecutor's job is to represent the state and present the state's case fairly to the trier of fact.

ADMISSIBILITY OF EVIDENCE AND EXPERTS

The remainder of this chapter will discuss the role of an expert witness and legal concepts that impact his or her ability to properly testify. In today's complex world many issues come before the court that neither the judge nor the jury may fully comprehend. The judicial system therefore allows for the use of expert witnesses. Based upon an expert's training, experience, and education he or she is allowed to present an opinion. This is in contrast to fact witnesses whose testimony is strictly limited to those things that were perceived by their own senses—what they heard, saw, smelled, etc. To arrive at his or her conclusions and therefore present an opinion, the expert may conduct tests or other activities that form the basis of the opinion as long as those tests and activities are grounded in accepted theory and practice.

Each court operates under a set of rules that dictate the conduct of the attorneys, the process of the trial and its proceedings, and how evidence is to be presented. Those rules encompass the use of experts and the giving of expert testimony. The rules vary somewhat between states themselves as well as federal courts. However, they do follow similar general guidelines in all systems. First and foremost, the attorney offering an expert's opinion must satisfy the court (and the opposing party(s)) of the *bona fides* of the expert and the basis of his or her opinion. The presiding judge ultimately decides whether or not to admit the testimony of the expert. There are several steps in the process. Initially, the attorney must (in most cases) inform the opposing party through the court that an expert has been retained. At the very least the expert's name must appear on the witness list whose disclosure to the opposing party is mandated. The opposing party may object at this early juncture (or may have an opportunity to object later). The opposing party may decide to retain its own expert(s) as well. There are complex rules in discovery that dictate whether not, and if so dictate whether a complete copy of the expert's report or merely a summary of the report must be disclosed to the opposing party and a time frame for doing so. As a general rule, in a criminal case an expert retained by the prosecution should expect disclosure of his or her report to the defense. Upon receipt of the report, the opposing party may petition the court to not allow the expert's report or testimony as evidence. The court may order a hearing to determine whether or not the evidence should be allowed. This may occur prior to trial or may actually be held during trial (out of the presence of the jury). The decisions made at this point often form the basis of an appeal should an unsatisfactory verdict be returned. In some jurisdictions the decision to admit or not admit the expert can be appealed as a separate matter while the case is progressing.

In 1975 the federal court system adopted the Federal Rules of Evidence to standardize practice and procedure in all federal district courts. Rule 702 discusses the testimony of an expert witness and Rule 703 addresses the basis for expert testimony. The seminal case for expert opinion was decided in 1923 by the District of Columbia Circuit Court of Appeals (a federal appellate court) and arose from a murder case in Washington DC, which occurred about a year earlier. It is known as the Frye Case because the accused murderer was one Robert Frye. The government offered the testimony of a well-known psychologist who had observed the defendant undergoing a forerunner of a polygraph examination. It was his opinion that the defendant was being truthful when he denied committing the murder (the defendant claimed he had falsely confessed to share the reward money in the unsolved case). The judge denied use of the testimony; however, the arguments between counsel (which included a discussion of the tests and the expert's opinion) were held in open court with the jury in attendance. Frye was convicted of second-degree murder (not first as originally charged—some observers attribute the jury's decision to their hearing the "evidence," which was not officially admitted). Frye appealed his conviction, which the federal appeals court upheld the conviction and denied the use of the expert with the comment:

"Just when a scientific principle or discovery crosses the line between the experimental and demonstrable stages is difficult to define. Somewhere in this twilight zone the evidential force of the principle must be recognized, and while the courts will go a long way in admitting experimental testimony deduced from a well-recognized scientific principle or discovery, the thing from which the deduction is made must be sufficiently established to have gained *general acceptance in the particular field* in which it belongs."(Emphasis added.)

This opinion, which is only two pages long with no citations, became known as the Frye test and was used in all federal courts and most state courts for nearly a half of a century. (*Frye v. United States*, 293F. 1013, D.C. Cir, 1923)

In 1993 the US Supreme Court decided the case of *Daubert v. Merrell Dow Pharmaceuticals* (509 U.S. 579, 1993) concerning the denial at trial of the admissibility of an expert's opinion regarding a drug marketed by Dow. The Court recognized the gatekeeper function performed by the judge in cases involving expert opinion and provided guidance to judges by listing four questions that should be answered.

1. Has the theory at issue been tested?
2. Has the theory been subject to peer review?
3. How reliable is the theory, what is the error rate associated with it?
4. What is the extent of general acceptance in the scientific community?

These questions came to be known as the Daubert test. Two subsequent cases added further definition and bounds to the admission of expert testimony and opinion. The second case is *General Electric Co. v. Joiner* (522 U.S. 136, 1997), which affirmed that the proper standard for an appellate court to apply in reviewing the trial court's decision to allow or exclude expert testimony is the abuse of discretion standard—giving the judge a wide latitude as gatekeeper in these matters. The final case in the trio is *Kumho Tire Co. v. Carmichael* (526 U.S. 137, 1999), which involved the testimony of an expert in tire failure in an automobile accident. The Court broadened considerably the list of questions that a judge might consider as a gatekeeper and ruled that "technical and other specialized knowledge" as written in the rule would be as likely as the "scientific" knowledge in question in the Daubert case to be beyond the grasp of the average juror bringing that type of expertise within the rule as well.

In the year 2000, the original Rule 702 and Rule 703 were amended to incorporate the rulings noted above. The majority of state courts in the United States today have adopted either verbatim or very similar wording, the federal rules. A few states still subscribe to Frye, California uses its own blend known as Kelley-Frye, and a few states have never "declared" their position. Interestingly the three underlying cases are all civil matters, but the rules are applied to

criminal matters as well. Motions to exclude evidence, particularly patterned injury evidence such as bitemark analysis, which might be used to include a particular individual as a perpetrator of a crime are hotly contested in the current legal setting. A prosecution bitemark expert should be prepared for a Daubert hearing, motion *in limine*, or other exclusionary tactic. Additionally, an expert in this situation should expect a vigorous cross-examination during *voir dire* concentrating on his or her training and on the science underlying the opinion to be offered. Careful attention should be given to the *curriculum vitae* that is offered.

The process of testifying is similar in most jurisdictions. The expert should work closely with the attorney who retained him or her. One overriding caveat is to be completely honest with that attorney. The expert does not have a "side" in the litigation, merely an opinion. That opinion must be truthful and complete. In a hotly contested case, especially in criminal matters where an individual's liberty or even life may be at stake, opposing counsel will leave no stone unturned and no avenue unexplored. Prior testimony, prior writings, prior presentations are all fair game—an attorney who is blind-sided by information that should have been disclosed cannot assist his or her client, much less rehabilitate an expert who has been made to look silly or ill-prepared on the witness stand.

Civil lawsuits against dentists are based on a claim of injury or harm brought about by the negligence of the dentist being sued. The plaintiff (the one bringing the claim) must prove in court via the presentation of evidence four things. First, the doctor—patient relationship existed by virtue of which the defendant was owed the duty of proper care and treatment. Second, this duty was breached by the defendant in an unlawful or negligent manner. Third, from this breach of duty damages directly occurred. And finally, the breach of duty was the proximate cause of the damage suffered. Damages are commonly expressed as a monetary figure.

Most of these cases allege that the treating dentist deviated from the standard of care to which a reasonable and prudent dentist would adhere. Expert opinion is required to demonstrate to the court the standard of care that exists in the particular field. For example, a dentist must testify that not completely removing the decay in a tooth about to be restored falls below the requisite standard and this failure could (or did) result in the loss of the tooth in the future. Without the presentation of such testimony demonstrating the expected level of service, the plaintiff's case will fail. Of course the defendant will seek to find an expert who will testify that due to the circumstances in this particular tooth, that leaving decay in place was the correct procedure or that perhaps this was only an intermediate step in the treatment of the tooth. In most jurisdictions, a general dentist who performs treatment normally done by a specialist will be held to the standard of care that applies to a specialist. Some states have rules that dictate which experts might be allowed to testify based upon whether the expert is in active practice or whether the defendant is a specialist or not, for example. The jury weighs the conflicting testimony along with all of the other evidence presented to arrive at a verdict. In most systems, not only must the jury return a verdict of liability against the defendant they must also determine how much damage occurred and that the negligent act (or omission) was the proximate cause of the injury. The burden of proof is the preponderance of the evidence.

The plaintiff normally retains an expert prior to filing suit—in most states, the attorney is required to perform due diligence before the case can be filed. The defense normally hires their expert during the pretrial, discovery phase of the suit. Often the defense expert has available deposition testimony from the victim, from the treating defendant dentist, as well as the report of the plaintiff's dental expert. Another important consideration is the discovery process, especially for experts employed by the prosecution in a criminal case. In some jurisdictions, the opposing party in a civil suit may assert a right through discovery to obtain more than the final report; they may be able to obtain test results and notes of the expert. An expert hired by the state in a criminal case whose investigation and/or tests performed tend to prove innocence (or at a minimum do nothing to prove guilt) must report those findings to the prosecutor, at least verbally. The prosecution has an affirmative duty to disclose all exculpatory evidence to the defense team; this is known as the Brady rule after a US Supreme Court case. In a civil case, neither the plaintiff nor the defense is under such duty, quite often the attorney may initially ask the expert for a verbal report only. If the opinion does not help to prove the party's assertion, the expert may be dropped from the case at that point. Expert witnesses communicate with the opposing party through the attorneys only, direct contact (an *ex parte* communication) is not allowed. In civil cases very often, the agreement signed upon hiring will contain language pertaining to confidentiality and will likely forbid any other participation in the matter at hand. In criminal matters as mentioned above, a prosecution witness who has been released by the prosecutor may have an ethical duty to consult with the defense team.

There are numerous rights granted to the defendant in a criminal matter, many specified in the US Constitution and the first 10 Amendments, the Bill of Rights. Among these are the right to counsel, the right to a speedy trial, and the right to an impartial jury all guaranteed by the Sixth Amendment; protection against illegal search and seizure that is guaranteed under the Fourth Amendment; and protection against self-incrimination guaranteed by the Fifth Amendment. The right to equal treatment under the law is guaranteed by the 14th Amendment, which was enacted after the Bill of Rights. A long chain of US Supreme Court cases outline and define these rights. Other US Supreme Court cases have added additional "rights" such as the

Brady rule mentioned above, the Miranda warning putting one on notice of arrest and the attachment of rights, which includes the right to refuse to answer questions without the presence of counsel, Mapp that limits the scope of a search (including those conducted pursuant to search warrants), Terry that limits the ability of law enforcement to stop and frisk citizens, and many others. The interpretation of law is a constantly changing landscape, complicated by the fact that each state also has a constitution and laws that might grant further rights to defendants as well as specify or proscribe conduct allowable in trials or trial preparation. The hiring attorney should help guide the expert through this potential minefield.

A *subpoena ad testificandum* is a court order requiring the person named to be present at a certain place and time to testify. A *subpoena duces tecum* compels the delivery of certain specific documents or evidence. Subpoenas may be served (or delivered) to persons by several routes, including personal service and by mail. Subpoenas are commonly issued to compel the expert to participate in a deposition and be questioned by opposing counsel. A subpoena is also used to notify a witness to be present to testify in court during the trial. A subpoena may direct the expert to deliver a copy of his or her report and other physical evidence in his or her possession to opposing counsel or to the court—the actual delivery is usually accomplished through the hiring attorney.

The pinnacle of a forensic dentist's participation in court is trial testimony. Once sworn and accepted by the court as an expert, the hiring attorney will begin a series of questions known as the direct examination. In essence, the expert will be asked to tell the story—training (if not already highlighted during qualification), his or her history with the case, what evidence was received and/or tested, and the results of those tests or examinations. Ultimately, the attorney will ask for an opinion—the expert's conclusion(s). How that opinion is stated will be influenced by the type of case and by legal requirements that must be met. The attorney and the expert will in most cases rehearse the line of questions to be asked and the types of answers that are proper. It is important to note that the attorney should not (and under legal ethics rules cannot) direct the expert to a certain answer. The expert must always remember that the testimony, including any opinions stated, is theirs and theirs alone. Once given under oath and transcribed by the court reporter, they cannot be easily retracted or modified. This is of course true for deposition testimony as well.

Once the direct examination is complete, counsel will tender the witness to the opposing party for cross-examination. Opposing counsel will seek through questioning to undermine any aspect of the testimony given in direct testimony that he or she can. These questions are generally limited to testimony given during direct examination; however, regardless of whether brought up during qualification, prior testimony and case work may be the subject of questions. The expert should expect to be questioned on training and education, on the materials received and examined, the guidelines and standards if such exists for such examinations, similarly for testing. The expert will be questioned on his or her familiarity and understanding with the current (and past, sometimes well past) literature on the subject. How the expert arrived at his or her conclusions will be probed. Opposing counsel will likely interject some hypothetical situations that vary the facts in the instant case and query if under those modified circumstances would the expert have a differing opinion. The expert must pay close attention and listen well as opposing counsel will attempt confuse the facts and may ask compound or complex questions that cannot be answered by a simple "yes" or "no." The questioning, in contrast to the direct examination, will be brutal and intense in many cases. The ultimate goal of the cross-examiner is to have the expert change his or her opinion or at least show some weakness or lessening of support for it. At the conclusion of the cross-examination, the original counsel may initiate redirect examination, which is designed to and to attempt to repair any damage done during cross-examination or reinforce the expert's opinion. The scope is limited to subjects covered in cross -examination. At the conclusion of redirect examination, opposing counsel may choose to counter with recross-examination—again the subject is limited to only those topics brought up in the course of redirect examination. At the conclusion, the witness will be excused. Unlike fact witnesses, an expert witness may be allowed in some instances to remain in court (an expert like, any witness is always subject to being recalled to the stand) and may have been allowed in court to hear prior testimony, including other experts. Counsel for either side may petition the judge to invoke the exclusion of witnesses rule and restrict experts from hearing any other testimony.

Forensic dentistry can be an interesting and enlightening addition to the clinical practice of dentistry. The field can give the forensic dentist expert an opportunity to work with individuals and systems outside the normal realm of dental practice and to advance justice. In this arena, a specialist holds no advantage over a general dentist, each starts with equal footing. Success in the field requires a willingness to learn, dedication, and becoming comfortable with law enforcement, the legal profession, the legal system, and the world of the coroner/medical examiner. One who enters this arena must adhere to the highest ethical standards and be well-grounded in the pursuit of truth. A good forensic dentist advances the cause of justice by presenting the truth on the stand and fulfilling the expert's role to educate the attorneys, the judge, and the jury about the dental facts at issue. In today's world, being a good witness can prove difficult and one must never breach ethical standards. Juries now have come to expect the razzle-dazzle spectacle of television shows such as CSI. The dental expert must remember that those very same CSI techniques can disprove expert opinions not soundly grounded in science and fact. An expert who strives to do his or her best should not have to be concerned about the reversal of criminal convictions based on failed bitemark or any other odontological expert testimony.

Glossary of Latin Legal Terms

bona fides **(in good faith)** A person's honesty and sincerity of intention; documentary evidence of a person's legitimacy.

curriculum vitae **(the course of my life)** (CV or vita) commonly in the United States a comprehensive document (as opposed to a resume) listing in detail education, publication, work experience, appointments, qualifications, and other information relevant to the issue at hand.

ex parte **communication (from a party)** Contact occurring between parties outside the presence of the party's attorney.

motion *in limine* **(at the threshold)** A motion asking the court to limit or prevent certain evidence from being presented.

stare decisis **(to stand by that which is decided)** The legal doctrine that judges are obligated to respect previous precedential decisions.

subpoena ad testificandum **(under penalty for testifying)** A summons ordering a named individual to appear before a duly authored body at a fixed time and place to give testimony.

subpoena duces tecum **(under penalty bring along)** A summons directed to a named individual to appear before a duly authored body at a fixed time and place to give testimony and produce documents and/or items.

voir dire **(to say what is true)** The questioning of prospective jurors by the judge and attorneys in court.

11

Expert Witness Guidelines & Testimony
Forensic Odontology Expertise Versus Expert Witness Expertise

Thomas J. David[1,2], Robert E. Barsley[3,4,5]

[1]Forensic Odontology Consultant, Georgia Bureau of Investigation, Division of Forensic Sciences, Decatur, GA, United States; [2]Clinical Assistant Professor, Department of General Dentistry, Forensic Dentistry Fellowship, The University of Tennessee Graduate School of Medicine, Knoxville, TN, United States; [3]Professor, Department of Diagnostic Sciences, LSUHSC School of Dentistry, New Orleans, LA, United States; [4]Chief Forensic Odontologist, Jefferson Parish Coroner, New Orleans, LA, United States; [5]New Orleans Forensic Center, Orleans Parish Coroner, New Orleans, LA, United States

OUTLINE

Legal Precedents Versus Cutting Edge Technology

Another difference in approach that I have seen cause misunderstandings over the years is the concept of precedent. Lawyers are taught that the oldest ruling on a subject is the guiding precedent. A lawyer who could cite the Magna Carta or, even better, the Code of Hammurabi, would, I imagine, be in judicial nirvana. Scientists, conversely, hold that the latest information that is validated and verified is the best information. We don't refer much to alchemy texts any more, and the four humors are positively out of style. Leeches are no longer cutting-edge medical treatment (although your HMO might favor them as they work cheap.) To our consternation, when we offer a new type of evidence, the courts go into spasms of legal heartburn over whether to accept it. This sometimes leads to tortured legal arguments and rather ludicrous court rulings. As an example, I cite the problems the courts had in the nineteenth century with the admission of photographs as evidence. Never before had the courts been confronted with evidence which could largely speak for itself. Even physical evidence such as a bloody hammer in a bludgeoning case needed a witness to explain its significance. But a picture often tells its tale quite clearly. This caused the courts great concern as it invaded the sacrosanct role of the jury to decide the facts. After much peptic acid had been secreted, the courts did decide that photographs could be admitted, as long as there was a witness to explain their significance, even if that was quite plain from the picture. Maybe a little silly, but at least the evidence came in.

Anonymous

INTRODUCTION

Unfortunately, being a proficient forensic odontologist does not make someone an accomplished expert witness. The requisite skills for becoming proficient in forensic odontology are acquired in the scientific arena. On the other hand, the essential skills for proficiency as an expert witness are attained in the legal arena. Since most forensic odontologists do not have legal training, these skills are generally unfamiliar to forensic scientists. Many forensic scientists assume that because they know more than attorneys about their field of expertise, they have the upper hand when testifying. Nothing could be further from the truth! What they fail to realize is that the rules governing all legal procedures are determined by lawyers, not scientists. Therefore, the adage "you're playing in someone else's sandbox" is an appropriate metaphor. That being said, the necessity of becoming familiar with legal procedures and their nuances is essential.

Like other professions, the practice of law has many "buzzwords" critical to understanding what an attorney is actually asking you. Without an understanding of what these terms really mean, a forensic scientist may respond erroneously (in a legal context). A classic example of a legal buzzword is the term "authoritative". The dictionary definition of authoritative is "having or showing impressive knowledge about a subject" (Merriam-Webster Learner's Dictionary). The legal definition of authoritative is as follows: "absolute, dogmatic, incontrovertible, and strict." (Burton's Legal Thesaurus). Needless to say, the legal definition is much more restrictive and conveys a sense of complete acceptance without exception. An expert witness who does not understand the difference can paint themselves into a corner in court. Regrettably, many expert witnesses learn these skills the hard way, by trial and error (no pun intended). Nevertheless, some forensic organizations are now providing opportunities to acquire these skills preemptively.

Over the past several years, the American Academy of Forensic Sciences (AAFS), the American Board of Forensic Odontology (ABFO), and the American Society of Forensic Odontology (ASFO) have all provided workshops or presentations on expert witness skills. The inevitable conclusion is that even an accomplished forensic scientist can have his or her opinion misconstrued or usurped without an essential understanding of expert witness skills.

EXPERT WITNESS SKILLS

Guidelines for expert witnesses fall into three different categories: (1) Testimony; (2) Reports; (3) Curriculum Vitae (CV). These guidelines will be discussed individually, since the recommendations for each are separate and distinct.

Testimony

Court Testimony

TENETS AND TACTICS

Some of the rudimentary expert witness guidelines are based on moral and principled behavior fundamental to all human conduct, not just expert witnesses. Since these precepts are an essential premise of expected conduct for expert witnesses, they will be discussed first and considered as fundamental tenets of ordinary behavior among experts.

TENETS

1. **Be honest**—Integrity is the most important asset of an expert witness. Once an expert's integrity is compromised, his opinion is worthless in that case and all those following. While a mistaken opinion can be overcome, an integrity issue will haunt a career forever. Future testimony will center on the expert's integrity and history, not the issue at the bar.

2. **Tell the truth**—Resist any temptation to "stretch the truth." One who always tells the truth does not have to continually remember what has been previously stated. Every written document and sworn testimony becomes part of a "paper trail." An expert, who tailors his opinion to conform to those who employed him, will be overtaken by the written record.

3. **Be yourself**—An expert witness should use his or her personality to its best advantage during testimony and not venture beyond their "comfort zone." Individuals who attempt to change their personality are usually doomed to failure. It seems to be a common failing (misconception) among expert witnesses to attempt to sound more assertive or appear more authoritative during testimony. An attempt to copy someone else's style will, most likely, come across as phony and will seem less credible to the judge or jury. An expert witness must strive to improve detrimental personality traits; experience teaches that comfort will be best achieved by adopting a natural, relaxed demeanor.

4. **Be polite**—Be polite to everyone in court. The judge is in charge of the courtroom and should always be shown appropriate respect. Other court officials should also be treated respectfully. This is a classic situation where the Golden Rule applies—"do unto others as you would have them do unto you." People treated with respect are more likely to reciprocate with respect.

5. **Handling mistakes**—If a simple mistake is made on the stand or in the report, admit it, and do not belabor the point. In some ways, admission of a mistake can actually make one appear more credible. Arguing about an obvious mistake can only result in a loss of credibility with the jury.

TACTICS

1. **Do not argue**—An expert's purpose in court is to present his or her opinion, not to argue about the opinion. The jury is there to evaluate the evidence, not judge a debate. Arguing with opposing counsel can cause the expert to appear biased. State the reasons for the opinion(s), but do not argue about the opinion(s). One who argues too much or too passionately may seem less than objective.

2. **Do not lose your temper**—Regardless of what happens when testifying, do not let your temper get the best of you. One who loses his temper has also likely lost concentration and often blurts out something later regretted. In addition, such verbal "faux pas" may be used against that expert in the future.

3. **If things are not going well and you find yourself in a hole**—Stop Digging (Fig. 11.1). If testimony is not going according to plan and the expert or the attorney has not been able to turn things around, stop the bleeding. The more attention focused on how badly things are going, the worse things will get. At some point the expert (or his attorney) must do what is necessary to bring that particular line of questioning to an end and move on to something else.

4. **Stick to the evidence**—Ultimately, an expert's opinion must be based on the evidence and materials reviewed. It is essential that the expert's opinion(s) and any report(s) or testimony is be supported by the evidence and materials reviewed. Opinions based on conjecture or hunches will seem biased and bring into question the motives and the expertise of the supposed "expert." In every case, the opinion(s) of the expert must be supported by an evidentiary basis.

5. **Opinions about other experts**—An expert witness is only present to offer an opinion about the evidence, not other expert(s). If asked about another expert, be polite and make general comments only. In many cases an expert for one party will have a different opinion from an opposing expert; and the expert should state only the reason(s) his or her opinion differs. Under no circumstances engage in "name-calling."

6. **Questions about written material**—Never respond to questions about written material without reviewing the material first. An expert witness has the right to review any material beforehand even if the question is posed on the stand. In many cases, opposing counsel does not have the material in question or has misrepresented it in some fashion.

7. **Opinions of written material**—An expert witness may be asked for an opinion about certain written material. Specifically, one may be asked whether or not a textbook or publication is "authoritative" or whether one agrees or disagrees with certain statements in the material. The word "authoritative" is a legal buzzword that carries a connotation far beyond what might be commonly thought (see legal definition of authoritative under Introduction). One should make general comments only and not be overly complimentary of the author(s). A general statement that this textbook or periodical is an acceptable reference can categorize its usefulness without conveying too much importance.

FIGURE 11.1   Stop digging yourself into a hole.

8. **Connecting with the jury**—Eye contact with jurors is an essential element in establishing rapport with the jury. When answering a question posed by an attorney, the natural tendency is to maintain eye contact with the person who is asking the questions—that is a mistake! To connect with the jury, the expert witness must make regular eye contact with them. Without regular eye contact, the jury will probably think one of several things, none of which are good for the expert: (1) he is lying; (2) he does not know what he is talking about; or (3) he is unsure of his opinion(s).

> **Corollary**: While initiating eye contact is important in establishing a rapport with the jury, it is not the only factor in creating a sense of credibility. Believable experts clearly state opinions without hesitation. One who continually has to refer to notes for basic information may not seem to be much of an expert at all.

9. **Use powerful analogies**—Jurors will not remember all, perhaps even much, of the testimony presented by witnesses; however, if keys points are summarized and testimony is presented with memorable phrases, the important ideas may be more easily recalled. Just remember, if "a picture is worth a 1000 words," then a powerful analogy is worth a least half of that.

10. **Get out of the witness stand**—Listening to someone sitting in a chair and talk can quickly become repetitious and boring to a juror. Getting out of the witness stand is a great way to break up the monotony. Convey an important point to the jury by standing up and pointing to a demonstrative chart or photo. This type of activity will quickly get the attention of the jury. The implied message to the jury is "listen carefully, this is important" as long as something important is said.

> **Corollary**: While getting out of the witness stand will get the jury's attention,

reading notes or reports from the witness stand will have just the opposite effect. Reading to someone from a sitting position is about as exciting as watching grass grow. A witness needing to refer to his notes should ask the judge "May I refresh my memory?" Additionally, some courts may require the permission of the judge prior to standing or moving about the courtroom—very few judges consider their courtrooms to be stages.

Strategic Responses

An expert witness does not ask questions, he or she only responds to the questions posed by counsel or opposing counsel. Therefore, it is critical each response conveys the expert's opinion as accurately as possible. During cross-examination the questions asked are intended to elicit agreement or disagreement with certain statements or assertions. Unfortunately, simple agreement or disagreement often results in a misunderstanding of the response implying something entirely different than what was intended to be said. In life, there are few absolutes and this is but another example of why most responses should be qualified, otherwise the speaker can be "painted into a corner."

1. **Absolute opinions**—Be careful about answering questions with absolute responses, such as always or never. Even a simple yes or no can be construed as an absolute reply unless it includes some sort of modifier. Instead of saying no, a better response would be "not normally" or "not that I can recall."
2. **Qualified responses**—The use of modifiers such as usually or normally help avoid an attorney mischaracterizing a response as unconditional. This adaptation also provides some "wiggle room" if someone later attempts to distort the reply or the question.
3. **Responses to yes or no only questions**—If a simple "yes" or "no" response is not accurate,

the response should be explained. This tactic, which may be attempted by opposing counsel, demonstrates why absolute responses should be avoided and may need qualification as explained above. The judge should permit a response, which includes "yes, with an explanation" or "no, with an explanation," followed by the explanation.

4. **Compound questions**—An attorney may ask a question containing multiple questions that often do not have the same answer. This is an attempt to elicit a damaging admission to the latter part of the question. If asked a compound question, request the question be simplified into several shorter questions. This is an area in which your counsel may prove helpful with a timely objection to the form of the question.

5. **Repetitive (or badgering) questions**—An attorney may ask the same question multiple times. Each time, the question will probably be worded a little differently. This strategy tests the consistency of the response to the same question. Inconsistent responses impeach the expert's credibility. However, consistent responses can be bolstered by politely pointing out to opposing counsel, "I think I have already answered the question but ...."

6. **Pregnant pauses**—An attorney may deliberately pause after a response before asking the next question. The silence is intended to imply additional information is required to complete the answer. The strategy here is to coax the expert into supplementing his or her response. A complete answer does not require any additional information.

7. **Compensation**—An expert witness is paid for his or her time (fees should be based on an hourly/daily rate, in fact in most jurisdictions an expert witness is prohibited from entering any type of compensation formula contingent on the outcome of the case). An expert witness is never paid for his or her opinion

per se. One who answers the question "how much have you been paid for your opinion" with an amount of money, will be portrayed as a "hired gun" who will say anything for a price. Instead, respectfully point out that the fee is earned on the basis of the time required for the case and not for the opinion.

Language Choices

Testifying in court is essentially a contest of words. Assuming one does not (proverbially speaking) shoot himself in the foot, the contest is between the expert and the opposing attorney. Therefore, it is important to choose the right words to get the point across. Words are the building blocks of conveying any message to the jury. The more words added, the more definition is provided to the jury. Just be aware that a message with too many words may miss the mark. Therefore, it is often better to say as much as possible with the fewest words—maximum clarity with minimum words. In addition to the number of words chosen, the type of word selected also helps to clarify the expert's message. Smaller words are almost always better than bigger ones. Each additional syllable is a verbal speed bump to the jurors. A witness using big words to sound smart has missed the point—the task is communication! The question —do these words establish a bridge to the jury or do they form a wall?

1. **Use of the collective "we"**—an expert witness may inadvertently refer to the attorney who retained him as "we." Since an expert is supposed to be independent and tell only the truth regardless of who retained him or her, the use of "we" implies taking "sides.' Needless to say, this may appear to compromise the objectivity of any witness using such language.

2. **Use of technical jargon**—The average juror has very little knowledge of technical terms in any given field of expertise. Avoid the use of technical language when testifying. Continual

use of technical terms, especially when not defined, may cause the jury to feel the expert is "talking down" to them. The use of simple words is a much better approach. For example,use teeth, not dentition; use cheek side, not buccal; or use jaw or jaw bone not mandible or alveolus.

3. **Choice of terms**—Be careful about the terms chosen to describe an analysis. A poor choice of words can create the impression the opinion may not be objective; e.g., using the term "manipulate" when describing how a patterned injury photograph was analyzed in Adobe Photoshop. Actually, digital data and filters were employed to improve the image for forensic analysis; therefore, the more appropriate term would be "enhance," rather than manipulate.

Summary
BASICS OF DIRECT TESTIMONY

Use simple understandable language and speak in conversational terms. Do not testify using a lecture format. Avoid long narratives. When answering questions, answer first, any necessary explanations can be made later. It is almost always preferable to mention any potential problems in an expert's testimony during direct testimony by "friendly" counsel in order that a cogent explanation can be given. Waiting until problems are raised on cross-examination (or worse, hoping the problems will not be raised at all) can result in the appearance that the witness has something to hide.

NOTEWORTHY DIRECT TESTIMONY Use visual exhibits to illustrate important points for the jury to remember. Get out of the witness stand when possible. Use memorable analogies to help explain opinions. A good witness tells the jury what they need to know, not all he knows. A witness who is perceived to be showing off either bores the jury or becomes disliked by some jury members. Finally, the use of self-deprecating humor can help to make a witness seem more likeable to the jury. Just remember, humor at the testifying expert's expense makes him seem more congenial, but humor at someone else's expense will probably have the opposite effect.

DEPOSITION TESTIMONY Depositions are similar in many respects to a court testimony; however, no judge or jury is present. All witnesses are sworn and there is a court reporter present to transcribe the proceedings. Unlike courtroom proceedings, attendance at a deposition is usually limited to involved parties. Typical attendees at a deposition include plaintiff and defense counsel, court reporter, witnesses to be deposed, and sometimes the plaintiff and defendant. In any case, all persons in attendance at a deposition are identified by the court reporter at the beginning of the deposition transcript. Depositions are a normal part of the discovery process in civil proceedings; however, depositions in criminal cases are rare. Florida is one of the few states permitting depositions in criminal matters. Because deposition testimony is sworn and transcribed, it will inevitably become part of the record in a case. Therefore, most of the previously mentioned advice concerning testimony applies equally to depositions.

A deposition is part of the legal discovery process. It is evidence given under oath and recorded for use in court at a later date. In the United States, it is given outside a courtroom in preparation for trial. Since the vast majority of depositions are given in regard to civil proceedings, an expert witness should be aware that the burden of proof is different (lower) in a civil court case. Unlike criminal cases, where the burden of proof is "beyond a reasonable doubt," the burden of proof in civil cases is a "preponderance of the evidence"—50% plus a smidgen more.

An expert asked to provide deposition testimony will usually receive a subpoena commanding his or her presence at a certain time and place. Typically, only the opposing attorney in a case will want to take a deposition. Expert witnesses are paid for their time in depositions. Therefore, it is allowable and proper to discuss your fees with the attorney who sent the subpoena and make necessary arrangements for payment prior to taking a deposition. In some cases, an expert may receive a subpoena *"duces tecum"* (Fig. 11.2), which not only requires the subpoenaed witness's presence at a certain time and place but also requires the expert bring certain materials specified in the subpoena to the deposition.

However, if any of the listed materials are not in the witness's possession or cannot be reasonably obtained, the witness should notify the attorney who originally retained his or her services. In addition to knowing what type of subpoena was received, it is also worthwhile to know whether the deposition is a "discovery deposition" or an "evidentiary deposition." A discovery deposition is typically used for purposes of discovery only and is not normally entered into evidence at any later trial. However, an evidentiary deposition is most often taken if there is a reasonable likelihood a witness may not be available for appearance later at trial. In this case, the deposition is often videotaped as well as transcribed.

STRATEGIES

Preparation for deposition—Prior to the deposition, the witness should make certain he or she has seen and is familiar with all of the records related to the case. In some cases, the expert may have been given only the records the attorney felt was necessary in reaching an opinion. Only the expert can assess and decide what records are relevant, not the attorney! It is important at the outset to request all the records pertaining to any allegations that have been made. Most especially, make certain you have read all previous depositions in the case. There is no more certain way to appear unprepared than to be presented with records or depositions by opposing counsel that have not been seen by the expert.

Timing of deposition—The timing of a deposition may be critical and dependent upon whether the expert has been retained as a plaintiff or defense expert. Typically, the plaintiff and the defendant are the first two witnesses deposed in a civil action. Afterwards, the order of deponents can vary somewhat. Nevertheless, an expert for the plaintiff should review the defendant's deposition before being deposed. The expert must be aware of any testimony made by the defendant that corroborates, contradicts, or provides new information concerning any documentation in the records. On the other hand, a defense expert should insist on reviewing the deposition of the plaintiff's expert before scheduling his deposition. Again it is imperative to know the opinions of the plaintiff's expert to respond appropriately.

Location of deposition—Choosing a location for your deposition may seem like a small matter. However, an incorrect choice can sometimes lead to regretful consequences. Ideally, a neutral location will be chosen. If provided the opportunity to choose, do not choose a location that may be distracting or create the possibility of mental or physical distress. For instance, a deposition at the expert's dental office creates the potential for too much distraction; while a deposition at the opposing attorney's office may place the expert at the mercy of someone who may not have the witness's best interest at heart. Often the best location for a deposition is at the office of the attorney who retained the expert.

Option to read and sign your deposition—At the beginning of the deposition, the court reporter should ask the expert witness if he or she would like to read and sign the deposition or if the expert "waives signature." Never waive the right to read and sign a deposition. A signature attests that the deposition is accurate, but an expert cannot determine whether this is true unless he or she has actually read the deposition before signing the errata sheet. Court reporters are human and they periodically make transcription errors. Any expert who waives his or her right to read and sign the deposition may be tacitly agreeing to critical errors in testimony.

SUBPOENA DUCES TECUM (CIVIL) –
ATTORNEY ISSUED VA. CODE §§ 8.01-413, 16.1-89, 16.1-265;
Commonwealth of Virginia Supreme Court Rules 1:4. 4:9

Case No.: ....

....
HEARING DATE AND TIME

.... Court

....
COURT ADDRESS

....**v./In re:** ....

TO THE PERSON AUTHORIZED BY LAW TO SERVE THIS PROCESS:

You are commanded to summon

....
NAME

....
STREET ADDRESS

....
CITY   STATE   ZIP

TO the person summoned: You are commanded to make available the documents and tangible things designated and described below:

....

at..at..
LOCATION   DATE AND TIME
to permit such party or someone acting in his or her behalf to inspect and copy, test or sample such tangible things in your possession, custody or control.

This Subpoena Duces Tecum is issued by the attorney for and on behalf of

....
PARTY NAME

....
NAME OF ATTORNEY   VIRGINIA STATE BAR NUMBER

....
OFFICE ADDRESS   TELEPHONE NUMBER OF ATTORNEY

....
OFFICE ADDRESS   FACSIMILE NUMBER OF ATTORNEY

....   _____
DATE ISSUED   SIGNATURE OF ATTORNEY

Notice to Recipient: See page two for further information.

RETURN OF SERVICE (see page two of this form)

FORM DC-498 (MASTER, PAGE ONE OF TWO) 7/01

FIGURE 11.2 Subpoena *"duces tecum."*

Even an inadvertent error as simple as omitting a word or misspelling a word can completely change the meaning of the responses.

Discoverable materials—Any written material brought to a deposition is discoverable. This includes records, reference articles, and written notes. Many experts take contemporaneous notes as records and depositions in the case are reviewed. Therefore, any handwritten notes should be professional in nature and not include editorial comments about anyone or anything, including notes taken during the deposition itself that may reveal something important which should remain confidential. Typically, the opposing attorney will ask to review the expert's records before beginning the deposition. The attorney may make copies of any written notes or reference materials in the file. Therefore, a meeting with the retaining attorney prior to the deposition can garner valuable information about what material should or should not be in the expert's case file.

Predeposition meeting—Another reason to meet with the attorney prior to a deposition is to determine how much information should be revealed during the deposition. During testimony the witness must answer all questions asked. However, the witness is under no obligation to volunteer any information. The attorney may determine it is strategically important to withhold certain information until trial. In cases unlikely to settle before trial, an attorney may want to hold back potentially damaging information for use at trial. On the other hand, if an attorney believes there is a strong likelihood of settlement, nothing might be held back. Therefore, the expert should discuss if questions should be simply answered as asked or "should let it all hang out."

Reports

The purpose of expert witness reports is to provide information to eliminate trial by ambush. Informed parties may enter into settlement talks, or the court may encourage settlement instead of using scarce and expensive court room time. It is part of the discovery process and is intended as an exchange of information by opposing parties. In most civil litigation, plaintiff and defense experts will submit reports. However, since the burden of proof is borne by the prosecution in criminal cases, defense experts may not be required to submit a report. Writing a report is not necessarily as easy as it may seem. In addition to the scientific elements of preparing a report, there is also an art to writing a report. The science of report writing contains three essential elements: (1) what items were examined, (2) what did the expert do with those items, and (3) what conclusion did the expert reach as a result of those actions.

The art of report writing is more subjective and requires balance of the information contained in the report. Many, perhaps most expert witnesses, consider a report to be a scientific document; however, most lawyers would consider it to be a legal document. Therefore, an expert witness must critique his or her report from the legal perspective. From a legal perspective, an attorney views a report as potential cannon fodder. Does it provide any information that may be used against the expert? This may include citing written materials in the report, the length (or brevity) of the report, the use of vague language in the report, or the use of absolute terms. Any of these items can provide potential avenues of impeachment of the expert's opinion(s). The bottom line is that a report is a balancing act between scientific diligence and legal ammunition. One must say the right amount—neither too much nor too little. Remember it is a scientific report, not a literary work and therefore should contain necessary information only. Highly detailed information is seldom necessary and should not be produced as part of the discovery process.

Factors outside the expert's control may also influence the content of the report including whether the report is court-mandated or is subject to discovery. In addition, the attorney who retained the expert may not wish to receive a written report if it contains opinions unfavorable to the case. Reports may be oral (verbal) or written. An initial oral report is often used to determine if a written report is desired. At least in a civil matter, it may allow the expert to report matters "off the record" and thereby shield unfavorable findings from opposing counsel. Oral reports are generally not discoverable. On the other hand, written reports are almost always discoverable and an expert witness may be encouraged to discuss his or her findings and how those findings might best be expressed in the report with the attorney. Some lawyers may want certain strategic information left out of the report. However, it cannot be overemphasized, the expert witness bears complete responsibility for the report; never allow an attorney to dictate or alter the findings

and opinion. If an agreement regarding how to express the opinion(s) cannot be reached, the attorney cannot force the expert to produce a report or testify against his or her better judgment.

The ABFO has guidelines for report writing specifically pertaining to bitemark analysis and comparison (Table 11.1). Although these guidelines are specific for bitemark reports, all sections of these guidelines can be used for any report, provided the specific type of analysis is modified accordingly (dental identification, age assessment, standard of care, etc.).

Report Writing Guidelines

CONTENT OF REPORTS

1. **Introduction**—This section of the report outlines the basic information explaining the expert's involvement in the case, what the

---

TABLE 11.1 American Board of Forensic Odontology Guidelines for Investigative and Final Bitemark Reports

The following ABFO Bitemark Report Writing Guidelines propose a format for written bitemark case reports. These guidelines are suggestions for the form and content of the report. Diplomats may be asked to provide preliminary or investigative reports. Those preliminary reports may follow the same general guidelines without being conclusive in nature.

Reports may be structured into the following sections:

Introduction

This section provides the background information, the "who, what, when, where, and why" data related to the case.

Inventory of Evidence Received

This section lists all evidence received by the forensic odontologist and details the source of the evidence.

Inventory of Evidence Collected

This section lists the nature, source, and authority for evidence collected by the forensic odontologist.

Opinion Regarding the Nature of the Patterned Injury or Injuries

This section states the author's opinion as to whether the patterned injuries in question are bitemarks, using ABFO terminology. Only one comparative term is used for each opinion in this part of the report.

Methods of Analysis

This section describes the analytic methods used for the patterned injuries determined to be bitemarks.

Results of Analyses

This section describes the results of the comparisons and analyses.

Opinion

This section states the author's opinion of the relationship between one or more bitemarks and a suspected biter or biters using ABFO Bitemark Terminology. Only one comparative term is used for each opinion in this part of the report.

Disclaimer

Disclaimer statements may be included to convey that the opinion or opinions are based upon the evidence reviewed through the date of the report. The author may reserve the right to file amended reports should additional evidence become available.

11. EXPERT WITNESS GUIDELINES & TESTIMONY

expert was requested to do. In general it answers the Five W's—Who, What, When, Where, and Why as appropriate. These basic facts explain the context of the case and set the stage for the analyses and opinions that follow.

2. **Inventory of evidence received**—This section is an itemization of evidence provided for analysis or examination and it identifies the individual or agency providing the evidence for review.

3. **Inventory of evidence collected**—This section of the report itemizes any evidence collected by the expert including the basis for the collection of evidence, e.g., a court order or a search warrant, etc.

4. **Method(s) of analysis**—This section of the report lists the types of analyses performed on evidence received or collected. The methods listed in this part of the report should be basic in nature. Any detailed discussion of these methods should be provided as necessary during the discovery process.

5. **Result(s) of analysis**—This section of the report summarizes the results of the analysis. Again, the results should be outlined briefly and detailed discussions of conclusions should be provided as necessary.

6. **Opinion(s)**—Many reports combine sections 5 and 6 into a single section, since the results of the analysis form the basis for any opinion(s). Regardless of the format, opinions should flow from the results of analyses and once again contain basic opinions only.

7. **Disclaimer**—The final section of the report should state opinion(s) held to a reasonable degree of certainty and based upon the evidence reviewed as outlined in sections 2 and 3 of the report. Finally, the report should acknowledge that an opinion is subject to revision should additional evidence become available at a later date and warrants a change.

STRATEGIES ABOUT REPORTS

As mentioned earlier, attorneys look at reports as potential cannon fodder. The more ammunition provided in your report, the less homework the opposing attorney has to undertake to learn about a particular field of expertise. Certain types of reports are typically viewed with skepticism by lawyers and usually raise a "red flag." Very short or very long reports will often provoke suspicion. Short reports may indicate to the attorney the expert is lazy or likes to cut corners, while long reports may indicate that the expert may talk too much and therefore is prone to making damaging admissions in deposition or on the stand if encouraged.

In addition to the length of a report, lawyers may also look at the type of language it contains. Reports containing vague language or use of many absolutes will also draw the attention of opposing attorneys. Vague language may be a sign the expert is not certain of his or her opinion and may be coaxed into changing his or her mind if challenged. On the other hand, the extensive use of absolute language may signal this expert is either biased or too sure of him or herself. In either case, there may be weaknesses in the basis for the opinions.

Since reports are typically provided long before any testimony, it is often advisable to avoid citing written materials in the report. Written material identified in a report will provide the opposing attorney ample time to obtain and vet a copy of the material, possibly using that information to impeach the expert or the expert's opinion(s). The mention of written material only at trial is unlikely to provide sufficient time to use this material for impeachment purposes.

CAVEATS ABOUT REPORTS

1. **Inconclusive reports**—If an expert is unable to reach a definitive opinion in his or her report, the opinion and disclaimer sections of the report will likely require more explanation. The reason(s) for the inability to reach a conclusion should be identified, which may well include problems with the quantity or quality of evidence reviewed. The expert should state what additional evidence (if any) would have been helpful in reaching a more definitive opinion.

2. **Statistical opinions**—An expert should avoid the use of statistical comparisons unless hard data exist to support those conclusions. For example, there is currently very little statistical data on which to base the frequency of occurrence of certain bite patterns. The use of unfounded statistical conclusions may result in rejection of the opinion by the trial judge or by the appellate courts.

3. **Distinct versus unique**—Experts often use these terms interchangeably, even though they mean different things. Distinct means uncommon or different from the norm. On the other hand, unique means one of a kind, rare, or exceptional. The use of the term "unique" denotes something highly unusual, extraordinary, or rare (Webster's New World Dictionary), while the term distinct denotes "distinguishable to the eye or mind as being discrete or not the same" (Merriam-Webster.com). Therefore, the use of the term unique should be avoided when comparing dental bite patterns to bitemarks.

4. **Explanation of ambiguous terminology**—If terminology used in a report is ambiguous or has multiple meanings, the expert should explain the meaning of the term in that report or use a different term. There should be no misunderstanding of any comparative or linkage term in an expert's report. A classic example of a term with ambiguous or multiple meanings is the use of the word "match." The use of the term "match" may imply that two (or more) items have been linked conclusively, or the listener may infer such. In reality, the term "match" merely means cannot exclude or consistent with. The use of the linkage term "match" should be avoided in favor of more definitive linkage terms.

DEFENDING YOUR REPORT

Once an opinion is reduced to writing, the expert who penned it must be prepared to defend the opinion. Every opinion in the report should be based on an analysis of the evidence reviewed. The expert should review the report and ensure each opinion contained therein can be unequivocally supported by the evidence and analysis. Any opinions not substantiated by the evidence must be removed from the report. Being more conservative with the opinion(s) stated in a report is not likely to create a legal problem. However, an opinion(s) not supported by evidence can create a legal dilemma. Once something is put in writing, it cannot be taken back. One final comment about reports—when in doubt, leave it out!

Curriculum Vitae

The term "CV" is taken from Latin and translates to "course of life." CV is a written description of an expert's work experience, educational background, and skills. It is more detailed than a resume and is commonly used by those looking for work. You should have only one CV. An expert with more than one CV invites vigorous cross-examination about what he or she is hiding and from whom is it being hidden. It is not uncommon that early in an expert's career there may be "fluff" items in his or her CV to keep it from being too short. As the expert gains professional experience, the "fluff" should be replaced with more relevant and topical information.

Contents of a Curriculum Vita

There are essential pieces of information that should be included in any CV. There are also some things that should not be included in an expert's CV.

1. What should be listed:
   a. **Biographical information**—Name, business address, telephone, email, date, and place of birth.
   b. **Educational background**—Beginning with undergraduate degrees list, dental school attended, as well as any specialty training; include name of institution, city/state, degree/certificate conferred and year granted.

c. **Board certifications**—List all certifications in chronologic order.

d. **Professional employment history**—Begin after dental school in reverse chronologic order; include name and address of employer and all positions held; include month and year employment began and ended, should be current to present date.

e. **Professional affiliations**—Include all professional organization memberships, both dental and forensic; include years of membership as well as committee work and chairmanships; also include any special recognition.

f. **Professional appointments**—Should begin after dental school in chronologic order; include appointing institution as well as years the appointment has been held; also include the appointment or title held.

g. **Professional publications**—Include exact title of the article as well as the name of the journal or periodical; also include the volume and page numbers of the article as well as the date of publication.

h. **Presentations**—Include exact title of the presentation as well as the date it was presented as well as the location; also include the name of the organization or meeting where the presentation was made.

2. What should not be listed:
   a. Anything irrelevant to the expert's professional practice.
   b. Anything related to religion.
   c. Anything related to politics.
   d. Continuing education (CE) required for licensure.

3. What may be listed:
   a. Community service affiliations.
   b. Volunteer activities.
   c. CE classes not required for licensure; in particular, the expert should list education pertinent to the expert's field of expertise.

Curriculum Vitae Caveats

A CV should be updated on a regular basis. The optimum time frame for updating a CV is at least annually. All pages of a CV should be numbered to insure it is complete. Be absolutely certain all information on the CV is accurate. In addition to the expert personally reviewing his or her CV, he or she should also have someone else who is familiar with the expert's background critically review it as well. Never misrepresent any information on a CV. Padding a CV may seem innocuous, but an expert who is caught distorting the truth will have his or her credibility immeasurably damaged. Just remember, without credibility, an opinion is worthless!

Further Reading

Babitsky, S., Mangrviti Jr., J.J., 2005. How to Become a Dangerous Expert Witness – Advanced Techniques and Strategies. Seak, Inc., Falmouth, MA, p. 15.

Barsley, R.E., David, T.J., Metcalf, R.D., 2013. Jurisprudence and expert witness testimony. In: Senn, D.R., Weems, R.A. (Eds.), Manual of Forensic Odontology, fifth ed. CRC Press, Boca Raton, FL, pp. 377–395.

Barsley, R.E., David, T.J., Pitluck, H.M., 2010. Jurisprudence and legal issues. In: Senn, D.R.S.P.G. (Ed.), Forensic Dentistry, second ed. CRC Press, Boca Raton, FL, pp. 379–393.

Brodsky, S.L., 1991. Testifying in Court: Guidelines and Maxims for the Expert Witness. Stanley L. Brodsky. American Psychological Association.

Burton's Legal Thesaurus, 4E. S.v. "authoritative". Retrieved from: http://legal-dictionary.thefreedictionary.com/authoritative.

Merriam-Webster.com. "distinct". Retrieved from: https://www.merriam-webster.com/dictionary/distinct.

Merriam-Webster Learner's Dictionary. "authoritative". Retrieved from: http://www.learnersdictionary.com/definition/authoritative.

Pozner, L., Dodd, R.J., 1993. Cross-Examination: Science and Techniques. The Michie Company, Charlottesville, VA.

"unique." Webster's New World Dictionary (of the American Language), Second College Edition, 1980. Simon and Schuster, p. 1552.

12

Expert Witness Liability
An Attorney's Perspective

Roger D. Metcalf[1,2]

[1]Chief of the Human Identification Laboratory, Tarrant County Medical Examiner's District, Fort Worth, TX, United States; [2]Assistant Professor, Center for Education and Research in Forensics, The University of Texas Health Science Center at San Antonio, San Antonio, TX, United States

Development of the theory of expert witness liability is a relatively recent and ongoing trend in the legal profession. Traditionally, the witness in court was afforded *absolute immunity* from civil lawsuit resulting from his/her testimony, noted as early as 1585 in the English case *Cutler v. Dixon*, 4 Co.Rep. 14b, 76 Eng.Rep. 886 (Q.B. 1585) and later *Anfield v. Feverhill*, 2 Bulst. 269, 80 Eng.Rep. 1113 (K.B. 1614), even if the testimony was malicious or knowingly false (*Hodgson v. Scarlett*, 1 Barn. & Ald. 232, 246–247, 106 Eng.Rep. 86, 91 (K.B. 1818) (Holroyd, J.)). Such immunity, however, would not protect the witness from criminal prosecution for perjury. Common-law witness immunity originally extended only to defamation claims by the opposing party, but the doctrine has been broadened over the years to the point expert witnesses have been shielded, until recently, even from claims of negligence in the performance of their duties (i.e., "malpractice") connected to their testimony. However, this ancient doctrine of absolute witness immunity is being eroded by recent decisions—for example, in *Jones v. Kaney*

[2011] UKSC 13, the Supreme Court of the United Kingdom in 2011 "...removed the 400-year-old protection providing expert witnesses immunity from suit for breach of duty whether in contract or negligence, in relation to their participation in legal proceedings." (*The Law Society Gazette*, http://www.lawgazette.co.uk/59804.article). In the United States, the seminal federal case on this topic is *Briscoe v. LaHue*, 460 U.S. 325 (1983), which states:

(a) The common law provided absolute immunity from subsequent damages liability for all persons—governmental or otherwise—who were integral parts of the judicial process. Section 1983 does not authorize a damages claim against private witnesses. Similarly, judges...and prosecutors...may not be held liable for damages under § 1983 for the performance of their respective duties in judicial proceedings. When a police officer appears as a witness, he may reasonably be viewed as acting like any witness sworn to tell the truth, in which event he can make a strong claim to witness immunity. Alternatively, he may be regarded as an official performing a critical role in the judicial process, in which event he may seek the benefit afforded to other governmental participants in the same proceeding. Nothing in § 1983's language suggests that a police officer witness belongs in a narrow, special category lacking protection against damages suits.

Briscoe, who had been convicted of burglary in Bloomington, Indiana, sued LaHue, a police officer, for his testimony that Briscoe was one of no more than 50–100 people in Bloomington whose fingerprint could "match" a partial print found at a burglary crime scene. Briscoe claimed LaHue committed perjury because FBI and State police fingerprint examiners declared the partial print to be of no value, and therefore, ultimately, Briscoe's right to due process was violated under 42 United States Code §1983. The United States Supreme Court held that a police officer giving testimony as a fact witness in a criminal trial was shielded by immunity for a number of public policy reasons—essentially witnesses, including public officials, must be free to give candid and forthright testimony without the chilling effect of fear of reprisal. This concept has grown over the years to include testimony given by other expert witnesses as well.

The use of expert witnesses in court has grown significantly since the decision in *Daubert v. Merrell Dow Pharmaceuticals*, 509 U.S. 579 (1993). Prior to *Daubert*, many jurisdictions followed, and several still do, the "Frye Standard" articulated in *Frye v. United States*, 293F. 1013 (D.C. Cir. 1923). This standard for admission of *novel* scientific evidence was based on "general acceptance" by experts in the relevant field. Mr. Frye had been accused of murder in Washington, DC, and his defense team wanted to introduce results of a then-new so-called "blood pressure deception test" (early forerunner of the polygraph), purported to show Mr. Frye was being truthful when he denied committing the murder. The trial court did *not* allow presentation of this novel scientific evidence, and Mr. Frye was duly convicted and perfected an appeal. The D.C. Circuit Court of Appeals (please note, this was not a US Supreme Court holding as is sometimes erroneously reported; at the time the trial court had the unfortunately confusing name "Supreme Court of the District of Columbia") upheld the conviction, and stated regarding the evidence:

> Just when a scientific principle or discovery crosses the line between the experimental and demonstrable stages is difficult to define. Somewhere in this twilight zone the evidential force of the principle must be recognized, and while courts will go a long way in admitting expert testimony deduced from a well-recognized scientific principle or discovery, *the thing from which the deduction is made must be sufficiently established to have gained general acceptance in the particular field in which it belongs* (emphasis added).

The *Frye* standard gave judges a "bright line" rule to follow for admission of novel scientific evidence—if the evidence had become "generally accepted" in the particular discipline, then it could be admissible at trial. Of course, the question immediately follows: just *who* is to affirm whether or not some evidence is "generally accepted" in the field? Enter the expert witness.

Fact witnesses are generally limited to providing testimony about things they actually perceived themselves. Contrary to popular misconception, however, fact witnesses are occasionally allowed to offer an opinion such as "I think he was drunk" or "I think he was speeding" as long as the subject is within the experience of the ordinary person. But for a witness to offer an opinion about a legal determination, such as, following the above example, "In my opinion, he was *intoxicated*," the witness must first be qualified as an expert in the relevant discipline. The expert witness in common law practice was one who "had ken beyond ordinary men" in some specialized area (here "ken" has the connotation of "knowledge"). In modern practice in the United States under the Federal Rules of Evidence (and Rules of Evidence in states such as Texas have adopted a version of the Federal Rules as their own), the witness can be qualified as an expert by virtue of his/her knowledge, skill, experience, training, or education (Federal Rules of Evidence 702). Note there is no specific university or college degree or particular type of training detailed by the Rule—it is up to the Judge to approve the expert and determine what evidence is admissible. From *Daubert*, *we* have the concept of Judge as the "gatekeeper" of the entrance through which scientific evidence and expert testimony must pass to be admitted at trial.

In the past, once an expert was qualified by the court, he/she had little concern about future liability for current testimony—as long as the expert witness did not commit perjury, he/she was immune from subsequent legal action for the proffered opinion testimony. After all, (1) the testimony had been given in the form of an *opinion*, not absolute scientific fact, and, in any case, as mentioned above, (2) the witness was simply afforded immunity from civil suit by the opposing party. Essentially, an expert could offer an opinion, and that opinion could be wrong, but as long as the expert witness really believed he/she was telling the truth, all was well for the expert.

But what if an expert is alleged to have committed perjury or some other illegal act in connection with his/her testimony, particularly in a criminal trial? Then liability certainly can attach. The reasoning is a bit convoluted, but so is this: a *private party* cannot violate another person's Constitutional rights (except for violations of the 13th Amendment); the Constitution protects us from such violations by the *Government*. The expert witness forensic odontologist may consider him/herself to be a private party but if employed by a Government agency, will likely be considered to be acting "under color of law" or, in other words, acting on behalf of and as part of the Government. In that case, the odontologist is no longer a private party, but would be an agent of the Government who could indeed be held liable for violating another person's Constitutional rights. The scenario would probably arise along these lines—the forensic odontologist would be engaged as an expert by the prosecution in a criminal case. The prosecution might be accused of violating the defendant's Constitutional rights in some way, and the odontologist named as a codefendant in the lawsuit. Such suits typically arise as so-called "1983 lawsuits"—named after the section of US Code where the pertinent regulation is found, 42 US Code §1983 "Civil Action for Deprivation of Rights." There have been at least two recent lawsuits of this nature: *Moldowan v. City of Warren*, 578 F.3d 351 (sixth Cir. 2009) and *Cristini v. City of Warren*, 30 F.Supp.3d 665 (E.D. Mich. 2014). If the odontologist is found to have committed perjury or some other "bad act" such as fabricating evidence, then immunity from judgement, whether in state or federal court, will not be available as a defense. In addition, it could also happen that, if the odontologist did indeed commit some bad act, the government agency hiring him/her might successfully claim the act was "outside the scope of the odontologist's duties" and refuse to defend or indemnify the odontologist. Obviously, it is better to always act in good faith and tell the truth on the stand.

Recently there have been civil cases as well, where expert witnesses have been held liable for damages in connection with their testimony. But again, consider, the "adverse" expert has witness immunity from civil suit by the opposing party, so who would sue the expert? The *expert's own employer*—the attorney who hired the expert! The attorney hires the expert witness—a "friendly" witness—and that witness testifies voluntarily and is compensated, often handsomely, for his/her time, knowledge, and expertise.

The seminal case in this area is LLMD of Michigan, Inc. v. Jackson-Cross Co., 740 A.2d

186 (Pa. 1999). The underlying case involved a plaintiff suing a group of lenders for failing to follow through with their commitment to fund a construction project. The plaintiff needed to show the value of the "lost business opportunity" and other damages caused by the lender's failure to fund the venture. The plaintiff engaged a firm to calculate the damages and prepare a report detailing the same, and to provide testimony at trial. The retained firm provided an expert witness to testify regarding the alleged damages, and it was elucidated by the defense team during testimony that a mathematical error had been made by the firm in the calculations, which made the calculations invalid. Further, the expert had to concede on the stand he had not performed the calculations himself, and did not know how to correct the error. The plaintiff in the underlying case ultimately settled the case with the lenders for a much lower amount than he had originally claimed, and then sued the expert witness and his firm for the difference, alleging expert witness malpractice. The appeals court found the expert here could be held liable for damages, writing:

> It is imperative that an expert witness not be subjected to litigation because the party who retained the expert is dissatisfied with the substance of the opinion rendered by the expert. An expert witness must be able to articulate the basis for his or her opinion without fear that a verdict unfavorable to the client will result in litigation, even where the party who has retained the expert contends that the expert's opinion was not fully explained prior to trial. Application of the witness immunity doctrine in Panitz was consistent, therefore, with the twofold policy of the doctrine: to ensure that the path to the truth is left as free and unobstructed as possible and to protect the judicial process.

> We are unpersuaded, however, that those policy concerns are furthered by extending the witness immunity doctrine to professional negligence actions which are brought against an expert witness when the allegations of negligence are not premised on the substance of the expert's opinion. We perceive a significant difference between Panitz and Wintoll's claim in this case that Jackson-Cross had been negligent in performing the mathematical calculations required to determine lost profits. The goal of ensuring that the path to truth is unobstructed and the judicial process is protected, by fostering an atmosphere where the expert witness will be forthright and candid in stating his or her opinion, is not advanced by immunizing an expert witness from his or her negligence in formulating that opinion. The judicial process will be enhanced only by requiring that an expert witness render services to the degree of care, skill, and proficiency commonly exercised by the ordinarily skillful, careful, and prudent members of their profession.

> Therefore, *we find that the witness immunity doctrine does not bar Wintoll's professional malpractice action against Jackson-Cross.* We caution, however, that our holding that the witness immunity doctrine does not preclude claims against an expert witness for professional malpractice has limited application. An expert witness may not be held liable merely because his or her opinion is challenged by another expert or authoritative source. In those circumstances, the judicial process is enhanced by the presentation of different views. *Differences of opinion will not suffice to establish liability of an expert witness for professional negligence* (emphasis added).

Courts have been careful to note the distinction between the *substance* of the opinion versus the *methods and care* used to arrive at an opinion—the content of the expert's opinion per se may not be actionable, but the way in which it was derived may be. State and federal courts are divided at this time on the issue of expert witness liability, so no general rule can be given whether or not a forensic odontologist might be subject to such liability—at the present it is not a well-settled law, it is highly case- and jurisdiction-specific, and it continues to evolve.

As dentists, we are well aware of the value of *prevention*, and the same principle applies here. Avoid legal problems by telling the truth, acting in good faith, and use accepted methods and principles.

An Insurance Risk Management Perspective

James A. Misselwitz[1,2,3]

[1]Vice President ECBM, LLP, West Conshohocken, PA, United States; [2]President, PLM & JAM Associates Inc., Millsboro, DE, United States; [3]Board member of CLEW (Consultants, Lawyers, and Expert Witnesses), Malvern, PA, United States

In this section of the chapter, I will discuss liability as it relates to a forensic odontologist's work in both testimony and depositions. The principle of "Judicial Immunity" varies significantly among state jurisdictions. Simply put, as courts needed experts to testify, they granted immunity to the expert to obtain their opinion and allow the "trier of truth" to make an informed decision. However, those simple days are long gone in most jurisdictions. The courts' understanding of what denotes an expert has been redefined by first *Frye*, then *Daubert*, and again by *Kumho Tire*. Experts are now paid for their testimony, which has certainly increased the likelihood that the other side may challenge either the result or counter with their own expert. Therefore, one needs to understand the playing field and some of the rules to protect oneself and one's assets.

For more than 50 years the standard for testimony was established in the courts by the *Frye* decision commonly referred to as the Frye standard.

This standard was used to determine the admissibility of an expert's scientific testimony, as established in *Frye v. United States*, 293 F. 1013 (D.C. Cir. 1923). A court applying the Frye standard must determine whether or not the method by which that evidence was obtained was generally accepted by experts in the particular field in which it belongs. The Frye standard has been abandoned by many states and the federal courts in favor of the Daubert standard, but it remains law in some states. The key Frye standard phrase is "Generally acceptable." This concept worked within the judicial system for a long time; however, in the 80s and 90s new

scientific discoveries and principles evolved faster than "general acceptance." Therefore, through case law the courts established a higher standard for expert testimony, the Daubert Standard.

This standard is used by a trial judge to make a preliminary assessment of whether an expert's scientific testimony is based on reasoning or methodology that is scientifically valid and can properly be applied to the facts at issue. Under this standard, the factors that may be considered in determining whether the methodology is valid are (1) whether the theory or technique in question can be and has been tested; (2) it has been subjected to peer review and publication; (3) it has a known or potential error rate; (4) the existence and maintenance of standards controlling its operation; and (5) whether it has attracted widespread acceptance within a relevant scientific community. See *Daubert v. Merrell Dow Pharmaceuticals, Inc.*, 509 U.S. 579 (1993). The Daubert standard replaced the Frye standard in the federal courts and some state courts. As a result, an expert must meet some very specific scientific criteria and establish the court as gatekeeper in deciding what is admissible as testimony.

District courts accepted *Daubert v. Merrell Dow Pharmaceuticals*, solidifying a gatekeeping role for trial judges in the admission of expert testimony. Under *Daubert*, certain factors contribute to the reliability, and hence the admissibility, of expert testimony. One of these is the general validity of the expert's methods. In *Carmichael v. Kumho Tire*, the district court found that a tire expert's methods were unscientifically valid, and hence excluded his testimony. This resulted in a decision that favored Kumho Tire. The Carmichaels appealed to the Eleventh Circuit.

The Eleventh Circuit reversed the district court's ruling. It reasoned that Daubert was expressly limited only to scientific expert testimony and did not apply to "skill- or experience-based observation." The tire expert's testimony rested on such unscientific "observation and experience." Additionally, the Eleventh Circuit reasoned the district court should have ruled differently based upon Federal Rule 702. Kumho Tire then requested the U S Supreme Court to review whether Daubert is to be applied solely to scientific evidence.

Applying that standard to the evidence proffered by the Carmichaels' tire expert, the Court concluded that the district court correctly refused to admit the expert's testimony. The district court had to determine whether the tire expert's methods could reliably determine what had caused the tire on the Carmichaels' van to explode. The expert's experience as a tire engineer was not the problem—the expert had worked for 10 years at Michelin. The fact that visual inspection of tires was generally a reliable method was not an issue either, because the issue before the court was specific to the tire on the Carmichaels' van. However, the expert said that his inspection of the tire led to the conclusion that a defect caused the tire to explode because he did not see evidence of other causes. "Nothing in either *Daubert* or the Federal Rules of Evidence requires a district court to admit opinion evidence that is connected to existing data only by the ipse dixit of the expert [i.e., only by the statement of the expert himself]." The district court acted within its discretion to exclude the evidence proffered by the tire expert in light of these concerns. Accordingly, the Supreme Court reversed the Eleventh Circuit's decision to overrule the district court.

Currently, scientific methodology can be applied to all testimony given by an expert, including their observations and opinions. This should give an expert some pause regarding

contemplation of providing testimony to the court.

It is the opinion of this author that "Judicial Immunity" has evolved to the point it simply cannot be considered as a reliable defense.

There are also misconceptions regarding negligence when it comes to providing expert opinion. The concept of negligence is based on a simple understanding that can be easily remembered as:

- Duty Owed
- Duty Breached
- Proximate Cause of the loss or injury (Loss or Injury)
- An Injury or loss (Loss)

Uninterrupted chain of events, often misunderstood by the untrained, is when we are not discussing the event itself but rather the examination of the event. In the insurance world this has caused many problems as underwriters focus on the event rather than the involvement of the professional that examines the event. If an expert uses a professional insurance agent or broker, it is fair to question them extensively on their understanding of the difference between scientific work as applied to the task and scientific work as applied to examining the cause or result of an event because if he or she does not clearly understand the difference and is going to rely upon your explanation, how is the agent or broker going to be able to respond or more importantly educate an underwriter as to the critical difference in the exposure and therefore policy terms, conditions, and pricing. This will be discussed at greater length as we examine the options for risk transfer.

In most jurisdictions, certainly at the federal court level, admission of testimony or deposition depends upon the evidence passing the Daubert standard. There are three (3) rules of negligence that apply: "Negligence per se," "Comparative Negligence," and "Contributory Negligence."

Negligence per se is conduct that violates standards of care as established by statute or law. Depending on the state law, violating a statutory standard of care can be interpreted as: (1) conclusive proof of negligence, making the defendant automatically liable without giving the defendant a chance to explain his or her actions; (2) presumptive proof of negligence, making the defendant liable unless the defendant can rebut the presumption of negligence by explaining the reasons for his or her actions; or (3) evidence of negligence, which can be considered when deciding whether the defendant should be liable at all. This rarely occurs in forensic testimony.

Comparative negligence is much more fertile ground for attorneys. Comparative negligence are rules used in some states that provide for commuting both the plaintiff's and the defendant's negligence. The plaintiff's damages are reduced by a percentage representing the degree of his or her contributing fault. If the plaintiff's negligence is found to be greater than the defendant's, the plaintiff will receive nothing. Contributory negligence occurs when a plaintiff partially causes or aggravates his or her injury. This doctrine bars relief to the plaintiff in a lawsuit if the plaintiff's own negligence contributed to the damage. Contributory negligence has been superseded in many states by other methods of apportioning liability. However, the concept is still applicable in several states and therefore requires an understanding which rules apply before you testify if you are going to assume the risk yourself.

Before beginning a career as a forensic expert, one might consider asking for professional advice from a lawyer, accountant, and insurance broker/agent regarding what they think about the new venture and what precautions should be taken.

Your attorney says: "You do not really need it. You have got judicial immunity. I have never heard of an expert being sued for their testimony. You will be fine. I can defend you if you need it, and you will not need it."

Your accountant says: "You are in great shape. All your records are up-to-date. I think the cost of professional insurance for your testimony is going to be very expensive and basically cost prohibitive. I recommend against it."

Your insurance agent/broker says: "You are in great shape. Your professional liability policy covering your dental operations covers automatically for all operations arising out of your dental practice. If you want I can add the name of your new company to the existing policy and we should be good to go."

I admit I have taken liberties with these responses, but, believe me, I have heard these statements more than once over the past 20 years. If you will indulge me just a little more, I will give you my observations about this advice. Common sense tells us that advice given for free is usually worth what you pay for it. If you really want to challenge this advice in a polite way you can just ask the professional to give it to you in writing for your file. You plan to rely on it. The answer should change almost immediately.

Let us talk about each piece of advice. "You really do not need it." There is some truth to this response. The likelihood of being for your testimony is very slight. Many things have to occur for that to happen, but the difference between possible and never is huge. The truth is an expert can be sued for court testimony. I think you know now that you can stand on judicial immunity, but if paid for your opinion, you have opened the door for that challenge. If the Daubert standard applies, then the opposing side has a multitude of ways to challenge your testimony. Most attorneys require retainers before they accept defense cases. The smallest retainer I have seen in an expert witness case is about $5000.00. And this retainer just starts the clock running. If your attorney has not handled an expert witness case before, then you will also pay for his time to learn the nuances of *FRYE, DAUBERRT, KUHMO*, as well as any additional statutes that may apply. In most cases, expert witness issues are resolved by the judge prior to trial; however, transferring the risk might be an alternative that you should consider.

An accountant clearly understands your assets, corporate structure, and what is at risk in the event someone tries to sue you. However, his understanding of the pricing of professional liability insurance may be based on his or her experience in doing taxes for medical doctors, even dentists, and of course his or her own accountant's professional insurance. If an accountant tells you that expert witness liability insurance is expensive, you have to understand that they do not have experience with this form of liability. The fact is that Errors and Omission (E&O) insurance for a forensic odontologist should run about $2000.00 per $1,000,000 in coverage. If you compare that to the legal cost of defending a liability suit, you might want to consider transferring the risk. In fairness, I have found that many forensic scientists come to this as a sideline, civic duty, or even at the end of their career. My rule of thumb in those instances is as follows. If your assets are less than $100,000.00 and your projected revenue is less than $10,000.00, then you can consider assuming the risk, as long as you do not mind the expense of litigation or the possibility of losing some or all of your assets.

It is important to discuss with your accountant how to structure your forensic practice to protect your personal assets. Potential practice structures include: C corporation, Subchapter S, or even an LLC. Each is a viable option to control the asset risk. Both your attorney and accountant can provide advice in this area.

Next we need to discuss the insurance agent or broker. A broker represents the insured in all his or her dealings and is paid by the insured. An agent represents the insurance company in all of his or her dealings and is paid by a commission for the product sold. Some insurance people are both. When an agent/broker advises you that forensic odontology is already covered, I urge caution. The reason is pretty simple but deserves some explanation directly related to the average Dental Professional Liability Policy.

The basic premise of a professional liability policy that covers a dentist is that he or she is dealing with patients and providing dental care and advice on oral hygiene. When the policy is designed, it will in most cases be dealing with bodily injury and property damage arising out of delivering that high level of care to your patients in those circumstances. It normally does not contemplate that you would also render service to the local coroner in the event of corpse identification. You might see it as your civic duty but that does not automatically make your insurance policy respond. As a matter of fact, most policies have contemplated that exposure and chosen to exclude things like testimony, depositions, independent medical exams, and any examination performed for a fee outside the routine practice of dentistry. This is particularly true of those relationships where privilege does not apply and where no doctor–patient relationship applies. One way of looking at your work to establish if your dental policy will cover the result is to simply ask yourself who gets the report? If the report is between you and your patient, then you are well within the dental professional policy. If, however, your report is going to a third party or someone else is paying for your opinion, you should use caution going forward, as this act is likely outside the scope of your dental professional policy.

We now have identified the risk in broad terms. But before we suggest ways to minimize your risk, we need to discuss risk in general terms. Risk is the exposure to loss. Nothing more complicated than that. However, what you can do about it deserves some thought.

As an odontologist you can deal with risk in a number of ways:

- *Avoidance.* You can simply not do this type of work. You can also from time to time choose not to respond to a certain cases because you do not like the jurisdiction, the judge, or even the circumstances of the case. All of these are excellent risk management techniques that you should use to minimize your exposure. Since you have bought this book and got to this chapter, I am quite sure that avoidance is not the preferred method that you are going to choose when it comes to risk.

- *Risk Acceptance.* This means you know your facts, you know your assets, and your decision is to go forward using your professional skill to be the ultimate defense of your work. A bold choice, and if you do not have much to lose, might be the most economical one to make.
- *Risk Reduction* is a series of techniques that allow you to reduce the amount of risk that you assume when applying your trade. We will discuss several of these you should consider.
- *Separation* can be used if you can find a way to separate yourself from part or all of the risk. In most cases I do not see this as a practical solution for your operations.
- *Duplication* can be used if the client is able to use two or more experts to establish the facts. This incurs more cost and while it works well for risk transfer it may not be a practical alternative.
- *Diversification* is a risk management technique whereby you perform work product for both plaintiff and defendant attorneys in the course of your career. You should also publish or edit prior articles if technology or procedures have changed conclusions in earlier works.
- *Contractual* is a risk transfer technique, using contracts to limit liability. Contracts can establish rules under which you can be held harmless of fault, and they can most importantly transfer your liability to someone else and the expense of your defense to another party. Retention usually refers to taking on a portion of the risk that you find manageable. Deductibles are a common example of this technique.
- *Risk Transfer* is simply using an insurance policy where you take a known loss (the premium) and transfer the unknown loss (the potential loss up to the limit of the policy) to an insurance carrier or underwriter. This often is the most economic choice that you can make in dealing with risk.
- *Risk Control or Prevention* is making sure that your practice minimizes the exposure to loss. Certainly making sure you testify to only the things you know, insure you are trained properly and staying current is essential. Testifying for both sides is a good practice. And, know what you have published.

There is nothing scary about what you are trained to do. It is a civic duty that clearly is needed by society. The pay is scant, and your profession is comprised of gifted individuals—some of the best people in the world. I trust that my insights are helpful in some small way as you make your contribution to society.

13

Ethical Issues in Forensic Science & Forensic Odontology

J.C. Upshaw Downs[1], Robert E. Barsley[2,3,4]

[1]Medicolegal consultant, forensX, LLC Savannah, Georgia; [2]Professor, Department of Diagnostic Sciences, LSUHSC School of Dentistry, New Orleans, LA, United States; [3]Chief Forensic Odontologist, Jefferson Parish Coroner, New Orleans, LA, United States; [4]New Orleans Forensic Center, Orleans Parish Coroner, New Orleans, LA, United States

O U T L I N E

INTRODUCTION

The terms morals and ethics are often confused, conflated, and/or misinterpreted. While similar, they have significant fundamental differences. "Morality is understanding the distinction between right and wrong and living according to that understanding, and ethics is the philosophy of how that morality guides individual and group behavior. The two are closely related, with morality being the foundation of ethics" (https://www.reference.com/world-view/difference-between-morality-ethics-e5a83d5135b93204). Put more simply, "… morals are how you treat people you know. Ethics are how you treat people you don't know" (Welsh, 2015). Over the past several decades, the general sense is that society's values are slipping. "Americans' views about the declining state of moral affairs largely reflect a belief that there is a deteriorating collective moral character …. [which has] more to do with matters of basic civility and respect for each other" (http://www.gallup.com/poll/183467/majority-say-moral-values-getting-worse.aspx?utm_source=Social%20Issues&utm_medium=newsfeed&utm_campaign=tiles).

Recent escalating political polarization and negative campaigning evidence this societal decline. Issues are no longer debated but rather the countervailing view is vehemently disparaged as opinion rather than fact. From an early age, students are taught that there are either facts (provable) *or* opinions (beliefs) "… and that all value and moral claims fall into the latter camp. The punchline: there are no moral facts. And if there are no moral facts, then there are no moral truths" (http://opinionator.blogs.nytimes.com/2015/03/02/why-our-children-dont-think-there-are-moral-facts/?_r=0). Without accepted proof, there are no absolute "right" or "wrong" positions, only personal opinions, which might be shared by others. If a group shares a certain view, then it becomes "consensus" and therefore may be considered valid or justified by the group's members. Simultaneously, those in disagreement with the group are dismissed as

"wrong" or worse. If progress is to be made on the moral front and thus in ethics, society must come to recognize that effort is required:

> "Facts are things that are true. Opinions are things we believe. Some of our beliefs are true. Others are not. Some of our beliefs are backed by evidence. Others are not. Value claims are like any other claims: either true or false, evidenced or not. The hard work lies not in recognizing that at least some moral claims are true but in carefully thinking through our evidence for which of the many competing moral claims is correct. That's a hard thing to do. But we can't sidestep the responsibilities that come with being human just because it's hard" (http://opinionator.blogs.nytimes.com/2015/03/02/why-our-children-dont-think-there-are-moral-facts/?_r=0).

Evidence that American society continues as an exemplar of serving self-interest by rationalization and self-justification is readily apparent in collegiate sports, where codes of conduct are established by rules enforced by mutual agreement. Transgressors face sanctions when they violate the agreed rules. When teams (players, coaches, administrators, and boosters) break the rules and get caught, they bemoan their sanctions since "everyone does it" and they were "only trying to stay competitive." Not surprisingly, the line between acceptable and unacceptable behaviors becomes blurred, with expectations lowered. In days past, collegiate athletics were lauded for institutionalizing the importance of camaraderie and teamwork. A new "standard" has emerged wherein elite amateur athletes in team sports eschew their opportunity to compete with their comrades to avoid potential injury, which might affect their future professional career and associated income. This is exemplified by college athletes skipping their final year(s) of eligibility and turning professional. The attitude of team before self has given way to "me first" and recently taken a step further with players skipping the final bowl game of their collegiate career to "prepare for the professional draft." Such self-serving behavior would have been unthinkable only a few decades ago. "That's just how society is right now …. I don't think it should be a shock to anybody that this is happening. Things have changed since the older days" (http://www.espn.com/college-football/story/_/id/18324453/miami-hurricanes-coach-mark-richt-critical-players-skipping-college-bowl-games). Such seems more and more to be the nature of cultural moral and ethical norms — a continued lowering of expectations for what is viewed as acceptable.

In considering formally structured ethics, particularly in an arena as complex as "forensics" where lives may literally hang in the balance, the underlying principles must be clearly understood as they provide the critical underpinnings of the eventual system derived from the foundational elements. The naïve perception of ethics—that is a universal "right versus wrong"—presumes uniform building blocks, interchangeable across societies, cultures, professions, and individuals. Such a perspective disregards varied perspectives, philosophies, purposes, and structures. To attempt some uniformity in understanding, and hopefully in implementation, potentially misunderstood terms such as morals, ethics, and professionalism should be clearly defined. Likewise, the several components of the forensic "system" need to be identified and the roles of each individual understood. With an established basis and roles, the practitioners can proceed to conclusion. Since the outcome of the interworking of the various functional components produces a finished product, the ultimate result desired is in fact the most critical element—one should define an end to begin. The desired goal drives the process. In other words, *the ends lead to the means, therefore the ends are justified by the means.* As such, a deconstruction from desired outcome to foundation may allow development of a useful and memorable script by which to perform.

THE SCRIPT

What is desired for ethical conduct in a forensic system? "The *basis* for ethics must be morals, not the other way around. Unless there is a strong and consistent moral base — founded on something substantial — ethics will be subject to convenience, vested interests and fudge factors. The underpinning for decent human conduct must be a consistent and easily understood code of morality" (Lloyd). The world's largest independent forensics practitioners' organization, "The American Academy of Forensic Sciences [AAFS] … provides leadership to advance science and its application to the legal system …. to promote professionalism, integrity, competency, education, foster research, improve practice, and encourage collaboration in the forensic sciences. *"Forensic Science is the application of scientific principles and technological practices to the purposes of justice in the study and resolution of criminal, civil, and regulation issues"* (https://www.aafs.org/about-aafs/). In other words, professionalism, integrity, and competency in the application of *science and technology in service of the justice system are at the core of the practice in the varied forensic disciplines. The AAFS ethics code is proscriptive, specifically addressing only four elements:* misconduct, misrepresentation of qualifications, data/science misrepresentation, and unauthorized public commentary (https://www.aafs.org/wp-content/uploads/Bylaws.pdf). At the heart of these ideals is the *individual* practitioner and assuring that analyses are *truthfully* performed, interpreted, and articulated. The simplicity allows significant room for interpretation in regards to what constitutes a transgression. Implicit is that the term "scientist" applies to one and all in the same way.

THE PLAYERS

The "one size fits all" designation of *Forensics Practitioner* incorporates a vast disparity of professional training, qualification, and experience. For example, AAFS members include "… physicians, attorneys, dentists, toxicologists, anthropologists, document examiners, digital evidence experts, psychiatrists, engineers, physicists, chemists, criminalists, educators, and others" (https://www.aafs.org/about-aafs/). The issue is that this rightfully inclusive collaborative philosophy puts all players on an equal professional footing.

The apparent goal is to ensure uniformity at all levels. However, well intentioned, blind adherence to parity may inadvertently conceal the important inherent differences among the various constituent elements—not all those involved perform the same tasks using the same methods.

Science is "[t]he intellectual and practical activity encompassing the systematic study of the structure and behaviour of the physical and natural world through observation and experiment." A scientist is "[a] person who is studying or has expert knowledge of one or more of the natural or physical sciences" Synonyms include researcher ("[a] person who carries out academic or scientific research") and technologist ("[a] person employed to look after technical equipment or do practical work in a laboratory") (https://en.oxforddictionaries.com). Without further clarification, the term "scientist" may indicate a technician who operates (or even maintains) equipment or an academic researcher. This is in no way intended as a slight, but to point a critical and oft overlooked distinction.

For example, an individual employed as a "toxicologist" might be an analyst with a B.S. degree whose job consists primarily of performing assays to obtain a quantitative result. The same designation of "toxicologist" can also be applied to a research PhD who not only has performed analyses but also can scientifically interpret those results as they might apply in an individual case. Without further exploration, one might conclude that "all toxicologists are created equal." The situation might be compounded if an employer designates the technician as a "toxicologist" and the individual is subsequently designated as an "expert" in court, putting them on an equal footing with the academician in the eyes of the court (and jury). Without a skilled examination, the differences may not be made public. The same can be said of an "investigator" whose job is merely to answer phone calls and transcribe second- or third-hand information regarding a case as opposed to an actual crime scene analyst. Either might be designated a "scene investigator" by their employer, but the qualifications and skill sets are hardly the same. Building on the sandy soil of inflated job titles may serve to stroke egos while simultaneously saving budget dollars, but it does disservice to the end user and as a result the structure crumbles from within.

More troubling is the simplistic lumping of the legal, engineering, and medicodental[1] professions under the umbrella of "forensic scientists." As professions in the forensic arena actually *requiring* extensive postgraduate training, licensing, and oversight as mere preliminaries to enter the respective field as a practitioner, these practices are unique. These disciplines may use scientific results, scientific methodology, and scientific principles as part of the practice; however, medicodental practice is not bench science any more than it is law or engineering, and vice versa. This distinction is highlighted by the lack of a jurisprudence section in the National Academy of Sciences (NAS) and the tripartite nature of the NAS—with separate engineering and medical academies (the National Academy of Engineering and the National Academy of Medicine), the purpose of which is "…to provide independent, objective analysis and advice to the nation .… encourage education and research, … and increase public understanding in matters of science, engineering, and medicine" (http://nationalacademyofsciences.org/about-nas/mission/).

Recognition that different specialties have fundamental differences—in methodology and purpose—is critical in developing and

---

[1] Medicine, dentistry, and nursing are included under the umbrella term medicodental practitioners. Although intrinsically a part of the medicolegal death investigation system, Coroners are not covered herein, since they may or may not be medical practitioners. A complete discussion of the nature of that office is beyond the scope here.

understanding ethics. Ethical behavior differs between various disciplines and sometimes within the same profession. Apparently divergent behavior may not only be appropriate but actually required to comply with ethical canons specific to a given profession. For example, most would consider lying to be wrong—the AAFS specifically condemns "misrepresentation" twice in its code of ethics (https://www.aafs.org/about-aafs/). Yet in the proper context, failure to lie may be considered evidence of incompetence or malfeasance. Similarities and significant differences exist between the various codes and practices of law enforcement, attorney, judicial, scientist, and medicodental professions.

Law Enforcement

Forensic cases generally start with law enforcement personnel by evidence discovery, documentation, collection, and eventual analysis. A *law enforcement officer has a sworn "... fundamental duty ... to serve the community; to safeguard lives and property; to protect the innocent against deception, the weak against oppression or intimidation and the peaceful against violence or disorder; and to respect the constitutional rights of all to liberty, equality and justice"* (http://www.iacp.org/codeofethics). Despite this ethical foundation, there has been an increasingly vocal demand for severance of law enforcement from the various forensics disciplines, most notably in the NAS report on Forensic Sciences: "Scientific and medical assessment conducted in forensic investigations should be independent of law enforcement efforts either to prosecute criminal suspects or even to determine whether a criminal act has indeed been committed" (https://www.ncjrs.gov/pdffiles1/nij/grants/228091.pdf). Heinous transgressions have been well documented, with "...police officers who, out of laziness, overzealousness or poor training, violated laws that protect suspects from abuse of police power, found damning evidence and then lied to cover up their flawed investigation." These failings frustrate the courts, which dismiss otherwise

legitimate prosecutions when faced with "...'highly reliable' proof of ... serious crimes 'cry out for a trial on the merits,' [but] they find the police misconduct the greater sin" (https://www.thestar.com/news/canada/2012/04/26/police_who_lie_how_officers_thwart_justice_with_false_testimony.html). One essential tool used by detectives in interrogation is that of lying during interrogation. Some might see this as a foundational element of police work (and malpractice if not properly employed), while others protest it as unethical misconduct. For almost half a century, the US Supreme Court has held that police can legally deceive a suspect during questioning: "The fact that the police misrepresented ... is, while relevant, insufficient ... to make this otherwise voluntary confession inadmissible. These cases must be decided by viewing the 'totality of the circumstances ...'" (https://supreme.justia.com/cases/federal/us/394/731/case.html). This important tool has been portrayed as a law enforcement power to lie at will to suspects—ethical oath be damned. Such an argument carefully prunes the nature of that oath, conveniently deleting certain key components of: *"to protect the innocent against deception... and to respect the constitutional rights of all to ... justice"* (http://www.iacp.org/codeofethics).

Such police "... trickery and deceit can be permissible (depending on the totality of circumstances) provided that it does not shock the conscience of the court or community" (http://policelink.monster.com/training/articles/1911-lying-to-a-suspect-how-far-can-an-investigator-go). "... [T]he U.S. Supreme Court has repeatedly acknowledged, 'Criminal activity is such that stealth and strategy are necessary weapons in the arsenal of the police officer.' (Sorrells v. U.S.) '... [T]he mere fact of deceit [will not] defeat a prosecution, for there are circumstances when the use of deceit is the only practicable law enforcement technique available.' (U.S. v. Russell)" (http://www.policemag.com/channel/patrol/articles/2007/01/point-of-law.aspx).

The problem is when the limited privilege becomes inculcated into the individual who then inappropriately expands it beyond the appropriate context. The result is that the individuals become tainted and cases are lost. "Police dishonesty makes a mockery of the courts, undermines the public's trust in the justice system and must be condemned.... [J]udges are frequently finding that police officers lie under oath....with little consequence to the officer...." Regrettably, not all such instances of transgression are handled similarly. "... [W]hen confronted with police dishonesty, some judges are reluctant to call it by its name, instead choosing innocuous language when assessing flawed officer testimony." Concealment may occur in a misguided attempt to protect the public's confidence in the police, to protect an agency from liability, or other equally flawed reasons. The essential reliance of the justice system on law enforcement integrity demands that breeches of the sacred trust be exposed for what they are. For example, one judge describing a case detective's testimony as "'inconsistent and inaccurate,' 'exaggerated,' 'almost inconceivable,' an 'embellishment,' 'misleading,' 'nonsensical' and 'patently absurd'" (https://www.thestar.com/news/canada/2012/04/26/police_who_lie_how_officers_thwart_justice_with_false_testimony.html). Remedies to *exposed* transgressions typically involve internal agency sanctions, up to and including termination. In addition, in particularly egregious cases, the officer may face criminal and/or civil prosecution. The ethical implications of seeing inappropriate conduct and turning a blind eye may somehow satisfy certain tenets of political correctness, but does a disservice in an individual case and virtually assures repeated and even expanded (types of) conduct, with resultant miscarriages of justice.

Attorneys

Attorney (both judges and lawyers) ethics appear quite formalized, with a lengthy code of professional conduct promulgated by the American Bar Association (ABA) dating to 1983. Although almost all states use this model as a basis for their individual ethics codes, the rule by jurisdiction—both at the state and national level. Prior to the conduct code was 1969's Model Code of Professional Responsibility (http://www.americanbar.org/groups/professional_responsibility/resources/links_of_interest.html). In fact, the last published ABA ethics code per se was the Canons of Professional Ethics, which lasted with amendments through 1963 and was finally replaced in 1969. This structure was intended, first of all, to ensure that the public had "absolute confidence" in the Justice system. "The future of the [American] Republic, to a great extent, depends upon our maintenance of Justice pure and unsullied. It cannot be so maintained unless the conduct and the motives of the members of our [legal] profession are such as to merit the approval of all just men." Simultaneously, the authors conceded that "[n]o code or set of rules can be framed, which will particularize all the duties of the lawyer in the varying phases of litigation or in all the relations of professional life.... [E]numeration of particular duties should not be construed as a denial of the existence of others equally imperative, though not specifically mentioned" http://www.americanbar.org/groups/professional_responsibility/publications/model_rules_of_professional_conduct.html). As an indicator of the high esteem the ABA held for the law, attorneys were referred to as no less than *ministers* of the law.

The present ABA Code sets out to delineate proper and ethical conduct involving the courts, other attorneys, and clients. Some of the major topics covered include: attorney—client relationship (including counsel and advocacy), third-party interactions, professional associations, pro bono services, professional integrity, and advertising (http://www.americanbar.org/groups/professional_responsibility/publications/model_rules_of_professional_conduct/model_rules_of_professional_conduct_table_of_contents.html). Certain aspects of behavior may seem unusual and perhaps in direct opposition to "ethical" behavior, from a certain perspective. For example, a criminal prosecutor is sworn to uphold the law and seek justice; however, at the very same time, if the District Attorney does not believe that a suspect will be convicted by a jury, the case should be dismissed—even if the attorney honestly believes the suspect to be guilty. The Justice system is predicated on the concept of "innocent until proven guilty." Toward that end, a prosecutor must turn over all potentially exculpatory evidence (so-called "Brady materials") to the defense—including that which might tend to reflect poorly on police officers and forensics practitioners involved in the case. Furthermore, the onus is on the state to err on the side of caution—if it might be Brady material, it should be disclosed. For example, a cop who has lied about evidence in a prior case must be revealed to the defense, even if there is no indication that such activity was repeated in the present case. In opposition to this principle is that a defense attorney is ethically bound to not disclose a defendant's private admission of guilt as it would violate the client's trust. In other words, defense is obligated to conceal the truth from the court. This might lead to the question "how can an attorney represent a defendant the attorney knows is guilty?"

The answer lies in the ethical foundation of the justice system and recognizing the designated roles of the attorneys involved. The prosecution's duty is to prove its case beyond a reasonable doubt while the defense's obligation is to protect the client's rights (even if guilty). Looked at from one perspective, this might seem an apparent ethical contradiction, but on the other hand, it is nothing less than "the Golden Rule" in action—do unto others as you would have them do unto you. The defense is ethically required to zealously protect the client's rights. Toward that end, the old adage: "If the facts are against you, argue the law. If the law is against you, argue the facts. If the law and the facts are against you, pound the table and yell like hell" (http://www.goodreads.com/quotes/918291-if-the-facts-are-against-you-argue-the-law-if) has been modified in practice to include "argue the science, and if the science is against you, argue the scientist. Then pound the table." Such is hardly surprising for a profession that practices centuries-old

methodology of "authoritative works" and precedent rather than scientific or medicodental methodology. Since the justice system is adversarial, it is hardly surprising that experts (both prosecution and defense) are routinely challenged. Professional ethical mandates demand scrutiny and confrontation. That certain techniques may be employed such as misrepresentation of reports, insertion of key modifiers raising doubt, obfuscation, arguing from the general to the specific and vice versa, misapplication of data, etc. can be anticipated and are not inherently unethical. Again a zealous advocate should demand viable answers.

One should note that the ABA's Code is only a *model*, and although 49 states have followed this lead, *"In each state it is the state Supreme Court that has the ultimate authority to adopt legal ethics and professional discipline standards that govern lawyer ethics in that state"* (http://www.americanbar.org/publications/youraba/2016/december-2016/a-brief-history-of-the-development-of-legal-ethics-standards-in-.html). The distinction between a code of ethics and one of conduct is important. Ethics involve compliance guidelines affecting personal choices while conduct involves actions, either mandatory or prohibited. Professional conduct implies regulatory oversight for compliance and enforcement, either by a professional society or by law. "In certain areas, where the public interest is considered to be heavily engaged, legislation has been enacted, either replacing professional regulation by statutory legislation, or by a form of supervision of the professional body by a statutory body" (https://en.wikipedia.org/wiki/Professional_conduct). As a result, in most states, these conduct rules have the force of law in that violation/conviction can result in disbarment (often for life and with effects in other states). In addition, there may be the potential for criminal and/or civil litigation.

Judges

Since judges are attorneys, all the foregoing applies as well. Additionally and in keeping with the stature of the office, specific judicial canons deal with certain behavior within and without the courtroom—including election practices in those states where judges are elected as opposed to appointed. These rules cover real or apparent impropriety regarding the sanctity of the bench, competence, and impartiality both professionally and in personal and extrajudicial settings, including in the political arena (http://www.americanbar.org/groups/professional_responsibility/publications/model_code_of_judicial_conduct.html). The crucible of the courtroom is the testing point for the forensics disciplines, which is fascinating since the law is grounded in experience and prior opinions, rather than scientific and/or medicodental methodology. "What makes scientific results different … is their conclusive [e]ffect on a judge and jury. If the lab report says so, then so it is. As much as judges and lawyers aren't scientists, neither are most jurors. We all bow to the god of science, even when we know that it's not omnipotent" (http://reason.com/blog/2009/12/18/report-new-york-state-crime-la). Despite the complexity of the subject, the present structure is such that the validity of some forensic disciplines is being argued in court rather than the facts of the case. "The reality is that the courtroom is the place where lawyers should be examining the case-specific science and not the basic underpinning value of the overarching scientific subject. The courtroom is not the classroom, so the time for teaching is during the preparatory stages before the business of testimony and evidence gets underway" (http://theconversation.com/we-need-to-rethink-the-relationship-between-forensic-science-and-the-law-37141).

The judge holds the unique position of the gatekeeper for forensics in the courtroom—deciding if such evidence is admissible. "… [I]t is the trial judge who must decide whether there is sufficient robust underpinning in scientific evidence to let it be heard by the jury. They have to be sufficiently confident that the science establishes the fact in question and will withstand reasonable cross-examination that will assist the triers of fact" (http://theconversation.com/we-need-to-rethink-the-relationship-between-forensic-science-and-the-law-37141). Two major standards for evidence exist—Frye and Daubert. Both recognize general acceptance within the respective scientific discipline but Daubert goes further, including "the factors that may be considered in determining whether the methodology is valid are: (1) whether the theory or technique in question can be and has been tested; (2) whether it has been subjected to peer review and publication; (3) its known or potential error rate; [and] (4) the existence and maintenance of standards controlling its operation…." (https://www.law.cornell.edu/wex/daubert_standard). The problem is that judges, like other lawyers, are typically not scientists or medicodental professionals yet they must understand and present such evidence to a jury. Often lost in the predicate for the Daubert criteria is the single modifier, "may." As in the court may *or may not* use any or all of these elements. Regardless, the general public and justice system sense is that a lab report is accurate and must be convincingly challenged to be disproved. Not surprising then that forensics in the courtroom turns to a battle of the experts—another area with apparent ethical conundrums. The judge must be fair to both sides but must also ensure that the jury hears valid and useful information.

The judge determines which witnesses are to be designated experts and thus have special privilege in testimony, such as formulating opinions and responding to hypothetical scenarios. Typically, for testing and testimony the prosecution relies on a governmental analyst who is supposed to be by nature of the job, a neutral party. In addition, the court may provide a contracted analyst on behalf of the accused. The defense may hire any number (assuming adequate resources) of similar analysts. If nine such hired analysts examine the evidence and concur with the prosecution's expert, this would be scientifically replicating the initial results thus validating the original conclusions. If a 10th defense expert contradicted the others, this would logically be the defense's courtroom expert, despite the overwhelming contradictory conclusions. By designating both the prosecution and defense witnesses' "expert" status, the judge would put them on equal footing, even though scientifically the defense contentions would be (arguably) considerably outside the consensus. Yet, such is the structure of the court, where deference is given to the defense.

Scientists

Even a basic term such as forensic practitioner needs to be defined. "A forensic science service provider [FSP] is defined by the NCFS as any forensic science agency or forensic science practitioner providing forensic science services. A forensic medicine service provider [FMSP] is any forensic medicine agency or forensic medicine practitioner providing forensic medicine services" (https://www.justice.gov/ncfs/file/839711/download). As noted earlier, the term "forensic scientist" may refer to individuals with widely different backgrounds, skills, qualifications, and duties. The designation by the employer as a job description does not in and of itself carry the inherent blessing as an actual scientist. Obviously, the individual has an ethical duty to disclose the true nature of their position, including personal limitations.

Classically, at the heart of the science is the scientific method: observations lead to hypotheses which lead to testing which eventually lead to theories which are then tested and the cycle repeats. "No single, identifiable method applies to all branches of science; the only method, in fact, is whatever the scientist can use to find the solution to a problem. This includes induction, a form of logic that identifies similarities within a group of particulars, and deduction, a form of logic that identifies a particular by its resemblance to a set of

accepted facts" (http://www.ssr.org/sites/ssr.org/files/uploads/attachments/node/16/rothchild_scimethod.pdf). *Deduction* proceeds from premises to conclusions, the latter which can be proved with certainty if the premises are accepted as fact. *Induction* flows from observations with linkage resulting in a "best fit" hypothesis, but the conclusion may or may not be correct. In most forensic sciences, the methodology is inductive, with testing resulting in observations. The results of analyses results in hypotheses based on prior work and experience—the past allows prediction of future results. A third type of reasoning, *abduction*, is used by medicodental professionals (see below). In application, the forensic scientist must select the appropriate evidence to be tested and perform the proper testing. In attempting to be ethical, both must be done correctly and in good faith. Concerns may arise if the foundational premises are subsequently challenged, particularly if there are limited and/or degraded materials to be tested. Analyses ideally proceed from least destructive to most destructive, since once evidence is consumed, it is gone. Questions and challenges might arise if evidence is consumed in testing, leaving no sample left for subsequent reanalysis or additional testing. Another consideration is the potential future development of improved methodology and/or equipment that might allow more refined examinations. If nothing remains, speculation about potential results may be a basis for challenging the original conclusions: "if only evidence remained, new testing would contradict the original work."

Numerous FSP organizations have attempted for decades to develop ethical codes and guidelines. The AAFS code referenced earlier covers acts of professional misconduct, misrepresentation (about qualifications or tests), and unauthorized commentary. Since this is a professional organization code, enforcement is from within by means of an ethics committee and established procedure. Comparison of numerous such codes established "… four major categories addressed by every code of ethics …: 1) working within professional competence, 2) providing clear and objective testimony, 3) avoiding conflicts of interest, and 4) avoiding bias and influence, real or perceived" (https://www.justice.gov/ncfs/file/839711/download). At the heart of these codes is that the purity of the impartial objective analysis of evidence in the pursuit of justice is first and foremost. This is significantly different from the law, where the integrity of the justice system comes first, followed by the client.

Both the NAS (2009) and the National Commission on Forensic Sciences (NCFS) have lamented the lack of a standardized single national code of ethics and as a result, the NCFS promulgated a National Code of Professional Responsibility for Forensic Science and Forensic Medicine Service Providers to address these concerns. This set of guidelines is significantly more extensive. It incorporates medicodental practitioners and adds lab management and is a responsible party in compliance and reporting. Topics addressed include qualifications, honesty and truthfulness, continued competency, continued learning, validated methodology and technology, evidence handling, conflicts of interest, detailed contemporaneous record-keeping, independent review, supported conclusions, bias, expertise, terminology, distinguishing data from opinion, limitations, record alteration and withholding, quality management systems, nonconformity reporting, full communications with parties, notification of stakeholders, and protecting whistle-blowers (https://www.justice.gov/ncfs/file/839711/download). However noble and well intentioned, there are several issues one might consider in evaluating this proposal. While extensive, the net result of this example may be counterproductive, since almost all elements would be covered under "professional competence" and the precise enumeration of specific components might be construed as limiting the areas covered to *only* those *precise*

elements. As a federal construct, this would apply to only federal practitioners. Although a separate specialty within the AAFS, there is no provision at all for any of these regulations to apply to attorneys. Finally, there is no means for enforcement if the proposed code is actually implemented.

Medicodental Practitioners

As the subspecialty of medicine dealing with the oral cavity and craniofacial structures, dentistry remains intertwined with other medical specialties, dating to antiquity. Furthermore, the forensic odontologist often works directly with and at the behest of the forensic pathologist. Likewise, nursing stands alongside the others. All three areas share the common thread of patient care, both in practice and in ethics. "… [A] physician must recognize responsibility to patients first and foremost, as well as to society, to other health professionals, and to self" (https://www.ama-assn.org/sites/default/files/media-browser/principles-of-medical-ethics.pdf). Likewise, "[t]he American Dental Association calls upon dentists to follow high ethical standards which have the benefit of the patient as their primary goal" (http://www.ada.org/~/media/ADA/Publications/Files/ADA_Code_of_Ethics_2016.pdf?la=en). "The nurse's primary commitment is to the patient, whether an individual, family, group, community, or population" (http://www.nursingworld.org/MainMenuCategories/EthicsStandards/CodeofEthicsforNurses/Code-of-Ethics-2015-Part-1.pdf). In short, unlike the other forensic-associated disciplines discussed herein, the *patient* comes first.

The ethical focus on the individual patient, rather than "the system" is not the only significant difference between medicodental practitioners and other forensic fields. Unique among the "forensic sciences," medicine, dentistry, and nursing deal with the healing arts rather than bench science. The medicodental process typically employs a different type of reasoning in problem solving. That is *abductive* reasoning, where incomplete observations lead to best fit hypotheses based on available data. For example, a patient presents with certain symptoms which are common to several different illnesses and through testing, some possibilities become more or less likely, termed a "differential diagnosis." Observation and testing is continued until the most likely final diagnosis is achieved. This same logical construct is employed by jurors in that they do not hear all of the evidence about a case, but only the portions available to the court and then render a verdict based on those data. Significantly, unlike the bench sciences, practice of the medicodental arts requires history. Indeed, the diagnostic process begins with history—a description of what is wrong. In the medicodental world, practitioners utilize a systematic approach to the patient—SOAP (subjective, objective, assessment, and plan). In fact, to neglect to obtain or consider available medical history can be considered malpractice. Proper interpretation of data requires a scaffolding of context. A similar mindset is employed in many nonforensic exercises. For example, in digital security analysis, "[a]ssessing a cyber attack is more art than [bench] science. Intelligence analysis deals with information that is often intentionally deceptive.... 'The significance of information is always a joint function of the nature of the information and the context in which it is interpreted.' This feels uncomfortable to those who want to be sure beyond a reasonable doubt" (http://savannahnow.com/column-opinion/2016-12-13/elaine-ou-don-t-assume-russia-meddled-us-election). Interestingly, this view directly contradicts the fact that juries employ the same abductive (incomplete data) reasoning as do physicians.

The difference between medicodental and other forensic disciplines has become even more important as the concept of "evidence-based medicine" (EBM) has taken hold. Unfortunately, those unfamiliar with medicolegal practices may misunderstand or misrepresent the nature of EBM.

While hailed by some as a "new" method, it actually dates to the early 1900s and the Flexner Report. In short, EBM ... is the conscientious, explicit, judicious, and reasonable use of modern, best evidence in making decisions about the care of individual patients. EBM integrates clinical experience and patient values with the best available research information." Thus pure EBM is about selecting best patient treatment options. The closely allied concept of "Evidence *Informed* Medicine" (EIM) is where the same experience, research, and patient are applied to all aspects of medicodental practice. In both EBM and EIM, the significance of evidence is stratified (from most to least reliable) to hopefully eliminate biases: meta-analyses, prospective randomized controlled studies, experiments, case studies, and experience (https://www.ncbi.nlm.nih.gov/pmc/articles/PMC3789163/). In the clinical treatment of patients, these strata usually—but not always—make sense. "While scientists concur that randomized trials are ideal for evaluating the average effects of treatments, such precision isn"t necessary when the benefits are obvious or clear from other data" (http://www.nytimes.com/2016/11/25/opinion/sunday/flossing-and-the-art-of-scientific-investigation.html). In medicodental practice where the immediate issue is not patient care but in correct collection, examination, and interpretation of generally static, variably degraded, or otherwise less than optimal evidence in an isolated case. Furthermore, many such medicodental examinations are inherently destructive—for example, performing an autopsy or excising a bitemark. The milieu generally precludes doing randomized controlled studies, since replicating specific case circumstances is difficult, if not impossible. Other shortcomings may not be so obvious.

"It's bad enough that expertise is under attack these days from populist political movements that dismiss specialist opinion as just another establishment ruse. But lately expertise is being criticized from another direction, too — from would-be defenders of science." Recently, the national media reported that dental flossing was not supported by good evidence; "In response, the Department of Health and Human Services, the American Dental Association and the Academy of General Dentistry reaffirmed the importance of interdental cleaning" (http://www.nytimes.com/2016/11/25/opinion/sunday/flossing-and-the-art-of-scientific-investigation.html). The reason evidence was lacking is precisely the subject of the reports. Ethical standards precluded the "best" type of scientific medicodental evidence, meta-analyses of randomized controlled studies because it would be grossly inappropriate to perform a study knowingly putting the patient at risk when there is no legitimate question to be answered. The adversarial system challenges the practitioner. "Distrusting expertise makes it easy to confuse an absence of randomized evaluations with an absence of knowledge. And this leads to the false belief that knowledge of what works in social policy, education or fighting terrorism can come only from randomized evaluations. But by that logic..., we don't know if parachutes really work because we have no randomized controlled trials of them" (http://www.nytimes.com/2016/11/25/opinion/sunday/flossing-and-the-art-of-scientific-investigation.html).

This is not to suggest in any way that science and medicodental practice are static, rather as Charles Darwin "...confirmed that truths themselves admit of differing interpretations, that new research can divulge new facts that need to be incorporated into existing meanings. In fact, all scientific work involves the recurrent disruptions and revisions of previous work. The world is in a constant state of development and so is our knowledge of it" (Crysdale). All forensic disciplines, particularly the medicodental arts, should work to foster understanding of the operative principles. "This requires greater co-ordination and understanding between two ancient academic disciplines who have rarely been easy bedfellows: law and science. Lifetimes of misunderstanding have built up around their gladiatorial arena and they no longer seem to speak a common language. It is time for a paradigm shift in their relationship, geared towards addressing areas of common and competing ground, talking about science in plain English and agreeing where the current research gaps exist and how we are best placed to fill them" (http://theconversation.com/we-need-to-rethink-the-relationship-between-forensic-science-and-the-law-37141). Ethical medicodental practice also requires the provider to work with attorneys and their agents for the purpose of justice.

Medical, dental, and nursing professional organizations are self-governing; however, all require formal jurisdiction licensure. Thus not only are practitioners subject to professional organization sanctions for ethical transgressions but they also have individual state board oversight, including ethics hearing with potential sanctions including censure and even loss of licensure. Despite these already significant controls, the proposed NCFS Code of Professional Responsibility is also intended to apply to the medicodental specialties. Since many practitioners, especially dentists and nurses, only perform forensic work on a part-time basis, imposing additional redundant or cumbersome requirements may be counterproductive, particularly if the intrusion is received with skepticism by practitioners. Common sense and life experience suggests that, particularly in medicodental areas, the more experienced the practitioner, the more likely a good outcome. Along that line of thought, the opinions generated by a rules committee of 30 members having one medicodental arts member with 10 years of postgraduate training (plus whatever years of actual practice experience) who is countered by a minimum of more than a century (up to 290 or more) years of nonmedicodental training (not to mention millennia of absent practice experience) might be seen as not representative of the state of the discipline. Focus should be on compliance with ethical requirements rather than trying to force an artificial homogeneity.

Engineers

Engineering is a discrete specialty, recognized by the NAS with a separate National Academy of Engineering. Engineering can be defined as "the application of science and mathematics by which the properties of matter and the sources of energy in nature are made useful to people" (https://www.nspe.org/resources/press-room/resources/frequently-asked-questions-about-engineering). As with attorneys and medicodental specialties, specialized education is required. Practitioners are subject to state licensure. In addition, professional organizations have established ethics codes covering fundamental canons, practice rules, and professional obligations. At the core is the recognition that "...the services provided by engineers require honesty, impartiality, fairness, and equity, and must be dedicated to the protection of the public health, safety, and welfare" (https://www.nspe.org/sites/default/files/resources/pdfs/Ethics/CodeofEthics/Code-2007-July.pdf). Similar to attorneys, the specialty is more geared to a general target (public welfare) than to the individual.

Experts

Special mention should be made of the expert witness. All the various forensics players might be called on in one capacity or another to serve as a court-designated expert witness. Obviously, most commonly this would involve the scientist, medicodental practitioner, or engineer. In addition to the practice and ethical duties described above, expert witnesses are subject primarily to voluntary codes of ethics. In general, these are those held by the AAFS: avoidance of unprofessional conduct, avoidance of misrepresentation of data or science, and avoidance of misrepresentation about credentials/expertise.

Unprofessional conduct can be seen as anything that might tend to put the discipline or the professional organization in a bad light. Purposefully obfuscating the truth by "spinning"

the techniques, limitations, results, or significance of the testing is simply put, lying. This may take the form of commission or omission—either can be equally misleading, depending on the context. Likewise, misstating one's training or abilities is prohibited. Personal misrepresentations can be uncovered through careful scrutiny of the witness' curriculum vitae. Scientific, engineering, or medical exaggerations and errors can be revealed through consultation with a qualified consultant; however, caution should be exercised in distinguishing professional differences of opinion or misunderstandings from actual misrepresentations.

Where there is a history of questionable (or worse) behaviors on the stand, the prosecutor has the ethical duty to disclose this information to the defense and the defense has the obligation to explore this information to best serve the client's interests. In the legal context, misrepresentations may rise to the level of perjury. In any instance with a bona fide transgression, the involved attorneys have an obligation to report actual discrepant behavior—to the witness' agency, professional organization, and/or state oversight board.

TOWARD CODES AND COMPLIANCE

Although generally applicable to both forensic services providers and to forensic medicine providers, this overview of ethical codes and compliance is targeted at the latter. Formal Anglo-American medical ethics dates to the beginning of the 19th century with Percival's *Medical Ethics* (Percival, 1803). Utilizing case-study approach and observation rather than theory, this ultimately became the basis for the American Medical Association's ethics code. Ethical dilemmas can be complex and challenging. Simplification of highly detailed information can enhance recall and improve compliance. Enhanced understanding may help in ameliorating conflicts. Toward this end, ethical violation can be classified as minor or major. The focus herein is the latter; minor lapses will not be covered. Antiquity and religious tradition have provided the model of the seven deadly sins. These classic major transgressions can be simplified by category: desire (envy and lust), possession (greed and sloth), and consumption (gluttony and anger). Overarching all is pride—the root of all sin. "For the love of money is a root of all kinds of evil. Some people, eager for money, have wandered from the faith and pierced themselves with many griefs. In contrast to the sins are the seven cardinal virtues (chastity, kindness, charity, diligence, abstinence, patience, and humility). Following a brief background, each category and countering ethic is briefly discussed with examples.[2] In reality, distinctions are seldom pure and vices tend to commingle. Recognition of the myriad forms of potential ethical danger and active defense against ensnarement provide the best opportunity to maintain professionalism throughout a challenging career, and in so doing, maintain excellence in patient[3] care.

The Need

The forensic profession can provide many challenges for the practitioner, particularly with regard to maintaining a high ethical standard. Forensic practice requires the medicodental professions to apply their highly specialized expertise to questions of legal (civil and criminal) import. Such knowledge, immersed in the crucible of the adversarial justice system, carries the danger of being consumed in the flames of rhetoric and confrontation. Applied ethics in forensic pathology is well beyond a brief review; however, some general considerations may facilitate discussion. Ethical transgressions may be considered "minor" or "major" breaches. In ancient times, some came to view these poles as represented by the "venial" or relatively inconsequential and the "capital" or serious offenses. The latter came to be known as the seven deadly sins. A brief overview follows with a series of discourses on each of these classic transgressions with case examples followed by a brief consideration of the countervailing virtue. The intent herein is to provide a means of recognition of human failings and in so doing provide a means for enhanced professionalism within the medicodental discipline.

> The problem is that it has become politically awkward to draw attention to absolutes of bad and good. In place of manners, we now have doctrines of political correctness, against which one offends at one's peril: by means of a considerable circular logic, such offences mark you as reactionary and therefore a bad person. Therefore if you say people are bad, you are bad. (Truss)

The reality that personal moral failings would prima facie jeopardize an expert's credibility can result in far bigger problems. In a justice system reliant in large part on expertise, foibles become magnified. As professionals who routinely appear in court and are publically challenged, one's actions—both public and private—are under

[2] Many statements herein are collected from newspaper articles and summary court documents. These are not inclusive of all the factual information and only represent the content contained therein. As such, these examples may not include complete and accurate final reportage. These are included with the intent of serving as exemplars and the veracity is not assured—these should not be construed as being authoritative in any way. The reader is referred to original source materials for explanation and/or exposition.

[3] Forensic medicodental professionals may deal with both the living and dead. Many Attorney-Physicians have argued eloquently and passionately that a decedent is not technically a "patient" because there can be no direct doctor–patient relationship, The largest physician member organization has acknowledged that the dead are so in practice, with the gross anatomy cadaver, the medical student's first patient (AMA).

increased scrutiny. Unfortunately, lessons are learned at inopportune times: "History and experience tell us that moral progress comes not in comfortable and complacent times, but out of trial and confusion" (Ford). Juries, demanding perfection, evaluate not only "… the evidence itself - the inconsistent testimony, the botched reports, … [and mishandled evidence]" (O'Donnell and John, 2001) but also the credibility of the witnesses providing such data. Personal failings serve as the cornerstone of an ad hominem attack. "…[I]n the hands of an expert defense lawyer, jurors say, hairline cracks in the evidence can become ruinous fissures…" (O'Donnell and John, 2001). Regardless of whether or not the argument is valid, a seed of doubt may be planted, potentially jeopardizing an individual case, or if repeated or particularly heinous, multiple prior cases. For over 200 years, organized medicine has sought to codify appropriate behaviors. It is imperative for professionals, who alone understand the myriad intricacies of their chosen discipline, to advocate for standards and self-regulation—particularly ethical guidelines—to preserve the veracity and dignity of the discipline. Such concerns should also be modulated by the recognition of human nature and the tendency to fall short of expectations. As such, the ultimate goal should be reasonable and allow for instances where the desired end may not be achieved. True camaraderie demands expecting the best as well as extending the hand of assistance whenever needed—a penny of prevention is worth a pound of cure.

"Since its appearance in 1803, Percival's *Medical Ethics* has been the dominant influence in Anglo-American medical ethics and the paradigmatic source for the first, and subsequent, Code of the American Medical Association" (Pelligrino, 1986). To be practicable, an ethics code must not only be in effect and enforced but also accessible and understood. As recognition is the first step to remediation, identifying reasonably anticipated snares should serve to facilitate the quest to effectively apply a moral standard. Those lessons most easily learned are those with which one has a memorable and effective reference, as with the medicodental case study model. In ethics, "Percival taught by giving examples rather than by abstract concept…. His philosophical approach accords well with his medical philosophy in which Percival insists on observations of cases, rather than theorizing about disease…. The 'cases' Percival used to illustrate his moral lessons reveal a wide range of reading in classical authors, the Bible, the history of Europe and his own country, and in the literature of his own times. All of his works are interspersed with quotations apposite to his moral argument" (Pelligrino, 1986). In keeping with this tradition, and toward the end of providing a simple workable code, a very basic but powerful ethical model—the seven deadly sins—is suggested from the wisdom of antiquity. There follows a brief case study illustrating each transgression and its converse.

The Seven Deadly Sins

In the Old Testament's book of Proverbs, Solomon cites seven detestable qualities: "… haughty eyes, a lying tongue, hands that shed innocent blood, a heart that devises wicked schemes, feet that are quick to rush into evil, a false witness who pours out lies and a person who stirs up conflict in the community" (Proverbs 6). Moral transgressions later became codified by the Roman Catholic Church as venial (inconsequential or lesser) and mortal (serious or capital). In The Divine Comedy, Dante described these as *luxuries* (extravagance or lust), *invidia* (envy), *avaritia* (greed), *acedia* (sloth), *gula* (gluttony), *ira* (wrath or anger), and *superbia* (pride) (Alighieri, 2012). Classically, each of these so-called seven deadly sins has a countering cardinal virtue: lust is countered by chastity, envy by kindness, greed by charity, sloth by diligence, gluttony by abstinence, anger by patience, and pride by humility (DeadlySins.com). As evident, indulgences are far from limited to the baser elements. As with so many things, transgressions rarely occur in isolation. An issue in one area might suggest the need to explore elsewhere.

The sins seem to break these down into three somewhat overlapping categories, based on the individual's underlying motivation: desire, accumulation, and consumption. *Wanting* that which one does not possess is the basis of envy and lust. *Possessing* yet not being satisfied are reflected in greed and sloth, where despite the gift of wealth or leisure, a "more is better" philosophy prevails. *Consumption* (physical or emotional) without regard to the eventual inevitable outcome is the hallmark of both gluttony and anger. Overarching all is pride, "the mother of all sins… the thin line between righteousness and self-righteousness" (Facaros and Pauls, 1998).

Lust Versus Chastity (Purity/Integrity) (Merriam-Webster)

Lust, or the pervasive desire for personal gratification, is usually considered predominately or exclusively in the sexual context. While this context can be encountered in medicolegal death investigation (MDI), such is the exception rather than the norm. Breaching this taboo is so shocking that failure to identify necrophilia may have profound repercussions. Case in point: a teenage victim sustained a subtotal decapitation during the course of being killed. Unknown at the time, her body was violated by an attendant while in the morgue cooler awaiting autopsy examination. The presence of ejaculate (presumably from the killer) served as an aggravating circumstance in securing the capital murder conviction—despite admitting brutally killing the victim (Huff, 2008), the convict maintained for over a quarter century that he was not the source. The truth was accidentally uncovered only after the morgue attendant underwent a routine DNA database entry following committing a probation violation. Subsequent investigation revealed at least two other bodies had been sexually violated by this individual. The attendant had been a long-term employee (6 years before the first event and

10 years following) without publically identified issue (Huff, 2008; Perry, 2009). Not surprisingly, such shocking events are often accompanied by aggrieved parties demanding justice in the civil courts (Gerhardstein et al., 2010), which has obvious ramifications for all involved.

More commonly encountered in professional fora are less licentious but no less lascivious behaviors; the world is replete with opportunities for inappropriate self-pleasuring. Medicodental practitioners, having direct access to pharmacopeia, may fall victim to substance abuse or other forms of moral turpitude. Such shortcomings are so widespread as to even be lampooned in popular culture (viz., the movie *Little Shop of Horrors*). Prescription medication transgressions often overlap with sexual, due to the intertwined nature of patient care issues and drug access with the potential for quid pro quo relationships not uncommon; however, the temptation can and does occur when circumstances provide a seemingly irresistible opportunity (Lattman, 2011). Situations can go so far as to sedate a patient, rendering them incapacitated, and then taking sexual liberties with an unconscious victim. State medicodental licensing boards routinely deal with a broad range of such drug-related issues, with various outcomes for those found in violation.

Case study: A medicolegal case involved the suspected homicide of a young child. The case had numerous evidentiary problems, including other experts challenging the state's conclusions. Despite this, the state took the case to trial as a homicide. To complicate matters, the original medical examiner had had his medical license suspended and "At his hearing, … [the physician] admitted to ordering large quantities of controlled drugs for 13 years and that he distributed them to people who were not his patients…. He also admitted he had self-medicated with hydrocodone, Valium and phentermine…" (Higgins, 2010). Issues continued once his license was reinstated "…after he agree[d] to 5 years' probation. But the same month, he was indicted … on three counts of unlawful distribution of a controlled substance, one count of failure to keep required records of controlled substances and two counts of obtaining a controlled substance by fraud" (Higgins, 2010). The prosecution was "…hoping to at least keep him presentable for a trial, knowing his credibility was going to be questioned" (Higgins, 2010) and admitted to being "…tired of baby-sitting" (Higgins, 2010) the pathologist. "… [The doctor's] own attorney had advised him to invoke his Fifth Amendment right to not answer questions, … [and the defense] attorney would attack the autopsy results" (Higgins, 2010). In light of the reality that the case was jeopardized, "[the prosecution] … could have hoped jurors didn't notice the state had no strong medical evidence… [but the] biggest problem in the … case was that the medical evidence is a matter of opinion…" (Higgins, 2010). Eventually, the father pled guilty. One could anticipate (correctly) that this was not an isolated anomaly for this troubled practitioner.

The converse of lust is *chastity*, commonly considered in only the sexual context but more properly defined as the broader concept of self-restraint or denial, derives from the Latin *castus* meaning morally pure or guiltless. The professional would be wise to consider potential outcomes of fulfillment of various desires and snares along the various pathways. As with so much in ethics, retrospection is helpful, "for all have sinned and fall short…" (Romans 3:23). Case in point—several years later, one of the experts in the example cited above was found in possession of illegal drugs and was subsequently sanctioned with the record expunged (Echegarary, 2010). Extremes of aberrant behavior such as substance abuse are obvious but likely not the starting point. Rather, these represent the terminus of a misguided path. The wisdom of the adage "moderation in all things" becomes obvious but is sometimes difficult in light of the tu quoque argument seeking to justify one's actions simply because others have done so. Consensus does not ensure propriety or correctness, only company. Ethical behavior

sometimes requires the individual to walk the road less traveled—that of propriety.

Envy Versus Kindness (Benevolence/Mercy) (Merriam-Webster)

Envy, or the desire to possess that which one sees in another, is often accompanied by a desire to see that very subject stripped of the prized commodity. "Envy is not the wish for the object or advantage that provoked the envy. Rather, envy is the much darker wish that the superior would lose the object or advantage. Envy is the perverse pleasure, the malicious joy (*Schadenfreude*) that is felt when the superior fails or suffers" (Clanton, 2006). In this sense, envy is far darker than mere jealousy. Money, power, authority, celebrity, etc. are ripe for the abuses of coveting. Embittered subordinates may come to feel entitled or that they might do a better job than their bosses. The narcissist's primary weapon invoked is gossip (Clanton, 2006). Collusion with others seeks to ostracize the target—the "haves" versus the "have nots." Problematic behaviors attempt to paint the objective in an unfavorable light, such as by disproportionate attention to trivial matters—any issues that the envious relator feels might gain traction. If emboldened, continued behaviors potentially damaging casework may include prevarication, misdirection, evasiveness, dissimulation, dawdling, and the like. Perversely, often the disgruntled party merely projects personal shortcomings onto others. Vociferous and excessive attacks bespeak ulterior motives: "The lady doth protest too much, methinks" (Shakespeare, 1999). Such an envious employee is little more than a bully and directly creates a hostile work environment—a particular danger for governmental agencies in allowing such a situation to develop (Isle of Man Government Officers Association; Isle of Man Government Officers Association, 2009). Failing to act when needed, the sin of omission, has consequences. When issues are not recognized and eradicated, organizational structure crumbles from within.

Distinguishing envy from concern is essential. Neglect in the face of overt commission is hardly benign—it only compounds troubles. No one is immune to occasional ethical lapses, typically these would fall into the venial category and may not even be perceptible. On the contrary, a track record of prior major issues should give pause: "A disgruntled medical examiner [who had] stored organs like brains and hearts in Tupperware containers and soda cups at a storage facility … [had been] fired for failing to file autopsy reports" (Gruesome discovery, 2012). "… [He] had already lost his job as a medical examiner and medical license in another state before coming to [the jurisdiction, when a] …court revoked his license for incorrectly stating on autopsy reports that sections of several brains he cut out were to be used for medical conferences and teaching purposes" (Gruesome discovery, 2012). Such history is telling and points to the need for adequate screening of potential hires and reevaluation of existing ones with regular objective performance analyses. In such processes, interjecting personal opinions or unjustly slighting an ambitious employee can do as much—if not more—harm than negative criticism. Office/departmental policies regarding such exercise should be carefully followed and documented with other agendas set aside. Arbitrary and/or inaccurate ratings bestowed on dedicated staff can be at least as damaging as falsely rewarding "difficult" employees, despite an implicit hope in so doing of perhaps "domesticating" the former and placating the latter. The reality is that overall morale can be irreparably damaged by this duality of applied envy such that behavior moderates to that of the stereotypical "bureaucratic employee" who is "just putting in time." Furthermore, unfairly creating a hostile work environment leaves the employer treading on the very thin ice of employment law.

Perversely but not surprisingly, one area where tensions can run high is in the process of office improvement. While a noble goal, the reality is that many laboratory systems lack the resources to achieve accreditation. Achieving such external recognition is a tangible index of progress. Change can be as hard to accept as it is to achieve. Initial responses to calls for betterment may be taken as personal attacks for real or perceived shortcomings. Seeking tangible success might be dismissed as envy of other jurisdictions when in truth the desire is to follow the easy path that has always worked well enough to "get by" in the past. "…[A]ny time you make major reforms, you're going to ruffle some feathers…. [Reformers] cannot be distracted by those people who are more interested in maintaining the status quo than in promoting change" (Harris and Hamil, 1999). The ideal for improvement is to set an attainable target and strive aggressively to achieve beyond the desired outcome in the belief that "The greater danger for most of us lies not in setting our aim too high and falling short; but in setting our aim too low, and achieving our mark" (Michelangelo).

For example, a chronically problematic office hires a new idealistic reformer who "… attacked what he called a 'frustrating and mystifying' culture of dysfunction…. [Stating he was] '…a no-nonsense guy, …sick and tired of the nonsense'" (Harris and Hamil, 1999) "… [So the new Chief] reformed with a vengeance. He … reduced the backlog … set up stricter autopsy criteria for suspicious deaths … [tried] to fire two of the office's seven forensic pathologists … dismissed or placed on leave the morgue's two office administrators and the senior autopsy technician. But his efforts at overhauling … fostered a climate of distrust and apprehension. [Leaving] remaining staff … on the verge of open revolt …" (Harris and Hamil, 1999). Such polarization is unhealthy and destructive for the office and the community. Tensions escalate and press accounts memorialize the discord. The net result is that cases reputations are potentially jeopardized.

The counterpoint to envy is *kindness*. The difficulty with unilaterally invoking benevolence is that suspicions run equally high with tensions and "the other side" may become convinced that an agenda is in place and that accepting the effort is tantamount to endorsing "the opponent's" view. The biblical admonition to turn the other cheek only works when passive resistance is a viable option. In countering "the green-eyed monster" maintaining neutral perspective is vital. Although a peaceable mutually accepted resolution is not always possible, the effective mediator understands that conveying an honest analysis of each side's strengths and weaknesses to the individual parties in a case engenders trust and confidence, maximizing the potential for success (Nations, 2012). Perspective demands taking a balanced view and consideration that each side has, or at least believes they have, a valid point. Recognizing that middle ground and making concessions—in advance of confrontation—connote strength of position. Unfortunately, recognizing and addressing valid counterpoints in advance of a debate shifts the center toward the opposite pole and, having already internally conceded ground, requires an even more tenacious argument to prevent unacceptable losses.

Greed Versus Charity (Philanthropy) (Merriam-Webster)

Greed is the excessive desire for more than is needed. Greed in medicodental practice compromises quality, access, and altruistic service (Crawshaw, 1993). Money, power, and fame are easily identified temptations. Other enticements, while readily apparent, may not commonly be recalled so quickly. In some instances, avarice (both monetary and ego) may become so enmeshed that an objective observer cannot distinguish a single underlying motive. "…[T]he most corrosive effect of greed and the [accompanying] tacit approval of greed is to the profession's philosophy of service" (Crawshaw, 1993).

The old belief was that medicodental professionals "…have, in effect, sworn an oath to place the interests of the patient ahead of their own interests — including their financial interests" (Brody, 2010). As discussed earlier, physician, dentist, and nursing ethical canons place the patient first. Another part of heeding the call to the medicodental profession is acceptance of certain fiscal realities, including student loans, practice acquisition costs, office operational expenses, malpractice coverage, reimbursement efforts, etc. In short, it is not—or at least it should not be—about the money. Despite this, the public perception is otherwise "…there is no end of opinion, verging on explicit protest, from patients, their families, insurance operators, legislators, and the general public that doctors are a greedy lot" (Crawshaw, 1993). "An egregious example is in the case of a doctor in the US whose yearly income exceeds $4m[illion]" (Crawshaw, 1993). "Without question doctors should earn incomes which genuinely reflect the training, time, effort, and trust that goes with their care of the sick. It is malignantly counterproductive for soaring medical reimbursement to diminish the stature of the vast majority of doctors" (Crawshaw, 1993). Four categories of physicians have been suggested: altruists, professionals, entrepreneurs, and money-grubbers; unfortunately, the avaricious 3—5% minority who taint the rest by association (Crawshaw, 1993). The impact of such biases carries over into management concerns for effective operations: "Society has effectively barred [the] physician's requests of more or 'adequate funding' with the knee jerk but politically effective canard of the doctor's greed" (Swerdloff, 2000). The result is that the chronically underfunded medicodental disciplines continue to lack adequate resources.

Ego greed, a desire for exaggerated reputation, may go hand in hand with monetary greed as a means to an end. "Under state and federal rules of evidence, judges decide whether prospective expert witnesses can testify, but they sometimes rely heavily on the titles and letters around someone's name" (Bartos, 2012). The reality is that credentials *do* matter in court and are considered not only by the judge in designating someone an "expert" but also to the jury, who determine the witness' veracity. The founder of one credentialing entity apparently disagrees, stating that "...credentials are not designed to qualify experts in court ... only a judge can make that determination..." (Bartos, 2012). "Credentials are often appealing shortcuts... Jurors have no way of knowing that this certifying body, whether it''s this one or any other one, exacts scientific standards or is just a diploma mill" (Bartos, 2012). "Experts in the field worry that inconsistent standards and training for forensic examiners can lead to miscarriages of justice — to the guilty walking free and the innocent being locked up or worse" (Bartos, 2012). Consider the example of a contracted autopsy assistant who "... provides medical examiner services for county coroners ... and private autopsies for families across the country. He says he has observed or helped with more than 1000 autopsies, and he's trained in gunshot wounds, strangulation and drug deaths. But some coroners and medical examiners ... [believe he] has inflated his qualifications and performed autopsies without a medical license. Others allege that doctors whose signatures were on some autopsy reports were not present at the autopsies, did not review the work or never actually signed the documents.... [His] online work profile is filled with inaccurate information" (Weich, 2013). He reportedly performed a homicide autopsy but "... argues that the work he did fell short of an autopsy" describing instead performing an evisceration while specifically defining the autopsy as "... the diagnosis of the cause and manner of death..." (Weich, 2013). Few would argue that both procedures are a part of the process of an autopsy, but professional guidelines demand that the physician be an active participant in the process. Lacking a medical degree, he "... uses the professional initials 'FPA,' which he says stands for Forensic Pathologist Assistant, a

designation he invented" (Weich, 2013). Important danger signs suggesting possible ego issues are the creation of nonexistent credentials and unique self-definition of terms.

Similarly, the forensic community as a whole is familiar with organizations having unflattering reputations. According to one former executive, his "'... operated like a certification mill...' [The] exams are designed so that anyone can pass... [with] the failure rate at less than 1 percent" (Bartos, 2012). Testing could hardly be described as rigorous, where "... study packets helped ... fill in the blanks, making it basically an open-book exam. The rest of the questions relied largely on common sense (i.e., When providing testimony, which of the following should you NOT do? Answer: Cross your arms and joke with the jury)" (Bartos, 2012). For example, one pathologist states he is "... board certified in anatomic pathology, clinical pathology, forensic pathology and forensic medicine." ... [with] credentials in anatomic and clinical pathology from the American Board of Pathology [ABP] ... but not in forensic pathology..." for which he cites other entities, including the one described above (Bartos, 2012). "When asked about this in court or in sworn depositions over the years, ... [he] has said that he walked out on the [ABP] test because he found the questions insulting to his intelligence. He claimed, for example, that one question asked about colors associated with death.... [T]he American Board of Pathology produced the test ... [he] took. There were no such questions" (Balko, 2012).

The remedy to greed is *charity*. Daily professional life leaves abundant opportunity for philanthropy. Giving freely of time and talent is a good step. Professional limitations may hinder the ability to assist those in need; however, creativity is a powerful ally. *Pro bono* efforts and consults are tangible means to counter a perceived "... strategy ... to attack the profession's integrity and label all attempts at asking for adequate funding as guided by greed and self interest" (Crawshaw, 1993). Classically, human nature has been labeled egoistic; however, recent research has indicated that the more rapid (intuitive) decisions tend toward cooperation and charity, while delayed (reasoning) choices favor selfishness (Ward). None can divine another's innate motivation, so the only tangible evidence is examining the track record: "actions speak louder than words." By cultivating a pattern of giving, philanthropy becomes second nature.

Sloth Versus Diligence (Merriam-Webster)

Sloth can be defined as having it all and doing nothing with it. Implicit in apathy is that emotion exists, but is ignored. The present state of disarray in the nation's medicolegal system serves as a testament to the mantra of "getting by" in that ultimately the work gets done. Public outcry and political repercussions tend to follow identified major public scandals rather than following a careful, structured path to improvement. Self-justification and "the better way" seldom know a single omniscient source. Medicodental practitioners have tried, individually and collectively, for decades to provide better services and have gone to great length to educate those in positions of influence about the discrepancies between needs and desires to have the ideal MDI system across the country. Despite powerful and persuasive arguments, little has changed. Compounding this direct lack of authority is a perhaps seldom acknowledged lack of impetus. Particularly with budget crises and escalating governmental responsibility, radical alterations to the status quo remain a difficult sell. Furthermore, if a jurisdiction were to modify the local MDI procedure, authorities would have to publically embrace that things had been imperfect. The latter is seldom a popular admission in efforts affecting such a broad segment of society, especially the justice system. The difficulty is compounded by the reality that in most of the country, where the coroner's office exists, the office is political. Public figures seldom relish

condemnation and disparagement, particularly from outsiders.

"In reality, as opposed to TV, crime scene investigators and crime labs are overworked and under-funded. This has led to backlogs of untested evidence, created problems with preserving evidence once it's collected, and [worse] ..." (Clark, 2012). Dysfunction is not synonymous with nonfunction. Insufficient resources may tempt but cannot compel. Right actions remain just that, regardless of outside distractions. One knows the full risks and stakes of any specific case only with the benefit of hindsight. Likewise, the full impact of shortcomings is complete only retrospectively. The danger done by inaction—by preferring not to offend rather than to act with integrity—harm not only in the short term but also have lasting impact, as the tentacles of lethargy extend far and ensnare relentlessly. Apathy proceeds from becoming pervasive to entrenched, followed by expected and enshrined. Thus the false synonym of political correctness with equity leads to those who fail to act for fear of offending or being challenged. Principle requires daring to act when action is required. Facts remain immutable, while interpretations may vary. Chronic systemic shortcomings then become a convenient excuse to explain away failures.

If there were indeed a compelling case to be made for system improvement and if a factual debate about the needs for such improvement were the only obstacles, then logically change should flow in short order. Reality is more complex. The system is anchored on the pillars of funding, power, and politics. Change—even or perhaps most often beneficial advances—are feared as an affront to the status quo. The proverb "Better the devil you know than the devil you don't know" (Taverner, 1539) has an operative codicil—either way, one faces evil incarnate. Accepting a bad situation because something worse might happen is the core of defeatism. Comfort replaces the desire to attain to a greater end with the result that little changes except the calendars. Those who dare not try are assured of failure—in fact, they already have.

Consider the example of an individual with direct knowledge of physical child abuse who fails to report or do anything to end an ongoing situation. "[He] knew the two babies were being abused and yet he did nothing…. [He] pleaded guilty to injury to a child by omission" (Muñoz, 2009). Although having done nothing directly to the victims, the subject, especially if a medico-dental professional with a mandated duty to report, is a voluntary coconspirator. According to the legal tenet, the hand of one is the hand of all. "[A] person who joins with another to accomplish an illegal purpose is criminally responsible for everything done by the other person which occurs as a natural consequence of the acts done in carrying out the common plan or purpose" (Judicial Department, 2007). Although criminal charges may not necessarily follow a professional's failure to report, certainly such inaction should be reported to the oversight and professional authorities for appropriate follow-up. A medicodental practitioner with knowledge of such a lapse has an ethical duty to inform. Maintaining the status quo can be easy, since those who "rock the boat" are often dismissed as troublemakers. Facile should never be mistaken for "right."

Diligence contrasts with sloth. No one strives for mediocrity—except in settings where routine and placation trump higher virtues. In human interactions, one has little to gain if the end is defined as merely achieving a specific goal of longevity in position. Growth requires challenge. In the professional life of MDI, the mission dictates an unending challenge to seek and document facts. A cynic could counter that this is merely finding the obvious by rote— the best that can be done is to find the obvious. Each and every decedent, each and every accused, indeed each and every human de-serves the same level of impartial diligence and dedication. The true test comes in the cruci-ble of the courtroom where the stakes are elevated, sometimes to the level of life and death. Yet such high profile cases are the excep-tion rather than the norm and as such, some might be inclined to pay special attention to those cases that "matter" as opposed to the gar-den variety cases seen on a daily basis. The duty is to try to find whatever facts exist. Every case, every time. Because the autopsy is inherently destructive, the forensic pathologist is accus-tomed to considering other possible avenues (medical records, lab testing, genetic informa-tion, etc.) to provide additional information. In the example of the 12-year-old girl cited above, such a mindset led directly to the exten-sive search for the missing sexual examination kit and to doing the best possible job with the available evidence. In the end, despite concerns expressed by some that admitting that evidence was lost might "look bad," the confirmatory testing ensured justice ultimately prevailed. "All courses of action are risky, so prudence is not in avoiding danger (it's impossible), but calculating risk and acting decisively. Make mistakes of ambition and not mistakes of sloth. Develop the strength to do bold things, not the strength to suffer" (Machiavelli). Politics should never trump ethics or morality.

Gluttony Versus Temperance (Moderation) (Merriam-Webster)

Gluttony or inordinate overconsumption is often erroneously limited to the gourmand inces-santly bolting food. While certainly fitting the definition, such unbridled excess has broad application. In medicodental practice, this might take the face of reveling in the status of being *the expert* on a given topic, with attorneys on both sides having a keen interest in one's professional opinion. In this context, gluttony may border on and even overlap with ego but the difference is in motivation—not the sense of power but the sense of satiety. Doing extreme numbers or types of cases is also a danger. A "glutton for punish-ment" performing extraordinary caseloads also may have a greed incentive but cloaks it with the euphemism of real or alleged "service" or "experience" to justify excesses. Suggested caseload limits exist for a reason. In medicodental practice, with excessive numbers come fatigue and the potential for error (ACGME Task Force, 2011). Demands imposed by resource encumbrances and/or volume, such as mass disaster events can have a profound impact, leading to burnout and posttraumatic stress issues. "'Continued exposure to violence, challenging cases with media exposure and confrontation in court, relatively low pay, and recent government cutbacks' were all cited as factors [in curtailing forensic practice]" (Breslow, 2012). Excessive caseloads and nonprofessionalism "...can result in increased errors, autopsies being performed by unqualified personnel (or not being performed at all), and manpower burnout and attrition" (NIJ National Association of Medical Examiners, 2006). Where service extenders are used, the temptation may be to increase delivery by utilizing assistants to even greater extents. Ultimately, the danger becomes "... someone doing autopsies without a medical license.... This is a huge atrocity, an invitation to disaster, and it needs to stop" (NIJ National Association of Medical Examiners, 2006).

Case Scenario: A single pathologist "performed 80–90 percent of the [jurisdiction's] autopsies ... that amounted to between 1200 and 1800 per year..." (NAME). NAME accreditation standards mandate an individual's range of 250–325 (INTUIT), thus in this scenario, a single physician worked the equivalent of six to seven full-time medical examiners. "For much of this time, he shouldered this workload while also holding down one, sometimes two full-time jobs..." (NAME). This pathologist's "... testimony helped put thousands of people in prison ....Critics say he was able to monopolize autopsy referrals from the state's prosecutors because he told them what they needed to hear in order to ring up convictions. He also testified in numerous lawsuits for medical malpractice and

wrongful death" (NAME). Such concerns, if accurate, jeopardize the very foundation of objective medicodental practice. For example, one court threw out his testimony wherein "... he preposterously claimed that he could tell by a murder victim's wounds that there were two people holding the gun that fired the fatal bullets" (NAME). Some are bound to challenge such extraordinary claims: one group complained to the State Medical Board "... seeking to revoke ... [his] medical license. ... [He] responded with a defamation suit, which the organization settled earlier this year for $100,000" (NAME). "Ironically, their investigation began with documents the team found during the discovery phase of ... [his] defamation suit ... What they've found since implicates not only ... [the pathologist], but a host of police officials, prosecutors, even judges who knew... [he] was deficient and offering dubious testimony, but did nothing to stop it" (NAME). "We've known for a while that there was a problem here... But I really had no concept of the depth and breadth of the malfeasance.... It's ... almost everybody. The state has known all along that it was pulling the wool over everyone's eyes" (NAME).

Temperance overcomes gluttony. The medicodental professional is well familiar with tangible improvements in patients' quality of life when personal excesses are moderated. The indoctrination process of medicodental education at the graduate and postgraduate levels may blunt the realization that good advice, when unheeded, is for naught. "She generally gave herself very good advice, (though she very seldom followed it)" (Carroll). The reality is that bureaucracies will endure despite the absence of any individual. Vacations, holidays, sick leave, flexible schedules, employee recognitions, and other benefits are provided to allow employees the opportunity to recover and revitalize, with the net effect that productivity goes up with such rewards (INTUIT). By extension, funding sources might be well served in actively pursuing such policies to enhance morale.

Anger Versus Patience (Tolerance/Sufferance) (Merriam-Webster)

Anger in the sense intended here is that consuming rage adversely impacts the individual. Given frustration can exist at many levels. The public may decry perceived unprofessionalism, staff may openly disagree, and professionals may become upset with one another. Such negativity, if made public, assures headlines. Due to the intense outcry when human remains are disrespected, scrutiny can be expected when such allegations are made (Ray_Brent_Marsh/index). The sudden appearance of leaked or planted stories in media accounts painting an individual or operations in a particularly bad light signify internal decay. Possible exaggeration or more nefarious motives should be considered. Dueling and escalating media accounts might be anticipated, as for example, when remains are improperly stored in the morgue: "… [Body] stacking photographs and at least five anonymous letters sent to county officials, office employees and the media are hurting morale" (Medical examiner, 1998). "… [The] chief medical examiner acknowledges that the improper practice of stacking bodies has occurred at the county morgue, but said it appears to have been the work of disgruntled employees violating official policy" (Medical examiner, 1998). In the situation where the supervisor contradicts or even blames the staff, the question begs why the supervisor tolerated such behavior. Answers may be myriad, ranging from ignorance of the acts to benign neglect to indifference to denial to malicious covert acts. Reportedly untenable and intolerable situations appearing as if overnight beg the question: why. Attempts to placate the press can be a challenge at best. "Wooing the press is an exercise roughly akin to picnicking with a tiger. You might enjoy the meal, but the tiger always eats last" (Dowd Maureen). The best that can be done is to be available, honest, open, and direct. Taking ownership of mistakes is the most effective means of ameliorating a bad situation and diffusing tensions.

Several examples of media exchanges involving several different MDI offices suggest a similar pattern of hostility:[4]

> … [The] office has come under frequent criticism in the past year for a series of controversies such as criminal investigations, lawsuits by two employees who contend they were fired for reporting illegal practices, the accidental cremation of a wrong body,

> *the employment of an unlicensed physician and questions about the reliability of autopsies in several high-profile homicide cases"* (Ford, 2012).

> Staff members at the morgue say the increased workload has worsened already unsafe and unsanitary conditions in the autopsy room and refrigeration unit… [and] criticism of the office has demoralized the staff. [With the majority of staff asserting that] …. "The morale has dropped to the lowest level in the past 15 years…. We are constantly insulted and accused of being incompetent, threatened to be removed from our positions, berated, harassed, belittled and disrespected …. We are often overworked and the Chief never, ever steps forward to contribute or give a word of thanks or compliment. It appears he only knows negative criticism" (Dardick, 2012). The latter point was seemingly reiterated by the pathologist's statement that some employees "…were actively insubordinate and intransigent and subverting the process… [Some] who were marginally competent and some who were incompetent" (Dardick, 2012). "We have some very seriously disgruntled employees… Because they're being held to levels of accountability they've never been held to before. I've upset the apple cart. Well, get used to it" (Dardick, 2012).

> [Governmental officials] … ordered the review after learning a cooler designed to hold 300 bodies was filled beyond capacity. Photos sent to the media

---

[4] These comments are compiled from several different jurisdictions and sequencing has been edited for readability.

showed adult remains stacked on metal shelving and movable trays, sometimes two per shelf. The remains of infants were shown stacked atop each other. Most of the bodies were wrapped in blue plastic bags, in several cases with their limbs exposed" (Donovan, 2012). "… [T]wo morgue employees were fired and one was disciplined… [and] a top aide [was sent] to monitor the medical examiner's office…" (Byrne, 2012) because "… she is a fine pathologist, but some have questioned her management skills" (Byrne, 2012). "[The] Medical examiner [is] standing in way of fixing morgue problems" (Finally Enough for Chief State Medical Examiner, 2012) "… [M]anagement issues … can't be summed up starting with one person. This is about a culture over time, and management is a component of that" (Byrne, 2012). "There have been recurring problems … [but the ability] to deal with it is limited by the fact that the person who is in charge of it has a term of office…" (Finally Enough for Chief State Medical Examiner, 2012). "The new rules allow … request that the medical examiner be removed for 'negligence, malfeasance, misfeasance, immoral, illegal or unethical conduct, or failure to properly execute the duties of such position'" (Byrne, 2012).

The "my way or the highway" mentality leaves no room for compromise and literally begs a counteroffensive. *Quid pro quo* allegations may be anticipated when each side feels— legitimately or not—threatened by the other. Ultimately, the truth can only be uncovered by a complete, objective, and unbiased external investigation. Even then, when difficulties are identified, attempts to rectify problems may be met with resistance, as for example, when the professional "…threatened to quit his job if the administration didn't quit meddling in the affairs of his office" (Finally Enough for Chief State Medical Examiner, 2012). The public has "…little sympathy with the … [practitioner's] intolerance of change. (He makes a breathtaking salary of $303,433 a year)" (Finally Enough for Chief State Medical Examiner, 2012). Thus the stroke of an editorial pen brushes aside as the shrill cries of a mercenary the, perhaps legitimate, concerns from an experienced medicodental professional. "With an ethic of greed doctors cease to base their motivation on compassion and caring to become merchants selling medical services to

the highest bidder" (Crawshaw, 1993). Anger, justified or not, is channeled into faultfinding with another and labelling them as having ethical failures. The ad hominem attack proceeds from a constructed base—whether flawed or not.

A very different form of anger might be anticipated with particularly egregious cases, especially from the public at large and the victim/survivors in particular. The communal sense of outrage is well familiar, particularly with the current polarizing high profile "case of the century" (Lewis, 1995; Medina, 2011; Alvarez, 2011; NY Daily News. George Zimmerman acquitted, 2013). No less passionate are those involved in death penalty cases where the stakes are literally life and death (Kinsella, 2012). Concerns over the stakes in wrongful conviction cases have created a powerful postconviction relief lobby, claiming hundreds of "DNA exonerations" [sic] including ~6% on death row (Innocence Project). Cases that shock societal mores can be challenging on many levels. Professionalism and ethics demand that justice be served, and in fairness to the truth, the nature of the case should not adversely impact the underlying science or medicodental principles. Facts remain facts, regardless of their significance or lack thereof. When truth is perverted by commission or omission, it becomes easy to understand angry outcries of miscarriage of justice. Opinion must never supplant fact.

Case example: A case appeal to the State Supreme Court included arguments that the state's expert presented "'junk science' testimony in support of … [the] allegation of anal sexual battery" and that his attorney had been "…ineffective for failing to object to … [the pathologist's] highly prejudicial testimony…." "In order to win this point, the defense "…must show that … testimony constituted plain error. 'Plain error exists where such error affects the defendant's substantive/fundamental rights, even though no objection was made at trial.' 'To determine if plain error has occurred, this Court must determine if the trial court has deviated from a legal rule, whether that error is plain, clear or obvious, and whether the error has prejudiced the outcome of the trial'" (Galloway v. State of Mississippi, 2013a,b). As such, the following state's expert testimony was allowed:

> "[F]orceful penetration of the anus ... caused injury... by the penetration of the anal canal. It's evidence of anal rape (Galloway v. State of Mississippi, 2013a,b).

> The injuries that were present in her inner legs and over the area of her vagina and anus were in no way produced by spreading of the legs. Her injuries were those of a rolling type of crush injury where her legs stayed together... These are classic patterns of penetration, forceful, resisted into [the] anus... (Galloway v. State of Mississippi, 2013a,b).

> The injuries that are produced by forceful penetration with a penis dilate the anus. It gets bigger and bigger and bigger with more penetration. The edges of the anal opening are rubbed away with repeated penetration, and finally it gets distended and stretched enough that it ... characteristically tears in the midline in back. And this is exactly what she had. She had the injury of forceful penetration by a penis of a sexual event, not a random injury of the area between her legs (Galloway v. State of Mississippi, 2013a,b).

> [It would have] caused enough pain that it would be resisted.... [Not] something that a person would want to have done to them. It would be painful enough to want to stop... or prevent it (Galloway v. State of Mississippi, 2013a,b).

In a prior case, cited as justification in the same ruling, the same expert had testified that

> ...[T]he injuries to the genital region, the stretching and scraping and tearing of the vagina and rectal tissues. These are produced by forceful penetration of the vagina and rectum by a structure that is able to distend and stretch and tear in a symmetrical pattern. In other words, a round—a roughly round structure... It has to be a part of a human body or something with that same texture consistency [- like a] male sex organ (Galloway v. State of Mississippi, 2013a,b).

Remaining calm in the face of serious ethical and professional misconduct is a thankless task. In a case where an expert's testimony clearly goes beyond the bounds of reasonable, the natural response of outrage is expected.

Patience stands in contrast to anger. Rather than being paralyzed by frustration over the outcome, the justice system provides avenues to redress grievances. In the exemplar above, an amicus curiae brief was filed by nine qualified experts who felt that the state's expert had claimed an inappropriate level of medical certainty for accepting his theory and rejecting the defense's theory of how the injuries had occurred. This panel of experts determined the injuries in question to be nonspecific and that "the most that can be said with professional propriety is that the [anal] findings are consistent with either a penis or other such smooth object." The brief concluded that the trial testimony amounted to "...little more than 'the ipse dixit of the [state's] expert.' '[S]elf-proclaimed accuracy by an expert is an insufficient measure of reliability'" (Galloway v. State of Mississippi, 2013a,b). The appeal was rejected; however, the efforts to maintain the ethics and integrity of the profession continue.

Pride Versus Humility (Merriam-Webster)

Pride is considered by many the most dangerous of all the sins, "... the queen of all vices; and vainglory, that immediately arises from pride, ... a capital sin. And reasonably so: for pride means an inordinate seeking to stand high. Now from everything that a man seeks he attains a certain perfection and high standing; and therefore the ends of all vices are directed to the end of pride; and therefore pride seems to exercise a *general* causality over the other vices..." (Aquinas, 1892). Although all are tempted, certain professions may tend to be associated with a general sense of repleteness. Medicodental professionals in particular are forced by training to wait—college, medical school, internship/residency, and fellowship training bring only the promise of continuing education, certification, licensure, etc. Inculcation of delayed gratification is the means to a never attained end. Combined with the difficulties and stress of daily practice, homicide autopsies, courtroom testimony, and limited resources, the career takes a toll, but "[b]etter to reign in Hell, then [sic] serve in Heav'n" (Milton). Hardly surprising then that once actively engaged in practice, a practitioner might exude a certain sense of accomplishment—just pride in a job well done. The concern is where a partisan bias could unduly influence the reporting of fact-finding. Of the three forms of reasoning: *deduction* (analysis with general rules applied to specific cases with results inferred), *induction* (specific case and result with rule inferred), and *abduction* (rule and result with case inferred), medicodental diagnostics chiefly utilize the latter process of abduction. "Neither inductive nor abductive reasoning leads to certainty; [therefore] we must hypothesize, and there may be several competing hypotheses that could be logically correct. This is the nature of most diagnostic tasks" (Morris et al., 1988). Although usually considered in a medicodental epidemiologic context, the Hill considerations have a place in the formation of a differential diagnosis: association, consistency, specificity, temporality, biological gradient, plausibility, coherence, experimentation, and analogy (Höfler, 2005). Finding the best fit between data and hypotheses is at the core of medical diagnostics.

Vexing is the well-intentioned practitioner who consults exclusively or predominately for one side in the partisan medicolegal milieu, rather than as an objective scientist. In such situations, partial and half-truths might be too easily substituted for fact. The consultant can develop an inscrutable ability to divine what other experts saw/should have seen and said, meant, or *intended* to say. "Possibilities" and "concerns" are given equal footing with medical certainty. This last is part of the heart of the issue, in that there exists no specific quantifiable degree of "certainty" in the medicodental arts, specifically *legal* medicodental practice. "… [Some] medical professionals … interpret "medical certainty" to require a very high degree of probability, others may not. Some cases even promote the

contrary, stating that an 'absolute,' 'unqualified,' or even 'scientific' certainty is not required of a medical professional's testimony in order for it to be admitted as evidence on causality" (Abbott and Magnusson, 2008). The issue is clouded by the message intended: "… was the doctor stating that he was certain beyond a reasonable doubt, or was the doctor testifying that he was absolutely certain …? When the jury applied the physician's testimony to the facts of the case, it is likely that the jury gave the testimony a different weight than the doctor intended" (Abbott and Magnusson, 2008). Furthermore, "[t]he idea that there is a reasonable degree of certainty implies that there exists an unreasonable degree of certainty, or a lesser degree of certainty, or a lesser degree of being indisputable. This begs the question, at what point does something become so "indisputable" that it becomes reasonable" (Abbott and Magnusson, 2008)?

Consider the following case where a man was convicted of shooting his wife. During the trial, the state's pathology witness testified that (Parvin v. Mississippi; http://law.justia.com/cases/mississippi/supreme-court/2013/2011-ka-01471-sct.html):

> "…the victim had suffered a "near contact wound," but maintained that the distance from the muzzle to the victim was "approximately four feet." He testified that this conclusion was based on the appearance of the entrance wound and the presence of gunpowder "tattooing." Although … he did not know what type of gun was used, his "impression" was that a 12-gauge shotgun … had caused the injury… Notably, the autopsy report did not include his conjectures regarding the measurement of the shotgun bore, or his opinion that the pellets were "right on the verge of separating."

At the same trial, the firearms examiner—also a state's expert,

> "…who actually had tested the gun in question but was unable to establish a conclusive shot distance… [T]he testing procedure complied with the generally accepted methods used by forensic firearms experts, and he identified authoritative publications which supported and explained these methodologies.

The pathologist had also testified to fairly precise trajectory angles of the shot, stating that he

> "… had used a protractor, which he placed at the wound site, to determine the angles.

> "… [T]he measurements provided … and the shooting's depiction … fell woefully short of the requirements for admissibility. … When asked to explain how he had calculated his distance and trajectory measurements, … [he] did not cite any scientific principle or method. He asserted that he could measure the trajectory of the shotgun pellets using

> only his naked-eye observations of the entrance wound and a protractor, despite his testimony that it would be "impossible" to track the fired pellets. The only explanation offered was his assertion that "this case was straightforward."

> As for the distance determination, … [the pathologist] claimed to know that the pellets were "right on the verge of separating," and made an unsupported statement that, when fired, "individual pellet strikes start appearing after four feet," no matter the type of ammunition or shotgun. Despite the conflicting testimony from the State's firearms expert that a conclusive muzzle-to-wound distance could not be determined, … [the pathologist] claimed to have been able to measure the distance by viewing the wound and the victim's clothing. In sum, the only scientific method or principle appearing in the record was the ipse dixit or self-proclaimed accuracy of … [the pathologist].

On appeal, the verdict was reversed and the case remanded for a new trial. Motivation for another's acts is difficult to ascertain with certainty, but certainly the temptation to be the omniscient expert can be a powerful driving force.

Humility is the most effective defense against pride. The most important consideration is perspective; for in looking at actions and events, one can be all too easily swayed by one's own biases—be those recognized or covert. The essence of all forensic casework is that practitioners seek to establish facts. Enhanced individual expertise logically might make one more skilled in that task, all else being equal. If some

detail is missed during an evaluation, it remains so: "Over that unseen, the heart grieves not" (John Upshaw Downs Sr, 1997), since myopia may commonly be associated with tunnel vision. Put another way, "Never read your own press releases" (Joe Davis). From a careful systematic evaluation of all available data, a forensics professional ultimately renders an opinion. If one has reasonable confidence in the conclusion, then one is obliged to render that opinion—even knowing that challenges may ensue. Ultimately, everything rests on perspective. *How* individual elements are interpreted, individually and collectively. Seldom is there a single unanimous interpretation of any set of complete facts in a forensic case. Even the esteemed Supreme Court of the United States, in establishing rulings, issues dissenting opinions, which have no legal authority but which serve to provide a rational basis explaining the discord. The vital component of humility is the recognition that despite best efforts, the other person might actually be right, with the implicit understanding that you are wrong. The experienced forensic scientist would be well served to remember the adage, "You are only as good as your next mistake" (Joe Davis).

Conclusion

As in most of life, isolating specific discrete elements is difficult, life does not occur in a vacuum. In many examples cited above, an argument could be made that each of the seven shortcomings is exemplified by various persons involved: lust, envy, greed, sloth, gluttony, anger, and pride. In truth, the curse of temptations is that they intersect and intertwine, ultimately seeking to insinuate themselves into one's character. "The heart of human sin lies in the lust for power, and the devil— the deceiver— is the epitome of this power mongering" (Crysdale). All are tempted. "I do not understand my own actions. For I do not do what I want, but I do the very thing I hate" (Rom). Shortcomings impact the practitioner and thus may adversely damage casework. The best defense is a good offense. The most efficacious weapon in the armamentarium is recognition and preemptive reciprocity by invoking the virtues of chastity, charity, kindness, diligence, patience, and humility. Encouraging virtuous behavior serves to enhance professionalism and improve patient care. Ethical medicodental practice demands the practitioner take a stand.

> It takes a great deal of courage to stand up to your enemies, but even more to stand up to your friends (Rowling).

ETHICAL SCENARIOS

Every forensic dentist must encounter that first case. In fact, most encounter it twice—a first ID case and a first bitemark case. In the abstract there should be no difference in the fundamental issues involved in analyzing, accepting, and completing either type. But each has a particular path to error that the dentist can inadvertently (or perhaps purposefully) choose. In the identification case, the authorities may pressure the forensic dentist for a fast definitive (and positive) identification. Often telling the dentist that the "family is waiting" for the ID or "we know it is him" and you are just confirming what we already know. In the bitemark arena the pressure may come from the authorities using phrases again like "we know he did it" or "Doc, you are our only hope to pin this terrible crime" on this guy and "help us get him off the streets" before he does it again. The forensic dentist must understand that the motivation and the duty of the investigating officers is to solve the crime and arrest a suspect. Law enforcement may use any lawful method to do so, which includes lying to the suspect(s). The prosecutor has a duty to investigate and, if warranted, accept the case (and evidence) generated

by the police to represent the people in the case in court. While the prosecutor does not have a duty to convict per se, many conflate their duty to that level (and the public expects convictions). Similarly, the defense attorney has the duty to zealously represent his client before the bar, again within the bounds of law. As both the prosecutor and defense attorney are sworn members of the bar, each must follow strict rules (canons), which preclude lying and also preclude offering false testimony. The forensic dentist on the other hand has only a duty to himself—to tell the truth. To do so he or she must remain free of bias, must thoroughly analyze the case materials, must be familiar with and properly apply the methodology, and must resist the temptation to "help" the authorities. Unfortunately, we cannot know how many of the "bad" cases in the field began with a first fateful step influenced not by the facts (truth) but by the desire to help. In the long run, the best help is to do the job accurately, correctly, and dispassionately—only in that way will the actual truth be found.

Another ethical dilemma that many will encounter in forensic practice revolves around what might be considered "completed" cases; that is, cases in which the expert has testified and/or submitted his or her findings and the matter has been adjudicated through the trial court. Not so fast! Convicted defendants have the right to appeal; these appeals can be numerous and may occur many years after the trial date. There have been several instances in which an expert, who testified to a particular conclusion in the original matter, may now by virtue of advanced technology, consideration of the theories and/or discoveries, or for other reasons hold a modified opinion in the matter. While the law is not fully settled in these types of matters, most commentaries on ethics suggest that the expert has an affirmative duty to contact someone involved in the matter—the old or new defense attorney or the prosecutor, which one may depend upon the previous affiliation.

However, certainly if the revised opinion would argue for innocence, the best course might be to contact the prosecution because such information would have to be disclosed to the current defense/appellate team.

Another dilemma that many faced in the past is now, at least in criminal matters, fairly cut and dry. An expert contacted (even contracted) by the prosecution arrives at a final opinion that does not indicate culpability on the part of the defendant, or may even point toward innocence. The prosecutor, under Brady, has an affirmative duty to disclose all information that is favorable to the defendant to his attorneys if requested. No defense lawyer would fail to make such a request and the prosecution would be bound to disclose the report/opinion and to furnish the name of the expert as well. There is no reciprocal duty on the art of the defense. In noncriminal matters (and in some criminal cases defense experts), the expert is required to sign a confidentiality/nondisclosure agreement prohibiting sharing the conclusions/opinion with anyone else. These types of agreements have been held to be enforceable. The freedom (or even life) of a defendant is not at stake in these situations.

One real life example to illustrate the dilemma that expert witnesses may face: a prosecution expert opined that the defendant could not be excluded as having made the bitemark in question. The defense expert stated that he could exclude the defendant as having made the bitemark in question. Based on these contradictory opinions, the prosecution hires another expert who opines that the defendant made the bitemark in question "without doubt". Based on this level of certainty, the prosecutor contacts the first expert and asks if (based upon the level of certainty of the last expert) he would "upgrade" his opinion to agree with the expert who is certain "without doubt." The implied message here is: if the expert whose opinion is equivocal is unwilling to "play ball," he may not be asked to offer his opinion at trial. And if the initial expert acquiesces, he has compromised not only his

impartiality but also his integrity. Expert witnesses need to be aware of the type of pressure that may be brought to bear by law enforcement and attorneys—always bear in mind that legal obligations are often far different from those of an expert witness.

References

Abbott, N., Magnusson, L., July 16, 2008. An enigmatic degree of medical certainty. Utah state bar. Utah Bar Journal. http://www.utahbar.org/utah-bar-journal/article/an-enigmatic-degree-of-medical-certainty/.

ACGME Task Force, 2011. MGraduate Medical Education > Duty Hours > Archive > Research & Testimony. Accreditation Councilfor Graduate Medical Education. http://www.acgme.org/acgmeweb/Portals/0/PDFs/jgme-monograph%5B1%5D.pdf.

Alighieri, D., November 30, 2012. The Divine Comedy, Complete: The Vision of Paradise, Purgatory and Hell. Gutenberg.org. http://www.gutenberg.org/files/8800/8800-h/8800-h.htm.

Alvarez, L., July 5, 2011. Casey Anthony Not Guilty in Slaying of Daughter. New York Times. http://www.nytimes.com/2011/07/06/us/06casey.html?pagewanted=all.

AMA. Humanizing anatomy: a medical student's first patient. Amednews.com http://www.amednews.com/article/20110418/profession/304189937/4/.

Aquinas St., T., 1892. Aquinas Ethicus: or, the Moral Teaching of St. Thomas. A Translation of the Principal Portions of the Second Part of the Summa Theologica, with Notes by Joseph Rickaby, S.J. Burns and Oates, London. Chapter: Question CXXXII.: of Vainglory. The Online Library of Liberty. http://oll.libertyfund.org/title/1967/124287.

Balko, R., November 29, 2012. Despite Evidence from Discredited Medical Examiner, Mississippi's Jeffrey Havard Nears Execution. HuffPost Politics @ HuffingtonPost.com. http://www.huffingtonpost.com/radley-balko/steven-hayne-jeffrey-havard b 2213976.html.

Bartos, L., April 17, 2012. Post Mortem Death Investigation in America No Forensic Background? No Problem. ProPublica.com. http://www.propublica.org/article/no-forensic-background-no-problem.

Breslow, J.M., August 8, 2012. More Deaths Go Unchecked as Autopsy Rate Falls to "Miserably Low" Levels. Frontline > Criminal Justice > Postmortem. http://www.pbs.org/wgbh/pages/frontline/criminal-justice/post-mortem/more-deaths-go-unchecked-as-autopsy-rate-falls-to-miserably-low-levels/.

Brody, H., 2010. Medicine's ethical responsibility for health care reform. New England Journal of Medicine 362, 283–285.

Byrne, J., June 29, 2012. State Agency Finds Nearly 2 Dozen Problems at Cook. ChicagoTribune.com. http://articles.chicagotribune.com/2012-06-29/news/ct-met-cook-county-morgue-report-20120629_1_morgue-bodies-racks.

Carroll, Lewis. Lewis Carroll: 10 favorite quotes on his birthday. unheeded wisdom. The Christian Science Monitor @ csmonitor.com. http://www.csmonitor.com/Books/2012/0127/Lewis-Carroll-10-favorite-quotes-on-his-birthday/Unheeded-wisdom.

Clanton, G., 2006. Jealousy and Envy. [book auth.]. In: Stets, J.E., Turner, J.H. (Eds.), Handbook of the Sociology Of Emotions. Springer, New York, pp. 410–442.

Clark, M., November 26, 2012. The Pew Charitable Trusts the Pew Charitable Trusts. The Pew Charitable Trusts. http://www.pewstates.org/projects/stateline/headlines/forensic-science-falls-short-of-public-image-first-of-two-parts-85899431 9082.

Crawshaw, R., 1993. Greed and the medical profession. Bmj: British Medical Journal 151, 306.

Crysdale, Cynthia S. W. Transformed Lives: Making Sense of Atonement Today (Kindle Locations 1471-1472). Church Publishing Inc. Kindle Edition.

Dardick, H., June 19, 2012. Preckwinkle to Announce Overhaul of Medical Examiner's Office. Chicago Tribune News chicagotribune.com. http://articles.chicagotribune.com/2012-06-19/news/ct-met-cook-county-medical-examiner-0619-20120619_1 preckwinkle-morgue-chief-forensic-pathologist.

DeadlySins.com. Contrary, Heavenly, and cardinal Virtues. 7 Deadly Sins > Virtues. http://www.deadlysins.com/virtues.html.

Donovan, L., January 18, 2012. Preckwinkle: Medical Examiner Standing in Way of Fixing Morgue Problems. Chicago Sun-Times.com. http://www.suntimes.com/photos/galleries/10090058-417/preckwinkle-medical-examiner-standing-in-way-of-fixing-morgue-problems.html.

Dowd, Maureen. Maureen Dowd. BrainyQuote.com. http://www.brainyquote.com/quotes/quotes/m/maureendow391343.html.

Echegarary, C., August 27, 2010. Former State Medical Examiner. WBIR.com > the Tennessean > News Headlines. WBIR.com. http://www.wbir.com/news/local/story.aspx?storyid=132130.

Facaros, D., Pauls, M., 1998. Traveller's Guide to Hell. S.L. Cadogan Books.

The Hartford Courant articles.courant.com Finally, 'Enough' For Chief State Medical Examiner, January 30, 2012. http://articles.courant.com/2012-01-30/news/hc-ed-chief-medical-examiner-steps-down-20120 127_1_malloy-administration-wayne-carver-ii-state-agencies.

Ford, Gerald R. Gerald Ford - Complacent. BrainyQuote.com http://www.brainyquote.com/quotes/quotes/g/geraldrfo402718.html.

Ford, R., February 24, 2012. Haggerty and Liam. 2 Workers Fired in Connection with Probe of Morgue. ChicagoTribune.com. http://articles.chicagotribune.com/2012-02-24/news/ct-met-cook-county-medical-examiner-20120224_1_medical-examiner-nancy-jones-preckwinkle-morgue.

Galloway v. State of Mississippi, June 6, 2013a. : Direct Appeal. NO. 2010-dp-01927-sct, s.L. Supreme Court of Mississippi.

Galloway v. State of Mississippi, June 6, 2013b. - Brief OfAmicus Curiae. NO. 2010-dp-01927-sct, s.L. State Supreme Court, Mississppi.

Gerhardstein, A.A., et al., July 20, 2010. Documents for case range. In: Kenneth Douglas, v., et al. (Eds.), Gerhardstein & Branch Co. LPA. http://www.gbfirm.com/litigation/documents/45_1-Complaint.pdf.

RT.com Gruesome discovery: Brains, Hearts Found in Florida Storage Unit, August 29, 2012. http://rt.com/usa/florida-storage-brains-heart-798/.

Harris, S.C., Hamil, R.A., September 12, 1999. Better Morgue, a Bitter Staff. Washingtonpost.com. http://www.washingtonpost.com/wp-srv/local/daily/sept99/arden12.htm.

Higgins, R., May 14, 2010. Final Twist Doomed Delashmitt Death Case. TimesFreePress > home >> local/regional >> final twist doomed delashmitt. http://www.timesfreepress.com/news/2010/may/14/final-twist-doomed-delashmitt-death-case/.

Höfler, M., 2005. The Bradford Hill considerations on causality: a counterfactual perspective. Emerging Themes in Epidemiology 2 (11). https://doi.org/10.1186/1742-7622-2-11.

Huff, S., July 29, 2008. Doubly Victimized: Karen Range. TrueCrimeReport.com. http://www.truecrimereport.com/2008/07/doubly_victimized_karen_range.php.

Innocence Project. Mission Statement. The Innocence Project. http://www.innocenceproject.org/about/Mission-Statement.php.

INTUIT. A Happy Staff is a Productive Staff: How to Motivate Employees. INTUIT > news > Achieving sales & profitability. http://smallbusiness.intuit.com/news/Achieving-sales-&-profitability/19439231/A-Happy-Staff-is-a-Productive-Staff:-How-to-Motivate-Employees.jsp.

Isle of Man Government Officers Association. Bullying and Harrassment. Isle ofMan Government Officers Association. https://www.gov.im/media/629669/preventionofbullyingharassmentbo.pdf.

Isle ofMan Government Officers Association, June 2009. http://www.gov.im/lib/docs/personnel/Information_Centre/preventionofbullyingharassmentbo.pdf.

Joe Davis (attributed), Dr.

John Upshaw Downs Sr., 1997. Managing Death Investigation, Revised 1997. National Criminal Justice Reference System. https://www.ncjrs.gov/pdffiles1/Digitization/196709NCJRS.pdf.

Judicial Department, S.C., February 5, 2007. 4159-State V. Curry. SC Judicial Department. http://www.judicial.state.sc.us/opinions/displayopinion.cfm?caseno=4159.

Kinsella, W., February 11, 2012. Reason over Passion in Death Penalty Debate. Toronto Sun. http://www.torontosun.com/2012/02/10/reason-over-passion-in-death-penalty-debate.

Lattman, P., December 5, 2011. Out of Galleon Scandal and Wall St. Excess, a Book. NY Times. http://dealbook.nytimes.com/2011/12/05/out-of-galleon-scandal-and-wall-st-excess-comes-a-book/.

Lewis, P., February 14, 1995. Discussion of the O. J. Simpson Murder Trial Is On-line as Well as on the Air. New York Times.com. http://www.nytimes.com/1995/02/14/us/discussion-of-the-o-j-simpson-murder-trial-is-on-line-as-well-as-on-the-air.html.

David F. Lloyd. Distinguishing Between Morality and Ethics. http://www.vision.org/visionmedia/ethics-and-morality/distinguishing-between-morality-and-ethics/731.aspx.

Machiavelli, Niccolò. The Prince. Project Gutenberg ebook. http://www.gutenberg.org/files/1232/1232-h/1232-h.htm.

texnews.com Medical Examiner Says Angry Workers 'staged' Body Stacking Photos, December 19, 1998. http://www.texnews.com/1998/texas/body1219.html.

Medina, J., November 29, 2011. Jackson's Doctor Is Sentenced to Four Years. NewYorkTimes. http://www.nytimes.com/2011/11/30/us/michael-jacksons-doctor-sentenced-to-four-years.html?ref=global-home&_r=0.

Merriam-Webster. Dictionary. Merriam-Webster. http://www.merriam-webster.com/dictionary/.

Michelangelo. Michaelangelo Quotes. BraineyQuote.com. http://www.brainyquote.com/quotes/authors/m/michelangelo.html.

Milton, J. Paradise Lost Book 1. The John Milton Reading Room. http://www.dartmouth.edu/~milton/reading_room/pl/book_1/.

Morris, Tim Finin, Gary, July 1988. Abductive Reasoning in Multiple Fault. ScholarlyCommons. http://repository.upenn.edu/cgi/viewcontent.cgi?article=1730&context=cis_reports.

Muñoz, J., December 22, 2009. Guilty by Omission Is Still Guilty: Man Gets Life for Baby Deaths. KENS 5 News. http://www.kens5.com/news/local/Guilty-by-omission-is-still-guilty-Man-gets-life-for-deaths-of-babies-79908222.html#.

NAME. NAME Inspection and Accreditation Checklist. National Association on Medical Examiners. https://netforum.avectra.com/temp/ClientImages/NAME/069196e4-6f95-437c-a2be-47649a70685e.pdf.

United Nations, September 2012. United Nations Guidance for Effective Mediation - UN Peacemaker. Peacemaker.org. http://peacemaker.un.org/sites/peacemaker.un.org/files/GuidanceEffectiveMediation_UNDPA20 12(english)_1.pdf.

NIJ, National Association of Medical Examiners, March 2006. Status and Needs of Forensic Science Service Providers: A Report to Congress. National Institute of Justice, Office of Justice Programs. https://www.ncjrs.gov/pdffiles1/nij/213420.pdf.

NY Daily News. George Zimmerman acquitted, July 15, 2013. Not Guilty Verdict Sparks Nationwide Protests. New York Daily News. http://www.nydailynews.com/news/protests-george-zimmerman-verdict-gallery-1.1398497.

O'Donnell, J.H., John, B., March 11, 2001. Jury Distrust, Bitter Verdict. The Baltimore Sun > Home > Collections > Police. http://articles.baltimoresun.com/2001-03-11/news/0103110274_1_stennett-verdict-jurors.

Parvin v. Mississippi. http://caselaw.findlaw.com/ms-supreme-court/1627980.html.

Pelligrino, E.D., 1986. Percival's medical ethics the moral philosophy of an 18th-century English gentleman. Arch Intern Med 146 (11), 2265−2269.

Percival, 1803. Medical Ethics.

Perry, K., October 19, 2009. Morgue Worker Admits to Sex with More Bodies. Cincinatti.com. http://news.cincinnati.com/article/20091019/NEWS0107/310180016/Morgue-worker-admits-sex-more-bodies.

Proverbs 6:19. BibleGateway.com. New International Version. http://www.biblegateway.com/passage/?search=Proverbs+6%3A16-19&version=NIV.

Ray_Brent_Marsh/index. NewYorkTimes.com. http://topics.nytimes.com/topics/reference/timestopics/people/m/ray_brent_marsh/index.html.

Rom. 7: 15,19− 24.

Romans 3:23. BibleGateway.com > New International Version. http://www.biblegateway.com/passage/?search=Romans+3%3A23&version=NIV.

Rowling, J. K. Quotation #35724 from Laura Moncur's Motivational Quotations. TheQuotations Page.com. http://www.quotationspage.com/quote/35724.html.

Shakespeare, W., 1999. The Tragedy of Hamlet, Prince of. W3C. XML markup © 1999 Jon Bosak. http://www.w3.org/People/maxf/XSLideMaker/hamlet.pdf.

Swerdloff, M.A., December 31, 2000. Comment: hamster health care. British Medical Journal @bmj.com. http://www.bmj.com/rapid-response/2011/10/28/greedy-doctors.

Adages Taverner Tr. Erasmus, R., 1539. The Oxford Dictionary of Proverbs, Reference.com, fifth ed. Oxford. http://www.oxfordreference.com/view/10.1093/acref/9780199539536.001.0001/acref-978019953953 6-e- 150.

Truss, Lynne. Talk To The Hand Quotes. GoodReads.com. http://www.goodreads.com/work/quotes/2881-talk-to-the-hand-the-utter-bloody-rudeness-of-the-world-today-or-six-g.

Ward, Adrian F. Scientists Probe Human Nature—and Discover We Are Good, After All. Scientific American. http://www.scientificamerican.com/article.cfm?id=scientists-probe-human-nature-and-discover-we-are-good-after-all.

Weich, S., May 05, 2013. Missouri coroners Question Practices of Forensics Company Operator. St. Louis Post-Dispatch. http://www.stltoday.com/news/local/metro/missouri-coroners-question-practices-of-forensics-company-operator/article_0662e5b 1-dcfa-578f-9487-8ab6a176ea4d.html.

Welsh, I., March 6, 2015. Ethics 101: The Difference between Ethics and Morals. http://www.ianwelsh.net/ethics-101-the-difference-between-ethics-and-morals/ (emphasis in original).

CHAPTER

14

Forensic Odontology Related Specialties

Craig O'Connor, Melissa Mourges, Murray K. Marks,
Darinka Mileusnic-Polchan, Heather Walsh-Haney

DNA

Craig O'Connor[1], Melissa Mourges[2]

[1]Criminalist IV, Assistant Technical Leader of DNA Operations, Department of Forensic Biology, New York City Office of Chief Medical Examiner, New York, NY, United States; [2]Chief, Forensic Sciences/ Cold Case Unit, Manhattan DA's Office, New York, NY, United States

DEOXYRIBONUCLEIC ACID HAS BEEN USED FOR HUMAN IDENTIFICATION FOR DECADES

The use of Deoxyribonucleic Acid (DNA) for human identification has had a rapid evolution over the last 30 years (Gill et al., 1985). From its first real exposure in the United States in 1993 during the O. J. Simpson murder trial (Linder, 1995) to the implementation of convicted felon DNA databases in 1998 to contemporary uses such as the identification of victims from the World Trade Center disaster, the murder trial of Amanda Knox, even on the documentary "Making a Murderer" (Ricciardi and Demos, 2015), accuracy in using DNA for identification of crime scene samples, whether from a blood stain, hair follicle, a tooth, skin cells, or other biological material, has come into sharp focus. For decades, the most used identification markers consisted of fingerprints and ABO blood groups (Caplan, 1990; Crow, 1993; Lee and Chang, 1992; Yamamoto et al., 1990). The use of DNA for identification quickly became the preferred method to individualize biological samples compared to other methods due to its increased capability to genetically differentiate people.

Research conducted in England by scientist Sir Alec Jeffreys in 1985 (Jeffreys et al., 1985a,b) paved the way for current human identification methods. While searching for markers for genetic research and gene discovery, he and his colleagues stumbled upon a new form of identification markers that dealt with fluctuating numbers of tandemly repeated DNA. They were then able to show that varying repeats differentiated individuals. Termed variable number of tandem repeats (VNTRs) and later short tandem repeats (**STRs**), it was shown that each location or **locus** had many forms (termed **alleles**) based on the number of tandemly repeated core sequences. These sequences produced different banding patterns when run on an agarose gel and the resulting banding pattern was unique to an individual.

WHAT IS SHORT TANDEM REPEAT TYPING?

First used in criminal cases in the early 1990s and extrapolating from the early VNTR work, currently the most commonly used method of DNA identification is the analysis of microsatellites, more commonly called STRs. STRs represent a class of microsatellite sequences seen throughout the human genome (Litt and Lutty, 1989; Edwards et al., 1991). They are used as molecular markers in a variety of situations such as gene mapping, disease diagnosis, human identification, and population studies (Fan and Chu, 2007; Hammond et al., 1994).

STRs are highly effective markers because of extreme variability within populations and between individuals. They are much more useful when dealing with very small amounts of DNA commonly found at a crime scene. STRs, coupled with the polymerase chain reaction (**PCR**) amplification, can accommodate certain levels of degradation and is highly adaptable to automation when dealing with hundreds of samples. Similar to VNTRs, STRs are series of short sequences (2–6 base pairs), repeated one after the other and vary in the number of repeats between individuals.

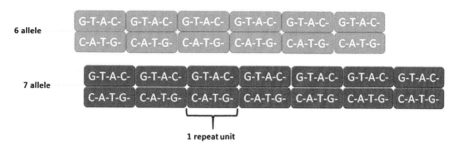

FIGURE 14.1 A schematic of alleles in a double-stranded short tandem repeat locus. There is a four base pair core motif that is repeated in tandem: six times for the top allele and seven times for the bottom allele. The alleles are designated by the number of repeats (i.e., 7 or 8) and the resulting DNA type would be 7, 8 for this individual.

Each locus contains a core sequence repeated in a head to tail fashion, and the number of repeats serves as the basis for differentiation (Fig. 14.1).

A major advantage to using STRs is the small amount of DNA (ideally 0.1–1 ng) needed to generate a full profile. With previous DNA typing methods using VNTRs, a great deal of DNA (~10–20 ng) was needed to achieve a result with high enough discriminatory capability to individualize the sample (Inman and Ruding, 1997). With the advent of PCR, STR use superseded other typing methods mainly because small product sizes (100–500 bp) could be generated. These small product sizes are beneficial for degraded DNA and contain discrete alleles that can easily be catalogued due to both the use of PCR and with other technological advances.

The small product size and the discrete nature of alleles enable the development of multiplex reactions, which allow one to amplify several loci in a single PCR reaction.

This process had the distinct advantages of gaining more information in the same amount of time with the same amount of material, while cutting down on the cost of the process (Butler, 2011). Instead of performing many different PCR reactions, one reaction can produce the same amount of information.

STRs can have large numbers of alleles due to varying repeat lengths (Lee et al., 1994) and exhibit a high degree of variability. They are abundant within the human genome. Thousands

of loci are known and have been classified with the possibility of millions being present (Edwards et al., 1991; Ellegren, 2004; Collins et al., 2003a,b). These loci comprise about 3% of the human genome (International Human Genome Sequencing Consortium, 2004; Collins et al., 2003a; Subramanian et al., 2003). One of the most important characteristics of STRs is that they are stable and consistent throughout the body. This means that the same profile is found in the nucleus of every cell of an individual. Therefore regardless what type of biological material (blood, semen, saliva, bone, teeth, hair) is deposited at a crime scene, the resulting DNA test performed will produce the same profile regardless of the cell type used.

EVIDENCE COLLECTION

The collection of DNA evidence is essential to case success. Without proper protocols in place, the samples could become compromised, contaminated, or lost prior to collection. Whether the evidence is biological in nature (semen from a rape case, blood from the victim of a homicide, teeth from skeletal remains) or it is from evidentiary material (skin cells from clothing or from a weapon), the sample location and volume is crucial. DNA may be found on anything that comes off of or out of one's body. Different sample types range from bodily fluids such as blood, semen, or saliva to items of evidence where DNA may have been deposited such as clothing, weapons, or touched objects. Bones, teeth and hair follicles are also rich in cells and therefore contain an abundance of DNA. Selecting the correct item to test is very critical to the overall success of the testing.

Evidentiary items from a crime scene are delivered to the forensic laboratory where it is received and stored in a secure location. Maintaining the **chain of custody** is extremely important to the integrity of the evidence. A written or electronic log is kept, documenting each person that has possession of the items and location they have been stored (Fig. 14.2). An incomplete chain of custody could lead to admissibility issues in a court of law as potential tampering and/or contamination of the evidence (Li, 2008).

The forensic analyst normally begins by examining the evidence packaging, making sure to note the appearance of the package and any identifying marks. Next, the item is described, noting size, shape, color, and other features followed by a visual examination looking for biological stains. When looking for blood, the stains appear reddish brown while a white/yellowish stain may indicate semen. If any stains are noted, they are then screened for that particular biological substance.

The primary screening tests performed in a forensic laboratory are presumptive and confirmatory. A positive presumptive test result means that the stain may potentially be a particular bodily fluid while a positive result from a confirmatory test confirms its presence by testing for specific characteristics of the substance. Presumptive tests are usually a simple color change reaction. These tests are extremely sensitive, with the ability to detect very small amounts of the substance, but not highly specific. For instance, a major presumptive test for blood is a phenolphthalein reaction also called the Kastle—Meyer (KM) test. A positive KM test yields a pink color change caused by a reaction to the hemoglobin content in blood, but it can also be caused by other substances such as rust (Kastle and Shedd, 1901; Meyer, 1903). Meanwhile, the Takayama test is considered a confirmatory test for blood because it forms hemochromagen crystals upon a reaction with

FIGURE 14.2 Evidence Chain of Custody. Each person who has possession of the item and the locations that it is stored is recorded. This is used to maintain the integrity of the evidence and to show that no tampering has taken place.

Item No(s):	Received From	Received by	Date

the iron in blood (Beam and Freak, 1915). Therefore a positive Takayama test confirms the presence of blood within a sample.

DEOXYRIBONUCLEIC ACID TESTING

After the screening tests are complete, the samples are sent for DNA testing. There are several major steps in the DNA testing process. The first is called DNA extraction. There are many methods available, but the ultimate goal is to get the DNA out of the cell. Chemical detergents such as sodium dodecyl sulfate or proteinase K are used to break open cells followed by separation and purification of the DNA.

Once the DNA is extracted, the next step is called quantification in which the amount of DNA within the sample is measured. If there is not any DNA or not enough within the sample, the process ceases. Earlier methods involved the use of gels or measured the amount of light absorbed by the DNA strands (Tataurov et al., 2008). Contemporary methods utilize **real-time PCR**, a technique where fluorescent dyes attach to the DNA as it is being replicated. This process is monitored in real time approximating the quantity of DNA present (Karsten et al., 2008).

Once the amount of DNA in the sample has been quantified, the specific STR loci are amplified. **PCR** mimics the natural replication process that happens in cells but takes place within a test tube. Synthesized fragments of DNA are used as primers to initiate the copying process (Hares, 2012). This is accomplished with a number of cycles of heating and cooling of the sample in an instrument called a thermocycler (Fig. 14.3).

Each cycle will double the amount of DNA in the sample and therefore after ～25–35 cycles of

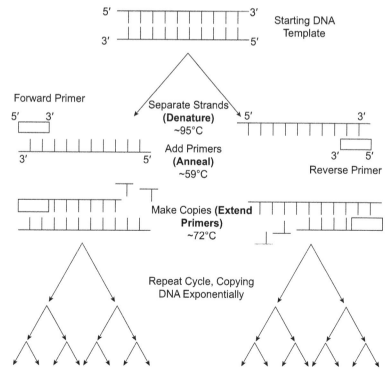

FIGURE 14.3 Polymerase Chain Reaction (PCR). DNA is amplified in a test tube in a similar fashion to the natural process of cell replication. The DNA is doubled with each cycle, exponentially increasing the amount of starting material. With one starting strand, one can have over a billion copies with just 25 cycles of PCR. *Adapted from Butler, J.M., (2009). Fundamentals of Forensic DNA Typing, first ed.* © *2010 Elsevier Academic Press.*

PCR there will theoretically be over a billion copies of the starting fragment of DNA. The STR locations were selected based on a number of factors including variability within the population, number of alleles per locus, and ease of amplification. Currently there are 13 loci that are termed the "CODIS core loci" and are needed for upload into the Federal Bureau of Investigation's database. In 2017 that number will increase to 20 providing additional diversity and variability, especially in respect to compatibility with European markers (Hares, 2015).

After replication, the samples are separated out by size during **capillary electrophoresis**. Using an electric charge, the negatively charged DNA molecules are propelled through a molecular capillary sieve where the smaller fragments move through faster than the larger fragments. Since the resulting products from PCR contain a fluorescent tag, after migrating through the capillary, they are fluoresced by a laser and recorded on a camera. The resulting picture, called an **electropherogram**, contains many peaks that represent the DNA fragments in the sample. The results are analyzed using a computer program that catalog and label the peaks, ending in a string of numbers called a **DNA profile**. Each number corresponds to the number of repeats present at the given STR loci. The results from an evidence item can then be compared to a DNA profile of a known individual (such as a victim or suspect) to determine if they match one another.

The genotyping process is complicated by the appearance of technical artifacts produced during the amplification or electrophoresis steps. One such technical artifact is called stutter. Stutter is the presence of amplification byproducts representing one more or one fewer repeat units than the actual allele. This "stutter" process can make analysis more difficult if not dealt with appropriately. Minimization of stutter byproducts was a key consideration when the currently used STR loci were selected.

RESULTS INTERPRETATION

Interpretation of a DNA result can be just as challenging and time consuming as the laboratory processes. When comparing DNA results, there are a number of conclusions that can be reached. The first step in the process involves determining the number of contributors to the sample. DNA from one person, such as from a blood stain or a saliva sample, is termed **single source**. Humans get half their DNA from each parent; and, each location should have no more than two alleles. When the sample contains DNA from more than one individual, it is classified as a **mixture**.

There are simple mixtures that allow one to deconvolute the profiles of the contributors and complex mixtures that are much more difficult to analyze. The major donor to a mixture is the person who contributed the most DNA, while the minor donor(s) contributed less DNA. In some mixtures, if the ratio of major to minor donors is large enough (usually 3—1 or greater), the full profile of each individual contributor can be determined. When there is ambiguity or missing information, it may only be possible to determine a partial profile of the contributor. In other mixtures, however, the amount of DNA from each contributor is comparable and therefore no deconvolution is possible (Fig. 14.4).

Once the sample is interpreted, it is then compared to a DNA profile of known individuals. If all the DNA alleles from a known person are the same as the alleles determined from a sample, one can conclude that the samples **match** (Fig. 14.5). If there are any inconsistencies between the two samples, then the two samples do not match. In a mixture where there is no distinct profile determined, a direct comparison to a known individual can still be done. If all or most of the DNA alleles from that person are present within the mixture, then the results indicate they can be included as a possible contributor. If most of that person's alleles are

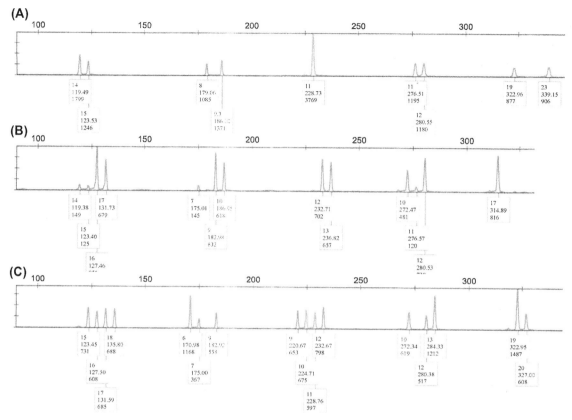

FIGURE 14.4 DNA typing results. (A). A single source sample from one person. Notice that since humans get half of their DNA from each parent, there are no more than two allelic peaks at each location. (B). Results from a simple mixture. The major and minor contributor allelic peaks can be easily deconvoluted. (C). Results from a complex mixture. The number of contributors and profiles of each of the donors, based on the visible peaks and peak heights are more ambiguous.

	Location #1	Location #2	Location #3	Location #4	Location #5
Evidence	12,13	21,23	7,8	10,11	12,12
Suspect 1	14,16	21,25	6,9	10,10	13,16
Suspect 2	12,13	21,23	7,8	10,11	12,12

FIGURE 14.5 DNA results from an evidence item are compared to DNA profiles from known individuals. If the profiles are consistent, then they are considered a match. If there are any inconsistencies, then the profiles do not match. Here, Suspect 2 matches the evidence profile while Suspect 1 is excluded as a contributor.

not present in the mixture, then they can be excluded as a possible contributor.

The process is not always definitive when it comes to comparing known individuals to mixtures. In fact, there can be times when no conclusions can be reached as to whether a person is a possible contributor or if they can be excluded. Inclusion and exclusion are very powerful statements. When there is uncertainty as to whether a person is included or not, caution should be invoked and the comparisons should be deemed inconclusive.

STATISTICAL ANALYSIS

Qualitative statements of inclusion or exclusion allow us to know what the overall interpretation of the results represent. Statistics are applied to provide weight to those conclusions. One of the most utilized statistics is a profile or **random match probability (RMP)**. This provides the probability that a randomly selected person from the population would match the evidence profile and is expressed mathematically as 1 in x people. In other words, the RMP can be viewed as a measure of the rarity of the DNA profile. For a full 13 locus single source profile, the RMP will generally be 1 in greater than 1 trillion people.

For more complex situations, especially those where a DNA profile from a contributor cannot be determined, the preferred method is calculating a **likelihood ratio (LR)**. The LR is a component of the long-established theorems of Thomas Bayes (Bayes's theorem, 2016). LR evaluates the probability of the evidence under two hypotheses; one with the comparison sample as a contributor and one without the comparison sample. Traditionally labeled as the "prosecution" and "defense" hypotheses, the LR is a ratio of these two probabilities. An LR greater than one indicates support for the numerator, and an LR less than one indicates support for the denominator. An LR of exactly one has no support for either hypothesis and is inconclusive.

OTHER MARKERS

There are several types of DNA-based markers. Autosomal STRs (previously discussed) are found on the nuclear DNA in each cell. There are also X chromosomal STRs found in all humans and Y chromosomal markers that are found exclusively in males. The Y chromosome will be passed down from father to son, virtually intact, in each generation. The Y chromosomal STR (YSTR) markers are used to help not only in criminal cases (identifying the male component in a mixture or the number of perpetrators in a gang rape scenario for instance) but can also be used for paternity testing, clinical applications, missing persons investigations, and historical genetic genealogy (Butler, 2006). Although not as discriminating as autosomal STRs, YSTRs can be very useful for identification purposes and as an exclusionary tool.

Mitochondrial DNA (mtDNA) is found in the cytoplasm of the cell outside of the nucleus. Like YSTRs, the mtDNA markers are passed down unilaterally through the maternal lineage. This means that mothers will pass their mtDNA down to all of their children, and all maternal relatives will subsequently have the same mtDNA profile. In this type of analysis, single nucleotide polymorphisms (SNPs) are the markers examined. When evaluating SNPs, the analyst is determining differences in the DNA at the sequence level and comparing those differences to any reference samples (Allen et al., 1998; Gill, 2002).

A distinct advantage of mtDNA use in forensics is that profiling can be accomplished with much smaller amounts of DNA from samples that do not traditionally provide autosomal results, such as hair shafts. Recent research efforts have resulted in more complete utilization of all the YSTR and mtDNA markers. These markers are routine analysis strategies of most crime labs.

COMBINED DNA INDEX SYSTEM AND OTHER DATABASES

In the spring of 1996, a nationwide project was launched to establish the core STR loci that would be used in the United States and eventually become the FBI's core set of 13 loci for their Combined DNA Index System (CODIS) (Butler, 2006; Budowle et al., 1998).

This database houses the DNA profiles of known and unknown individuals. It contains several indices and is used primarily to find matches to unknown profiles from crime scenes, missing persons investigations, and convicted felons. Today, CODIS houses over 15 million profiles and is a key investigatory tool in the criminal justice process.

Acceptance of the use of STRs for human identification was well received in the scientific community in its infant stages but met with some resistance in the criminal justice community. Throughout the decade of the 1990s, the forensic science community accepted STRs as an identifier of an individual but was hesitant to allow its use in court cases until the statistical analysis was strengthened and the definition of a "match" was solidified. There were several cases in the 1990s (Lynch, 2003; Schlotterer and Tautz, 1992) where analysis of DNA evidence was not allowed in court. Although not criticizing the science, judges claimed, and attorneys inevitably argued, that this type of evidence was too powerful and difficult for juries to understand without strict scrutiny. There was also uneasiness about the lack of adequately trained personnel (during the sample collection and storage phases) who understood the ease of contamination in these new analysis methods.

The mid 1990s brought about a number of changes that eased concerns over the use of DNA identification techniques in criminal cases. One such change involved moving from the non-discrete Restriction Fragment Length Polymorphism system to the PCR-fueled STR system of identification. In addition, the development of population databases and of general guidelines, procedures, and accreditation standards to be followed by the entire forensic community propelled acceptance in courtrooms. Concordance between analysts led to concordance between labs and later nations (Gill, 2002) enabling this type of analysis to become the gold standard of forensic identification systems used today.

FUTURE TECHNOLOGIES

As the use of forensic DNA analysis methodology increases so does the continuing research and innovation of these techniques. The most crucial area for examining these types of samples is to obtain additional genetic information out of smaller samples. Massively parallel sequencing (MPS) is one technology that is enhancing these testing capabilities. This technology has been used in clinical and other settings for years and is on the cusp of routinely being used in forensic laboratories (see reference: Ilumina Inc.). MPS analysis sequences the DNA strand hundreds of times and provides much more information allowing researchers to observe not only DNA sequences during STR analysis but also permits examination of coding regions within the DNA thereby providing phenotype characteristics (eye color, hair color, skin color, etc.).

There has been urgency in recent research to decrease the time it takes to process a sample. Rapid DNA analysis produces useable DNA profiles (CODIS 13 core loci) in less than 2 h (Date-Chong et al., 2016). Marketed as "bringing the laboratory to the crime scene," this technology has found its way into some police stations to aid in quickly identifying samples.

DEOXYRIBONUCLEIC ACID AND BITEMARK CASES

If a bitemark is swabbed for DNA of the biter and a profile foreign from the victim's is recovered, that DNA profile can be uploaded into the forensic or crime scene index of the national forensic DNA database, the CODIS. This national DNA database compiles and compares DNA from crime scenes and offenders within and among the 50 states and includes samples provided by federal law enforcement.

DNA from bitemarks represents the one time that statistics are routinely used in bitemark cases. It is almost always possible for the forensic biology lab to generate a statistic indicating the rarity of that DNA profile; it is not unusual for a single source profile to be so rare (i.e., 1 in greater than 6.80 trillion) that it constitutes "source attribution" for a particular individual. In the case of a profile indicating a mixture of DNA from the victim and one other person, the DNA lab may be able to generate a similar statistic. In the case where DNA from a victim and more than one other person is present, statistics may be generated by use of "probabilistic genotyping software," which calculates statistics in complex DNA mixtures.

Of course, the presence of an individual's DNA at a crime scene (as in bitemark cases—on a victim's body) is not necessarily probative of guilt. Innocent explanations for the presence of DNA must always be considered. For this reason, DNA evidence may not be compelling proof of the assailant's identify in cases where the suspect is an acquaintance coming into regular contact with the victim, or if the suspect is a parent or caregiver in a child abuse case or cases of abuse of elderly or otherwise vulnerable victims.

References

Allen, M., Engstrom, A.-S., Myers, S., Handt, O., Saldeen, T., Von Haeseler, A., Paabo, S., Gyllensten, U., 1998. Mitochondrial DNA sequencing of shed hairs and saliva on robbery caps: sensitivity and matching probabilities. Journal of Forensic Sciences 43, 453–464.

Bayes's theorem. In: Encyclopædia Britannica, 2016. Retrieved from: http://www.britannica.com/topic/Bayess-theorem.

Beam, W., Freak, G.A., 1915. On a greatly improved haemin test for blood with notes on some recently proposed methods. The Journal of Biochemistry 9, 161–170.

Budowle, B., Moretti, T.R., Niezgoda, S.J., Brown, B.L., 1998. CODIS and PCR-based short tandem repeat loci: law enforcement tools. In: Proceedings of the Second European Symposium on Human Identification, Innbruck, Austria. Promega Corporation, pp. 73–88. In: http://www.promega.com/geneticidproc/eusymp2proc/17.pdf.

Butler, J.M., 2006. Genetics and genomics of core short tandem repeat loci used in human identity testing. Journal of Forensic Science 51 (No. 2), 253–265.

Butler, J.M., 2011. Advanced Topics in Forensic DNA Typing: Methodology, first ed. Elsevier Academic Press.

Caplan, R.M., 1990. How fingerprints came into use for personal identification. Journal of the American Academy of Dermatology 23 (No. l), 109–114.

Collins, F.S., Morgan, M., Patrinos, A., 2003a. The human genome project: lessons from large-scale biology. Science 300 (No. 5617), 286–290.

Collins, J.R., Stephens, R.M., Gold, B., Long, B., Dean, M., Burt, S.K., 2003b. An exhaustive DNA micro-satellite map of the human genome using high performance computing. Genomics 82, 10–19.

Crow, J.F., 1993. Francis Galton: count and measure, measure and count. Genetics 135, 1–4.

Date-Chong, M., Hudlow, W.R., et al., 2016. Evaluation of the RapidHIT™ 200 and RapidHIT GlobalFiler® express kit for fully automated STR genotyping. Forensic Science International: Genetics 23, 1–8.

Edwards, A., Civitello, A., Hammond, H.A., Caskey, C.T., 1991. DNA typing and genetic mapping with trimeric and tetrameric tandem repeats. American Journal of Human Genetics 49 (No. 4), 746–756.

Ellegren, H., 2004. Microsatellites: simple sequences with complex evolution. Nature Reviews Genetics 5, 435–445.

Fan, H., Chu, J., 2007. A brief review of short tandem repeat mutation. Genomics, Proteomics, and Bioinformatics 5 (No. 1), 7–14.

Gill, P., 2002. Role of short tandem repeat DNA in forensic casework in the UK- past, present, and future perspectives. Biotechniques 32, 366–385.

Gill, P., Jeffreys, A.J., Werrett, D.J., 1985. Forensic application of DNA 'fingerprints. Nature 318, 577–579.

Hammond, H.A., Jin, L., Zhong, Y., Caskey, T., Chakraborty, R., 1994. Evaluation of 13 short tandem repeat loci for use in personal identification applications. American Journal of Human Genetics 55, 175–189.

Hares, D.R., 2012. Expanding the CODIS core loci in the United States. Forensic Science International: Genetics 6 (2012), e52–e54.

Hares, D.R., 2015. Selection and implementation of expanded CODIS core loci in the United States. Forensic Science International: Genetics 17, 33–34.

Ilumina Inc. Introduction to Next-Generation Sequencing Technology. http://www.illumina.com/content/dam/illumina-marketing/documents/products/illumina_sequencing_introduction.pdf.

Inman, K., Ruding, N., 1997. An Introduction to Forensic DNA Analysis. CRC Press LLC, Boca Raton FL.

International Human Genome Sequencing Consortium, 2004. Finishing the euchromatic sequence of the human genome. Nature 431, 931–945.

Jeffreys, A.J., Wilson, V., Thein, S.L., 1985a. Hypervariable 'minisatellite' regions in human DNA. Nature 314, 67–73.

Jeffreys, A.J., Wilson, V., Thein, S.L., 1985b. Individual-specific 'fingerprints' of human DNA. Nature 316, 76–79.

Karsten, M., Mogensen, H.S., et al., 2008. Comparison of five DNA quantification methods. Forensic Science International: Genetics 2, 226–230.

Kastle, J.H., Shedd, O.M., 1901. Phenolphthalin as a reagent for the oxidizing ferments. American Chemical Journal 26 (6), 526–539.

Lee, J.C., Chang, J.G., 1992. ABO genotyping by polymerase chain reaction. Journal of Forensic Science 37 (43), 1269–1275.

Lee, H.C., Ladd, C., et al., 1994. DNA typing in forensic science. I. Theory and background. American Journal of Forensic Medicine & Pathology 15 (No. 4), 269–282.

Li, R., 2008. Forensic Biology. CRC Press.

Linder, D., 1995. Famous American Trials: O.J. Simpson Trial 1995. March 25th 2008. http://www.law.umkc.edu/faculty/prqiects/ftrials/Simpson/simpson.htm.

Litt, M., Lutty, J.A., 1989. A hypervariable microsatellite revealed by in vitro amplification of a dinucleotide repeat within the cardiac muscle actin gene. American Journal of Human Genetics 44, 397–401.

Lynch, M., 2003. God's signature: DNA profiling, the new gold standard in forensic science. Endeavor 27 (No. 2), 93–97.

Meyer, E., 1903. Beiträge zur Leukocytenfrage. Fermente der Leukocyten (Contributions on the leukocyte question. Enzymes of the leukocytes). Münchener Medizinische Wochenschrift 50 (35), 1489–1493.

Ricciardi, L., Demos, M., 2015. Making a Murderer [Documentary]. Retrieved from: http://www.netflix.com.

Schlotterer, C., Tautz, D., 1992. Slippage synthesis of simple sequence DNA. Nucleic Acids Research 20 (No. 2), 211–215.

Subramanian, S., Mishra, R.K., Singh, L., 2003. Genome-wide analysis of microsatellite repeats in humans: their abundance and density in specific genomic regions. Genome Biology 4 (No. 2), R13.

Tataurov, A.V., You, Y., Owczarzy, R., 2008. Predicting ultraviolet spectrum of single stranded and double stranded deoxyribonucleic acids. Biophysical Chemistry 133 (1–3), 66–70.

Yamamoto, F., Clausen, H., White, T., Marken, J., Hakomori, S., 1990. Molecular genetic basis of the histo-blood group ABO system. Nature 345, 229–233.

Forensic Anthropology in Medico-Legal Death Investigation

Murray K. Marks[1,2], Darinka Mileusnic-Polchan[3], Heather Walsh-Haney[4]

[1]Associate Professor, Department of General Dentistry, University of Tennessee Medical Center, Knoxville, TN, United States; [2]Forensic Anthropologist, Regional Forensic Center, Knoxville, TN, United States; [3]Chief Medical Examiner for Knox & Anderson Counties, Regional Forensic Center, Knoxville, TN, United States; [4]Forensic Anthropologist, Program Leader & Associate Professor, Florida Gulf Coast University, Department of Justice Studies, Fort Myers, FL, United States

INTRODUCTION AND GRADUATE TRAINING

The expertise of the anthropologist is more than a traditional biological assessment of unidentified skeletal remains. Pathologists often request expert opinion regarding partial or complete human and nonhuman vertebrate skeletons. The anthropologist's skeletal interpretations have become a necessity to the forensic pathologist's understanding, reporting, and testifying on ante-, peri-, and postmortem trauma, taphonomy, time since death estimation, and victim identification (Blau and Ubelaker, 2008; Crowder et al., 2016; Ross and Abel, 2011; Schmitt et al., 2006). In fact, the September 2016 issue of *Academic Forensic Pathology* is devoted to the forensic anthropologist's role in the medical examiner system.

The utilization of forensic anthropology in medicolegal death investigation has evolved as a direct result of pathologists' request for information. It has generated research and a close working relationship between anthropologists and pathologists (Berryman and Lanfear, 2012;

Cunha and Cattaneo, 2006; Dirkmaat and Cabo, 2012; Ubelaker and Smialek, 2009). This teamwork has been demonstrated in the production of case-based exemplars (Fairgrieve, 1999; Buikstra and Rathbun, 1984; Reichs, 1988; Steadman, 2009), collaborative efforts in working cases involving human rights issues, and challenging recovery situations (Adams and Byrd, 2008; Cox et al., 2008; Ferlinni, 2013). The human rights work conducted by the Forensic Anthropology Foundation of Guatemala (FAFG) stands as a tacit example of the work forensic anthropologists perform in association with national and international truth commission teams. The FAFG was started by National Academy of Sciences honoree, Clyde Collins Snow. Under the direction of Fredy Peccerelli, this organization continues to discover, recover, and document the Guatemalan genocide (1960–96) This work has demonstrated the value of utilizing a holistic, collaborative approach between anthropologists, scene investigators, pathologists, and dentists at all levels of government, academia, and bureaucracy.

Anthropologists are the most prolific researchers and writers in the American Academy of Forensic Sciences (AAFS) community. Recent introductory texts describe the traditional tried and true means of establishing the biological profile as well as the collaborative and expansive nature of anthropology (Christensen and Passalacqua, 2014; Iscan and Steyn, 2013; Tersigni-Tarrant and Shirley, 2013; Thompson and Black, 2007). Anthropologists have produced specialized texts on the subjects of child abuse (Love et al., 2011; Ross and Abel, 2011), skeletal trauma (Passalacqua and Rainwater, 2015; Wedel and Galloway, 2014), fundamental forensic excavation methods (Conner, 2007; Killam, 2004), human rights trauma and archaeological methodology (Kimmerle and Baraybar, 2008; Cox et al., 2008), taphonomy (Adams and Byrd, 2014; Pokines and Symes, 2014; Haglund and Sorg, 1997), and burned remains (Schmidt and Symes, 2015). Forensic anthropologists are not saddled with the responsibilities of autopsy or clinical practice. Their focus is on the practical application of their training to answer forensically generated questions. In turn, this stimulates academic research in the field of forensic anthropology.

The traditional academic path for becoming a forensic anthropologist begins with specific graduate training in human and vertebrate skeletal biology, including musculoskeletal gross anatomy. This educational foundation is in biological anthropology with foci in bioarchaeology/biohistory, paleopathology, and archaeology, and more remote specialties like dental anthropology, primatology, nonhuman primate anatomy, paleoanthropology, and zooarchaeology, among others. Essentially, any PhD in physical anthropology with the proper postgraduate training is eligible for American Board of Forensic Anthropology (*theabfa.org*) (ABFA) certification. AAFS membership and board certification credentialing in the ABFA is the current standard of excellence achieved by anthropologists as collaborators in death investigation. In addition to skeletal biology, forensic anthropologists are trained and experienced in radiologic techniques. This permits the anthropologist to assist medical examiners in cases involving antemortem–postmortem comparisons for nondental identification, ballistic, blunt- and sharp force trauma, child abuse archaeology, surface scattered remains, and clandestine grave discovery and recovery. The forensic anthropologist's skills are enhanced through collaboration with the pathologist to understand soft tissues; dentists and oral surgeons to understand therapeutic and traumatic aspects of dentistry; orthopedic surgeons to understand mechanisms of fracture and repair; and radiologists for guidance with comparison of subtle structural skeletal nuances.

DUTIES

The traditional graduate training in human and vertebrate skeletal biology provides the anthropologist the educational skills to generate a biological assessment toward identity of human remains when extended postmortem time, temperature, and the elements have rendered visual identification and soft tissue trauma recognition impossible. The basic biological assessment of age, sex (not "gender"), ancestry estimation (not determination), and calculation of a stature range provides law enforcement a biologic profile assisting in the identification of unidentified human remains. The anthropologic assessment parameters have expanded to include ante-, peri-, and postmortem evaluation of trauma focusing on perimortem ballistic, blunt- and sharp force, and thermal injury. Unlike soft tissues whose gross and cellular integrity has an abbreviated postmortem longevity, bone and teeth retain a mineralized memory of growth, development, degenerative, and therapeutic nuances that may permit identification. These structures are key in providing peri- and postmortem indicators of traumatic events crucial to the pathologist's investigation.

HUMAN?

It is not uncommon for a quarter of an anthropologist's casework to involve nonhuman remains. While seemingly a straightforward exercise for an experienced osteologist to determine if bones and teeth are human or nonhuman, most law enforcement and crime scene personnel and even some medical examiners may be perplexed by single cranial bones or groupings of bones when the skull is lacking, not to mention commingled sets of remains. Incomplete bones or fragments pose even a greater challenge to the expert. These may require more detailed examination beyond reference literature and comparative collections used for differentiation. For example, an incomplete or shattered turtle carapace or plastron may appear like a human cranial fragment of a human cranium (see Fig. 14.6). If the remains are more complex, fragments may require a histological analysis to confirm genera. Having confronted this dilemma for a long time, anthropologists have produced comprehensive texts and comparative atlases to facilitate identification of regionally specific, nonhuman vertebrate skeletons (Adams and Crabtree, 2011; Beisaw, 2013; France, 2008, 2010, 2016). And, while these aids include description of nonhuman dental remains, the Ungar (2010) text provides the most comprehensive in-depth material identifying single and grouped mammalian dentitions.

BIOLOGICAL AFFINITY: AGE, SEX, ANCESTRY (RACE), AND STATURE

Once remains are recognized as a human "forensic" concern, they sometimes require processing to remove adherent wet/moist and/or

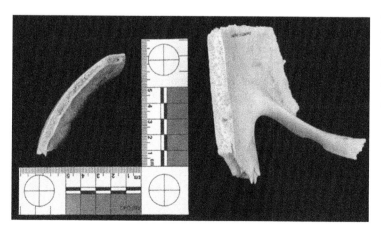

FIGURE 14.6 A near-cross section of human parietal fragment (left) and partial turtle plastron (right). Human evinces spongy bone (diploe) between the inner and outer cortical tables while the plastron lacks the spongy bone layer. Metric scale. *Photograph by Micki David.*

desiccated soft tissue to permit examination of surface detail. Age, sex, and ancestry known as the "biological affinity," (Berg and Ta'ala, 2015) is an initial and developing "gestalt" estimated during the earliest phase of analysis. Sex and ancestry is necessary for adult stature estimation techniques as they are population specific. Of note, the anthropologist estimates a "sex," not "gender" designation from decomposed and skeletal remains. The latter term is a social and cultural construct and is not biologic.

Some skeletal remains, primarily those belonging to prehistoric Native Americans, have spiritual importance to their descendent community, but no forensic significance regarding cause and manner of death. Both state and federal laws mandate protection of human biological remains, their associated mortuary cultural items, and the archaeological context beginning at the moment of discovery through the treatment/handling and return to the correctly designated descendant community. Most state archeology offices have a burial rights commission or commissioner accountable to the desires of the local, regional, or state Native American tribal authority. For example, Florida Statute §872.05 was written with the intent to protect archaeological human remains, lands, and artifacts from prehistoric and historic burials. Violators can be convicted of third-degree felonies and sentenced to prison, payment of fines, or both. Historic mortuary remains of nonnative American ancestries are also subjected to protective state laws overseen by a state archaeologist and subject to identical protection by the state and descendant community (often church elders).

Forensic anthropology follows best practice guidelines created by the Scientific Working Group for Forensic Anthropology (SWGANTH) in 2008 by a cadre of ABFA anthropologists collaborating with the Department of Defense's Central Identification Laboratory and the FBI (Adams and Lothridge, 2000). These guidelines recommend methodology and traditional qualitative and quantitative data collection procedures partially outlined in Buikstra and Ubelaker (1994) and best illustrated in White et al. (2012), and Christensen et al. (2014).

Age is most accurately estimated through the assessment of a variety of developmental and degenerative skeletal and dental features using multiple methodologies (İşcan, 1989; Iscan and Steyn, 2013; Latham and Finnegan, 2010). As long as the skeletal system is undergoing morphologic development (fetus through age 20—25), age is accessed by evaluating the degree of skeletal development. The teeth provide the most accurate indicator of age while they are undergoing development (Deutsch et al., 1983; Demirjian and Goldstein, 1976; Harris et al., 2010; Lewis and Senn, 2013; Liversidge, 2009). Once morphologic skeletal development is complete, age is assessed through the evaluation of degenerative features. Occasionally, fetal age assessment cases arise requiring the use of complex and comprehensive skeletal morphometric approaches Fazekas and Kósa (1978) including specific diaphyseal metrics (Huxley, 2010).

Epiphyseal appearance, fusion, and sequencing of closure is useful to assess age in subadult skeletons that have the presence of mixed dental development (Baker et al., 2005; Latham and Finnegan, 2010; Scheuer and Black, 2000). In the adult, degenerative regions most accurately correlating with chronological age include the pubic symphysis and auricular surface of the os coxae (Miranker, 2016). The costosternal articulation of the fourth rib and cranial sutures are much less reliable regions. Osteoarthritic accentuation of single or multiple articular margins, while generally indicating advanced age, may or may not be associated with occupational stress (İşcan and Kennedy, 1989).

Humans, like most primates and most mammals, are sexually dimorphic. While the entire juvenile female skeleton changes at puberty, pelvic maturation in size and shape (for parturition) is more pronounced than in males. In males, overall size changes are consistent with muscle attachment site development/reinforcement (White et al., 2012). A fully mature (adult) female pelvis will be smaller and have a "smaller" more paedomorphic skeleton than a male of similar age. Primary pelvic features utilized in sex estimation include the ventral arc, subpubic concavity, ischiopubic ramus of the pubis, and auricular surface and sciatic notch of the ilium. Secondary regions include the skull where the muscle attachments of the nuchal, mastoid, and gonial regions are robust in the males and gracile in the females. These features help clarify pelvic findings. Because adult females are smaller, have less muscle mass, and smaller joint surfaces than males, "smaller" female and "larger" male skeletons can be quantitatively differentiated through detailed metric analyses. Jantz and Ousley (2005) developed *ForDisc*, a computer software program currently in its third version, permitting population-specific, sex- and stature-discriminant function analyses to estimate sex.

For several generations, forensic anthropologists estimated "race" as part of the biological assessment. This term originated from the race concept entrenched in the history of biological anthropology (Gill and Rhine, 1990; Little and Kennedy, 2010; Marks and Synstelien, 2005; Ta'ala 2015). Today, the more politically correct terminology is "ancestry" or population affinity/membership. However, when using either term, anthropologists performing race analysis are cognizant of the difference between the biological and sociological constructs of population identity. The most difficult skeletal component in biological assessment to research, study, and ascertain is race, yet it is as relevant as age, sex, stature, and pathology when providing law enforcement with criteria to help secure records to identify the unknown.

The craniofacial skeleton is the region targeted for estimating ancestry. Previously, the seemingly straightforward assignment of American Whites, Blacks, Native Americans, and Asians was utilized. Today, analyses have become increasingly more challenging with the admixture, microevolutionary/secular change and a growing influx of immigrants, namely Latin American/Hispanic populations, into the country (see Berg and Ta'ala, 2015). More than ever, the anthropologist is now concerned with the detailed examination of Hispanic-based populations and their osteological parameters (Anderson and Spradley, 2016). The traditional morphoscopic trait list relied upon by Gill and Rhine (1990) has evolved into complex analyses (Hefner, 2015) and quantitative methods using *ForDisc* (Jantz and Ousley, 2005).

Stature estimation is a simple mathematical calculation or software-based exercise derived from measurements of complete or portions of single or grouped long bones. The rationale of estimating living stature is plausible given the positive correlation between height and long bone length. The pelvic and pectoral bones of the appendicular skeleton provide the most accurate correlation to stature. However, vertebrae, metacarpals, tarsals, and metatarsals may be utilized, but these methods produce larger error estimates. Estimation of sex and ancestry is required to apply the appropriate population-specific regression equation and standard error. Complete and/or segments of long bones are measured on an osteometric board or a sliding caliper. Range of variation (prediction intervals including 90%—99% of the target population) are calculated using the same *ForDisc* program applicable for craniometric sex and ancestry estimation.

TRAUMA

The forensic pathologist's interpretation of perimortem homicide events relies upon skeletal trauma adjacent to injured soft tissues. In a majority of trauma cases involving bone, the damage to bone has greater postmortem longevity over the surrounding soft tissue and becomes the "go-to" medium to reconstruct causation. The combined high mineral and collagenous component of the skeleton insures that bone retains a memory of impact, penetration, and perforation even in the most arduous postmortem environments. Arguably, no other realm of the anthropologist's expertise has evolved and expanded as quickly as perimortem bone trauma reconstruction. Recent texts by Kimmerle and Baraybar (2008), Passalacqua and Rainwater (2015), and Wedel and Galloway (2014) underscore the importance of understanding perimortem bone trauma. Most introductory forensic anthropology textbooks, taphonomy texts (Pokines and Symes, 2014), and thermal breakage/disturbance texts (Schmidt and Symes, 2015) have chapters strictly devoted to this topic (Dirkmaat, 2012a).

Published surgical and trauma accounts reported by orthopedic, oral surgery, and otolaryngology physicians provide the clinical, biostructural, and physiological roadmaps that guide the anthropologist's understanding and context of fracture. Galloway's (1999) first text and Wedel and Galloway's (2014) text illustrate, bone-by-bone, the clinical and interdisciplinary application of bone trauma mechanics. Examples include: complex comminution of the small, fragile bones of the internal midface, greenstick fractures from ligature, or manual strangulation that may mark the hyoid and laryngeal cartilages (partially or completely ossified over time) (Fig. 14.7), to the load-bearing physics of fracturing in long bones.

Bone has a predictable response to the three main sources of perimortem trauma: ballistic, blunt-, and sharp force trauma (including postmortem saw mark analysis in dismemberment). The sequence and microscopic fracture pattern(s) inform the anthropologist to direction, proximity, and magnitude of force of the device used to injure the tissue. In addition, the effects of thermal injury have become a specialized area of interpretation (Schmidt and Symes, 2015).

No other death engenders the immediate attention, humbled respect, and professional vigilance more than an abused infant or child. Ross and Abel (2011) demonstrate the necessary breadth of the interdisciplinary collaboration. One key arena of study in abuse victims focuses on bone healing rates of the fracture callus from gross (Love et al., 2011; Ubelaker and Montaperto, 2011) to histological evaluation (Marks et al., 2009). These researchers are involved with interpreting the mechanism of osseous repair to estimate time since injury for estimating an acute or chronic history of abuse. Kleinman (2015) is the landmark forensic pathology reference manual portraying key soft and mineralized tissue trauma.

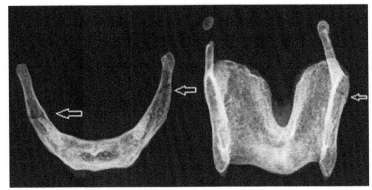

FIGURE 14.7 Radiographs of the hyoid (left) and ossified thyroid cartilage (right) showing perimortem trauma (*white arrows*). The hyoid contains bilateral fractures to the greater horns while the thyroid reveals a fracture to the left lamina and posterior border. *Photograph by Austin Polonitza.*

TAPHONOMY

Estimating a postmortem interval or time since death is of critical value to the forensic pathologist for linkage of a victim with a suspect(s). An individual may be included or excluded as a suspect if it can be determined approximately how long the victim has been dead. Once the traditional early soft tissue indicators (*algor-* and *rigor mortis*) of time since death have diminished, time since death estimates rely upon decomposing soft tissues and the appearance of skeletal surfaces. Haglund and Sorg (1997) and more recently Pokines and Symes (2014) have produced texts demonstrating the tremendous breadth of case-based and experimental research that anthropologists have undertaken in soft and mineralized gross and histological tissue deterioration.

The University of Tennessee's Forensic Anthropology Center has managed an outdoor human decomposition research facility for more than 30 years (Shirley et al., 2011) and has long been the research center for many of these longitudinal research studies. Most forensic pathologists understand postmortem interval from a cross-sectional perspective. Longitudinal research projects permit a greater qualitative and quantitative appreciation for the dynamics of decomposition. Besides the University of Tennessee, academic forensic anthropologists at Texas State University, Michigan State University, Western Carolina University, and Boston University have developed decomposition research facilities and laboratories to study the chronological relationship of decomposition to terrestrial and aquatic temperature, humidity, body position/coverage, etc., not to mention the entomological nuances that fine-tune the estimation of time since death (Amendt et al., 2010; Byrd and Castner, 2002; Rivers and Dahlem, 2014).

POSITIVE IDENTIFICATION

Nondental positive identification from individualistic skeletal features is a common, long-standing, anthropological practice requiring graduate training in radiology and in gross morphology. With guidance from the pathologist, radiologist, and/or orthopedic surgeon, the anthropologist can pattern recognize subtle, incongruent contours in cortical and trabecular structures under inspection. This technique to obtain identification requires an antemortem, pre- or postsurgical diagnostic radiograph and utilizes a similar point-by-point comparative approach as in dental radiographic identification techniques.

The most common antemortem radiographs utilized by anthropologists for identification come from A-P head films illustrating frontal sinus configuration, assessing orthopedic surgical appliance intervention—placement, or to discover a series of normal or pathological cortical and/or trabecular bone structural nuances. For example, because cervical and upper thoracic spinous processes tend to be captured in antemortem A-P head films, and the standard operating procedure for many medical examiner offices include A-P postmortem "presentation" radiographs of the same anatomical areas, the contour of the spinous processes and the presence of osteophytes and enthesophytes on vertebral body margins have proven useful in positive identification (Derrick et al., 2015; Watamaniuk and Rogers, 2010). A single antemortem diagnostic skeletal feature, developmentally normal or pathologically derived, may not satisfy criteria for positive identification, but several such findings confer identification.

Advanced digital imaging modalities, i.e., CT and MRI (Thali et al., 2010), aid in identification. Qualification (morphology) and quantification (measurement) of frontal sinus structure provides similar individualized characteristics for identification as the maxillary sinus floor viewed in dental bitewing and/or panorex radiographs. Surgeons assist in prosthetic appliance recognition and the clarification of presurgical diagnostic radiographic features. Dental or skeletal manipulation of the decedent/specimen, whether fleshed, decomposed or skeletal, is necessary to reproduce the most accurate angle for comparative pattern matching to the antemortem radiograph. With increased dental and medical use of cone-beam computed tomography, anthropologists are becoming more familiar with these images and their use in postmortem comparison techniques (Sarment and Christensen, 2014).

THE SCENE

The autopsy begins at the crime scene where the forensic pathologist is responsible for the decedent, clothing, location, and the recovery process. Although secured and protected by uniformed officers, the crime scene belongs to the forensic pathologist, medical examiner, or coroner regardless of their presence. The nonmedical experts who process the scene (death investigator, criminalist, detective, anthropologist, etc.) act as agents for the medical examiner/coroner in the collection of evidence. Forensic pathologists rely heavily upon the expertise of the death investigator and the anthropologist.

By virtue of the extensive archaeological field training of the anthropologist, decomposed and skeletal surface scatter and buried remains are properly recovered. Learning about bones in a discovery context, albeit archaeological, is far more realistic than the study of bones and teeth in an anthropology or anatomy laboratory. Discovering, recovering, and documenting skeletal remains in a burial context, prehistoric or historic, are an unheralded training experience for a clandestine forensic recovery. The anthropologist's crime scene duties may include: determining and documenting scene surface scatter significance (Dirkmaat, 2012a; Schultz, 2012), evidence collection (Hochrein, 2012), GRP (ground penetrating radar) for burial discovery, and GIS technology (geographic information system) from surface and burial documentation during recovery. Forensic archaeology has become a near standalone discipline (Dirkmaat, 2012b) within the AAFS Anthropology Section.

Unless the dentist goes to the crime scene, reliance on the anthropologist to recognize and recover the dentition is necessary.

TESTIMONY

Because the complexity of analyzing skeletal remains has increased, specifically in regard to perimortem-based trauma, the frequency the anthropologist testifies on behalf of their findings is increasing. As mentioned, the pathologist welcomes the opinion(s) of the anthropologist to assist in her/his conclusions. While the pathologist is ultimately responsible for the investigation, anthropological findings are often part of the collaboration between the pathologist, anthropologist, and attorney. When the legal team delineates the direction of the formal proceedings, it is up to the prosecution (or defense), under advisement of the pathologist, whether the anthropologist's contribution would be a positive addition to, or create confusion related to, the pathologist's rendition of facts in the courtroom. Most anthropological testimony is for the prosecution and, depending upon jurisdiction, he or she may be called several times a year to present their findings in conjunction with or independent of the pathologist's testimony.

As an expert witness, the anthropologist should rely on the exact skeletal findings as a basis for their testimony. Two common testimony requests posed primarily by the defense have been made to the senior author (Marks): "From your findings, can you establish a cause of death?" and "How did you make the positive identification (when teeth were the medium of identification)?" Whether there is mention in the anthropologist's report on either topic of those expert's findings, those two areas are the expertise of the pathologist and dentist, respectively. Knowing and understanding the boundaries of your expertise is crucial to the success of an expert witness. Being lured outside those boundaries provides fertile grounds for failure as an expert witness. An astute attorney, creating the slightest doubt in the jury's mind about your statements, may place your whole testimony in jeopardy—"Well Professor, if you are not sure about that, what else are you not sure about?"

Just as each scene recovery situation, laboratory analysis and findings, and the degree and mechanism of trauma differ, so are jury composition and court room dynamics. In the past, the anthropologist has not only presented specific findings primarily about trauma but also regarding discovery and recovery of remains. The direct testimony was lengthy and was challenged in cross and redirect testimony. Occasionally, attorneys begin with page one of a forensic anthropology report reading each sentence so that the jury can follow. This has implications well beyond results and discussion in report writing. Identification procedures performed by the dentist on a decedent are often stipulated; however, very little of the bone trauma findings are accepted without discussion. Therefore the anthropologist typically appears on the stand more frequently than the dentist.

A final note involves the expert presentation of evidential remains in the courtroom. The judge rules what biological evidence is inflammatory to a jury. In Tennessee, the judge may allow the victim's bones and teeth, especially when traumatized, to be presented and explained to a jury. While powerpoint images seem more visually practical, using the actual remains is a humbling experience—especially when the victim's relatives are in the gallery. It is important to remember the audience you are testifying before and to tactically include the judge in your presentation as s(he) needs to witness every detail shared with the jury. Keep in mind, a courtroom is not a university classroom or a demonstration or lecture for law enforcement or medical examiners. Jury composition

and education level ranges from less than a high school education to well-educated professionals. Finally, remember that the remains become the property/evidence of the state as soon as the pathologist or anthropologist removes them from the scene and/or body; and at trial, when entered as an exhibit they likely become part of the legal system for years.

THE ANTHROPOLOGIST AND THE DENTITION

Teeth belong to the skeleton. The reverse is not true. To that end in the Medical Examiner/Coroner system, forensic odontology is part of forensic anthropology and both are part of forensic pathology. Forensic anthropologists know far more about teeth than dentists know about bones. Our training, from the archaeological and crime scene burial and surface scatter setting to the laboratory, allows us to recognize, recover, and document the entire skeleton(s) and reconstruct loose, fractured, and compromised dentitions. And while some forensic anthropologists are also dental anthropologists, we are not forensic dentists and are not familiar with the clinical subtleties that allow positive identification. Hence, we do not and will not attempt positive identifications. Our duty is to understand the ante-, peri-, and postmortem traumatic and taphonomic agents impacting the victim and getting those remains into the hands of the expert. One should utilize the anthropologist's skills from the introduction of remains at the scene and nurture their basic dental knowledge to enrich your knowledge base and the consultation you do for the forensic pathologist. Until dentists go to crime scenes, it is the anthropologist's responsibility to identify, assemble, and recover the dentition of skeletal, decomposed, incinerated, or disfigured victims. We are trained in recognition of the dentition and our main goal is recovery for the expert. For the dentist, it does not get any better than that.

References

Adams, B.J., Byrd, J.E., 2008. Recovery, Analysis, and Identification of Commingled Human Remains. Humana Press (Springer Science+Business Media, LLC), New Jersey.

Adams, B., Byrd, J., 2014. Commingled Human Remains: Methods in Recovery, Analysis, and Identification. Academic Press (Elsevier), New York, NY.

Adams, B., Crabtree, P., 2011. Comparative Osteology: A Laboratory and Field Guide of Common North American Animals. Academic Press (Elsevier), Amsterdam.

Adams, D.E., Lothridge, K.L., 2000. Scientific working groups. Forensic Science Communications 2 (3).

Amendt, J., Campobasso, C.P., Goff, M.L., Grassberger, M., 2010. Current Concepts in Forensic Entomology. Springer Science+Business Media, Heidelberg.

Anderson, B.E., Spradley, M.K., 2016. The role of the anthropologist in the identification of migrant remains in the American Southwest. Academic Forensic Pathology 6 (3), 432–438.

Baker, B.J., Dupras, R.L., Tocheri, M.W., 2005. Osteology of Infants and Children. Texas A&M University Press, College Station, TX.

Beisaw, A.M., 2013. Identifying and Interpreting Animal Bones: A Manual. Texas A&M University Press, College Station, TX.

Berg, G.E., Ta'ala, S.C., 2015. Biological Affinity in Forensic Identification of Human Skeletal Remains, beyond Black and White. CRC Press, Boca Raton, FL.

Berryman, H.E., Lanfear, A.K., 2012. Forensic anthropologists in medical examiner's and coroner's offices: a history (Chapter 26). In: Dirkmaat, D.C. (Ed.), A Companion to Forensic Anthropology. Wiley-Blackwell John Wiley & Sons, Ltd., UK, pp. 534–548.

Blau, S.E., Ubelaker, D.H., 2008. Forensic Anthropology and Archaeology. West Coast Press, San Diego, CA.

Buikstra, J.E., Rathbun, T.A. (Eds.), 1984. Human Identification: Case Studies in Forensic Anthropology. Thomas, Springfield, IL.

Buikstra, J.E., Ubelaker, D.H., 1994. Standards for Data Collection from Human Skeletal Remains. Arkansas Archaeological Survey Report Research Series, Fayetteville, AR.

Byrd, J.H., Castner, J.L., 2002. Forensic Entomology: The Utility of Arthropods in Legal Investigations. CRC Press, Boca Raton, FL.

Christensen, A.M., Passalacqua, N.V., Bartelink, E., 2014. Forensic Anthropology: Current Methods and Practice. Academic Press, San Diego.

Conner, M.A., 2007. Forensic Methods, Excavation for the Archaeologists and Investigator. Alta Mira Press (A Division of Rowman & Littlefield Publishers, Inc., Lanham, UK.

Cox, M., Flavel, A., Hanson, I., Laver, J., Wessling, R., 2008. The Scientific Investigation of Mass Graves, Towards Protocols and Standard Operating Procedures. Cambridge University Press, New York.

Crowder, C.M., Wiersma, J.M., Adams, B.J., Austin, D.E., Love, J.C., 2016. The utility of forensic anthropology in the medical Examiner's office. Academic Forensic Pathology 2016 (3), 349–360.

Cunha, E., Cattaneo, C., 2006. Forensic anthropology and forensic pathology: the state of the art (Chapter 3). In: Anthropology, F., Medicine (Eds.), Complementary Sciences from Recovery to Cause of Death. Humana Press, New Jersey, pp. 39–56.

Demirjian, A., Goldstein, H., 1976. New systems for dental maturing based on seven and four teeth. Annals of Human Biology 3 (5), 411–421.

Derrick, S.M., Raxer, M.H., Hipp, J.A., Goel, P., Chan, E.F., Love, J.C., Wiersema, J.M., Akella, N.S., 2015. Development of a computer-assisted radiographic identification method using the lateral cervical and lumbar spine. Journal of Forensic Sciences 60, 5–12.

Deutsch, D., Pe'er, E., Gedalia, I., 1983. Changes in size, morphology and weight of human anterior teeth during the fetal period. Growth 48 (1), 74–85.

Dirkmaat, D.C (Ed.), 2012a. A Companion to Forensic Anthropology. Wiley-Blackwell-Blackwell Companions to Anthropology. A John Wiley & Sons, Ltd., UK.

Dirkmaat, D.C., 2012b. Documenting context at the outdoor crime scene: Why bother? (Chapter 2). In: Dirkmaat, D.C. (Ed.), A Companion to Forensic Anthropology. Wiley-Blackwell-Blackwell Companions to Anthropology. A John Wiley & Sons, UK, pp. 48–65.

Dirkmaat, D.C., Cabo, L.L., 2012. Forensic anthropology: embracing a new paradigm (Chapter 1). In: Dirkmaat, D.C. (Ed.), A Companion to Forensic Anthropology. Wiley-Blackwell Blackwell Companions to Anthropology, A John Wiley & Sons, Ltd., UK, pp. 3–40.

Fairgrieve, S.I., 1999. Forensic Osteological Analysis, a Book of Case Studies. Charles C. Thomas, Springfield, IL.

Fazekas, I.G., Kósa, F., 1978. Forensic Fetal Osteology. Akademiai Kiado, Budapest, Hungary.

Ferlinni, A.S., 2013. Forensic Archaeology and Human Rights Violations. Charles C. Thomas, Springfield, IL.

France, D.L., 2008. Human and Nonhuman Bone Identification: A Color Atlas. CRC Press, Boca Raton, FL.

France, D.L., 2010. Human and Nonhuman Bone Identification: A Concise Field Guide. CRC Press, Boca Raton, FL.

France, D.L., 2016. Comparative Bone Identification: Human Subadult to Nonhuman. CRC Press, Boca Raton, FL.

Galloway, A., 1999. Broken Bones, Anthropological Analysis of Blunt Force Trauma. Charles C. Thomas, Springfield, IL.

Gill, G.W., Rhine, S., 1990. Skeletal Attribution of Race: Methods for Forensic Anthropology. Maxwell Museum Anthropological Papers no. 4. University of New Mexico, Albuquerque.

Haglund, W.D., Sorg, M.H., 1997. Forensic Taphonomy: The Postmortem Fate of Human Remains. CRC Press, Boca Raton, FL.

Harris, E.F., Mincer, H.H., Anderson, K.M., Senn, D.R., 2010. Age estimation from oral and dental structures. In: Senn, D.R., Stimson, P.G. (Eds.), Forensic Dentistry, second ed. pp. 263–303.

Hefner, J.T., 2015. Cranial morphoscopic traits and the assessment of american black, american white, and hispanic ancestry (Chapter 3). In: Berg, G.E., Ta'ala, S.C. (Eds.), Biological Affinity in Forensic Identification of Human Skeletal Remains, beyond Black and White. CRC Press (Taylor & Francis Group), Boca Raton, FL, pp. 27–43.

Hochrein, M.J., 2012. Crime scene perspective: Collecting evidence in the context of the criminal incident (Chapter 5). In: Dirkmaat, D.C. (Ed.), A Companion to Forensic Anthropology. Wiley-Blackwell-Blackwell Companions to Anthropology. A John Wiley & Sons, Ltd., UK, pp. 101–112.

Huxley, A.K., 2010. Estimation of age from fetal remains (Chapter 10). In: Latham, K.E., Finnegan, M. (Eds.), Age Estimation of the Human Skeleton. Charles C. Thomas, Springfield, IL, pp. 147–160.

Iscan, M.Y., Kennedy, K.A.R., 1989. Reconstruction of Life from the Skeleton. Wiley-Liss.

İşcan, M.Y., 1989. Age Markers in the Human Skeleton. Charles C. Thomas, Springfield, IL.

İşcan, M.Y., Steyn, M., 2013. The Human Skeleton in Forensic Medicine, third ed. Charles C. Thomas, Springfield, IL.

Jantz, R.L., Ousley, S.D., 2005. Fordisc 3.0 Personal Computer Forensic Discriminant Functions. The University of Tennessee, Knoxville.

Killam, E.W., 2004. The Detection of Human Remains, second ed. Charles C. Thomas, Springfield, IL.

Kimmerle, E.H., Baraybar, J.P., 2008. Skeletal Trauma, Identification of Injuries Resulting from Human Rights Abuse and Armed Conflict. CRC Press, Boca Raton, FL.

Kleinman, P.K., 2015. Diagnostic Imaging of Child Abuse, third ed. Cambridge University Press, Cambridge, UK.

Latham, K.E., Finnegan, M., 2010. Age Estimation of the Human Skeleton. Charles C. Thomas, Springfield, IL.

Lewis, J.M., Senn, D.R., 2013. Dental age estimation (Chapter 8). In: Senn, D.R., Weems, R.A. (Eds.), Manual of Forensic Odontology, fifth ed. CRC Press, Boca Raton, pp. 211–256.

Little, M.A., Kennedy, K.A.R., 2010. Histories of American Physical Anthropology in the Twentieth Century. Lexington Books, Plymouth, UK.

Liversidge, H.M., 2009. Permanent tooth formation as a method of estimating age. In: Koppe, T., Meyer, G., Alt, K.W. (Eds.), Comparative Dental Morphology. In: Sharpe, P. (Ed), Frontiers of Oral Biology, vol. 13. Karger, Basel, Switzerland, pp. 153–157.

Love, J.C., Derrick, S.M., Wiersema, J.M., 2011. Skeletal Atlas of Child Abuse. Humana Press-Springer Science+Business Media, New York.

Marks, M.K., Synstelien, J.A., 2005. Determination of racial affinity. In: Payne-James, J., Byard, R., Corey, T., Henderson, C. (Eds.), Encyclopedia of Forensic and Legal Medicine. Elsevier Science, pp. 136–142.

Marks, M.K., Mileusnic, D., Marden, K., 2009. Forensic osteology of child abuse (Chapter 15). In: Steadman, D.W. (Ed.), Hard Evidence: Case Studies in Forensic Anthropology, second ed. Prentice-Hall, Upper Saddle River, NJ, pp. 205–220.

Miranker, M., 2016. A comparison of different age estimation methods on the adult pelvis. Journal of Forensic Sciences 61, 1173–1179. https://doi.org/10.1111/1556-4029.13130.

Passalacqua, N.V., Rainwater, C.W., 2015. Skeletal Trauma Analysis: Case Studies in Context. Wiley-Blackwell/John Wiley & Sons, Ltd., West Sussex, UK.

Pokines, J.T., Symes, S.A., 2014. Manual of Forensic Taphonomy. CRC Press, Boca Raton, FL.

Reichs, K.A., 1988. Forensic Osteology. Charles C. Thomas, Springfield, IL.

Rivers, D.B., Dahlem, G.A., 2014. The Science of Forensic Entomology. Wiley Blackwell.

Ross, A.H., Abel, S.M., 2011. The Juvenile Skeleton in Forensic Abuse Investigations. Humana Press-Springer Science+Business Media, LLC, New York.

Sarment, D.P., Christensen, A.M., 2014. The use of cone beam computed tomography in forensic radiology. Journal Forensic Radiology and Imaging 2 (4), 173–181.

Scheuer, L., Black, S., 2000. Developmental Juvenile Osteology. Academic Press, San Diego.

Schmidt, C.W., Symes, S.A., 2015. The Analysis of Burned Human Remains, second ed. Academic Press, San Diego.

Schmitt, A., Cunha, E., Pinheiro, J., 2006. Forensic Anthropology and Medicine: Complementary Sciences from Recovery to Cause of Death. Humana Press, NJ.

Schultz, J.J., 2012. Determining the forensic significance of skeletal remains (Chapter 3). In: Dirkmaat, D.C. (Ed.), A Companion to Forensic Anthropology. Wiley-Blackwell-Blackwell Companions to Anthropology. A John Wiley & Sons, Ltd., UK, pp. 66–84.

Shirley, N.R., Wilson, R.J., Jantz, L.M., 2011. Cadaver use at the univeristy of tennessee's anthropological research facility. Clinical Anatomy 24 (3), 372–380.

Steadman, D.W. (Ed.), 2009. Hard Evidence: Case Studies in Forensic Anthropology, second ed. Prentice-Hall, Upper Saddle River, NJ.

Ta'ala, S.C., 2015. A brief history of the race concept in physical anthropology (Chapter 1). In: Black, B., White, Ge, B., Ta'ala, S.C. (Eds.), Biological Affinity in Forensic Identification of Human Skeletal Remains. CRC Press (Taylor & Francis Group), Boca Raton, FL, pp. 1–16.

Tersigni-Tarrant, M.A., Shirley, N.R., 2013. Forensic Anthropology, an Introduction. CRC Press, Boca Raton, FL.

Thali, M.J., Viner, M.D., Brogdon, B.G., 2010. Brogdon's Forensic Radiology, second ed. CRC Press, Boca Raton, FL.

Thompson, T., Black, S., 2007. Forensic Human Identification, an Introduction. CRC Press (Taylor & Francis Group), Boca Raton, FL.

Ubelaker, D.H., Montaperto, K.M., 2011. Biomechanical and remodeling factors in the interpretation of fractures in juveniles (Chapter 4). In: Ross, A.H., Abel, S.M. (Eds.), The Juvenile Skeleton in Forensic Abuse Investigations. Humana Press-Springer Science+Business Media, LLC, London, pp. 33–48.

Ubelaker, D.H., Smialek, J.E., 2009. The interface of forensic anthropology and forensic pathology in trauma interpretation (Chapter 17). In: Steadman, D.W. (Ed.), Hard Evidence: Case Studies in Forensic Anthropology. Prentice Hall, Upper Saddle River, NJ, pp. 221–224.

Ungar, P.S., 2010. Mammal Teeth: Origins, Evolution and Diversity. The Johns Hopkins University Press, Baltimore, MD.

Watamaniuk, L., Rogers, T., 2010. Positive personal identification of human remains based on thoracic vertebral margin morphology. Journal of Forensic Sciences 55, 1162–1170. https://doi.org/10.1111/j, 1556-4029.2010.01447.x.

Wedel, V.L., Galloway, A., 2014. Broken Bones: Anthropological Analysis of Blunt Force Trauma, second ed. Charles C. Thomas, Springfield, IL.

White, T.D., Black, M.T., Folkens, P.A., 2012. Human Osteology, third ed. Elsevier Academic Press, Boston.

Further Reading

Black, S., Aggrawal, A., Payne-James, J., 2010. Age Estimation in the Living, the Practitioner's Guide. Wiley-Blackwell, West Sussex, UK.

Crowder, C.M., Stout, S., 2011. Bone Histology — an Anthropological Perspective. CRC Press, Boca Raton, FL.

Mincer, H., Harris, E., Berryman, H.E., 1993. The A.B.F.O. Study of third molar development and its use as an estimator of chronological age. Journal of Forensic Sciences 38 (2), 379–390.

Pilloud, M.A., Hefner, J.T., 2016. Biological distance analysis: forensic and bioarchaeological perspectives. Academic Press, San Diego.

Educational Outcomes

Edward E. Herschaft[1,2]

[1]Department of Biomedical Sciences, UNLV School of Dental Medicine, Las Vegas, NV, United States;
[2]Forensic Odontology Consultant, Clark County Office of the Coroner/Medical Examiner, Las Vegas, NV, United States

Goals are measured using learning objectives.
Gail March, PhD

By completing the chapters in this textbook the reader will be able to achieve the cognitive, psychomotor, and affective competencies required to function as a dentist in a forensic setting by attaining the following abilities:

CHAPTER 1: FORENSIC SCIENCES AND FORENSIC IDENTIFICATION

1. Evaluate the various perspectives of forensic science and identification based on a law enforcement, prosecution, or defense approach to the discipline and its practices.
2. Describe the terms forensic science, forensic analysis, and forensic identification.
3. Compare the scientific disciplines/analytical methodologies that can facilitate human forensic identification.
4. List the three ways that information preserved from forensic analysis of bitemark injuries can assist in a legal investigation.
5. Describe how a "positive identification" of a victim resolves legal issues and provides closure to their family.
6. Summarize the history of bitemark litigation involving modern cases since 1954.
7. Discuss the problem related to the challenges to bitemark testimony initiated by postconviction advocacy groups and their reliance on the 2009 National Academy of Science (NAS) advisory report, *"Strengthening Forensic Science in the United States: A Path Forward,"* to support the claim that bitemark analysis is scientifically unsound.
8. Describe the cases in which federal and state courts have interpreted the NAS report regarding pattern-matching evidence to signify that it *does not* "imply that evidence of forensic expert identifications should be excluded from judicial proceedings until the particular methodology has been validated."
9. Assess the impact of the "moratorium" regarding admission of bitemark analysis and comparison evidence issued by the Texas Forensic Science Commission in 2016.
10. How have popular culture and the media contributed to the lay public's often flawed perception that forensic science practitioners are infallible regarding analysis of patterned evidence.
11. Contrast how opinions and conclusions generated by forensic scientists differ from those proffered by other scientific disciplines.
12. Summarize the issues described in the William Richards (2001) homicide case, which exemplify situations that may lead to a false conviction based on forensic dental evidence.

13. Describe how the evolution of forensic science in the 20th century led to potential manipulation of the criminal justice system to secure a conviction.
14. Illustrate how forensic DNA evidence differs from other scientific evidence in regard to its ability to solve cases through database comparison and reliance on statistical probability even when there is no suspect.
15. Compare results of the 2009 NAS publication regarding the state of forensic science with those of the report from the President's Council of Advisors on Science and Technology, which focused on the science supporting forensic odontology, fingerprint analysis, hair analysis, DNA, firearms analysis, and shoeprint identification
16. Assess whether the current state of forensic science is truly impartial and unbiased, considering the concept that forensic science is used to assist the state in the development of its case against a suspect
17. Indicate how the current development of forensic science investigation can be used to definitively identify perpetrators, exonerate the innocent, and improve the justice system for all who come in contact with it.

CHAPTER 2: HISTORY AND SCOPE OF FORENSIC ODONTOLOGY

1. List the historical cases that reflect the evolution of forensic odontology from the era of the Roman Empire to the middle of the 19th century.
2. Identify the various procedures that a forensic dentist may have to perform within the scope of the practice of forensic odontology.
3. Describe how dental age assessment can assist the legal community in identification of missing and unidentified individuals, determination of assignment of judicial matters to adult or juvenile court, and

evaluation of an individual's status prior to deportation.
4. Discuss the role of the dentist in the recognition of signs and symptoms of human abuse.
5. Clarify the rationale for review and revision of bitemark analysis methods and techniques by the American Board of Forensic Odontology (ABFO).
6. Explain the role of the forensic odontologist as a potential expert witness in civil and criminal litigation cases.

CHAPTER 3: DENTAL IDENTIFICATION AND RADIOGRAPHIC PITFALLS

1. Explain the role of the forensic odontologist when providing an opinion regarding the identity of a decedent or living individual based on dental scientific best practices.
2. List the important reasons for determining a positive identification for a decedent or living individual.
3. Compare and contrast the five accepted methods of identification, including the scientific acceptance and morphometric advantages and disadvantages of each procedure.
4. Identify the components related to the collection and preservation of postmortem dental evidence.
5. Compare the accepted procedures for accessing the oral cavity of viewable human remains as opposed to those that are nonviewable.
6. Describe the protocol for ethically and professionally performing a surgical exposure of the oral cavity to gain access.
7. List the five photographic views required to document the dentition of a decedent.
8. Discuss the rationale for obtaining a complete series of correctly oriented and exposed periapical and bitewing

postmortem dental radiographs and others (i.e., panoramic, occlusal, and computed tomography radiographs) if available.

9. Evaluate the significance of incorporating postmortem cone beam computed tomography (CBCT) imaging technology into the future radiological armamentarium of forensic odontologists.
10. Describe the components of a forensic odontology autopsy kit.
11. List the five factors that should be illustrative components of the postmortem dental record and can be supplemented by a narrative description using standardized dental nomenclature and numbering systems.
12. Summarize the requirements for collection, assessment, and retention of antemortem dental records.
13. Identify the sources for acquisition of antemortem dental records and the components of these records, which may be used for comparison with postmortem dental records.
14. Assess the problems that may be associated with the transmission of antemortem digital radiographs, including Digital Imaging and Communications in Medicine (DICOM) accessibility, the transfer of potentially reversible phosphor storage plate images, and radiographic film orientation dot placement.
15. Illustrate the advantages provided by CBCT technology regarding image magnification and distortion that two-dimensional radiographic imaging does not provide.
16. Contrast the advantages and disadvantages of antemortem orthodontic and head and neck medical radiographs, including medical CT images, when comparing data from this evidence to postmortem dental radiographs.

CHAPTER 4: FORENSIC PHOTOGRAPHY

1. Recognize the importance of proper collection, preservation, and accurate reproduction of visible photographic evidence acquired by the forensic odontologist in identification, bitemark, and abuse cases.
2. Understand the basics of photography and the operation of the digital camera.
3. Describe the physics related to the optics of lenses and image formation.
4. Define the terms digital single lens reflex (DSLR) camera, point and shoot camera, iris diaphragm, aperture, f-stop, focal point, depth of field, diffraction, spherical aberration, sharpest acuity, sensor, pixels, high resolution, dynamic range, "crop factor," ISO settings, through the lens exposure, macro (close-up photography), reproduction ratio, and hot boot.
5. Compare the four types of lenses and their use in the acquisition of forensic dental photographic evidence.
6. Explain the term perspective distortion and lens selection factors and positional requirements that influence its development.
7. List the four sensor sizes commonly used in DSLR cameras.
8. Describe the relationship between sensor size and determination of optimal focal length for a given task.
9. List the nine advantages of digital sensors over film, including archiving and proof that evidence has not been falsified.
10. Identify the four exposure variables that the photographer can control and how each influences the contrast of an image.
11. Indicate why spectral highlights (glare) are created by flash photography.
12. Select the appropriate formula to calculate the required lens extension to achieve the desired magnification of a macro photography digital image.
13. Evaluate how "flat field" macro lenses can correct perspective distortion and softened focus at the margins of an image while optimizing depth of field using hyperfocal distance techniques.
14. Identify the components of the electromagnetic spectrum, the four effects (reflection, absorption, transmission,

fluorescence) that this radiation has on an object, and how its wave lengths are applied in forensic photography.

15. Appraise how DSLR cameras are designed to prevent recording of unwanted ultraviolet and infrared (IR) wavelengths.

16. Explain why high-resolution images offer the most versatility in terms of ability to enlarge and crop photographs and produce sharp images.

17. Create a standard operating protocol and methodology, which includes demographic information, careful and complete cataloging of all images taken, equipment used, camera settings, orientation images depicting evidence location using visible light photography, progressively closer images to the subject until final macro images are made with an appropriate photographic scale as a size reference, and without a scale to permit the entire area of interest (injury) to be seen without obstruction.

18. Program a DSLR camera to the highest possible image resolution with the camera set in "auto" mode to default to programmed image capture settings for aperture, exposure time, and amount of supplemental light (flash) necessary to create the image and produce adequate visible light photographs.

19. Archive native, original, nonenhanced images and copies used for image enhancement, enlargement, and examination to ensure complete photographic documentation of a forensic dental case.

20. List the six guideline objectives for acquisition and retention of recommended forensic photographic images employed in dental identification cases.

21. List the three guideline objectives for acquisition and retention of recommended forensic photographic images employed in patterned injury cases.

22. Clarify why acquisition of forensic photographic images employed in patterned injury cases should be obtained after trace evidence collection.

23. Outline the reasons for making macro visible light photographs in patterned injury cases and the procedures required to insure that this evidence is measureable, appropriately exposed and labeled, not distorted, and identified with orientation images and case numbers.

24. Discuss the requirement to obtain informed consent or a court order prior to making photographs of suspects in forensic dental cases.

25. List the six guideline objectives for acquisition and retention of recommended images employed when photographing suspects in forensic dental cases.

26. List the locations photographed for documentation of the variety of injuries sustained from abusive behavior.

27. Define alternate light imaging (ALI), narrow band illumination, and monochromatic light imaging, and the six uses for this technology in forensic science.

28. Describe the use of fluorescent light as an ALI source and the wavelengths associated with IR photography and the Stokes shift phenomenon.

29. Explain why a special, yellow band pass (cut) filter and other technique-sensitive considerations (i.e., tripod camera mounting, darkened room, long exposure times) are required when making images with low-energy fluorescence.

30. Contrast the wavelengths and skin penetration abilities of nonvisible light photography: ultraviolet (UV) photography with those of IR photography.

31. Describe the two uses of UV photography in forensic dental cases.

32. Appraise how ALI and UV photography was used in the cases presented at the end of this chapter.

CHAPTER 5: DISASTER VICTIM IDENTIFICATION

1. Define the terms disaster, disaster victim identification (DVI), and multiple fatality incident (MFI).
2. Classify disasters according to the cause of the event.
3. List the five priorities of a medical examiner/coroner (ME/C) when processing MFI victims.
4. Describe the essential requirements necessary to fulfill the tasks of an MFI operation.
5. Name the federal authorities responsible for disaster response in the United States.
6. Indicate which federal agencies have authority over the 15 emergency support functions (ESFs) described in the National Response Framework.
7. Explain the mission of the various federal agencies responsible for the management of a disaster incident under the authority of ESF #8 (Public Health and Medical Services).
8. Identify the supervising authority, composition, and role of Disaster Mortuary Operational Response Teams (DMORTs), and the contribution of forensic odontologists to these units.
9. Describe the contents of the three Disaster Portable Morgue Units (DPMUs) and indicate where they are located.
10. Differentiate among the responsibilities assigned to the three specialty DMORTs (i.e., DMORT, Victim Identification Center, and DMORT-All Hazards.)
11. Name other federal, military, state, and private DVI units established to facilitate identification of civilian and armed forces—related decedents.
12. Explain disaster site management protocol, including which agencies have jurisdiction over processing and identifying the deceased, investigation of transportation accidents, and terrorist events.
13. Recognize the four requirements to consider when selecting a temporary morgue site.
14. Discuss the process of search and recovery in an MFI regarding site preservation, artifact and human remains retrieval, and coordination with HAZMAT and security and safety personnel.
15. Describe the composition and roles of the three components of a Search and Recovery Team.
16. Summarize the primary purpose of mortuary operations in a disaster.
17. List the five mandatory provisions required for mortuary operation regardless of the magnitude of the disaster.
18. List the 12 workstations that comprise the mortuary annex examination area that is staffed by forensic scientists and supporting personnel.
19. Discuss the organization, materials, supplies, software, and procedures performed in each of the 12 workstations to achieve documentation of victim identity, which can be certified with a death certificate issued by the local ME/C.
20. Explain the 1994 American Dental Association resolution regarding the policy for the establishment of state dental identification teams and the need to form them before an MFI occurs.
21. Summarize the requisite requirements, roles, and responsibilities of a dental section team leader.
22. Compare the roles and responsibilities of members of a "go team" and those of a "support team."
23. Indicate the composition, responsibilities, and tasks performed by the postmortem dental section team.
24. Indicate the composition, responsibilities, and tasks performed by the antemortem dental section team.

25. Explain the exemption to the 1996 US government HIPPA legislation protecting patient privacy.
26. Indicate the composition, responsibilities, and tasks performed by the dental comparison section team.
27. Describe the requirement to have morgue shifts based on the equipment and supplies available, computer access, magnitude of the MFI incident, and requirement for team members to rest and be rotated.
28. Assess the usefulness and safety considerations of portable dental X-ray generators as components of the postmortem dental section team armamentarium.
29. Assess the usefulness of digital dental radiography sensors as components of the postmortem dental section team armamentarium.
30. Compare and contrast dental identification software programs, including Computer-Assisted Postmortem Identification (CAPMI), WinID3, DVI System International, and Unified Victim Identification System/UVIS Dental Identification Module (UVIS/UDIM)
31. Evaluate how each dental identification software program interfaces with the DEXIS Digital X-ray System to incorporate digital radiographs into the digital dental record.

CHAPTER 6: MISSING AND UNIDENTIFIED PERSONS

1. Describe the magnitude of the problem of missing and unidentified persons in the United States and internationally.
2. Identify the national and international organizations supporting intergovernmental resolution of the missing and unidentified person problem and the databases that maintain information regarding these individuals.
3. List the reasons that individuals may "go missing" that are not associated with criminal activity on the part of the victim.
4. Contrast the requirements involved when reporting a missing minor (subadult) as opposed to an adult individual.
5. Discuss the legal, moral, and ethical factors that are essential regarding the necessity to obtain a positive identification of a decedent.
6. Explain the contributions made by the forensic odontology community regarding resolution of the missing and unidentified human remains problem.
7. Assess how inconsistencies in the manner in which law enforcement jurisdictions respond to the missing and unidentified human problem has impeded its resolution.
8. Assess how inconsistencies in the manner in which ME/Cs respond to the missing and unidentified human problem has impeded its resolution.
9. List the three factors that contribute to the difficulty of accurately using large databases of unidentified decedents to determine identity.
10. Describe the demographics and risk factors associated with unidentified decedents.
11. Indicate how natural and man-made disasters and armed conflicts contribute to the missing and unidentified human problem.
12. Provide a summary of the procedures to follow and contacts, resources, agencies, and services to which the family of a missing individual can turn to for assistance and support while seeking resolution of the situation.
13. List the public and private agencies that may assist in filing missing person reports and create a 19-item missing person checklist.
14. Identify additional areas in which forensic odontologists can interface with other forensic professionals to assist in the determination of identity besides the

comparison of antemortem/postmortem dental records.

15. Evaluate the case studies presented regarding the specific contributions of forensic odontology and involvement of other forensic specialties in their resolution.

CHAPTER 7: DOMESTIC VIOLENCE

1. List those factors associated with violent behavior within a relationship that may appear besides physical injury to the maxillofacial complex.
2. Describe the five helpful features that can differentiate between accidental injuries and nonaccidental trauma.
3. Explain the association between aggressive, violent behavior and prevalence of intimate partner or family member victimization.
4. Clarify how all forms of familial and intimate partner violence (IPV) are potentially interrelated.
5. Recognize the importance of proper collection and analysis of data and record management using the SOAP protocol in domestic violence cases.
6. Discuss how the subjective, objective, assessment, and plan information in the SOAP protocol are documented and recorded in a domestic violence case file.
7. Identify the universal demographic patterns associated with violent human behavior.
8. Choose appropriate techniques and resources to enhance evidence documentation of hard and soft tissue physical injuries in IPV and elder abuse cases.
9. Define physical dating violence (PDV).
10. List the serious psychological and physical sequelae that PDV, cyberbullying, and sexting can initiate in a victim.
11. Review the percentages of college-age men and women reporting sexual assault victimization in a study from one university.

12. Summarize the results of the United States Bureau of Justice Statistics, FBI Supplemental Homicide and Medscape reports, and the Centers for Disease Control and Prevention information regarding the physical/psychological injuries and financial burden of IPV.
13. Name the most common sites for injury associated with IPV.
14. List the seven findings related to perinatal IPV developed from a meta-analysis study conducted between 2001 and 2006.
15. Contrast the types of craniofacial injuries sustained by female IPV victims from those detected in victims assaulted by unknown or unidentified assailants.
16. Review the United States Health and Human Services Administration on Aging—National Center on Elder Abuse (NCAE) definitions of physical, emotional, sexual, exploitation, neglect, abandonment, and self-induced aspects of elder abuse.
17. Summarize the results of the NCAE (The United States Department of Health and Human Services, 2005 report) demographics related to elder abuse in the United States.
18. Discuss the reasons that special attention must be paid to the head and neck complex during initial stages of elder abuse evidence collection, including signs of nonaccidental physical trauma.
19. List the five indicators of elder abuse reported by the National Committee for the Prevention of Elder Abuse.
20. Provide a step-by-step procedure algorithm for making accurate film or digital photographic images to document the location and severity of a suspected abusive injury.
21. Collect salivary evidence from a patterned injury suggestive of a bitemark to insure that no genetic contamination has been introduced into the sample.
22. List the contact information available for clinicians and investigators provided by

governmental and private support agencies and advocacy centers concerned with the human abuse problem (i.e., child, intimate partner, elder abuse).

23. Evaluate the knowledge base regarding the epidemiology, prevention, recognition of physical/emotional/sexual/neglect-related child abuse, and treatment developed by a pediatrician specializing in this field.

24. Clarify why forensic interviews of children suspected of being abused are best conducted by professionals with specific training in forensic interviewing.

25. Recognize the state and federal laws that mandate health-care providers to report "reasonably" suspected abuse and authorize providers to disclose otherwise confidential information in the context of a mandated report.

26. Define good faith reporting and those factors that are disincentives to reporting abuse.

CHAPTER 8: ASSESSMENT OF DENTAL AGE

1. Define forensic age assessment.

2. Summarize how age assessment has been used historically and the reasons that this discipline of forensic science has been underutilized currently.

3. Describe how age assessment, when used with other morphometric determinants, is advantageous in providing authorities a quick and inexpensive means to ascertain a reliable age and identification of the missing and unidentified, MFI victims, and living individuals.

4. List the civil/criminal legal situations and forensic occurrences in which scientific age determination of individuals is an important factor.

5. Identify the three scientific categories employed to determine dental age.

6. Recognize the dental morphological development criteria that are the most reliable and accurate means to correlate growth and development to true chronologic age in subadults (i.e., infants, children, and adolescents).

7. Explain why utilization of any dental morphologic staging system to determine age requires trained dental and anthropological investigators who must rely on written descriptors that fully describe the tooth developmental spectrum of each stage.

8. Recognize the gross and histological postformation dental maturation criteria that are most reliable and accurate when used to determine true chronologic dental age in adults.

9. Clarify how biochemical dental techniques (i.e., dentinal amino acid racemization and enamel carbon 14 [14C] dating) is used to determine age at death and date of birth $\pm$ 3 years of age for individuals born after 1943.

10. Contrast how genetics, gender, anthropological ancestry, environmental factors, disease, and hormonal changes impact the forensic odontologists' assessment of dental development.

11. Discuss the components and parameters of a normative statistical analysis and the rationale for using this statistical method to evaluate dental age estimation.

12. Identify the scientifically accepted threshold for error (confidence level) when determining results of a dental age estimation.

13. Explain the rationale for using statistical regression formulas to estimate dental age in adults with postformation dental changes.

14. Evaluate the usefulness of the ABFO dental age estimation techniques selection chart and the need to utilize all available methods and exact procedures when conducting a dental age assessment.

15. Summarize the criteria for evaluating dental age in infants and children and the advantages and disadvantages of atlases created by Schour and Massler, Ubelaker, and AlQahtani et al. in this regard.

16. Summarize the criteria for evaluating dental age in infants and children, the advantages and disadvantages of charts in this regard, and the requirement for quality radiographs when using either atlas or chart techniques.

17. Define tooth eruption, gingival emergence, alveolar emergence, tooth mineralization, early/late adolescence, "censoring" of data collection, and adult age range.

18. Illustrate how the Moorrees, Fanning and Hunt chart and Demirjian and Goldstein chart produce more accurate assessments of human dental chronologic age than those of the atlases previously mentioned.

19. Summarize the criteria for evaluating dental age in early and late adolescents and the advantages and disadvantages of methodologies developed for these populations by Moorrees et al., Demirjian et al., and Mincer.

20. List the manner in which the United States legal system currently uses dental age assessment obtained from the forensic odontologist.

21. Describe why, in the statistical analysis of third molar age assessment, probability is calculated by using the continuous distribution function (e.g., NORMDIST in Microsoft Excel).

22. Clarify which of the six traditional postformation dental variables used to assess adult chronological age are the most and least useful and which are most affected by environmental dental factors.

23. Contrast those dental age assessment techniques that should be used in the living from those that should be used in decedents.

24. Use Draft Age Estimation Quicksheets (DAEquicksheets@gmail.com) to evaluate results of the noninvasive, nondestructive Kvall et al. technique to determine an estimated adult dental age from dental radiographs of intact maxillary and mandibular single-rooted teeth according to the tooth selection hierarchy established for this procedure.

25. List two advantages and four disadvantages of the Cameriere et al. technique for adult dental age determination.

26. Name the adult dental age estimation techniques, including advantages and disadvantages that are used invasively or noninvasively on deceased individuals.

27. List those dental age estimation protocols that require analysis of extracted and sectioned teeth.

28. Describe the protocols and advantages and disadvantages of the Johanson, Maples, Bang and Ramm, Lamendin et al., and Prince and Ubelaker dental age estimation techniques.

29. Appraise the biochemical and histological dental age assessment techniques regarding age groups targeted, degree of accuracy, and disadvantages.

30. Define the terms enantiomers, racemization, tooth dentin aspartic acid racemization (AAR), aspartic acid L-form/D-form, and bradytrophic tissue.

31. Discuss how combining AAR dentin analysis with 14C enamel analysis can significantly improve the ability of investigators to identify unknown decedents' date of birth (14C), age at death (AAR), and date of death—calculated by comparison of the results of the two techniques.

32. Name additional techniques that can supplement dental age estimation protocols to provide additional demographic and genetic information concerning the life of the subject.

33. Integrate forensic dental age assessment guidelines developed by national and international forensic organizations into the practice of forensic odontology.

34. Review the scientific literature to become familiar with the evidence-based studies, which have added to the body of knowledge regarding skeletal and dental age estimation techniques.

CHAPTER 9: PATTERNED INJURY ANALYSIS AND BITEMARK COMPARISON

1. List the historical cases that reflect the evolution of bitemark analysis from the era of William the Conqueror to the 20th century.
2. Compare the Frye and Daubert standards for admissibility of scientific and nonscientific expert witness testimony and the other cases that refined these standards to allow judges to act as gatekeepers regarding admissibility of expert testimony and district court judges to exclude expert testimony in some situations.
3. Discuss the current situations that have deemed bitemark analysis "junk science," and led to increased scrutiny and criticism of bitemark evidence, and eventual exoneration of 21 individuals whose convictions were associated with this testimony.
4. Assess the significance of modern criminal cases in which bitemark evidence was admitted from Doyle v. State.1954 to Stewart v. Florida.1982.
5. Define patterned injury and the requirements deemed necessary for these injuries to be useful for evidentiary purposes.
6. List the variables associated with human bitemarks and the differences in impression quality made by this subset of patterned injuries on human skin or inanimate objects.
7. Clarify how distinctive features in a human bitemark can be helpful in eliminating some

suspects in cases where the number of suspected biters is defined.
8. Determine if a patterned injury has been caused by a human or animal bite or inanimate object (i.e., watch, EKG pad, pendant, catheter tube).
9. List the three terms used in the ABFO Standards and Guidelines for pattern, patterned injury, and bitemark evidence to describe the degree of confidence that a patterned injury is or is not a bitemark and can be linked to the dentition of a suspect.
10. Define bitemark according to the six criteria listed in the ABFO manual as well as class characteristics, pattern recognition, bench science, bias, opinion and linkage opinion.
11. Identify the four factors essential to the determination of whether a patterned injury is a bitemark.
12. Describe the procedures that are used to eliminate bias in the analytical process of comparing a suspect's dentition with the patterned injury.
13. Identify the direct and indirect methods for comparing a suspect's dental casts with the patterned injury.
14. List the three ABFO guideline terms used to state the opinion(s) of the forensic odontologist relating the various suspects' dentitions to the bitemark(s) in question after all comparisons are completed.
15. Discuss the components of a bitemark report.
16. Evaluate the variables regarding the evidentiary value of bitemark evidence and its powerful and important use to exclude suspects.
17. Identify the six factors that eventually reduced the exoneration rate of cases involving bitemark evidence from 8.0% (28/350) to 2.3%–0.8% (8/350 & 3/350).
18. Compare the exoneration rates related to bitemark testimony, DNA, and fingerprint evidence.

19. Evaluate the scientific validity of patterned (e.g., bitemarks, ballistics, and fingerprints) image analysis and evaluation as an effective nonbench science utilizing observation, measurement, and comparison to detect patterns and regularities/irregularities to formulate hypotheses that ultimately develop and produce general conclusions.

20. Distinguish between the processes of deductive and inductive reasoning regarding the effects of acquisition of new evidence, the intentions of the observer or investigator, and the influence of the forensic odontologist being trained and educated as a clinician.

21. Describe how abductive reasoning differs from inductive and deductive reasoning and how it is used by jurors to reach a verdict.

22. Explain how the three components of the totalitarian ego process allow the ego to fabricate and revise information or justify a conclusion through cognitive biases, which must be avoided by the forensic odontologist.

23. Summarize how blinding, independent verification (second opinions), following patterned injury analysis methodology, and providing conservative opinion statements can minimize the bias of the forensic odontologist reviewing evidence and providing expert testimony in a bitemark pattern case.

CHAPTER 10: UNITED STATES JURISPRUDENCE

1. Clarify why a forensic dentist should have a basic understanding of the law and legal system in the country in which his or her work is performed.

2. Compare the powers and duties granted to the federal and district courts by the United States Constitution, and state courts by their respective constitutions.

3. Explain how some state systems further subdivide "entry-level" courts by jurisdictional methods (i.e., specific courts and judges for criminal or civil matters, and some for family/juvenile matters such as divorce, custody, wills, and probate).

4. Name the court level in which a forensic dentist will be called upon to testify regardless of whether the case is in federal or state jurisdiction.

5. Contrast the requirements between the selection processes of judges in federal and state courts.

6. Describe the factors that differentiate the jurisdiction of "lesser" courts from district courts.

7. Define felony, misdemeanor, appellate court, circuit court, remanded appellate cases, oral argument, stare decisis, a brief, tort, negligence, malpractice, punitive damages, trier of fact, directed verdict, bona fides, double jeopardy, direct-, cross-, and redirect examination, Daubert hearing, motion in limine, voir dire, curriculum vitae, standard of care, Brady Rule, Miranda Warning, ex parte communication, subpoena ad testificandum, and subpoena duces tecum.

8. Identify the basic rules that apply to the appellate process and procedures in the ultimate appeals court in federal and state systems—"supreme court."

9. Discuss the reasons that decisions in appellate cases form the basis for what is considered the "law."

10. Compare the three types of legal cases in which a practicing dentist may be involved regarding the parties responsible for bringing the case, and the party having the burden of proof and at what standard (i.e., preponderance of evidence, beyond a reasonable doubt.)

11. Describe the two foundational principles of the American judicial system not always embraced in the legal systems of other countries.

12. Discuss the differences between the roles of an expert witness and fact witness in the American judicial system.

13. Illustrate the procedures required to admit a witness as an expert.

14. Explain how the Federal Rules of Evidence (Rule 702 and Rule 703) standardize practice and procedure in all federal district courts regarding admission of expert testimony, which has gained general acceptance in the particular field and the expert witnesses presenting such evidence.

15. List the four questions that judges require answered as the gatekeepers responsible for admitting an expert opinion in a case.

16. Explain how General Electric v. Joiner (522 U.S. 136, 1997) and Kuhmo Tire Co. v. Carmichael (526 U.S. 137, 1999) added further definition and bounds to the admission of expert testimony and opinion.

17. Identify the four factors that a plaintiff must prove when bringing a suit for negligence against a dentist in civil court.

18. Describe the rights granted to a defendant in a criminal matter, which are specified in the US constitution and its first 10 amendments, The Bill of Rights.

19. Contrast the questioning of an expert under direct examination with that experienced by an expert under cross-examination.

20. Prepare to provide forensic dental expertise according to the highest ethical standards and in the pursuit of truth and advancement of the cause of justice while fulfilling the expert's role to educate attorneys, judges, and juries regarding the dental facts at issue in a case.

CHAPTER 11: EXPERT WITNESS GUIDELINES AND TESTIMONY

1. Illustrate why the forensic odontologist must attain proficient legal skills in addition to those of a scientific nature to be an effective expert witness.

2. List the three categories that represent the guideline subdivisions for the expert witness.

3. Discuss the five tenets that form the basis for moral and principled behavior for an expert witness.

4. Discuss the 10 tactics that are the basis for professional conduct and behavior for an expert witness.

5. Evaluate the strategic responses that an expert witness should consider when replying with an absolute opinion, qualified response or responses to yes or no questions, compound questions, badgering questions, and questions related to compensation.

6. Describe the strategic response by an expert witness to a prolonged pause prior to the next question by an attorney.

7. Explain the rationale for establishing language choices that create a communications bridge between the jury and the expert witness presenting dental information.

8. Summarize the importance of avoiding the use of the collective "we" term, technical jargon, and terms, which can create the impression that the expert opinion may not be objective.

9. Recognize the importance of presenting potential problems in an expert's testimony during direct testimony.

10. Compare the similarities and differences between court testimony and deposition testimony.

11. Describe the difference between a discovery deposition and an evidentiary deposition.

12. Identify the six strategies that should be considered as a forensic odontologist prepares to provide expert testimony in a deposition.

13. List the three essential elements of the science of report writing and factors that may influence the content of the report.

14. Use the ABFO guidelines for report writing, which specifically pertain to bitemark analysis and comparison.
15. List the seven components that comprise the contents of a report.
16. Explain why the length of a report and its language style may raise "red flags" and be viewed with skepticism by opposing attorneys.
17. Identify the four caveats that must be considered when preparing a report as an expert witness.
18. Defend the opinion of a report written by a forensic dental expert witness based on analysis of evidence reviewed.
19. Describe the eight sections that should be included in a curriculum vitae, the four items that should not, and the three that may be listed.

CHAPTER 12: EXPERT WITNESS LIABILITY

1. Discuss how the absolute immunity from civil lawsuit resulting from fact and expert witness testimony is being eroded by recent decisions in the courts of England and the United States.
2. Explain why an expert witness had little concern regarding future liability by offering an opinion in court unless perjury was committed.
3. Compare the risk of liability for the forensic dentist testifying as a private party or providing testimony when employed by a government agency.
4. Summarize the significance of US Code 42 U.S. Code §1983 "Civil Action for Deprivation of Rights" in regard to an odontologist being named as a codefendant in cases where the government agency retaining them have been accused of violating the constitutional rights of the defendant.

5. Describe the seminal case and those circumstances that distinguish between the substance of an expert opinion versus the methods and care used to arrive at that opinion, which determine whether an expert witness is or is not immune from a civil suit brought by the attorney who hired them.
6. List the five factors used in the Daubert standard to determine whether the methodology used by the expert witness is valid.
7. Discuss the case that clarified the fact that the scientific method can be applied to all testimony given by an expert, including their observations and opinions.
8. Identify the four factors that depict the concept of negligence.
9. Compare the three rules of negligence regarding proof of negligence and the impact of the degree of negligence ascribed to defendant or plaintiff.
10. Summarize the factors that a forensic dental expert should consider when structuring a forensic practice to protect personal assets and deciding to purchase Errors and Omission expert witness liability insurance.
11. Recognize the differences between the coverage provided by an average dental professional liability policy and those tasks not covered in forensic dental practice.
12. Define risk and the nine factors that can impact the exposure to risk for the forensic odontologist.

CHAPTER 13: ETHICAL ISSUES IN FORENSIC SCIENCE AND FORENSIC ODONTOLOGY

1. Compare the terms morals and ethics.
2. Compare the terms facts and opinions
3. Provide examples of how the cultural moral and ethical norms of American society are exhibiting a continued lowering of

expectations for what is viewed as acceptable.

4. Clarify why the concept that "the ends lead to the means therefore the ends are justified by the means" is a desired concept, which may allow development of a useful ethical conduct and memorable script by which to perform as a forensic odontologist.

5. Summarize the American Academy of Forensic Sciences (AAFS) definition of forensic science and the methods employed by this organization to provide leadership to advance science and its application to the legal system.

6. List the four proscriptive components of the AAFS ethics code.

7. Describe how the apparent goal to ensure uniformity among all levels and disciplines of forensic practice may inadvertently conceal important inherent differences in methodology and purpose among the disparate forensic science fields.

8. Identify the components of the sworn duties of a law enforcement officer.

9. Explain the rationale for the NAS's report on forensic sciences to affirm that, "Scientific and medical assessment conducted in forensic investigations should be independent of law enforcement efforts either to prosecute criminal suspects or even to determine whether a criminal act has indeed been committed."

10. Review the evolution of the current American Bar Association (ABA) Code of Professional Conduct which delineates proper and ethical conduct involving the courts, other attorneys, and clients.

11. Illustrate how the ABA code is only a model and that, "in each state it is the state Supreme Court that has the ultimate authority to adopt legal ethics and professional discipline standards that govern lawyer ethics in that state."

12. Describe the specific judicial canons regarding certain ethical behaviors that

judges must follow in addition to the ABA code and their impact on the admission of forensic scientific evidence at trial.

13. Discuss the process by which witnesses are designated experts and granted special privilege in testimony including the ability to formulate opinions and respond to hypothetical scenarios.

14. Define the terms forensic practitioner and forensic medicine service provider according to the National Commission on Forensic Science (NCFS).

15. Evaluate the circumstances in which questions and challenges are generated when evidence is consumed during forensic testing, leaving no sample remaining for subsequent reanalysis or additional testing.

16. List the four major categories included in every code of ethics established to guarantee impartial, objective analysis of evidence in the pursuit of justice.

17. List the 21 topics included in the National Code of Professional Responsibility for Forensic Science and Forensic Medicine Service Providers developed by the NCFS.

18. Assess the potential practical limitations to the National Code of Professional Responsibility for Forensic Science and Forensic Medicine Service Providers.

19. Identify the similar practice and ethical standards shared by physicians, dentists, and nurses, which distinguish these practitioners from other forensic-associated specialists.

20. Explain how abductive reasoning in medicodental practice is identical to the reasoning employed by jury members when incomplete observations lead to best-fit hypotheses based on available data.

21. Define the terms "evidence-based medicine" (EBM) and "evidence informed medicine" (EIM).

22. Describe the shortcomings related to the use of EBM and EIM practices when evaluating correct collection, examination, and

interpretation of generally static, variably degraded, or otherwise less than optimal evidence in an isolated forensic case.

23. Assess the current relationship between the disciplines of law and science and the need for a paradigm shift, which addresses the requirement that forensic medicodental practitioners and members of the legal profession work collegially in the interest of justice.

24. Define the term engineering.

25. Compare the ethical codes related to engineering that are similar to those established for attorneys.

26. List the three AAFS voluntary codes of ethics to which expert forensic witnesses are subject in addition to practice and ethical duties created by respective professional organizations and licensing authorities.

27. Compare seven major (capital) and minor (venial) ethical violations and contrast them with the seven cardinal virtues.

28. Define the term ad hominem attack.

29. Recall the "case-based" philosophical approach that Percival's Medical Ethics employed to illustrate ethical and moral principles.

30. Summarize the ethical and moral principles described in the forensic case studies used to exemplify the seven deadly sins (lust, envy, greed, sloth, gluttony, anger, and pride) and seven cardinal virtues (chastity, charity, abstinence, kindness, diligence, patience, and humility).

31. Describe the various ethical scenarios that may create legal dilemmas for the forensic dental expert during the course of their practice of this dental specialty.

CHAPTER 14: FORENSIC ODONTOLOGY—RELATED SPECIALTIES

1. Summarize the scientific history related to forensic use of DNA analysis for human identification.

2. Explain why DNA has become the preferred method to individualize biological samples compared with other methods of identification.

3. Define the terms variable number of tandem repeats (VNTRs), short tandem repeats (STRs), and polymerase chain reaction (PCR).

4. Describe the rational for using STRs as the most common method of DNA identification.

5. Collect DNA evidence from biological and evidentiary material using proper protocols required to maintain chain of custody.

6. Compare the sensitivity and specificity regarding presumptive tests (e.g., KM test) and confirmatory tests (e.g., Takayama test) for bodily fluids.

7. List the major steps in the DNA testing process, which generate a DNA profile for comparison with that of a known individual (e.g., victim or suspect) to determine correspondence.

8. When interpreting results of a DNA analysis, differentiate between single and mixture sources in a specimen sample.

9. Discuss how an investigator can determine a match between two samples in a forensic DNA analysis and how random match probability statistics are applied to provide weight to those conclusions.

10. Define likelihood ratio and apply this statistical ratio to cases in which the DNA profile from a contributor cannot be determined.

11. Illustrate how other genetic markers (e.g., X chromosomal STRs, Y chromosomal STRs) can be useful in the resolution of forensic cases requiring identification.

12. Describe the transmission and cellular location of mitochondrial DNA (mtDNA).

13. Clarify why single nucleotide polymorphisms are markers used to determine differences between mtDNA sequences and reference samples.

14. Describe how the Combined DNA Index System (CODIS) database is used to find matches to unknown profiles from crime scenes, missing person investigations, and convicted felons.

15. Summarize the legal challenges to DNA evidence and eventual acceptance of this evidence by the legal and forensic science communities.

16. Discuss how future technologies are providing capabilities to harvest DNA from smaller samples, provide phenotype characteristics, and significantly decrease the time required for laboratory analysis.

17. Summarize the advantages and disadvantages regarding the analysis of DNA evidence obtained from a bitemark.

References

The United States Department of Health and Human Services, Administration on Aging, National Center on Elder Abuse available at: http://www.ncea.aog.gov.Library/Data/index.aspx.

Further Reading

Anderson, L.W., et al. (Eds.), 2001. A Taxonomy for Learning, Teaching, and Assessing: A Revision of Bloom's Taxonomy of Educational Objectives (Complete Edition). Longman, New York. http://www.celt.iastate.edu/teaching/effective-teaching-practices/revised-blooms-taxonomy.

Gronlund, N.E., 1991. How to Write and Use Instructional Objectives. MacMillan, New York.

Kern, D.E., et al., 1998. Curriculum Development for Medical Education. The John Hopkins University Press, Baltimore, MD.

March, G., 2015. http://www.bumc.bu.edu/fd (Gail March (Ph.D.) (617) 414–7440, gmarch@bu.edu).

Mayer, R.E., 2010. Applying the Science of Learning to Medical Education. http://onlinelibrary.wiley.com/doi/10.1111/j.1365-2923.2010.03624.x/full.

Index

'*Note*: Page numbers followed by "f" indicate figures and "t" indicate tables.'

Printed and bound by CPI Group (UK) Ltd, Croydon, CR0 4YY

08/06/2025

01896870-0018